RASTAFARI AND THE ARTS

Drawing on literary, musical, and visual representations of and by Rastafari, Darren J. N. Middleton provides an introduction to Rasta through the arts, broadly conceived. The religious underpinnings of the Rasta movement are often overshadowed by Rasta's association with reggae music, dub, and performance poetry. *Rastafari and the Arts: An Introduction* takes a fresh view of Rasta, considering the relationship between the artistic and religious dimensions of the movement in depth. Middleton's analysis complements current introductions to Afro-Caribbean religions and offers an engaging example of the role of popular culture in illuminating the beliefs and practices of emerging religions. Recognizing that outsiders as well as insiders have shaped the Rasta movement since its modest beginnings in Jamaica, Middleton includes interviews with members of both groups, including: Ejay Khan, Barbara Makeda Blake Hannah, Geoffrey Philp, Asante Amen, Reggae Rajahs, Benjamin Zephaniah, Monica Haim, Blakk Rasta, Rocky Dawuni, and Marvin D. Sterling.

Darren J. N. Middleton is Honors Faculty Fellow and Professor of Religion in The John V. Roach Honors College, Texas Christian University. He has published eight books, received several teaching awards, and he lives in Fort Worth.

RASTAFARI AND THE ARTS

An Introduction

Darren J. N. Middleton

Routledge
Taylor & Francis Group

NEW YORK AND LONDON

First published 2015
by Routledge
711 Third Avenue, New York, NY 10017

and by Routledge
2 Park Square, Milton Park, Abingdon, Oxon, OX14 4RN

Routledge is an imprint of the Taylor & Francis Group, an informa business

© 2015 Taylor & Francis

The right of Darren J.N. Middleton to be identified as author of this
work has been asserted by him in accordance with sections 77 and 78 of
the Copyright, Designs and Patents Act 1988.

Library of Congress Cataloging-in-Publication Data

Middleton, Darren J. N., 1966-
  Rastafari and the arts : an introduction / Darren Middleton.
    pages cm
  Includes bibliographical references and index.
  1. Rastafari movement.   2. Arts and religion.   I. Title.
  BL2532.R37.M53 2015
  299.6'76167—dc23   2014029637

ISBN: [978-0-415-83188-8] (hbk)
ISBN: [978-0-415-83189-5] (pbk)
ISBN: [978-0-203-48165-3] (ebk)

Typeset in Bembo
by Apex CoVantage, LLC

Printed and bound in the United States of America by Publishers Graphics,
LLC on sustainably sourced paper.

In honor of
Asante Amen, Rocky Dawuni, Geoffrey Philp, and Benjamin Zephaniah,
for teaching me how to drop it metaphysical
and to
S. Brent Plate,
for bringing my religious theory to its senses

CONTENTS

ACKNOWLEDGMENTS

Back in the early 1980s, when I was not day-dreaming of captaining England's cricket team, I would watch my father on his way to work, jostling with the striking coalminers recently arrived from Yorkshire—the hostile pickets who keyed his car and called him a 'scab.' In retrospect, I was caught somewhere between fantasy and reality, a liminal figure, though at the time I did not recognize, much less use, such fancy phrasing. Still, I am here today because my mates and our music rescued me. Time and again reggae's drum-and-bassline, the soundscape for the Nottingham housing estate where I was born and raised, made me smile and kept me real. Friends who spun such records were mostly Jamaican Rastafari, children of postwar immigrants to England, and all of them were eager to evangelize—to help me grasp the sadness and grace and joy and rage of reggae, its easygoing good times and its militant uprightness. I was an easy convert. Day after day I unplugged my ears, released the madness, and heard the Siren's Song. In 1985, the song was "Picture on the Wall" by Natural Ites, a hometown band who put a local face on this global sound and word; after heeding their hymn to the divinity of His Imperial Majesty Emperor Haile Selassie I, my life was never the same.

Although I never took a course in 'Rastafari Studies' from the three British universities I attended, independent research has taken me to several continents, keen to hear the soundings of sistren and brethren as well as to participate in their reasonings. I have been fortunate to spend a year journeying throughout Jamaica; to DJ a 'religion and the arts' reggae show on Tennessee community radio; to conduct ethnographic research on devotees who have made their home in Ghana and Senegal; and, to develop alliances with Rastafari artists around the globe. Again, looking back, I realize that I have learned more from such people and places than what is contained within my book's covers. Written after careful observing, reading, and listening, *Rastafari and the Arts* is intended primarily for undergraduate students with little or no prior awareness of the movement, but other people are also welcome to read it.

Various individuals kept me driven as well as well-versed during my research and writing. I would like to take this opportunity to acknowledge them now with abiding appreciation; naturally, any remaining errors are my own: Komla Aggor; anonymous peer-reviewers with Routledge; Asante Amen; Katie Bain; Anna Carroll; the late Barry Chevannes; Lois Cordelia; Raghav Dang; Rocky Dawuni; Ennis B. Edmonds; Betsy Flowers; Iva Lou Hill and Bob Flowers; Rob Garnett; Bob Goode; Helena Araba Grahl; Monica Haim; Barbara Blake Makeda Hannah; Ejay Khan; Maggie King; Linda and Ray Love; Arnau Macia; Joan and Alan Middleton; Nathaniel Samuel Murrell; Serigne Ndiaye; Aliou Niang; Ann Nicholas-Green; Lauren Nixon; Kristian Petersen; Geoffrey Philp; S. Brent Plate; Micky Prince; Reggae Rajahs; Blakk Rasta; Greer Richardson; Paul John Roach; Roundtable Class (University Christian Church, Fort Worth, Texas); Saints and Sinners Class (Arborlawn United Methodist Class, Fort Worth, Texas); Richard Salter; Yushau Sodiq; Matt Spangler; Nicolette Stanley; Marvin D. Sterling; Cary Sullivan; Ben Taylor; True Love Graphic Design; Lisa Vanderlinden; Ryan 'Ishence' Willard at Higher Bound Productions; Glen Wilson; and Benjamin Zephaniah.

This study owes a great deal to Betsy Flowers, my wife, whose keen eye improved my writing and whose love, in more ways than one, rescued me from myself. Our son, Jonathan, kept me honest; and, I am delighted he knows and appreciates his reggae! I am especially in the debt of Luke and Mark Ehrhardt, my diligent and unfailing student assistants, for their comments on parts of this text. They also helped me build the website (www.darrenjnmiddleton.com) that now houses material germane to the study of Rastafari and the Arts. I should add that students in my Texas Christian University (TCU) Honors College class, 'Africa and the African Diaspora,' were kind enough to respond so well to early drafts of my work. Dr. Bonnie Melhart, TCU's Associate Provost of Academic Affairs, and Dr. Peggy Watson, Founding Dean of The John V. Roach Honors College at TCU, provided assistance for research trips to Ghana, Japan, and Senegal. In addition, I appreciate Dr. Sarah Robbins, Acting Dean of The John V. Roach Honors College at TCU, for help with securing funds for last-minute copyright clearance fees. My sincere thanks extend as well to Steve Wiggins and Andrew Beck, my editors at Routledge, whose deft wisdom made my task so much easier.

Permission to reprint current copyrighted material in this book is gratefully acknowledged. The dustjacket photograph of Rocky Dawuni is reproduced by permission of Glen Wilson; for help with securing Mr. Wilson's permission, I acknowledge Cary Sullivan at Aquarian Records. The paintings of E.J. Khan are reproduced by permission of E.J. Khan. And the paintings of Lois Cordelia appear by agreement of Lois Cordelia. Ryan 'Ishence' Willard at Higher Bound Productions worked with me to secure permission to use the cover art for Ishence's *Space N Time* album; the graphic design is by True Love (www.Fikir-studios.com), the artist is Ras Terms. I also owe a special debt to Ryan for helping me acquire permission to use Marcus Wilson's "New Name" painting; again, the graphic design is by True Love.

Portions of chapter two first appeared in Darren J.N. Middleton, "Fictional Dread: Two Early Novels about the Rastafarians of Jamaica," *Modern Believing* 41.4 (2000): 23–33. Reproduced by permission of *Modern Believing*; thank you to Jonathan Clatworthy and Anthony Freeman. Extract from Macmillan Caribbean Writers: *Brother Man* © Roger Mais 2004, published by Macmillan Publishers Ltd. Used by Permission. All rights reserved. For permission to use material from *Joseph: A Rasta Reggae Fable,* I thank Barbara Blake Makeda Hannah and Jamaica Media Productions. I thank Hannah Bannister and Peepal Tree Press for kind permission to incorporate Jean Goulbourne's *Excavation,* Orlando Patterson's *The Children of Sisyphus,* and N.D. Williams's *Prash and Ras* into chapter two. Also, Geoffrey Philp granted permission to use words from *Benjamin, My Son*; thank you, friend.

An earlier version of chapter three appeared in Darren J.N. Middleton, "Chanting Down Babylon: Three Rastafarian Dub Poets," in Angela M.S. Nelson, editor, *"This Is How We Flow": Rhythm in Black Cultures* (Columbia, SC: University of South Carolina Press, 1999), 74–86. Reproduced by permission of University of South Carolina Press; thank you to Vicki Sewell. I am most grateful to Bloodaxe Books for permission to quote excerpts from three poems, "The arrival of Brighteye" and "simple tings," and "Tongue Your Funky Rhythms in My Ear," which appear in Jean 'Binta' Breeze, *Third World Girl: Selected Poems, with Live Readings DVD* (Northumberland, England: Bloodaxe Books, 2011); thank you to Suzanne Fairless-Aitken.

Elements of chapter four first surfaced in Darren J.N. Middleton, "Benjamin Zephaniah," in David Scott Kastan, editor, *The Oxford Encyclopedia of British Literature* (Oxford: Oxford University Press, 2006), 371–375. Reproduced by permission of Oxford University Press; thank you to Brendan O'Neil. In addition, I thank Louise Manning and Penguin Books for permission to use Zephaniah's "The British (serves 60 million)."

Although the Ghana section of chapter six first appeared in *Black Theology: An International Journal* 4.2 (2006): 151–172, it has been reworked to account for subsequent research trips to West Africa; I thank Equinox Publishing for permission to revisit and re-use my published research.

Many musicians and poets were most generous in allowing me to incorporate their song lyrics and verse into my book; I appreciate the generosity of Asante Amen, Benjamin Zephaniah, Blakk Rasta, and Rocky Dawuni.

I have made every effort to clear permissions for all copyright material. Any omissions brought to my attention (d.middleton2@tcu.edu) will be corrected in future editions. I should clarify that most of my copyright concerns arose from non-responsive rights holders, especially to paintings I discuss, and unfortunately this is nothing rare. For the images where permission was not forthcoming, I have found the image on the internet, created two galleries (one for "Rastafari Visual

Art" and one for "Commodifying Rasta") within my own website, and then I have provided a URL in the book (www.darrenjnmiddleton.com) for further perusal.

If this book has a playlist or soundtrack, then I must mention Black Uhuru's *The Complete Anthem Sessions*, which evokes more memories than I can say here or anywhere. Clive Middleton introduced me to the original, Grammy Award-winning *Anthem*; Clive, I owe you one.

Portions of this book were first presented as "Jah Live!: Art, Religion, and the Internationalization of the Rastafari," which was my contribution to TCU's AddRan College of Liberal Arts Distinguished Faculty Lecture Series, March 2011. I am indebted to Dr. Andrew Schoolmaster, Dean of the AddRan College of Liberal Arts, for supporting this series. Dr. Nadia Lahutsky, my department chair, was kind enough to arrange for a course reduction in my teaching schedule, which enabled me to finish and bring this scholarship to publication.

Darren J. N. Middleton, Autumn 2014

PREFACE

From Belize's palm-covered tropical paradise of Caulker Cay to the appreciative crowds at Japan's Yokohama Reggae Festival, from the Shashemene settlement in Ethiopia to the youth subculture(s) of various post-Soviet states, Rastafari is on the world's cultural map.[1] Assuredly, this new religious movement has grown substantially since its modest beginnings in and around the first Rastafari commune ("Pinnacle") in the hills of St. Catherine, Jamaica, circa 1940. "Rastas dem everywhere," as Senegalese brethren put it to me lately, and in this book I invite readers to travel in the mind's eye and see Rastafari from a multivisioned, global vantage point. Examining the movement in this manner confirms that its adherents have transitioned "from outcasts to culture bearers," as Ennis B. Edmonds holds, and it shows that Rastafari represents one of the twenty-first century's most vibrant, durable, and pervasive religions.[2]

Rastafari and the Arts is intended primarily for undergraduate students and those with little or no prior awareness of Rastafari. Its goal is neither to defend Rastafari nor to attack it, but to understand Rastafari by introducing its range of philosophies and practices, by breaking down stereotypes that surround it, and by illustrating the movement's diversity. Art is largely my explanatory tool, and I address painting, reggae music, literature, and documentary film. I also explore how these artistic expressions have become entangled with globalization and commercialization in a still ongoing process. I do not attend to all art forms. One book cannot accomplish everything, which is the reason I see my work as an enterprise still in process; other scholars are welcome to join in its development, researching and writing texts that give consideration to how Rastafari has, among other things, contributed greatly to theatrical and dance production in Jamaica and elsewhere.

Readers will notice that I consider presentations and re-presentations of Rastafari in art by outsiders (the etic approach) as well as insiders (the emic approach). While some might say that the insider's viewpoint offers the devotee's unmediated, authentic voice, and that it fosters sympathy that the outsider overlooks or disregards, others might claim that the outsider's perspective presents an educational explanation of how the wider culture receives and uses religious lifestyle practices—'livity,' in the language of Rastafari.[3] Given Rastafari's rich variety after eighty years, and because there is no perspective entirely outside everything and no stance totally inside, *both* emic *and* etic approaches appear instructive. *Rastafari and the Arts* features interviews with Rasta musicians like Asante Amen, a rapidly rising vocalist from Jamaica's St. Andrew parish, and Rocky Dawuni, an established singer-songwriter from Ghana, West Africa; such materials help us engage Rastafari's inner vitality, especially the claims it makes, and they give my book its own authenticity.[4] Yet, I also involve non-Rastas by exploring the image of the Rastafari within mass communication and popular culture, emerging with the observation that Rastafari, like *any* religion, has been branded or commodified over time.[5] In the end, choices had to be made, and I trust readers will conclude that I have sustained an appropriate balance between the voices of Rastas on the one hand and the voices of non-Rastas on the other.

In my first chapter I scrutinize Rastafari through the lens of Ninian Smart's dimensional theory of religion, paying attention to how Rastafari's material or artistic dimension serves as the primary mechanism for the faith's transmission.[6] Scholars have furnished ethnographic as well as historical accounts of the movement for some years now.[7] I complement such studies by showing how art, broadly construed, fosters Rastafari's global growth, especially in this "dawn of the fifth epoch," as Michael Barnett terms the latest period in the movement's development.[8] With this aesthetic approach, then, I explore the evolution of Rastafari as a religious way of life that has been shaped almost exclusively by its artistic or material dimension. And I dispute the traditional idea that religion primarily pertains to beliefs and doctrines, to which art and artefacts are secondary or minor.[9]

Chapter two surveys renowned Rastafari literary art from the last fifty years or so—an assortment of novels, plays, and novellas crafted by movement insiders and outsiders. I begin my overview by situating Roger Mais's *Brother Man* (1954) and Orlando Patterson's *The Children of Sisyphus* (1964) within their arduous mid-twentieth century contexts—a time when Jamaican society, and the world, knew very little about the movement. Taken together, Mais and Patterson markedly raised the Rasta profile. I then address present-day Rastafari literary art, focusing on Jean Goulbourne, Masani Montague, and N.D. Williams. These artists create works that reflect, and even predict, the movement's emerging trends, particularly issues linked with gender and globalization. Interviews with Barbara Blake Makeda Hannah, Rasta cultural critic and one-time Independent Opposition Senator in the Jamaican parliament, as well as

Geoffrey Philp, one of Jamaica's rising literary stars, currently based in Florida, enable me to develop the notion that literature is an informative resource for learning about Rastafari.

One cannot write about Rastafari without addressing its primary artistic expression in music, and so in chapter three I outline reggae's history. Additional interviews with Reggae Rajahs, India's premier sound system operators, and with Asante Amen, surface in this chapter, along with performance poetry. Here, I also address three Rastafari dub poets (Mikey Smith, Mutabaruka, and Jean 'Binta' Breeze), noting how their trenchant verse tests late modern capitalism, 'Babylon' in the language of the Rastafari, and how, in the case of Breeze, poetry challenges Rastafari's traditional patriarchy. Relatedly, my fourth chapter focuses on Benjamin Zephaniah, the United Kingdom's premier Rasta wordsmith, crossover artist, and sometime nominee for Great Britain's Poet Laureate. As we see, Zephaniah's Bible-soaked Rastafari consciousness was, among other things, the main impetus behind his famous refusal to accept an Order of the British Empire (OBE) from Her Majesty Queen Elizabeth II.

In chapter five I offer a selected survey of documentary films featuring Rastafari. Such films are instructive, not simply because they show how flesh-and-blood brethren and sistren articulate as well as find their voices, however harmonious or inharmonious they sound in the final analysis, but because such documentaries describe the movement's transcultural presence. An interview with Monica Haim, director of *Awake Zion* (2006), which investigates the links between Jews and Rastafari, forms a part of my fifth chapter.

Chapter six considers artful Africans at home and abroad, using Ghana and Japan as case studies. First, Rastas have always made a point of returning to Africa. And some have made it back to Ethiopia, home of His Imperial Majesty Emperor Haile Selassie I, but equally significant, many have made their home in Ghana, historic site to slave forts and pan-Africanism.[10] This chapter analyzes Ghanaian Rastafari. Based on ethnographic work conducted across the last decade, it also discusses Ghanaian reggae, and it features interviews with Blakk Rasta, Accra-based musician and radio presenter, and with Rocky Dawuni. Second, this final chapter engages Marvin D. Sterling's *Babylon East: Performing Dancehall, Roots Reggae, and Rastafari in Japan* (2010). What has Trench Town, Jamaica, to do with Tokyo, Japan? In his answer to this question, Sterling, an anthropology professor at Indiana University, has penned an arresting, multisited ethnography of Afro-Asian cultural exchange, tracing the development of Jamaican dancehall reggae culture through five phases. I outline Sterling's work, showing how it complicates our sense of the African diaspora, and an interview with him brings the chapter to a close.

My epilogue explores the paradox behind the postmodern branding or commodification of Rastafari. Briefly, I consider how the anticapitalist message of earlier artists has morphed into more consumer-driven material forms. I then provide Appendices, a Selected Bibliography, and a Selected Webliography.

Notes

1 In deference to Rastafari, who strongly object to 'isms,' I do not use the term 'Rastafari-anism' in my book, and in keeping with custom in Rastafari studies, I use other terms instead. I speak of *Rastafari* for the collective way of life, or the experiential philosophy of religion, allied with the *Rastafari movement*. The primary meaning of the term, then, is to refer to the group or those persons who align themselves with it. When I highlight an individual member or members of the movement, I use *Rasta* or *Rastas*. For a lively discussion of this definitional concern, see the essays in Werner Zips, editor, *Rastafari: A Universal Philosophy in the Third Millennium* (Kingston, Jamaica; Miami: Ian Randle Publishers, 2006).

2 Ennis B. Edmonds, *Rastafari: From Outcasts to Culture Bearers* (Oxford and New York: Oxford University Press, 2003). Although I, an outsider, use Ninian Smart to view Rastafari as a religion, I acknowledge that many insiders, Rastas themselves, contest this classification; chapter one takes up this debate.

3 On the emic and etic approaches to religion, see Russell T. McCutcheon, editor, *The Insider/Outsider Problem in the Study of Religion: A Reader* (London: Cassell, 1999). On the politics of insider/outsider definition in Rastafari studies, see the essays in Zips, editor, *Rastafari*.

4 See https://myspace.com/asanteamen and http://rockydawuni.com/. Accessed March 30, 2014. Here and elsewhere, all websites (URLs) are current at the time of writing.

5 Consider "Rastamouse," one of the UK's most popular children's TV shows. See: http://www.rastamouse.com/#/1 Accessed March 30, 2014.

6 Ninian Smart, *Dimensions of the Sacred: An Anatomy of the World's Beliefs* (Berkeley and Los Angeles, CA: University of California Press, 1996). Also see Ninian Smart, *Worldviews: Cross-Cultural Explorations of Human Beliefs*, third edition (Englewood Cliffs, NJ: Prentice Hall, 1999).

7 Nathaniel Samuel Murrell provides an instructive bibliography of such studies in an appendix to his 1998 primer on the Rastafari. See Murrell, "Who Is Who in the Rasta Academy: A Literature Review in Honor of Leonard Barrett," in Nathaniel Samuel Murrell, William David Spencer, and Adrian Anthony McFarlane, editors, *Chanting Down Babylon: The Rastafari Reader* (Philadelphia: Temple University Press, 1998), 429–441. Another review of the literature on Rastafari may be found in Edmonds, *Rastafari*, 127–139.

8 In Barnett's recent and helpful timeline of the Rastafari movement, history may best be viewed as divided into five periods or epochs: November 1930 until 1948 (first epoch); 1948 until April 1966 (second epoch); July 1966 until 1981 (third epoch); 1981 until September 2007 (fourth epoch); and, September 2007 to the present day (fifth epoch). See Michael Barnett, "Rastafari in the New Millennium: Rastafari at the Dawn of the Fifth Epoch," in Michael Barnett, editor, *Rastafari in the New Millennium: A Rastafari Reader* (Syracuse: Syracuse University Press, 2012), 1–10.

9 S. Brent Plate deserves critical plaudits for launching the first peer-reviewed journal devoted to religion's material or artistic dimension. For details, see: http://www.bergpublishers.com/BergJournals/MaterialReligion/tabid/517/Default.aspx. Accessed March 30, 2014. In addition, see S. Brent Plate, *A History of Religion in 5½ Objects: Bringing the Spiritual to Its Senses* (Boston: Beacon Press, 2014).

10 Rastafari often insist that Haile Selassie's name and title be noted in full each time it is used: His Imperial Majesty Emperor Haile Selassie I. Since I intend no disrespect, I state the full name and title the first time I use it in every chapter of my book; for stylistic reasons alone, I use an abbreviation in subsequent appeals or references to the last Ethiopian Emperor. I should add that sometimes Rastafari use their own abbreviation, 'H.I.M.,' which stands for 'His Imperial Majesty.' Thus, readers should expect to see this term throughout my text.

1
A SMART WAY TO VIEW RASTAFARI

Introduction

When I, an Englishman, assumed a position teaching religion in the American South, I thought of it more as an experimental exercise in social dislocation and one which would, if I am honest here, probably prove short-lived. Fast forward twenty years, I am now a Full Professor at Texas Christian University in Fort Worth, Texas. Even more surprising, as a transplanted Limey devoted to liberal politics and the Labour Party, I actually delight in my students, most of whom come from and remain immersed in the conservative, evangelical world. They are, after all, in the Lone Star State, home to the mega-church and cowboy Jesus, though they might be more apt to describe Texas as a model of Christian America. While the disconnect between my own theological leanings and that of my students invites numerous challenges, my students do, nevertheless, take religion and matters of faith seriously. Or to reverse the phrase, faith matters to those who sit in my classroom.

My 'World Faiths' course is typical. Students might not personally agree with the principles and practices of the major global traditions or even the varied forms of Christianity explored. They are confronted and disturbed by religious diversity and pluralism. But they readily grasp the idea of the Holy as *mysterium tremendum et fascinans* (fearful and enthralling enigma); they treat sacred texts like the Torah and the Qur'an with a certain reverence; and they wrestle honestly with the problem of evil and suffering. Religious doctrines, rituals, and experiences—and the people who embody them—make sense to my students. I find it refreshing to share this starting point with them. It also helps that when making biblical references, I can assume a certain literacy and working knowledge of the major characters and stories such as Moses in the Bulrushes, the cleansing of the Temple, and the descent of the Spirit at Pentecost. Class, then, involves a sense of immediate emotional investment and intellectual seriousness—that is, until we get to Rastas.

"Rastas, a religion," they scoff; but still, "what fun," they also exclaim enthusiastically, sensing a break from the 'heavy stuff.' And so, I go with it for the first class period. Students share stories about their images of and encounters with Rastas—as few know the term Rastafari. One male student described a plush toy, a Rasta banana-man (aka 'Rastanana') complete with dreadlocks, which he won at the Texas state fair.[1] Rasta is a hairstyle, say many. Another woman thought Rasta was more about cuisine as she detailed her favorite meal at a local eatery—Jamaican jerk chicken and Caribbean spices flavoring this 'Rasta Pasta.' Most know that Rastas listen to a rhythmic music but they see it as the Jamaican version of The Beach Boys and Bob Marley as the Caribbean equivalent of Jimmy Buffett. If my students tend to stereotype Buddhists as awfully serious individuals who are not allowed to desire anything and Hindus as world-negating polytheists, Rastas are laid-back, beach-wandering, marijuana-smoking 'dudes' with distinct hair and chillin' tunes. And so, a very different challenge emerges, that of helping students view Rastas as religious and thus, as part of the density of the course. It is this challenge that my first chapter addresses.

Before we engage issues of artistic production, commercialization, and globalization, all of which have led to positive as well as negative stereotypes and are essential to this book's argument, we need to assume a particular starting point—Rastafari is a religion with much to teach us about the nature of beliefs and practices outside of institutional life and power-driven establishments. When I push students to analyze Marley's music and lyrics, for example, they begin to recognize that he is not so much the black version of Buffett, but an Amos-like prophet of Old Testament proportions, keen to criticize capitalism, 'Babylon' in the language of Rastafari, as well as to promote social justice (Gen 11; 2 Kgs 20:12–19; Dan 4:30; Rev 17:2–5). We also learn that while Rastafari do not eat 'Rasta Pasta,' at least as a rule, they do consume their own symbolic foods, just like Jews (Passover *seder*) and Christians (Eucharist). In fact, Rastafari adhere to a strict dietary code, often consuming only organic fruit and vegetables, which Rastas see as natural or 'ital' sustenance. Practicing this austere lifestyle facilitates 'livity,' which is 'dread talk' (the language of Rastafari) for living in concert with the vital, pulsating energy that inhabits and animates most, if not all, natural phenomena.[2] Generally speaking, Rastafari religion lives and breathes through such ital food rituals and charismatic musician-leaders.

The purpose of studying Rastafari, and one reason for writing this book, is to move beyond preliminary stereotypes and summary judgments by introducing students to the many and varied ways Rastafari shapes patterns of religious practice and belief in today's world. Here, I am not trying to 'prove' that Rastas are 'religious,' for Rastafari often resist this category, as we will see, but I am eager to show, from a scholarly standpoint, how and why they *might* be viewed in this manner. Reading Rastafari religiously pushes us past what we think we know about one of the world's most misunderstood groups, and it brings us to the point where we explore the many questions that Rastas ask about life's meaning. This opening chapter focuses on such questions, using Ninian Smart's dimensional theory of religion to investigate the observable features of Rastafari as it is experienced, practiced, and believed. I pay special attention to the material or artistic dimension of Rastafari because, without the arts, the most famous form of Rastafari creativity and practice, our grasp of this religion would be greatly diminished.

Defining Rastafari

A massive scholarly consensus emphasizes the difficulties of trying to classify or pinpoint Rastafari. Historically, Rastas have affiliated to one of the three major mansions or houses (Jn 14:2)—akin to a religious denomination or a spiritual subgroup—within the movement.[3] But because there is extensive diversity both between and among the Nyabinghi, the Bobo Shanti (The Ethiopia Africa Black International Congress), and the Twelve Tribes of Israel, distinguishing between essential and non-essential ideas and practices has proved challenging. Although the Twelve Tribes of Israel and the Bobo Shanti consult the Bible, for example, the Nyabinghi shelve it, or they did so until fairly recently, because they believe it symbolizes white, Christian, and colonial cruelty. Instead, the Nyabinghi structure their ritual action around a finely calibrated liturgical calendar, which observes dates linked to Ethiopia and its last Emperor, His Imperial Majesty Haile Selassie I—dates like January 7 (Ethiopian Christmas); April 21 (anniversary of Selassie's 1966 visit to Jamaica); July 23 (Selassie's birthday); September 11 (Ethiopian New Year); and November 2 (Selassie's coronation). In contrast, the Bobo Shanti congregate for weekly sabbath, a more biblical structuring, and the Twelve Tribes of Israel worship together during monthly meetings. A fourth mansion, the School of Vision, which Priest Dermot Fagan founded in 1994, only complicates the task of defining Rastafari because Fagan's group, which resides in Jamaica's Blue Mountains, mixes traditional Rastafari Afrocentrism with atypical claims about UFOs, extraterrestrial biological entities, and government-mandated microchips; an interview with musician and baptized member of the School of Vision, Asante Amen, appears in chapter three.[4] The Kingston-based Rastafarian Centralization Organization has tried to unify the above-mentioned mansions, without much success, and thus, for the foreseeable future, many commentators expect that practical as well as ideological diversity will prevail among Rastafari. British Rasta poet Benjamin Zephaniah writes:

> My friend who is a brain surgeon is continually being told that he's not a real Rasta because he doesn't sound Jamaican enough; another friend who is a psychiatrist has been told she can't be a Rasta because she doesn't cover her hair, and, because I don't smoke weed, absolutely no one believes I am a real Rasta … [Rastafari is] a place to go for young black people that don't

want to join gangs, the Nation of Islam, or go to their parents' church. Those who are interested in black and African history, and those who are not prepared to buy into western consumerism will join the Rastafarian family to try to see the world through alternative spectacles.[5]

Eighty years ago, Rastafari seemed restricted to Kingston's projects. These days, the "Rastafarian family" spreads out across the world, as Donisha Prendergast's documentary film, *Ras Ta—A Soul's Journey* (2010) confirms.[6] And the movement's internationalization will only boost, not diminish, the variety or hetereogeneity that Zephaniah notes.

Recent studies on Rastafari in West and South Africa, in Japan, and in New Zealand reveal assorted behaviors and beliefs; and, such accounts stimulate scholars to be circumspect.[7] "There are those both within and outside the Rastafari community who seek to authoritatively delimit the boundaries of the movement," Richard Salter says, but "Rastafari's rapid global expansion affords us few commonly observable elements by which to do so," which explains why he thinks that to address what is Rastafari, "we first must acknowledge that there is no such thing as Rastafari, but rather only Rastafari*s.*"[8] I agree. Wherever two or three Rastas are gathered, either in Malmo or Mumbai, there one can expect to find difference or otherness, even disagreement; and thus, if we hope to grasp this wide-ranging and relevant movement, we must proceed cautiously.

Emphasizing Selassie's centrality represents a careful place to start and understand Rastafari practice. False adherents trust in King James (and his Bible), reggae musicians Morgan Heritage sing in "Hail Rastafari," but true believers trust in Haile Selassie I, earth's rightful ruler. Generally speaking, Rastas hold to the divinity of His Imperial Majesty Emperor Haile Selassie I (1892–1975), King of Kings, Lord of Lords, Conquering Lion of the Tribe of Judah. Such eminent titles echo biblical passages, including Ps 68:31, 87:3–4; Rev 5:5, 17:14, and 19:16. In Amharic, an Ethiopian language, Haile Selassie denotes 'Power of the Trinity.' He was also known as Lij Tafari Makonnen, formerly Ras, which means 'Crown Prince' Tafari (the family name). Selassie was crowned in 1930, deposed in 1974, and died in 1975; in 1992 Rastafari throughout the world made pilgrimage to Ethiopia, Africa's Holy Land, or Zion, to celebrate the centenary of the late Emperor's birth, and some Rastas returned in late 2000 to participate in the ritualized reburial of the Emperor's remains in Addis Ababa's Trinity Cathedral. Conferences and concerts also marked the 120th anniversary of Selassie's birth in late July, 2012; here, Rastafari gathered to recite scripture and read poetry.[9]

Numbering between 700,000 and one million followers internationally, present-day Rastafari continue to ponder Selassie's place in their worldview, as recent studies show.[10] Some Rastas, like those in Brazil and Mali, qualify the movement's initial convictions, viewing the Emperor as God's emissary, not God-in-the-flesh, and as an arresting symbol of Africa's ancient wisdom and beauty. Other Rastafari, like those in most Caribbean islands, persist in paying tribute to Selassie's cosmic or divine supremacy. Also available through my personal website (www.darrenjnmiddleton.com), the following three paintings depict such divinity, or Christ in his "Kingly Character," to invoke the title of Garnett Silk's much-admired reggae song.[11] And these paintings, like Silk's music, shape as well as reflect followers' beliefs about Selassie. From Carriacou, Grenada, which is located in the Southern Caribbean, the "Last Supper" mural (n.d.)—the result of an unknown outsider or self-taught artist/group of artists—is equal parts New Testament, Leonardo da Vinci, and local Rasta creativity.

Notice how Christ-Selassie, complete with Ethiopian crown, presides over the Last Supper and uses coconuts instead of bread; how the disciples are black and dreadlocked (Num 6:1–21; Jer 8:21; Dan 7:9); and, how the chillum pipe, which Rastas use for sacramental marijuana-smoking (Gen 1:12, 3:18; Ex 10:12; Ps 104:14; Prov 15:17; Rev 22:2), nestles nearby, waiting to be passed on the left-hand side when the occasion permits.

Created by a movement insider, Ras Terms's "Space N Time" (2007) also gestures toward transcendence. Here Selassie situates himself between heaven and earth, between visions of teleology (purpose) and disteleology (purposelessness), at the intergalactic center of things.[12] Notice the undetonated bombs beneath Selassie's feet, an allusion to an iconic photograph of the historical Selassie with his feet on top of two bombs dropped by Benito Mussolini's Italian forces when they invaded Ethiopia in 1935. Also consider the enormous dreadlocks, inextricably intertwined with Africa, and with roots to the world beyond. And observe, on the lower right-hand side of the painting, 9/11's Twin Towers, an event in time that appears after Selassie's death, yet figured as something Selassie explains,

FIGURE 1 "Last Supper" mural, Grenada (artist and date unknown). Photo: Katie Bain.

ISHENCE

Higher Bound Productions

SPACE N TIME

FIGURE 2 Ras Terms, "Space N Time" (2007).

like the African paradise to the left-hand side; like infinity itself; or, like the stars, represented by the constellation of Leo, an allusion to the pride of Africa as well as to one of Selassie's many titles. I should add that September 11, 2001 is "widely viewed within Rastafarian circles" as denoting the demise of 'Babylon,' where 'Babylon' signifies late modern capitalism's radical depersonalization of men and women through the cash–nexus alliance, which phrases like 'you are what you earn' have come to reflect.[13] By focalizing Selassie, having him appear larger than life and looming above the burning towers, as it were, "Space N Time" visualizes Zion's victory over Babylon, the victory of good (Selassie) over evil (Italian bombs, the World Trade Center). Whatever else it declares, this painting upholds Rastafari as a reclamation of a self and cultural identity denied by Babylon. Similar themes surface throughout *Coping with Babylon: The Proper Rastology* (2007), Oliver Hill's documentary film about the difficulties faced by Rastafari living in the West, and in "Babylon Release the Chain," Junior Reid's song of lamentation for Jamaica's disenfranchised blacks.[14] Finally, it is worth noting that Ras Terms's painting, which graces the cover of Ishence's reggae album, "Space N Time," also takes the shape of an open text, an occurrence that invites connections to the Book of Life or the Good Book. Ryan 'Ishence' Willard, via e-mail, wrote to me about his work with Ras Terms. "I commissoned him to do the piece for the album. I gave him an idea that I was thinking about and he elaborated on it. To me, the art compl[e]ments the music by encompassing and accentuating different realms of Rastafari," Willard explains. "The music and the artwork are like parables to be deciphered by each individual and their own connection and experience with the creator."[15]

Selassie occupies the center of "Ital Farm" (n.d.), another painting by Ras Terms, which portrays the all-natural or 'ital' Rasta as an unshaven cultivator of the land. Festooned in military regalia, His Imperial Majesty reigns as the Black Lord of the Sun and the Moon, without which there can be no leaves on the tree for the healing of the nations (Rev 22:2). Like the celebrated reggae anthems of Peter Broggs ("International Farmer") and Dennis Brown ("Promised Land"), Ras Jah Terms's painting evokes thoughts of Shashemene, land that is 155 miles south of Ethiopia's capital, which Selassie gifted to African expatriates in 1948. Today's Rastas, like Kaleb Martin, a twenty-something musician based in Shashemene, cultivate and harvest this land, with an eye towards sustainability, because they see it as their spiritual homeland.[16] Rastafari is thus a new religious movement tied to Ethiopia, the only African country to remain untouched by European colonialism.[17] More recently, Ethiopia has suffered famine and war. Yet its connection to the past by way of the ancient Axumite kingdom, the Beta-Israel (Falasha, black Jews), and the Ethiopian Orthodox Church (one of Christianity's oldest forms) guarantees its prestige. Concluding his search for the lost Ark of the Covenant in Ethiopia, Henry Louis Gates Jr. proclaims the wonder of this country's history and heritage:

> So many of Africa's genuine contributions have been denied or appropriated by non-Africans that many of us who love the continent and its cultures have a tendency to err on the side of optimism, or even wishful thinking, making dispassionate scholarly assessments difficult if not impossible at times. Let me make clear that the odds of the Ark being housed in the Sanctuary of the Tablet at St. Mary's Church at Axum are overwhelmingly against the Ethiopians. Nevertheless, I must confess I am haunted by the claim, and I started this journey hoping most ardently that it would turn out to be true. If it remains frustratingly impossible to know for certain, I did at least end my journey with an even fuller realization of another truth: the overwhelming importance of this symbol to Ethiopia's traditional Jewish and Christian communities. The profound faith that the Ethiopians share in the tangible presence of the Ark in their country inspires a sense of cultural heritage that is incomparably galvanizing. It is in itself something of a wonder.[18]

Ras Terms's "Ital Farm" painting links the divinity of Selassie to the centrality and wonder of Ethiopia as Africa. If Selassie is divine, then Africa serves as his, and therefore Rastafari's, sacred throne. Similar themes of sacred geography and messianic definition appear in the music video for Ancient King's "Ethiopie."[19]

The wonders of the African world never escaped Marcus Mosiah Garvey, one of the last century's major political activists, and Rastafari can also be linked to his fervent desire to centralize race consciousness in the global tussle for black freedom from white repression. Garvey mobilized blacks by valuing their person-hood, by inspiring their autonomy, and by urging them to tell their own stories in the context of Africa's own unfurling narrative. On this last issue, Garvey castigated white Christian control of the continent, which means his message was energetically anticolonial, yet it is important to note that he was as religiously evocative as he was politically potent:

> If the white man has the idea of a white God, let him worship his God as he desires. If the yellow man's God is of his race let him worship his God as he sees fit. We, as Negroes, have found a new ideal. Whilst our God has no color, yet it is human to see everything through one's own spectacles, and since the white people have seen their God through white spectacles, we have only now started (late though it be) to see our God through our own spectacles. The God of Isaac and the God of Jacob, let Him exist for the race that believes in the God of Isaac and the God of Jacob. We Negroes believe in the God of Ethiopia, the everlasting God—God the Father, God the Son and God the Holy Ghost, the one God of all ages. That is the God in whom we believe, but we shall worship Him through the spectacles of Ethiopia.[20]

In addition to urging blacks to Africanize God, Garvey advised all descendents of slaves brought to the New World between the fourteenth and nineteenth centuries to go 'back to Africa.' In 1919 he founded the Black Star Line, ostensibly to provide transportation to the Motherland. And many individuals invested in this shipping fleet; by 1922, however, the Black Star Line had failed, and Garvey was arrested on charges of fraud.

Undeterred by Garvey's disastrous attempt to facilitate mass repatriation, Albert Artwell, one of several self-taught painters featured in Wolfgang Bender's *Rastafarian Art* (2005), has crafted "The Black Star Liner" (2001), which depicts diaspora blacks—some of whom seem Rasta—recapitulating the journey through the Middle Passage by leaving the Caribbean and returning, full steam ahead, to the African continent.[21] Artwell is not alone in his Garvey-veneration. Reggae singers around the world, from Jamaica's Burning Spear ("Marcus Garvey") to Great Britain's Maxi Priest ("Marcus"), regularly rhapsodize this herald of African nationalism. And even though some scholars, like Adolph Edwards, think Rastas misrepresent Garvey, there are others, like Noel Leo Erskine, who describe him as the "unseen hand that guided Rastafari from its initial impulse."[22] Officially,

Jamaicans view Garvey as a National Hero, and African Americans esteem his founding role in the Universal Negro Improvement Association. In Garvey's philosophy, then, race and religion commingle; and this provocative mix may best be seen in his belief—Rastas often say "prophecy"—that diaspora blacks should turn their eyes upon their ancestral home and look for the crowning of a black-king redeemer.[23]

The coronation of Lij Tafari Makonnen (Haile Selassie) as Emperor of Ethiopia on November 2, 1930, was an event that attracted several European notables, including British novelist Evelyn Waugh. And almost immediately, the awareness of a potentially new era in black history grew as far away as Jamaica.[24] Garveyites in Kingston, such as Archibald Dunkley and Leonard P. Howell, became expressly animated when they heard that "the Conquering Lion of the Tribe of the Judah" (Rev 5:5) was among his titles. They were also intrigued by his claim to be a direct descendent of King Solomon and the Queen of Sheba—a claim traceable to 1 Kgs 10 and to the *Kebra Nagast* ("Glory of the Kings"), a fourteenth-century national myth or legend cycle concerning the Solomonic ancestry of Ethiopia's Emperors.[25] Horace Campbell writes:

> The crowning of Haile Selassie was to provide a new deification, replacing the white God in heaven and the white representative at Buckingham Palace with the Coptic version of a God who was both divine and human. The beliefs of the first Rasta were a profound response to the sickness of the colonial society. Those who preached the divinity of Ras Tafari were rejecting the link between Christianity and whiteness, and were inexorably breaking with the philistine white West Indian society, thus linking their cultural and spiritual roots with Ethiopia and Africa. As a first step, this was progressive.[26]

Looking back, we observe that the first Rastafari scrutinized sacred writings from their social location, practiced an ingenious form of mother-tongue exegesis or vernacular interpretation, and then created what Theo Witvliet labels Caribbean liberation theology.[27] Brandishing scripture as a decolonial weapon, early leaders like Robert Hinds upheld Ethiopia's Emperor as the black Messiah. More modern Rastas, like reggae artists Exco Levi ("Kebra Nagast") and Tarrus Riley ("Marcus Garvey"), continue to use the *Kebra Nagast*, Garvey's teaching, and the Bible to exalt Selassie's magnitude, to chant down twenty-first-century slavery, and to condemn the heaven in the sky untruth of traditional Christian eschatology or end-times thinking.

The Bible mentions Ethiopia quite frequently.[28] It declares the Redeemer's Ethiopian origins: "I will make mention of Rahab and Babylon to them that know me; behold Philistia and Tyre, with Ethiopia, this man was born there" (Ps 87:4). And again: "Princes shall come out of Egypt; Ethiopia shall soon stretch forth her hands unto God" (Ps 68:31). On the basis of these and other related biblical passages, such as Jer 8:21 and Dan 7:9, Rastas believed, and many still believe, in Selassie's divinity. Basically, they claim that the Emperor is Jah (an abbreviated form of Jehovah) Rastafari, the Living God. Even though there is an audio recording of Selassie distancing himself from such claims, Rastas I know frequently allude to the Apostle Paul's famous hymn on Jesus's unselfish character, recorded in Phil 2:6–11, and many tell me that His Imperial Majesty's humble comments only underscore his divinity, which means the Emperor's words cement rather than dislodge their faith. Today, many brethren and sistren concur with Black Uhuru, the Rasta-inspired vocal group and winners of the first Reggae Grammy Award (1985), when they intone worshipfully: "I Love King Selassie."[29]

First-generation Rastafari rejected white dominance, especially in the form of European colonization as well as postcolonial influence, and they hoped for an eventual return to Africa from Babylon.[30] Even though white Rastafari are now more common, given the movement's internationalization, and this phenomenon has been covered in fiction as well as non-fiction, Rastafari tends to attract many black men and women because a black person's divinity stimulates rituals as well as beliefs that contest Christianity's perceived reliance upon, and basic support for, white dominance.[31] The lifestyle, including reggae music, helps to identify Rastafari as a religion of protest against white capitalist and Christian values; indeed, it is not uncommon to hear Rastas 'chant(ing) down Babylon,' an allusion to weakening Western imperialism either through anticolonial resistance or in seeking an exodus back to Africa—a strategy captured in songs like Lutan Fyah's "Burn Babylon" and Jah & I's "Rasta and Babylon." This said, the sometimes artistic and always spirited act of blasting Babylon tells only part of the story. Although it is accurate in some respects to refer to Rastafari as a religion of protest, doing so risks characterizing Rastafari negatively, and Rastafari is so much more than a negative force. Put positively, Rastafari is a reclamation of a self and ethnic character denied by Babylon, as I explain here and elsewhere in my book.

Whereas many early Rastas believed repatriation (read: exodus) was imminent and would be at the hands of the Emperor, numerous contemporary Rastas favor rehabilitation. By rehabilitation, I mean that the majority of the movement's followers currently reside outside Africa, with many in the Caribbean, Europe, and North America, where they work for the Africanization of the West, which involves opposing racial discrimination, seeking regime change, and affirming black family as well as community life.[32] For those engaged in Africanization, Rastafari is a hymn to black somebodiness, as Jah Bones suggests:

> What is Rasta? Rasta is the totality of a life's experience, which is reflected in history and projected into the future. Rasta is the spiritual/material foundation of a livity that has its roots in Africa. Rasta is the result or find of a search for cultural identity and racial security; a means by which individuals can be redeemed into the heaven of a collective togetherness that is seen as an answer to selfish individualism and anarchy of the personality. Rasta is

even a socio-religious medium, whereby a people possess the opportunity to enunciate and project their images, concepts and lifestyles onto wider societies and the world at large.[33]

To Bones's point concerning Rasta as a "socio-religious medium," which is his way of describing Rastafari's contribution to the West's Africanization, consider the following case studies. Horace Campbell's research shows how Rastas were involved in the Grenadian Revolution in 1979.[34] Barry Chevannes upholds how modern Rastas challenge the Jamaican middle class to eradicate bigotry and intolerance.[35] Barbara Bush sees similar trends within the United Kingdom, thus offering a European milieu for the Rastafari's internationalization.[36] Also consider socialist Cuba where, as Katrin Hansing shows, Rastas "question and resist officially established and popularly accepted notions and norms with regards to race as well as explore and express new narratives of blackness."[37] Since the 1960s and 1970s, furthermore, Rastafari in the United States have been growing in number—gathering in diaspora, as Randal L. Hepner notes.[38] Hepner draws from media announcements, law-enforcement reports, and his own ethnography to conclude that devotees are thriving in the eastern seaboard's urban centers, such as New York City and Miami, Florida, as well as in Los Angeles, San Francisco, and Houston. In these places, Rastas flourish by crossing the usual lines of social marginalization (race, class, and gender), largely, though by no means exclusively, through the success of reggae music, an art form that Rastafari across the world employ to communicate their convictions.[39] Patrick Taylor summarizes the last eighty or so years:

> Rooted in a radical Afro-Christian, Jamaican tradition, Rastas have forged a new religion and culture out of African, European, and even Indian roots. The Bible of King James was reread through the *Kebra Nagast* of Ethiopia and both texts reflectively applied to the Caribbean historical reality in an upsurge of orality that Rastas refer to as 'reasoning.' Rasta ingenuity helped to awaken first in Jamaicans and then in other peoples of African descent a new sense of themselves as Africans in a struggle for social and political change. At the same time, its universal appeal, popularized in reggae, thrust it into the global arena, attracting people of different races, including both Jews and Christians.[40]

Ninian Smart's Religious Theory

Until his unexpected death in 2001, Ninian Smart was a comparative theologian, past president of the American Academy of Religion, and holder of professorships on both sides of the Atlantic. His phenomenological and cross-cultural method views religion through the lens of worldview analysis. By worldview, Smart means an "incarnated worldview, where values and beliefs are embedded in practice.

That is, they are expressed in action, laws, symbols, organizations."[41] Religion is what religion does. And Smart has done much to advance an inquisitive, serious, and appreciative approach to religion's *observable features*. Such informed empathy, which "tries to bring out what religious acts mean to the actors," fosters a dimensional analysis of worldviews, where the aim "is to provide a realistic checklist of aspects of a religion so that a description of that religion or a theory about it is not lopsided."[42] There are seven dimensions in Smart's schema, and he gives each one "a double name, which helps to elucidate them and sometimes to widen them." Although he acknowledges a "rather random" order to the seven dimensions, each one comes together to highlight religion's irreducibility.[43] Indeed, Smart holds that religion's complexity can never be simplified to doctrine *or* ethics, myth *or* ritual, et cetera; rather, he holds that a balanced religious theory sees and values religion's multidimensional character, especially in its individual and communal expression in the world.

This first chapter uses Smart's dimensional theory of religion because it enables me, an outside scholar, to provide a methodological map, an atlas designed to help readers explore the world of Rastafari practices and ideas, and to trace the link between the way Rastas think and act. What follows, then, is instructive, because it provides for an investigation of Rastafari's origins and leaders, sacred writings, rituals, personal experiences, community life, moral teaching, theological beliefs, and artistic achievements. This said, insiders often qualify outsiders, and vice versa. Consider current trends in U.S. Christianity. Scholars might say there is a Smart way to view Christianity, for instance, since outsiders are able to probe its myths and rituals, to outline its ethics, and to explore its administrative structure(s). We can see Smart's seven dimensions within Christianity, in other words, and therefore we have reason to conclude that Christianity is a religion. At some point, though, we must concede that some Christian insiders complicate matters when they self-identify as "spiritual but not religious"—a lifestyle that equates "being Christian" with resisting the leadership hierarchies and doctrinal watchdogs frequently associated with the term "organized religion."[44] Insider convictions therefore qualify outsider descriptions. And in deference to those Rastas—like poet Mutabaruka—who strongly object to viewing Rastafari as a religion, because 'religion' denotes public affiliation with an official religious institution and/or assent to authorized denominational ideas and ethical positions, I acknowledge that Rastafari is an intense lifestyle, and that it is often marked by disconcerting diversity. Mutabaruka declares:

> There is no Rasta religion per se! There is not a Rasta religion. People want say Rasta religion. There is a Rastafari experience. The experience is a way of life. And the man in New York City, who is experiencing Rastafari, will not say the same thing like the man who is living in Kingston, like the man who is living in Westmoreland. It's a total different experience.

But the nucleus of this experience is Haile Selassie. That mean you will hear the man in New York saying Haile Selassie and you will hear the man in the hill saying Haile Selassie and you will hear the man on the ground in Kingston saying Haile Selassie. But how he got to Haile Selassie is totally different, totally different. And this is what is confusing the sociologists. It is confusing the sociologists, because they want a pattern to study. A lot of people, they want a pattern. How do we study Rastafari when you have one Rasta saying one thing and a next Rasta saying a next thing? Yes, because it's an experience. So most Rastas will tell you that Rasta is not a religion, even though the form, having a theological nucleus, appears like a religion to some.[45]

Benjamin Zephaniah, another poet insider, shares Mutabaruka's sentiments, even as he appears to modify them. Commenting on Snoop Dogg's 2012 conversion to Rastafari, Zephaniah concedes how easy it is for outsiders to misconstrue the movement. This said, he calls for "ambassadors"—insiders like Snoop Dogg (now Snoop Lion), and perhaps outsiders, like scholars in Rastafari studies—to better explain Rastafari's distinctive features, and the diverse uses to which Rastas put them in assorted contexts:

Snoop Lion says he wants to spread the message of Rastafari, but does Rastafari need an ambassador? Yes, is my answer, we need as many as we can get. I think we are one of the most misunderstood groups of people in the world. People don't know if we should be thought of as a religion, a political movement, a cult, or black hippies. Christians and Muslims call themselves broad churches, but we have a church so broad that no one knows where it starts or where it ends. We think of this as a strength, but for outsiders it breeds misunderstandings. Snoop, it seems, like many misunderstanders, believes that to be a Rastafarian you have to make, or listen, to reggae music, he believes that you have to wear red, gold and green hats, he believes that you have to smoke marijuana, all stereotypes that on the whole have done us no favours. Dear misunderstanders, did you know that there are groups of Rastas who shun reggae music, and that most Rastas on this planet don't smoke? We need enough ambassadors to show the range of ideas within Rastafari. We need people to break down the stereotypes and show the diversity within our community, but sadly I don't see that happening any time soon.[46]

Although Mutabaruka's words show us that he—like many Rastas—will not allow us *finally* to categorize Rastafari as 'religious,' I hold that scholars, with their "pattern," may teach us *something* about the movement's challenging and varied nature. A "Smart Way to View Rastafari" is an explanatory device, and it is open to question and qualification but, in the last analysis, it may help us "break down the stereotypes and show the diversity" within and among Rastafari across the globe. Therein lies no small virtue.

Religion's Ritual or Practical Dimension

Religion's ritual or practical dimension involves informal as well as formal activities such as "worship, meditation, pilgrimage, sacrifice, sacramental rites and healing activities."[47] Because of Rastafari's acephalous (lacking a controlling or presiding authority) nature, there are few *prescribed* activities within the movement. Even so, ritual as sacred action appears to govern the way Rastas behave, as Carol D. Yawney's work explains—daily prayers, reading the Bible as well as other special texts, community gatherings or reasoning sessions ('groundings' or 'groundation'), drumming as well as chanting ('Nyabinghi'), and the use of marijuana ('ganja') typify the ritual dimension of the movement.[48] On this last issue, many but by no means *all* brethren and sistren use ganja for therapeutic as well as explanatory reasons; an all-natural or 'ital' herb, divinely designed for the healing of the nations (Rev 22:2), ganja, the 'weed of wisdom,' helps Rastafari become mindful of Babylon's injustices *and* their devotion to Jah. As the song by S.N.T. Soundsystem voices it, "Ganja Heal Rasta."

Smoking marijuana is illegal in many countries, and Rastas around the world have encountered problems with governing authorities, especially after being caught passing the 'chalice,' the communal pipe. In the United States, for example, ganja smoking repeatedly tests the limits of American cultural pluralism and the law.[49] And Zimbabwean President Robert Mugabe, who once declared that dreadlocked Rastas have "moths and mud" in their hair, recently bewailed Jamaican Rastafari for smoking cannabis and expressing no interest in higher education.[50] Illegalities and disparaging comments notwithstanding, the ritual use of the holy herb fosters Rastafari identity, as William F. Lewis shows.[51] Lewis focuses on Jamaican and North American Rastafari. Yet his understanding carries wider or transcultural application, given Pauline Bain's work on marijuana and identity formation among Rastafari in South Africa's Eastern and Western Cape.[52]

Other rituals include, but are not restricted to, the practice of cultivating a distinctive hairstyle ('locks' or 'dreadlocks'), which some but not *all* Rastafari see as biblically inspired (Num 6:5–6), and as an outward sign of their inner vitality—a physical reminder of their covenant with Jah, as echoed in The Mighty Diamonds's song "Natural Natty."[53] Ritualized speech is important to Rastafari, as Velma Pollard's work on dread talk shows. Rastas deploy an inventive form of African English, for example, and this patois means that words such as 'InI' (we; you and I), 'overstand' (to understand; to comprehend); 'downpress' (to oppress; to quell or to overwhelm); and 'reason' (dialogue; to converse religiously, often when smoking ganja) come together to create a new lexicon of meaning.[54] In addition, the ritual of natural or organic living, known as 'ital livity,' means that Rastas frequently set themselves apart from non-Rastas by following a strictly vegetarian—sometimes vegan—diet. Here, as elsewhere, Rastafari appeal to scripture, especially

FIGURE 3 Lois Cordelia, "Ital Offering" (2006).

to the instructions surrounding ritual purity and cleanness in Leviticus, which they approach with reverence and rehearse in obedience.[55] Songs by Turbulence ("Rastafari Livity"), Ini Kamoze ("Ital"), and Konshens ("Good Life & Livity") reflect this ancient rule. Also see Lois Cordelia's "Ital Offering" painting (2006). Inspired by Egyptian tomb reliefs and by the Rastafari way of life, this visual art depicts an African priest and priestess receiving Jah Sun's blessings of warmth and light upon an offering of wholesome, succulent ital food.[56]

Generally, Rastafari does not render pilgrimage—the ritual of sacred travel—essential but Ethiopia attracts Rastas all over the world to visit regions and cities associated with their movement: Addis Ababa, Shashemene, Lake Tana, Gondar, Lalibela, and Axum. Some Rastafari, like the Sudanese Ras Lumumba, journeyed to Ethiopia and joined Bob Marley's widow, Rita, for emotional services marking the late Emperor's reburial on November 5, 2000.[57] Other non-Rastas, like Peruvian Nobel prize-winning novelist Mario Vargas Llosa, often swell the ranks of those brethren and sistren making pilgrimage to Trench Town, Bob Marley's unofficial shrine in Jamaica. Pilgrimage rituals exude tremendous power, as scholars well know, and the force field created by sacred sites and holy places frequently seems so powerful that even non-believing pilgrims become engrossed by their experiences. Llosa confesses:

> One doesn't have to be religious to realize that without religion life would be infinitely emptier and grimmer for the poor and the downtrodden

and that societies have the religions they require. When I discovered that a son of mine and a group of his friends from school had become practitioners of the faith, I hated the Rastas' picturesque theological syncretisms, their marijuana communions, their horrible dietary laws, and their matted locks. But on the sad streets of Trench Town, or amid the poverty and neglect of the villages of St. Ann, the faith that for my son and his friends was doubtless a passing fad, a fickle extravagance of privileged youth, seemed to me a moving bid for spiritual life, a bid against moral disintegration and human injustice. I ask forgiveness of the Rastas for what I once thought and wrote about them, and, along with my admiration for his music, I proclaim my respect for the ideas and beliefs of Bob Marley.[58]

Marley's reggae has helped to situate Rastafari globally, as commentators from Sebastian Clarke to Stephen Foehr avow; and, in 2007, the Anglican church in Jamaica included Marley's lyrics in its hymnal—a choice that sparked a national debate about using Rastafari convictions in the ritual of Christian worship.[59] For his part, Smart recognizes that rituals may comprise words and music. But since I view reggae as a transnational art form, one that symbolizes Rastafari's material or artistic dimension, I address it later in this chapter.[60]

Religion's Doctrinal or Philosophical Dimension

Religion's doctrinal or philosophical dimension refers to its ideological convictions or viewpoint(s) concerning life, meaning, and sacred power. There are many ways of defining religion but most religions make reference to beliefs, Smart says.[61] In deference to Mutabaruka's aforementioned remarks, Rastafari may best be viewed as an experiential philosophy, a way of life characterized by commitments to certain Afrocentric truths that brethren and sistren enliven by religious ritual or sacred action. I outlined such truths—Ethiopianism; Selassie's divinity; the rejection of white privilege and the retrieval of black somebodiness; the disavowal of Babylon; and, some form of this-worldly concept of salvation (repatriation or rehabilitation)—earlier. Ennis B. Edmonds summarizes such "Rastology":

> Certain elements of Rastology and livity, such as the deification of Haile Selassie I, dreadtalk, and the cultivation of dreadlocks, have been discounted by critics of Rastafari as inspired by the inebriation of those who have consumed ganja in excess. However, a closer look will reveal that Rastafari, though steeped in the symbolic and the mythic, represents a commitment to reconstitute an African self that has been trampled by slavery and Western cultural imperialism. Rastafari represents a people disaffected by and dissatisfied with the forces of Western civilization, which have assigned

them a place in the margins of history and society. Drawing on the cultural resources of their African past and the myth-making capacity shared by humans, they have created a movement and a culture that represents their sense of self as divine and empowered.[62]

To these and other, aforementioned features of Rastology, which I, following Smart, see as Rastafari's doctrinal or philosophical dimension, I would add one further and general belief: gender relations.

Rastafari is clearly patriarchal in its practices and beliefs regarding men and women. This understanding emerges out of its cultural context. But it is also connected to Rastafari's doctrinal or philosophical assumption about the divinity of Selassie, who is perceived as a strong, powerful, and manly king. Many male Rastas often use scripture to prooftext their belief that women are subordinate to men (Gen 2:15–24; 1 Tim 2:8–15). These days, however, such convictions are changing—as Rastafari become increasingly more diverse, according to Michael Barnett.[63] In Great Britain, for example, progressive Rastafari women write and publish *Jus Jah*, the UK's first lifestyle magazine dedicated to the Rastafari community. More globally, The Empress of Zion Incorporated—a non-profit organization—has organized international conferences and launched anthologies to give voice to women within the movement. A new crowd of performers, from Empress Ayeola ("Rastafari Works") to Queen Omega ("Jah Dawta"), has appeared, to sing away the themes of marginality and invisibility. Also, Donisha Prendergast's *Ras Ta* uses the device of a young Rastafari woman to film and tell the global story of Rastafari.[64] Such voices challenge religious patriarchy within Rastafari, furnishing us with another example of the faith's varied or heterogenous character. Book-length studies, like Jeanne Christensen's *Rastafari Reasoning and the RastaWoman: Gender Constructions in the Shaping of Rastafari Livity* (2014) and Obiagele Lake's *RastafarI Women: Subordination in the Midst of Liberation Theology* (1998) have joined documentaries, like Bianca Nyavingi Brynda's *Roots Daughters: The Women of Rastafari* (1992), in describing this fluid phenomenon.[65] And Imani M. Tafari-Ama's survey of attendees at the 2010 International Rastafari Studies Conference, which was held in Jamaica's capital, also shows how an emerging black feminist consciousness in Jamaica is beginning to shape Rastafari sistren's sense of identity and agency.[66]

Religion's Mythic or Narrative Dimension

"Every religion has its stories," Smart declares, and many come together to illustrate religion's mythic or narrative dimension.[67] I have noted the Bible's role in the Rastafari movement, from its concern for ritual purity to its high regard for Ethiopia, and I have placed this text beside another special writing—the *Kebra Nagast's* account of the Solomonic ancestry of African kings—and urged readers to view them together. Steel Pulse vocalize this Afrocentric interpretation

FIGURE 4 Marcus Wilson, "New Name" (2008).

of scripture in their song, "Not King James Version." And the cover art for *New Name*, a 2008 reggae anthology featuring Jah Rubal, Xkaliba, and others, illustrates a certain style of Rastafari biblical hermeneutics.

Crafted by Marcus Wilson, a St. Croix Rasta, this painting situates Selassie close to one of the famous rock-hewn churches of Lalibela, which are located in northern Ethiopia and date to the twelfth and thirteenth centuries. Here, one of the eleven Lalibela churches bears an inscription from Dan 2:31–34. This passage speaks of a five-part statue, which symbolizes the five empires—including Babylon—that would dominate Judea before God's own kingdom arrived. In Wilson's 2008 painting, light streaming from the Lalibela church engulfs the unsteady statue of Nebuchadnezzar, Babylon's king; and an axe, which looks set to topple and send the king into the vortex beneath him, appears to issue from Jah's hands. Ethiopian Orthodox clergy regard Lalibela as the new Jerusalem, and here Wilson connects Selassie and Africa's holy land to Babylon's defeat and the creation of Jah's kingdom.[68]

Other texts about Ethiopianism, like Leonard P. Howell's pamphlet, *The Promised Key* (1935), together with *The Holy Piby* (1924), a black man's Bible, written and published by Athlyi Rogers, and Fitz Ballatine Pettersburgh's *The Royal Parchment Scroll of Black Supremacy* (1926), also exemplify Rastafari's mythic or narrative dimension. William David Spencer discusses Howell's fourteen-page work, concluding that it reveals early Rasta nostalgia for Africa, strict prescriptions concerning Rasta livity, and that it repudiates traditional Christianity before it describes Selassie as the promised key that will unlock salvation's door to those trapped in diaspora.[69] Nathaniel Samuel Murrell works on *The Holy Piby*, emerging from careful study and commentary to claim that it is an important Rastafari text.[70] Michael Hoenisch concurs. "Howell and Rogers evidently were steeped in a tradition of Ethiopianism. Through their Africanized re-reading of certain biblical stories, they addressed blacks as the chosen people, whose promised land, Ethiopia, offers liberation and the solution of the present crisis [colonialism]."[71] Here again, though, Rastafari approach texts like the Bible differently. Members of the Twelve Tribes of Israel read its narratives regularly, as Luciano's "Chapter a Day" song reveals, even as other mansions, like the Nyabinghi, consult and discuss written scriptures with ferocious ambiguity.

Religion's Experiential or Emotional Dimension

Examples of religion's experiential or emotional dimension include, but are by no means restricted to, testimonies, illuminations, and prophetic visions, sometimes under the ritualized use of ganja.[72] Numerous instances of this dimension occur within Rastafari. One of the most informative examples may be found in *Book of Memory* (2004), the eyewitness testimony of Jamaican Rasta elder Prince Williams, who describes his experience during pivotal moments in the movement's early days, like the 1963 persecution of Rastafari in Jamaica's Coral Gardens.[73] Also consider Steven D. Glazier's work, which features case studies involving both incremental and radical conversions to Rastafari.[74] After encouraging his informants to describe their experiences and emotions, Glazier concludes that Rastafari conversion narratives typically invoke notions of spiritual journey or pilgrimage, appear intensely poignant, and seem unavoidably idiosyncratic. The same could be said for Rita Marley's turning-point encounter with Selassie in 1966; her testimony alludes to the Doubting Thomas story in Jn 20:24–29:

> Rastafarianism, the religion that holds that Emperor Haile Selassie I of Ethiopia was the risen Christ who would lead blacks the world over to freedom, was beginning to exert a powerful influence in Kingston during the late 1960s, but Rita Marley remained skeptical. When Selassie visited the island, she turned out with thousands of others to see him for herself, hoping for a sign. As his motorcade passed her, he waved and nodded to her; in his open palm, she believed she saw the nail prints of the crucifixion, and from that moment on, her faith was unwavering. Her conversion deeply impressed her husband and influenced him to study and accept the Rastafarian beliefs that became so essential to his music and philosophy.[75]

Early B's reggae classic, "Visit of King Selassie," announces similar sentiments. Snoop Dogg's 2012 trip to Jamaica was also transformative, if eccentric, given his decision to convert to Rastafari after reasoning with Rasta elders, to be baptised as Snoop Lion, and then to publically proclaim himself Bob Marley's reincarnation, even as one of Marley's children sat in the audience at the press conference.[76]

"It is obvious that certain experiences can be important in religious history," Smart declares, and I would also add 'identity formation,' because a "psychology of blackness, resistance, and somebodiness," to cite phrasing used by Clinton Hutton and Nathaniel Samuel Murrell, is embedded in the experiences of Rastafari, whether that be in Christ-like visions or highly emotional conversion tales.[77]

Described as a "narrative of ethnogenesis," Charles Price's recent work explores this psychology of black somebodiness by showing how early Rastafari incorporated "a morally configured conception of Blackness" into "struggles for freedom, justice, and for a positive Black identity."[78] With the advent of Rastafari's globalization, however, fresh perils and possibilities have emerged, he says:

> Anciency [intense reverence for Africa's history and heritage], Black redemption, repatriation, righteous living, and the Godly Emperor Haile Selassie I, cornerstones of the identity of those who came into the faith through the late 1960s, must now jostle with a movement in abeyance and a people who now position Rastafari identity in diverse ways within their self-concept. Selassie I, Black redemptions, and the moral aspects of Blackness may be less important to new adherents of Rastafari identity.[79]

Such "new adherents" include white Rastafari, such as Robert and Julia Roskind, whose 2001 memoir shows how the culturally creolized or blended experiences of white Rastas challenge what Price calls the movement's customary appeal to "the centrality of Blackness."[80] Of course, those who follow trends in popular culture will know how easy it is to satirize this phenomenon, as 'Ras Trent' shows; this 'SNL digital short' features a privileged white kid using his fluency in Rastafari patois or Africanized English—dread talk—to chant down bourgeois conformism, even as he embodies it. All comedy aside, it seems that scholars like Michael Loadenthal find white Rastafari riveting, even the so-called Trustafarians and Impostafarians, because they complicate the issue of what and who constitutes an 'authentic' Rasta, an issue that appears unlikely to be resolved soon.[81]

Religion's Ethical or Legal Dimension

Moral imperatives, which may or may not be enshrined in law, represent religion's ethical or legal dimension.[82] The Rastafari salutation, 'peace and love,' which may be heard both inside and outside reasoning sessions, provides a guide for moral action, and thus represents the faith's fundamental example of this dimension. Much of what passes for ital livity—vegetarianism, avoidance of alcohol and tobacco, herbal healing, and the cultivation of locks—also falls into this category. Specifically, Barry Chevannes's ethnography of the Bobo Shanti details the situational ethics of this idealized, utopian community located in Bull Bay, nine miles east of Jamaica's capital.[83] The commune's entrance indicates that violent weapons are forbidden, for example, and one of the compound's several structures allows menstruating women to observe specific ritual imperatives set forth in scripture and strictly reinforced by King Emmanuel Charles Edwards VII, the community's founder-leader. Chevannes also notes how the Bobo Shanti are unlike other Rastafari, because the Bobo Shanti agree to live together, wrap their hair in turbans, wear flowing vestments or robes, and many even gesture differently from that of other *locksmen* and *-women* (dreadlocked Rastafari).

Despite this pronounced sense of self and other, the local community praise the Bobo Shanti for their hospitality and kindness, Chevannes concludes.[84]

There are variations within the Rastafari movement, as the work of Chevannes and others makes clear, and perhaps such differences may best be seen in the ethical realm. Consider the principle of spiritual and political revolution. Rastas believe in chanting down Babylon, as I have noted, and yet they often seem divided on how to accomplish this task. Some mansions favor repatriation, and the Bobo Shanti exemplify this ethic, and others, like the Twelve Tribes of Israel, prefer rehabilitation. Either way, Rastafari dedicate themselves to the principles of spiritual revolution and political resistance, and these entangled commitments produce moral codes that shape the varieties of Rastafari religious experience.[85] Reggae songs such as Army's "Rasta Awake," Chronixx's "Selassie Souljahz," Jah Mali's "Blood Thirsty," and Lorenzo's "Trod in the Valley" enunciate such codes, revealing Rastafari's ethical imagination.

Religion's Organizational or Social Dimension

Religion's organizational or social dimension refers to how and why it institutionalizes itself across time and through charismatic figures, visionaries, and/or leaders. Groups are also important in this dimension. The Bobo Shanti, the Nyabinghi, and the Twelve Tribes of Israel, signify the three most noticeable mansions in Rastafari, as noted earlier, and such subdivisions or denominations display different approaches to Rastafari livity. Emily Raboteau explains:

> These groups don't all share the same beliefs and practices. Some require dreadlocks and believe that ganja is a telephone to God, but some don't. Some shun the Bible as a book of lies while others repeatedly read it cover to cover. Some embrace all races while others take a black-supremacist, militantly antiwhite stance. Many, but not all, adhere to a strict, salt-free, vegetarian, Ital (vital) diet. What, then, do the houses of Rastafari have in common? A defiant, anticolonialist mind-set, a spirit of protest, a reverence for former Ethiopian emperor Haile Selassie, and a notion that Africa is the spiritual home to which they are destined to return.[86]

Famous Bobo Shanti include musicians such as Anthony B., Capleton, and Sizzla Kalonji. Still more reggae artists, such as Luciano and Freddie McGregor, associate with the Twelve Tribes of Israel. Other, smaller mansions, such as African Unity, Covenant Rastafari, Messianic Dreads, and the Selassian Church, which emerged in the final throes of the last century and in the early part of our own, may partition the movement even further in coming years. Such growth is an important part of religion's life. And like any other developing body of believers, Rastafari are not immune to growing pains, which often appear in the form of power struggles, such as the energetic bickering that followed Sizzla Kalonji's inauguration as head of the Rastafari movement in late 2012. Numerous Nyabinghi resisted Sizzla's move and their complaints, along with those of other brethren and sistren, underline Rastafari's time-honored disavowal of a presiding authority. Yet there are groups, like the Rastafarian Centralization Organization, which foster intra-religious cooperation among Rastafari—of the sort that revived Trinidadian Rastas in 2009.[87]

The Rastafari movement has had its fair share of key figures, despite its decentralized structure, and besides Marcus Garvey and Haile Selassie, I have noted the roles played by Archibald Dunkley, King Emmanuel Charles Edwards VII, Robert Hinds, Leonard P. Howell, and Rita as well as Bob Marley. Stately songs praising such trailblazers, such as Everton Blender's "Leonard Howell," Junior Reid's "Emmanuel Calling," and Tarrus Riley's "Love Created I," are now part of reggae's urgent detail, delivered amid growling drum-and-basslines or else through coolly restrained, sensuous acoustic riffs. Other notable leaders include Vernon Carrington, widely known as the Prophet Gad, leader of the Twelve Tribes of Israel. Bob Marley belonged to this organization, whose houses are scattered throughout the world, and reggae mix master Scientist has crafted several dub soundscapes, including "Gad Man the Prophet," in honor of Carrington's spiritual and moral authority. Reflections on the Prophet Gad's leadership, together with an interview, appear in William David Spencer's *Dread Jesus* (1999), which was released before the Prophet Gad's passing in 2005. Also, the contribution of the late Ras Sam Brown—Rastafari elder as well as leader of the Suffering People's Party in the 1960s—to Jamaican politics has been recorded in recent years.[88]

When initial leaders or early visionaries die, other leaders often emerge, and fresh authority steps in and begins to take the movement in new directions. Original charisma becomes routinized or settled over time, as sociologists like Max Weber say, or, to switch the trope, the bones of the infant group ossify, enabling it to stand up as well as walk, even to run. Scholars call this occurrence 'institutionalization.' And after eighty years, Rastafari may best be viewed as moving through this complex process, emerging from its childhood years into its adult stage, part of which involves group inquiry into its postcharismatic fate, according to Barry Chevannes.[89] As an example of such fine-tuning, Chevannes mentions the changes underway in how Rastas now theologize death. In the movement's nascent stages, Rastafari held "no truck with death and funerals," and they believed "that those who died had no part with the living God."[90] After various and early leaders transitioned to the ancestor realm, though, many Rastas internalized death's certainty, and now plan accordingly:

> The internal adjustment that the Rastafari movement as a whole has had to make to their belief concerning the natural phenomenon of death is the most convincing evidence of a process of routinization underway. From a stance of resolute denial of the necessity of death for the truly faithful to the acceptance of its inevitability is quite a distance. There was a time when

the word 'dedaz' (dead things) was commonly used by the righteous to heap scorn on meat eaten by the unrighteous. While there is no reason to suggest any change in food ways, it can no longer be said that the Rastafari have no truck with death. All that remains to be done is for the movement to develop its own liturgy of the final rite of passage. Until one emerges, the Ethiopian Orthodox Church will continue to oblige.[91]

Chevannes makes instructive use of Weberian sociological theory in his work. The same can be said for Ennis B. Edmonds's grasp of Rastafari's present and future directionality. It is no coincidence, as I turn to consider religion's material or artistic dimension, that Edmonds links reggae to the routinization of Rastafari at home and abroad.[92] As Rastafari globalizes, we discover vast changes in Rastafari identity. Over time, as whites join and identify with the movement, Rastafari experiences a stretching of cultural and racial boundaries. This change in group dynamics is related to artistic production. The growing consumerism of Rastafari means that identity with the movement often gets purchased.

Religion's Material or Artistic Dimension

"A religion or worldview will express itself typically in material creations," Smart observes, "from chapels to cathedrals to temples to mosques, from icons and divine statuary to books and pulpits."[93] When Smart speaks of such creations, though, he refers to the production of the religious group itself, which in this case entails everything from Rastafari architecture to dancehall concert posters, and yet my book engages visual, literary, and musical elements from both etic and emic sources.[94] This approach need not trouble us, because terms such as 'inside' and 'outside' signify two ends of an invented continuum; in the cut-and-thrust of everyday life, things seem less simple and more complex, because religion, *any* religion, is almost always shaped by the viewpoints of the outsider *as well as* the insider. Given film's transnational appeal, for example, Western Christian views of Jesus owe as much, if not more, to Hollywood movie moguls than they do to church theologians.[95]

Whether or not Rastafari craft and distribute them, artistic treatments of transcendence facilitate the movement's intercontinental spread. In summer 2013, the Institute of Jamaica (IOJ) in association with various members of the island's Rastafari community showcased artefacts, paintings, and utensils at Kingston's Water Lane Gallery; the "Rastafari Exhibition" emphasized "the contributions of Rastafari to the Jamaican society and the world, while at the same time revealing the response of the Jamaican society towards the movement," the IOJ's assistant curator, Makabe Trott, informed *The Jamaica Gleaner*. The IOJ exposition was not the first of its kind. "One Love: Discovering Rastafari!" was curated by Jake Homiak, a cultural anthropologist with over thirty years' experience researching Rastafari, and it appeared throughout 2008 at the Smithsonian's National Museum of

Natural History, Washington DC. Although both exhibitions moved spectators beyond an exclusive focus on reggae music, in this section I note that reggae has been the strongest and most effective medium of broadcasting Rastafari livity to an international audience.[96]

Bob Marley's music placed Rastafari on the world's cultural map, as Kevin Macdonald's documentary film (*Marley*; 2012) shows, and the Tuff Gong warrior continues to inspire artists—from solo performers in Ghana, like Blakk Rasta, to Jah Division, a sound system based in the Slovak Republic—to spread Rastafari's vibe around the globe, sometimes with intriguing results.[97] Marvin D. Sterling testifies to a thriving reggae dance scene in Tokyo, Osaka, and even rural Japan, for example, and Timothy Rommen shows that reggae's globalization has created the space for novel re-inscriptions of Rasta livity, in the United States and in the Caribbean especially, where Protestant reggae bands fuse Rastafari and Christian ideologies without concern.[98] Bands like Three Plus are creating brand new genres, like Jahawaiian, in Honolulu. Also consider Reggae Rajahs, India's first reggae sound system, who represent a fresh, killer sound for New Delhi and other parts of South-east Asia. Global Rasta websites, like WorldofJah, showcase these and other, similar performers. According to Sarah Daynes, such social media not only fosters our globalized self-understanding, it represents an imperative issue for contemporary Rastafari:

> Music is now present everywhere through this medium, and reggae fans organize networks for discussion, information and meetings through the medium of the Internet. Irie FM, the Jamaican reggae station, can be listened to from any computer, whether it is in Wisconsin or on a Greek island. Music has never been so easy to diffuse and distribute, and whether it will lead either to a uniformity of what reggae fans listen to, or on the other hand to a multiplicity of sounds that will be found everywhere instead of limited to their place of emergence only, is an open question, and one that deserves interest.[99]

Rastafari and the Arts profiles Asante Amen, Rocky Dawuni, and other reggae musicians, to stress the movement's material or artistic dimension and yet, to complicate matters, it also moves beyond the customary example of reggae to emphasize how other imaginative expressions—novels, documentary film, dub poetry, drama, and intuitive painting—serve as instructive mechanisms for the transcultural transmission of the faith's message. Two examples illustrate my point. Films like Oliver Hill's *Coping with Babylon* feature concert footage as well as behind-the-scenes interviews, and by engaging Rastafari's inner vitality and the claims its spokespersons—such as Luciano, Freddie McGregor, and Half Pint—make, such documentaries help us grasp how Rastas confront the spiritual and moral issues that arise out of living in Jamaica and elsewhere. Also, the self-taught visual artists featured in Wolfgang Bender's *Rastafarian Art* likewise portray the possibilities and perils faced by today's Rastas. Consider Ras Dizzy, an insider to the movement, whose work has appeared in two major surveys (1987, 2005) of intuitive art at The National Gallery of Jamaica. His compositions, like "Rastas are Religios" (1989), display broad brushstrokes, and they serve as the visual analog to his philosophical writings, which espouse something I have tried to ponder in this chapter—the notion that Rastafari is a living, vibrant, and durable religion.[100]

The painting of Ejay Khan, an outsider, also publicizes Rastafari. Khan lived and worked in Westmoreland, Jamaica in the 1990s; and her first marriage, to Ras Prophet, introduced her to, and inspired her to identify with, the movement's message and livity. These days she creates Rastafari art from her studio in northeastern Massachusetts, and the following interview testifies to her sense of the importance of the material or artistic dimension of the Rastafari religion.

An Interview with Ejay Khan

DJNM: How has Rastafari shaped your sense of spirituality or religion? What representative practices, or livity, do you incorporate into your life, for example, and do you consider yourself an 'insider' or an 'outsider' to the movement?

EJK: I was on a deep, all-encompassing spiritual path, just beginning to expand my understanding of my spirituality beyond the fundamental Christian dogma of my upbringing, when I traveled to Jamaica and met my future husband, a powerful spiritual being and Rasta known as Ras Prophet. We married a few months later and I spent the next four years living in the tiny seaside country ghetto of Little Bay. During those years, my beliefs, faith, and spirituality were tested and stretched repeatedly, as I learned the livity of Rastafari, and how to live in the moment in love and faith without all the conveniences and things Babylon teaches us are necessary for happiness. I have the greatest respect for the Rasta way of life, and for His Imperial Majesty Emperor Haile Selassie. I do not consider myself an insider to the Rastafari movement, or to any specific movement or religion, but I connect more with Rasta than any other. I do not specifically incorporate some Rasta practices (I do not smoke ganja—I am not opposed to it in any way, but just don't feel the need; I cook relatively ital, but not as strictly as when I lived in Jamaica and was cooking for Prophet; I shave my legs and under arms—something I gave up during my years in Jamaica because it was an offense to Prophet and not worth arguing over); however, I do continue to incorporate the love, peace, tolerance, unity, and compassion of Rasta in my daily life, and I continue to live outside the Babylon system as much as possible.

DJNM: Your website houses your growing gallery of Rasta-inspired art [http://www.khanstudiointernational.com/galleryrastafarian.htm]. And here, you talk of the "positive influence of Rastafarians in the world." Care to elaborate?

EJK: As I said in my answer to the previous question, I think the love, peace, tolerance, unity, and compassion Rasta exhibit in their daily lives, and living outside of and free from the Babylon system as much as possible, are very positive teachings and livity that the whole world community could benefit from more of. The thing I most admire about true Rastafari is their refusal to be politically correct or become a social organization, which I think is the downfall of many churches today. They are more concerned about political correctness and providing something for everyone rather than speaking the truth (even if it offends) and providing spiritual nourishment (rather than just bean suppers and coffee hours).

DJNM: Do you think Rastafari visual art parallels other religious painting? If so, how? If not, why not?

EJK: Yes, and I believe it logically would because most Rasta I have known grew up in Christian families, and the Rastafari beliefs are based on teachings contained in the Bible, and fulfillment of biblical prophesies. Haile Selassie himself was a devout Ethiopian Orthodox Christian. Of course other religious paintings throughout history have not focused on black, African, or dreadlocked religious figures, so Rasta art is unique in that regard, but still has a religious feel to it whether Rasta consider Rastafari a religion or not, at least from what I have seen. Also, I believe all religious art is inspired, so would have a similar feel and parallel message, whether Rastafari, Islamic, Buddhist, Christian, Jewish, Krishna, Hindu, etcetera.

FIGURE 5 Ejay Khan, "Rastafarian Last Supper" (2009).

DJNM: Your "Rastafarian Last Supper" painting (2009) radiates rich golds and reds, yet it seems quite unlike some of the traditional depictions of Christ's final meal, which feature perplexed or shocked disciples. What were you aiming for with this regal, Africanized landscape and portraiture?

EJK: "Rastafarian Last Supper" was done as a result of many people contacting me over the years asking if I had painted one. Of course, there was no Last Supper in the Rastafarian ideology; however, I have long believed that Jesus and his apostles would have looked more like the way I depicted them in this painting. Like Rasta, I believe Africa is the motherland, so I placed the event under an acacia tree, which to me symbolizes Africa more than anything else I could think of. Also, the acacia is used as a symbol to represent purity and endurance of the soul, and to signify resurrection and immortality. Egyptian mythology associated the acacia tree with the tree of life, connecting all of creation. Of course I was going for the regal aspect of Haile Selassie (Christ in his "Kingly Character," to cite Garnett Silk's song), and the regal aspect of Rastafari in general. Many people ask me about the woman in the painting. She has no specific identify (although she would be Mary in the Christian Last Supper), and she was included because there would have been a woman there, even though most depictions of the Last Supper do not include one.

DJNM: Paintings such as "Signs and Wonders" (2009) and "Looks Like Redemption" (2009) appear to be linked, at least to me, and I note that the former painting features a lion, a lamb, and Bob Marley, set against a night sky shot through with meteors or comets. The latter painting retains the lion, but this time we see a night sky *sans* Marley and the lamb, though the comets are present, and everything is focalized by a single shaft of light. Are the two paintings connected?

EJK: "Looks Like Redemption" was based on the Leonid meteor shower of 2009 and a cloud formation that appeared in the shape of a lion. "Signs and Wonders" was a subsequent version that just naturally took off in more of a Rastafarian direction with the addition of Bob Marley and the lamb. Selassie, being the Conquering Lion of the Tribe of Judah, always comes to mind for me when a lion enters the scene. Lambs also always come to mind for me when there is a lion (Isa 11:6). I look forward to the day when they and all will figuratively lie together and eat grass.[101] Bob Marley, as the ambassador of reggae and spreading the word about Rastafari to the world, had to be included in a piece that focused on redemption.

DJNM: Eschatological or 'end times' themes seem to prevail in "Earth's Rightful Ruler" (2006), because His Imperial Majesty sits at planet Earth's center and, at his feet, we find the lion and the lamb, so evocative of the peace that many religious assume will mark the end of time. Thoughts?

EJK: The Rasta saying: "Jah is earth's rightful ruler and he runs no wire fence" was in my mind when I did this painting. Selassie was said to always have lions around the palace and often accompanying him, as well as the fact that he was

FIGURE 6 Ejay Khan, "Earth's Rightful Ruler" (2006).

given the title "King of Kings, Lord of Lords, Conquering Lion of the Tribe of Judah" at his coronation, so there had to be a lion at his feet. The lamb of course represents the world peace and unity that will exist when Rasta rules the world—when the day of revelation comes and everyone suddenly remembers that we are all one: 'One Love, One Heart, One Destiny.'

DJNM: When I first found your website, and thus looked through your gallery of images, I was struck by your "Conquering Lion" (2007) painting. This arresting image depicts a militant, sword-brandishing and dreadlocked Rasta against a blood red sky, together with an angry lion, which seems to have morphed into, or has emerged from, a thunderous or threatening sky. A meteor shower descends, as it does in several of your works; and, I am keen to know what was going through your mind when you painted this 'Rasta-pocalypse,' for want of a better term.

EJK: Rasta are very peaceful, loving people; however, they can also become filled with explosive righteous indignation, passionately wanting to figuratively

FIGURE 7 Ejay Khan, "Conquering Lion" (2007).

'burn down Babylon' (kind of like Jesus overturning the seller's tables in the Temple [Mk 11:15–19]). We have become too complacent and just roll over in the face of the oppressor and show our soft underbellies because they promise us material stuff, and an illusion of safety and security. I have the greatest respect for the righteous indignation of Rasta confronting the machine, their David and Goliath story. This painting depicts a conquering lion (Rasta) after winning his battle against the ways of the world (comparing again to Jesus, after his forty days in the wilderness being tempted by Satan [Mk 1:9–13]). It could also represent the greater 'Rastapocalypse' term you coined. That's the great thing about art, it can be whatever you see and however you interpret what you see.

DJNM: Some of your paintings are paired with your poetry—why is this? Your "Rasta Lion" (2005) painting has a man's face (Ras Prophet?) on a lion's body, for example, and the accompanying poem speaks of each Rasta finding the "kingdom of Zion" within his or her soul—is Zion a state of mind, then, or is it a destination (Africa, Ethiopia), or is it both?

EJK: To me the Kingdom of Zion/Heaven are states of mind/being as opposed to external physical places. And once again, I have a Garnett Silk song in mind. I have an affinity for Silk's lyrics because they speak to me more directly and personally than many other artists, and his "Zion in a Vision" reminds me of a waking vision I had that forever changed my view of Zion/Heaven and physical death. In any event, Silk likens Zion/Heaven to a family reunion, an atmosphere of love, communitarianism, and righteousness. That state of being exists here and now, without the need to go anywhere. Rastas know that and it is their job for each one to try to teach one, until everyone knows.

DJNM: "Free to Soar" (1998) depicts a Rasta whose dreadlocks become entwined in an old tree; a lion; a bird of prey clutching an artist's brush; and an infant sleeping at the tree's base. The artwork appears to gesture towards the possibilities and perils of being Rasta and of making Rastafari art today. How would you describe the changes and challenges Rastafari face in the new millennium? And what's next for you, vocationally and spiritually?

EJK: "Free to Soar" is actually a painting about myself and my experience living in Jamaica. I am the baby at the lion's feet when I first arrive in Jamaica, being aware but having much to learn. Through my years of living and growing with Prophet (in the tree), I emerge wiser and free to soar on the other side of the experience. The soaring owl clutching the paintbrush is me. As far as the challenges Rastafari face in the new millennium, they are the same challenges faced by everyone: keeping our focus, not forgetting who and what we are, and staying in the present in the face of a world that wants us to believe the opposite of what is true. As for me, I continue creating new

FIGURE 8 Ejay Khan, "Free to Soar" (1998).

work, currently mixed-media photo montages focused on the abstract grit and glory of the working side of Gloucester, America's oldest working sea port, which is in a major state of flux due to state and federal regulations impacting the fishing industry. Spiritually, I can't say what is next for me, since the path is ever shifting and moving in directions I never expect or can anticipate in advance.

Conclusion

Drawing on etic as well as emic sources, my first chapter has outlined the major dimensions of the Rastafari religious movement, culminating in my focus on the material or artistic dimension of Rastafari. I now turn to another example of my aesthetic approach to this religion, situating two early novels depicting Rastafari in the context of the movement's first few and somewhat tense years in Jamaica. After this initial investigation, I survey more contemporary examples of Rastafari literary art, penned by insiders and outsiders alike.

Notes

1 Actually, my student's experience is not unusual. For additional details, see: http://www.huffingtonpost.com/2013/05/01/rastanana-rasta-banana-photos_n_3193916.html. Accessed March 30, 2014.

2 On the distinctive language of Rastafari, see Velma Pollard, *Dread Talk: The Language of Rastafari*, revised edition (Montreal: McGill-Queen's University Press, 2000).

3 On Rastafari mansions, especially their differences, see Ennis B. Edmonds, *Rastafari: A Very Short Introduction* (Oxford and New York: Oxford University Press, 2013), 52–70. Also see Ennis B. Edmonds, *Rastafari: From Outcasts to Culture Bearers* (Oxford and New York: Oxford University Press, 2003), 67–96.

4 On this School, see: http://www.youtube.com/watch?v=0OgOXzLvX3o and http://www.youtube.com/watch?v=dDwT9Amf9NI. Accessed March 30, 2014.

5 On Zephaniah's observations regarding Rastafari's diversity, see: http://www.guardian.co.uk/commentisfree/2012/aug/07/snoop-dogg-rastafari. Accessed March 30, 2014.

6 Rita and Bob Marley's granddaughter, Prendergast, travels to eight countries in search of Rastafari's international presence. For the official trailer, see: http://www.youtube.com/watch?v=VAWQt329n0U. Accessed March 30, 2014.

7 For such studies, see: Neil J. Savishinsky, "Transnational Popular Culture and the Global Spread of the Jamaican Rastafarian Movement," in Morton Klass and Maxine K. Weisgrau, editors, *Across the Boundaries of Belief: Contemporary Issues in the Anthropology of Religion* (Boulder, CO: Westview Press, 1999), 347–366; Fortune Sibanda, "The Impact of Rastafari Ecological Ethic in Zimbabwe: A Contemporary Discourse," *Journal of Pan African Studies* 5.3 (2012): 59–75; Marvin D. Sterling, *Babylon East: Performing Dancehall, Roots Reggae, and Rastafari in Japan* (Durham, NC: Duke University Press, 2010); Edward Te Kohu and Ian Boxhill, "The Lantern and the Light: Rastafari in Aotearoa (New Zealand)," *IDEAZ* 7 (2008): 70–97; Carmen White, "Rastafarian Repatriates and the Negotiation of Place in Ghana," *Ethnology: An International*

Journal of Cultural and Social Anthropology 49.4 (2010): 303–320; Frank Wittmann, "The Global-Local Nexus: Popular Music Studies and the Case of Rastafari Culture in West Africa," *Critical Arts* 25.2 (2011): 150–174. Finally, see Edmonds, *Rastafari: A Very Short Introduction*, 71–93.

8 Richard Salter, "Rastafari in a Global Context: Affinities of 'Orthognosy' and 'One-ness' in the Expanding World," *IDEAZ* 7 (2008): 11.

9 On Haile Selassie, see Harold G. Marcus, *A History of Ethiopia* (Berkeley, CA: University of California Press, 1994), 116–180. Also see Clinton Chisholm, "The Rasta-Selassie-Ethiopian Connections" in Nathaniel Samuel Murrell, William David Spencer, and Adrian Anthony McFarlane, editors, *Chanting Down Babylon: The Rastafari Reader* (Philadelphia: Temple University Press, 1998), 166–177. In addition, see Edmonds, *Rastafari: A Very Short Introduction*, 32–51. The centenary celebrations were captured in a documentary film. See John Dollar, *The Emperor's Birthday* (New York: Filmakers Library, 1992). I review this film in my book. For an account of this special journey, see Neville Garrick, *A Rasta's Pilgrimage: Ethiopian Faces and Places* (San Francisco: Pomegranate Communications, 1998). In an online article, Ayele Bekerie describes the event celebrating the 120th birthday-anniversary of Selassie by the Rastafari community in Ethiopia. See: http://www.tadias.com/07/30/2012/photo-journal-haile-selassies-120th-birthday-anniversary-in-shashemene-ethiopia/. Accessed March 30, 2014.

10 This number is an estimate. See Ennis B. Edmonds and Michelle A. Gonzalez, *Caribbean Religious History: An Introduction* (New York: New York University Press, 2010), 201. Exact figures are unavailable. On different views of Selassie, see Eleanor Wint in consultation with members of the Nyabinghi Order, "Who Is Haile Selassie?: His Imperial Majesty in Rasta Voices," in Murrell *et al.*, editors, *Chanting Down Babylon*, 159–165. Wint's interviews took place in Jamaica. I observed something similar—changing perceptions regarding Selassie—during fieldwork in West Africa, as my book makes clear. Also see Samuel Furé Davis, "A Voice from Cuba: Conceptual and Practical Difficulties with Studying Rastafari," *IDEAZ* 7 (2008): 28–40; Jan DeCosmo, "Globalization and Rastafari Identity in Salvador, Bahia, Brazil," *IDEAZ* 7 (2008): 52–69; and Adeline Masquelier, "'Rasta' Sufis and Muslim Youth Culture in Mali," in Linda Herrera and Asef Bayat, editors, *Being Young and Muslim: New Cultural Politics in the Global South and North* (New York: Oxford University Press, 2010), 241–259.

11 Financial and copyright concerns prevent the use of some images in my book. Much of the artwork may be found on the internet, intriguingly, and interested readers will notice that I have assembled a gallery of "Rastafarian Visual Art," culled from the web and with citation, at my website: www.darrenjnmiddleton.com. Accessed March 30, 2014.

12 For Ras Terms's website, see: http://www.rasterms.com/. Accessed March 30, 2014.

13 Jahlani Niaah, "The Rastafari Presence in Ethiopia: A Contemporary Perspective," in Michael Barnett, editor, *Rastafari in the New Millennium: A Rastafari Reader* (Syracuse, NY: Syracuse University Press, 2012), 81.

14 Oliver Hill, *Coping with Babylon: The Proper Rastology* (Oaks, PA: MVD Visual, 2007). For additional details, including a thoughtful review, see: http://www.popmatters.com/pm/review/coping-with-babylon-the-proper-rastology. Accessed March 30, 2014. I engage *Coping with Babylon* in my book.

15 E-mail with the author, March 2014. Willard is the owner and founder of Higher Bound Productions. For details, see: http://www.higherboundprod.com/. Accessed March 30, 2014. Readers who navigate this site will find a gallery of Rastafari album

cover art, which represents Willard's thoughtful and artistic approach to the musical transmission of Rastafari's message. Ras Terms is the artist for "Space N Time," as noted, and the graphic design for the album is by True Love (www.Fikir-studios.com). Accessed March 30, 2014.

16 On today's Shashemene, see Erin C. MacLeod, "Water Development Projects and Cultural Citizenship: Rastafari Engagement with the Oromo in Shashemene, Ethiopia," in Barnett, editor, *Rastafari in the New Millennium*, 89–103. On Kaleb Martin, see: http://www.youtube.com/watch?v=Z1fOmAJWF8M&sns=em. Accessed March 30, 2014.

17 On Ethiopianism among the Rastafari, see Leonard E. Barrett, *The Rastafarians*, with a new afterword (Boston: Beacon, 1997; 1988), 68–102. Also see Erin C. MacLeod, *Visions of Zion: Ethiopians and Rastafari in the Search for the Promised Land* (New York: New York University Press, 2014); Niaah, "The Rastafari Presence in Ethiopia," 66–88; and, Neil J. Savishinsky, "African Dimensions of the Jamaican Rastafarian Movement," in Murrell *et al.*, editors, *Chanting Down Babylon*, 125–144.

18 Henry Louis Gates, Jr., *Wonders of the African World* (New York: Alfred A. Knopf, 1999), 107. This book accompanies the PBS television series; for details, see: http://www.pbs.org/wonders/. Accessed March 30, 2014.

19 See http://www.youtube.com/watch?v=NWtNavPGdZg&feature=youtu.be. Accessed March 30, 2014.

20 Marcus Garvey, *The Philosophy and Opinions of Marcus Garvey* (London: Frank Cass & Co. Ltd., 1983), 33–34.

21 On Artwell and other intuitive artists, see Randall Morris, *Redemption Songs: The Self-Taught Artists of Jamaica* (Winston-Salem, NC: Winston-Salem State University, 1997). Also see Alan Bagshaw's online essay, "Rastafarian Visual Symbolism in the Visual Arts": http://debate.uvm.edu/dreadlibrary/bagshaw.html. Accessed March 30, 2014.

22 See Adolph Edwards, *Marcus Garvey, 1887–1940* (London; Port of Spain, Trinidad: New Beacon Books, 1967), 36. Also see Noel Leo Erskine, *From Garvey to Marley: Rastafari Theology* (Gainesville, FL: The University Press of Florida, 2005), 116. Barry Chevannes notes that while Selassie resisted Garvey's philosophy and opinions, and although Garvey disdained Selassie and Rastafari, most brethren and sistren revere Selassie and Garvey in their beliefs and rituals. See Chevannes, *Rastafari: Roots and Ideology* (Syracuse: Syracuse University Press, 1994), 109, 180. Also see Rupert Lewis, "Marcus Garvey and the Early Rastafarians: Continuity and Discontinuity," in Murrell *et al.*, editors, *Chanting Down Babylon*, 145–158. Lewis wonders if Rastafari's "decentralized and less organized (than Garveyism) nature will prove to be Rastafari's own salvation" in the immediate future (156). On Garvey's assessment of Selassie, see: http://www.jamaicans.com/culture/rasta/MarcusGarveyeditorial.shtml. Accessed March 30, 2014.

23 On Garvey and the UNIA, see the research project site at the University of California (Los Angeles): http://www.international.ucla.edu/africa/mgpp/. In addition, see the Marcus Garvey Foundation: http://www.garveyfoundation.com/. Both sites accessed March 30, 2014. Also see James G. Spady, Samir Meghelli, and Louis Jones, editors, *New Perspectives on the History of Marcus Garvey, the UNIA, and the African Diaspora* (New York: Marcus Garvey Foundation Publishers, 2011). On Garvey's prophecy, see Barrett, *The Rastafarians*, 81.

24 On the coronation, see http://www.youtube.com/watch?v=TO3Kes35UgI. Accessed March 30, 2014. Also see Evelyn Waugh, *The Coronation of Haile Selassie* (London: Penguin, 2005). On the movement's initial phase, see: Barrett, *The Rastafarians*, 80–102;

Horace Campbell, *Rasta and Resistance: From Marcus Garvey to Walter Rodney* (Trenton, NJ: Africa World Press, 1987), 69–120; Edmonds, *Rastafari: From Outcasts to Culture Bearers*, 29–40; Erskine, *From Garvey to Marley*, 59–84; Robert A. Hill, *Dread History: Leonard P. Howell and Millenarian Visions in the Early Rastafarian Religion* (Chicago: Miguel Lorne Publishers, 2001); William F. Lewis, *Soul Rebels: The Rastafari* (Prospect Heights, IL: Waveland Press, Inc., 1993), 1–16; Joseph Owens, *Dread: The Rastafarians of Jamaica* (London: Heinemann, 1976); M.G. Smith, Roy Augier, and Rex Nettleford, *Report on the Rastafari Movement in Kingston, Jamaica* (Mona, Jamaica: University College of the West Indies, Institute of Social and Economic Research, 1960); and Cadence Wynter, "Rodney and Rastafari: Cultural Identity in 1960s Jamaica," in Barnett, editor, *Rastafari in the New Millennium*, 300–309.

25 See Gerald Hausman, *The Kebra Nagast: The Lost Bible of Rastafarian Wisdom and Faith from Ethiopia and Jamaica* (New York: St. Martin's Press, 1997). An English translation of *The Kebra Nagast* is available online: http://www.sacred-texts.com/chr/kn/. Accessed March 30, 2014. For specifics on the lineage claims, see Chisholm, "The Rasta-Selassie-Ethiopian Connections," 167–169. Finally, see Patrick Taylor, "Sheba's Song: The Bible, the *Kebra Nagast*, and the Rastafari" in Patrick Taylor, editor, *Nation Dance: Religion, Identity, and Cultural Difference in the Caribbean* (Bloomington, IN: Indiana University Press, 2001), 65–78.

26 Campbell, *Rasta and Resistance*, 65. As the June 2011 Leonard Howell Symposium at the University of West Indies illustrates, Howell was one of the most significant contributors to the movement's development. Also see Hélène Lee, *The First Rasta: Leonard Howell and the Rise of Rastafarianism* (Chicago, IL: Lawrence Hill Books, 2003).

27 Theo Witvliet, *A Place in the Sun: An Introduction to Liberation Theology in the Third World* (London: SCM Press, 1985), 104–117. For Rastafari within the broader context of black theology, see Theo Witvliet, *The Way of the Black Messiah: The Hermenetical Challenge of Black Theology as a Theology of Liberation* (London: SCM Press, 1987). On Rastafari biblical hermeneutics, see the following selected sources: Laurence A. Breiner, "The English Bible in Jamaican Rastafarianism," *Journal of Religious Thought* 42.2 (Fall–Winter 1985): 30–44; Nathaniel S. Murrell, "Wresting the Message from the Messenger: The Rastafari as a Case Study in the Caribbean Indigenization of the Bible," in R.S. Sugirtharajah, editor, *Voices from the Margin: Interpreting the Bible in the Third World* (Maryknoll, NY: Orbis Books, 2006), 169–188; Nathaniel Samuel Murrell and Lewin Williams, "The Black Biblical Hermeneutics of Rastafari," in Murrell *et al.*, editors, *Chanting Down Babylon*, 326–348; and finally, Taylor, "Sheba's Song," 65–78.

28 Rastafari are not alone in noting Africa's place in the Bible. Edward Ullendorff's, *Ethiopia and the Bible* (Oxford: Oxford University Press, 1968) is a classic treatment of the topic. Also see Edwin M. Yamauchi, *Africa and the Bible* (Grand Rapids, MI: Baker Academic, 2004), especially 100–105 (on the Queen of Sheba in Ethiopian traditions).

29 The Emperor's words appear in an interview with Canada's CBC news in 1967, one year after his official visit to Jamaica. Selassie emphasizes his mortality. See: http://www.jamaicans.com/culture/rasta/interview_popup.shtml. Accessed March 30, 2014. The Apostle Paul speaks of how Jesus did not boast about his divine status; rather, he voluntarily evacuated (*kenosis*) his divinity and humbled himself, became human and served others (Phil 2:6–11). Rastas I have encountered often cite this text and make the comparison with Selassie.

30 On Babylon, see Owens, *Dread*, 69–89. Owens points out that the term refers to the police, state, and church structures in Jamaica, Britain, and North America. All

forms of organized religion, especially Roman Catholicism, are the 'downpressors of dread.' For a more recent account of how Babylon-thinking works among Rastas, see Edmonds, *Rastafari: From Outcasts to Culture Bearers*, 41–66.

31 Today, the Twelve Tribes of Israel mansion, which has a long history of racial inclusivity, appears to be the subgroup of choice for white converts to Rastafari. See Edmonds, *Rastafari: A Very Short Introduction*, 68. Barbara Makeda Blake Hannah discusses white Rastas in her book *Rastafari: The New Creation*, sixth edition (Kingston, Jamaica: Jamaica Media Productions, 2006; 1981). References to white Rastas abound in Norman Stolzoff's anthropological study *Wake the Town and Tell the People: Dancehall Culture in Jamaica* (Durham, NC: Duke University Press, 2000). Also see Campbell, *Rasta and Resistance*, 117; Hausman, *Kebra Nagast*, 150; and Timothy White, *Catch a Fire: The Life of Bob Marley* (New York: Holt, 1998), 281. For fictional treatments of white Rastas, see recent novels by Adam Davies (*The Frog King*), Nicola Griffith (*The Blue Place*), David Liss (*The Ethical Assassin*), Emily Listfield (*Best Intentions*), and Christopher Moore (*A Dirty Job*). White Rastas notwithstanding, the anticolonial call of the Rastafari is heard by black people everywhere, from Jamaican peasant life to major British cities. See the essays in Barry Chevannes, editor, *Rastafari and Other African-Caribbean Worldviews* (New Brunswick, NJ: Rutgers University Press, 1998).

32 On Rastas rehabilitating their wider society, see Edmonds, *Rastafari: From Outcasts to Culture Bearers*, 79–96. In saying that many modern Rastas favor rehabilitation, I do not imply that Rastas have abandoned the hope of repatriation. This is not the case among the Bobo Shanti mansion, for example, and Werner Zips writes about this and other, related issues in "'Repatriation is a Must!': The Rastafari Struggle to *Downstroy* Slavery" in Werner Zips, editor, *Rastafari: A Universal Philosophy in the Third Millennium* (Kingston, Jamaica; Miami: Ian Randle Publishers, 2006), 129–168. In addition, see Werner Zips, "'Global Fire': Repatriation and Reparations from a Rastafari (Re) Migrant's Perspective," in Franz von Benda-Beckmann, Keebet von Benda-Beckmann and Anne Griffiths, editors, *Mobile People, Mobile Law: Expanding Legal Relations in a Contracting World* (Burlington, VT; Aldershot, Hampshire, UK: Ashgate Publishing Company, 2005), 69–89. Also see Lewis, *Soul Rebels*, 105–114. In addition, I do not imply that the Rastafari lack an African presence; as my book indicates, this is not the case. Chapters on Ghanaian Rastafari in the Zips collection are also instructive. In addition, the Rastafari Community of Shashemene has been politically active in recent years, writing to the United Nations to ratify its existence in Ethiopia legally. See Katherine McKittrick and Clyde Woods, editors, *Black Geographies and the Politics of Place* (Toronto; Cambridge, MA: Between the Lines; South End Press, 2007), 247–248. Moreover, see Erin C. MacLeod, "Water Development Projects and Cultural Citizenship," 89–103. On what would have been Marley's sixtieth birthday in 2005, newspaper reports cited the singer's widow, Rita, as saying she had plans to repatriate her husband's remains to Shashemene: http://www.guardian.co.uk/world/2005/jan/13/artsnews.ethiopia. This report was denied: http://news.bbc.co.uk/2/hi/entertainment/4172495.stm. On the difficulties in Shashemene, see Norimitsu Onishi, "Uneasy Bond Inside a Promised Land," *New York Times*, August 4, 2001: A4. For more recent news, see: http://www.guardian.co.uk/world/video/2010/jul/23/rastafarians-shashamane-ethiopia. All sites accessed March 30, 2014. Finally, see Campbell, *Rasta and Resistance*, 211–231.

33 Jah Bones, *One Love: Rastafari: History, Doctrine and Livity* (London: Voice of Rasta Publishing House, 1985), 12.

34 Campbell, *Rasta and Resistance*, 153–174. This research is part of his argument about Rastas becoming politically active in the Eastern Caribbean. "That these Rastas were not wanting to go back to Africa, but were participating in the fall of 'Babylon' in the Caribbean, was not lost to those who were horrified at the sight of Dreadlocks with guns" (163).

35 Barry Chevannes, *The Case of Jah Versus Middle Class Society: Rastafari Exorcism of the Ideology of Racism in Jamaica* (The Hague, Netherlands: Institute of Social Studies, 1989). Also see Barry Chevannes, "Rastafari and the Exorcism of the Ideology of Racism and Classism in Jamaica," in Murrell *et al.*, editors, *Chanting Down Babylon*, 55–71. Fran Jan van Dijk says something similar in an earlier article. See van Dijk, "The Twelve Tribes of Israel: Rasta and the Middle Class," *New West Indian Guide* 62.1 (1988): 1–26. Also see Adisa Andwele, "The Contribution of Rastafarianism to the Decolonization of the Caribbean" in Zips, editor, *Rastafari*, 7–20. For more recent commentary, see Anita M. Waters, "Reluctant Candidates?: Rastafarians and Partisan Politics in Jamaica and Elsewhere," in Barnett, editor, *Rastafari in the New Millennium*, 291–299. In addition, see Erskine, *From Garvey to Marley*, 189–198. Finally, Ennis B. Edmonds has documented this 'coming in from the cold' approach on the part of Jamaican Rastas. See Edmonds, *Rastafari: From Outcasts to Culture Bearers*, 79–96.

36 Barbara Bush, "The Dark Side of the City: Racialized Barriers, Culture and Citizenship in Britain, c.1950–1990s," in Zips, editor, *Rastafari*, 169–201. Also see Campbell, *Rasta and Resistance*, 181–209. Finally, see Ellis Cashmore, "The De-Labelling Process: From 'Lost Tribe' to Ethnic Group," in Chevannes, editor, *Rastafari and Other African-Caribbean Worldviews*, 182–195.

37 Katrin Hansing, *Rasta, Race and Revolution: The Emergence and Development of the Rastafari Movement in Socialist Cuba* (Berlin: Lit Verlag, 2006), 237. Interestingly, Hansing shows how Cuba represents a different kind of Babylon for the Rastas who live on the island (183–234).

38 Randal L. Hepner, "Chanting Down Babylon in the Belly of the Beast: The Rastafari Movement in Metropolitan USA," in Murrell *et al.*, editors, *Chanting Down Babylon*, 199–216. Also see Randal L. Hepner, "The House That Rasta Built: Church-Building and Fundamentalism Among New York Rastafarians," in R. Stephen Warner and Judith G. Wittner, editors, *Gatherings in Diaspora: Religious Communities and the New Immigration* (Philadelphia: Temple University Press, 1998), 197–234. For other perspectives on Rastas in the North American context, see Campbell, *Rasta and Resistance*, 175–181, and Lewis, *Soul Rebels*, 83–94.

39 Hepner focuses on gender especially. See Tricia Redeker Hepner and Randal L. Hepner, "Gender, Community, and Change among the Rastafari of New York City," in Tony Carnes and Anna Karpathakis, editors, *New York Glory: Religions in the City* (New York: New York University Press, 2001), 333–353. This article shows how and why Rastafari women are finding their voice within communities of faith in and around New York City.

40 Taylor, "Sheba's Song," 75.

41 Ninian Smart, *Dimensions of the Sacred: An Anatomy of the World's Beliefs* (Berkeley and Los Angeles: University of California Press, 1996), 2–3. Also see Ninian Smart, *Worldviews: Cross-Cultural Explorations of Human Beliefs*, third edition (Englewood Cliffs, NJ: Prentice Hall, 1999). For a robust assessment of Smart's approach, see the contributions to Ninian Smart, Peter Masefield, and Donald Wiebe, *Aspects of Religion: Essays in Honour of Ninian Smart* (New York: Peter Lang, 1994).

42 Smart, *Dimensions of the Sacred*, 2, 8.

43 *Ibid.*, 9–10.

44 For details, see Robert C. Fuller, *Spiritual But Not Religious: Understanding Unchurched America* (New York: Oxford University Press, 2001).

45 Mutabaruka, "Rasta from Experience," in Werner Zips, editor, *Rastafari*, 29–30. Relatedly, Mutabaruka versifies such sentiments in his "Spirituality" song-poem. For another insider's more trenchant opposition to identifying Rastafari as a religion, see Jah Bones, *One Love*, 4–8.

46 For the full text of Zephaniah's commentary on Snoop Lion's conversion to Rasta, see: http://guardiannews.com/commentisfree/2012/aug/07/snoop-dogg-rastafari. Accessed March 30, 2014.

47 Smart, *Dimensions of the Sacred*, 10. A fulsome account of this dimension is included in chapter two of Smart's book (70–129).

48 Carol D. Yawney, "Dread Wasteland: Rastafarian Ritual in West Kingston, Jamaica," in N. Ross Crumrine, editor, *Ritual, Symbolism and Ceremonialism in the Americas: Studies in Symbolic Anthropology* (Greenley, CO: Museum of Anthropology, University of Northern Colorado, 1978), 154–174.

49 Jill Norgren and Serena Nanda, *American Cultural Pluralism and Law*, third edition (Westport, CT; London: Praeger, 2006), 139–153. The authors offer a comparative study on religion and illicit drug use among Rastas and the Native American Church. Also see Ansley Hamid, *The Ganja Complex: Rastafari and Marijuana* (Lanham, MD: Lexington Books, 2002).

50 On President Mugabe, see: http://atlantablackstar.com/2012/09/13/robert-mugabes-disparaging-comments-bring-anger-in-jamaica/. Accessed March 30, 2014.

51 Lewis, *Soul Rebels*, 15–16; 60–61; 115–126.

52 Pauline Bain, "Identity, Protest and Healing: The Multiple Uses of Marijuana in Rastafari," in Debie LeBeau and Robert J. Gordon, editors, *Challenges for Anthropology in the 'African Renaissance': A Southern African Contribution* (Namibia: University of Namibia Press, 2001), 111–122.

53 On the history and symbolism associated with dreadlocks, see the two essays by Barry Chevannes in Chevannes, editor, *Rastafari and Other African-Caribbean Worldviews*, 77–126.

54 Pollard, *Dread Talk*. Also see Edmonds, *Rastafari: A Very Short Introduction*, 45–47.

55 See Lev 11–20. For details on ital livity, see Barrett, *The Rastafarians*, 140–142; Edmonds, *Rastafari: From Outcasts to Culture Bearers*, 67–78; Hansing, *Rasta, Race and Revolution*, 94–96; and John P. Homiak, "Dub History: Soundings on Rastafari Livity and Language," in Chevannes, editor, *Rastafari and Other African-Caribbean Worldviews*, 127–181.

56 For Lois Cordelia's website, see: http://www.loiscordelia.com/. Accessed March 30, 2014.

57 See: http://news.bbc.co.uk/2/hi/africa/1007736.stm and http://news.bbc.co.uk/2/hi/africa/1008721.stm. Rastafari were—and are—divided on the issue of the Emperor's death, burial, and reburial; see: http://news.bbc.co.uk/2/hi/africa/1007894.stm. All sites accessed March 30, 2014.

58 Mario Vargas Llosa, *The Language of Passion: Selected Commentary* (New York: Farrar, Straus and Giroux, 2003), 60.

59 Sebastian Clarke, *Jah Music: The Evolution of Popular Jamaican Song* (London: Heinemann, 1980) and Stephen Foehr, *Jamaican Warriors: Reggae, Roots, and Culture* (London: Sanctuary Publishing, 2000). On the Anglican church in Jamaica, see: http://www.christianpost.com/news/anglican-church-in-jamaica-to-add-bob-marley-to-hymn-books-28954/. Accessed March 30, 2014.

60 Support for this understanding of reggae, especially its transnational or transcultural qualities, appears in Michael Barnett, "From Warieka Hill to Zimbabwe: Exploring the Role of Rastafari in Popularizing Reggae Music," in Barnett, editor, *Rastafari in the New Millennium*, 270–277; Sarah Daynes, "The Musical Construction of the Diaspora: The Case of Reggae and Rastafari," in Sheila Whiteley, Andy Bennett, and Stan Hawkins, editors, *Music, Space and Place: Popular Music and Cultural Identity* (Burlington, VT; Aldershot, Hampshire, UK: Ashgate Publishing Company, 2004), 25–41; Edmonds, *Rastafari: From Outcasts to Culture Bearers*, 97–115; Erskine, *From Garvey to Marley*, 169–188; and Hansing, *Rasta, Race and Revolution*, 99–106.

61 Smart, *Dimensions of the Sacred*, 10. A fulsome account of this dimension is included in chapter one of Smart's book (27–69).

62 Edmonds, *Rastafari: A Very Short Introduction*, 51. For additional commentary on Rastafari ideology, philosophy, and praxis, see part three of Barnett, editor, *Rastafari in the New Millennium*, 123–174.

63 Michael Barnett, "The Many Faces of Rasta: Doctrinal Diversity within the Rastafari Movement," *Caribbean Quarterly* 51.2 (June 2005): 67–78. Barnett also shows how Rastafari's theological and political aspects commingle and diversify in Barnett, editor, *Rastafari in the New Millennium*.

64 On *Jus Jah* magazine, see: http://www.jusjahmagazine.com/. On the Empress of Zion, see: http://mjmagazine.wordpress.com/2011/03/14/sistahfestempress-of-zion-conference/. For Prendergast's film, see: http://rastajourney.com/. All sites accessed March 30, 2014.

65 See Jeanne Christensen, *Rastafari Reasoning and the Rasta Woman: Gender Constructions in the Shaping of Rastafari Livity* (Lanham, MD: Lexington Books, 2014); Bianca Nyavingi Brynda, *Roots Daughters: The Women of Rastafari* (Toronto: Fari International Productions; Oaks, PA: MVD Visual, 1992); Obiagele Lake, *RastafarI Women: Subordination in the Midst of Liberation Theology* (Durham, NC: Carolina Academic Press, 1998). Note the capital I in the title of Lake's book. Her book is one of the first attempts to reclaim a womanist or black feminist stance for Rastafari women, so she capitalizes the final letter to indicate the personhood of women in what was/is an essentially patriarchal religious worldview. For additional information on gender relations and the Rastafari, see Loretta Collins, "Daughters of Jah: The Impact of Rastafarian Womanhood in the Caribbean, the United States, Britain, and Canada," in Hemchand Gossai and Nathaniel Samuel Murrell, editors, *Religion, Culture and Tradition in the Caribbean* (New York: St. Martin's Press, 2000), 227–255; Maureen Rowe, "Gender and Family Relations in RastafarI: A Personal Perspective," in Murrell *et al.*, editors, *Chanting Down Babylon*, 72–88; Imani M. Tafari-Ama, "Rastawoman as Rebel: Case Studies in Jamaica," in Murrell *et al.*, editors, *Chanting Down Babylon*, 89–106; and Carol D. Yawney, "To Grow a Daughter: Cultural Liberation and the Dynamics of Oppression in Jamaica," in A. Milles and G. Finn, editors, *Feminism in Canada* (Montreal: Black Rose Press, 1983), 119–144. On how changing gender relations is an example of Rastafari's development, see Charles Price, *Becoming Rasta: Origins of Rastafari Identity in Jamaica* (New York: New York University Press, 2009), 213–217. Price believes "that the idealized patriarchal orientation adopted by some of the Rastafari, male and female, is giving way to more fluid understandings of gender based in the realities of the new terrain of the twenty-first-century" (216).

66 Imani M. Tafari-Ama, "Resistance Without and Within: Reasonings on Gender Relations in RastafarI," in Barnett, editor, *Rastafari in the New Millennium*, 190–221.

67 Smart, *Dimensions of the Sacred*, 10. A fulsome account of this dimension is included in chapter three of Smart's book (130–165).

68 Marcus Wilson is the artist for "New Name," as noted, and the graphic design for the album is by True Love (www.Fikir-studios.com). Accessed March 30, 2014.

69 William David Spencer, "The First Chant: Leonard Howell's *The Promised Key*, with commentary by William David Spencer," in Murrell *et al.*, editors, *Chanting Down Babylon*, 361–389. Also see Dereck Daschke and W. Michael Ashcraft, editors, *New Religious Movements: A Documentary Reader* (New York and London: New York University Press, 2005), 205–223. This anthology contains instructive excerpts from Rastafari sacred texts.

70 Nathaniel Samuel Murrell, "*Holy Piby*: Blackman's Bible and Garveyite Ethiopianist Epic with Commentary," in Gossai and Murrell, editors, *Religion, Culture and Tradition in the Caribbean*, 271–306.

71 Michael Hoenisch, "Rastafari-Black Decolonization," in Paola Boi and Sabine Broeck, editors, *CrossRoutes: The Meanings of 'Race' for the 21st Century* (Münster: Lit; Piscataway, NJ: Distributed in North America by Transaction Publishers, 2003), 145. For a similar assessment, see Anthony Bogues, *Black Heretics, Black Prophets: Radical Political Intellectuals* (New York: Routledge, 2003), 153–165.

72 Smart, *Dimensions of the Sacred*, 10–11. A fulsome account of this dimension is included in chapter four of Smart's book (166–195).

73 Prince Williams with Michael Kuelker, *Book of Memory: A Rastafari Testimony* (St. Louis, MO: CaribSound Ltd., 2004).

74 Stephen D. Glazier, "Being and Becoming a Rastafarian: Notes on the Anthropology of Religious Conversion," in Zips, editor, *Rastafari*, 256–281.

75 See: http://www.musicianguide.com/biographies/1608001329/Rita-Marley.html. Accessed March 30, 2014.

76 On Snoop Lion's 2012 conversion, as documented by his film crew, see: https://www.youtube.com/watch?v=MTqyV5Kw9Ss&feature=player_embedded. On Snoop Lion as the reincarnated Bob Marley, see: https://www.youtube.com/watch?v=EX7EqelDuQg&feature=player_embedded. Both sites accessed March 30, 2014.

77 Smart, *Dimensions of the Sacred*, 10. Also see Clinton Hutton and Nathaniel Samuel Murrell, "Rastas' Psychology of Blackness, Resistance, and Somebodiness," in Murrell *et al.*, editors, *Chanting Down Babylon*, 36–54.

78 Price, *Becoming Rasta*, 2, 18.

79 *Ibid.*, 211.

80 *Ibid.*, 213. Also see Robert Roskind and Julia Roskind, *Rasta Heart: A Journey into One Love* (Blowing Rock, NC: One Love Press, 2001).

81 On Ras Trent: http://www.youtube.com/watch?v=TcK0MYgnHjo&feature=kp. For Michael Loadenthal's research on White Rastafari, see: http://www.academia.edu/1470305/_2003_Jah_People_The_Cultural_Hybridity_of_White_Rastafarians. Both sites accessed March 30, 2014. Finally, see Brian Griffin, *The Trustafarian Handbook: A Field Guide to the Neo-Hippie Lifestyle—Funded by Mom and Dad* (Avon, MA: Adams Media, 2010).

82 Smart, *Dimensions of the Sacred*, 11. A fulsome account of this dimension is included in chapter five of Smart's book (196–214).

83 Chevannes, *Rastafari*, 171–188. For the Bobo Shanti's website, see: http://www.houseofbobo.com/. Accessed March 30, 2014.

84 Chevannes, *Rastafari*, 184–188.

85 Evidence for this point may be found in Jack A. Johnson-Hill, *I-Sight: The World of Rastafari: An Interpretive Sociological Account of Rastafarian Ethics* (Metuchen, NJ; London: The American Theological Library Association and The Scarecrow Press, Inc., 1995).

86 Emily Raboteau, *Searching for Zion: The Quest for Home in the African Diaspora* (New York: Atlantic Monthly Press, 2013), 71. Also see Edmonds, *Rastafari: A Very Short Introduction*, 62–70.

87 On Sizzla's controversial inauguration, see: http://yardienews.com/rastafari-reject-sizzla-as-their-president/. On the Trinidadian Rastafari, see: http://www.rastafarisp eaks.com/rastafari/221109.html. Both sites accessed March 30, 2014.

88 William David Spencer, *Dread Jesus* (London: SPCK, 1999). Additional details on Rastafari's early leaders and organizations may be found in Chevannes, *Rastafari*, 119–144. On Sam Brown, see: http://knowearth.blogspot.com/2007/03/historical-light-on-rasta-involvement.html. Accessed March 30, 2014.

89 Barry Chevannes, "The Rastafari of Jamaica," in Timothy Miller, editor, *When Prophets Die: The Postcharismatic Fate of New Religious Movements*, with an introduction by J. Gordon Melton (Albany, NY: SUNY Press, 1991), 135–147.

90 Barry Chevannes, "Rastafari and the Coming of Age: The Routinization of the New Rastafari Movement in Jamaica," in Barnett, editor, *Rastafari in the New Millennium*, 19.

91 *Ibid.*, 31.

92 Edmonds, *Rastafari: From Outcasts to Culture Bearers*, especially 7–28; 97–115.

93 Smart, *Dimensions of the Sacred*, 11. A fulsome account of this dimension is included in chapter seven of Smart's book (275–288).

94 See Elizabeth Pigou-Dennis, "Spatial Responses of the African Diaspora in Jamaica: Focus on Rastafarian Architecture," in Michael A. Gomez, editor, *Diasporic Africa: A Reader* (New York: New York University Press, 2006), 147–169. Film producer Maxine Walters has assembled an impressive collection of dancehall posters. See: http://www.largeup.com/2012/09/12/largeup-interview-maxine-walters-talks-jamaican-dancehall-signs/. Accessed March 30, 2014.

95 W. Barnes Tatum, *Jesus at the Movies: A Guide to the First Hundred Years and Beyond*, third edition (Santa Rosa, CA: Polebridge Press, 2012). Additionally, see Darren J.N. Middleton and S. Brent Plate, "'Who Do You *See* That I Am?' Global Perspectives on Jesus Films," *New Theology Review* 23.3 (2011): 17–28.

96 See: http://jamaica-gleaner.com/gleaner/20130609/arts/arts1.html. Also see: http://www.smithsonianmag.com/arts-culture/rasta-revealed-200801.html. Both sites accessed March 30, 2014. The National Museum of Ethiopia in Addis Ababa hosted a multi-media exhibit on Selassie and the Rastafari movement, summer 2014.

97 Tuff Gong was one of Marley's nicknames. It was also the record label that he, along with The Wailers, formed in the 1960s. Today, Tuff Gong also represents a line of Rasta-inspired clothing, which may tell us something about the movement's branding.

98 Marvin D. Sterling, *Babylon East: Performing Dancehall, Roots Reggae, and Rastafari in Japan*. Also see Timothy Rommen, "Protestant Vibrations?: Reggae, Rastafari, and Conscious Evangelicals," *Popular Music* 25.2 (May, 2006): 235–263.

99 Sarah Daynes, "The Musical Construction of the Diaspora," 39. For the WorldofJah website, see: http://www.worldofjah.com/. Also see this gateway for Rasta websites: http://links.dubroom.org/conscious-rastafari.htm. Both sites accessed March 30, 2014.

100 Wolfgang Bender, editor, *Rastafarian Art* (Kingston, Jamaica; Miami: Ian Randle Publishers, 2005), 109. On Jamaica's intuitive artists, see: http://www.nytimes.

com/2004/09/02/style/02iht-jamart_ed3_.html?pagewanted=all&_r=1&. In addition, see I. Ras Dizzy, "The Rastas Speak," *Caribbean Quarterly* 13.4 (1967): 41–42. On Ras Dizzy at The National Gallery of Jamaica: http://nationalgalleryofjamaica.wordpress. com/2012/08/28/jamaicas-art-pioneers-ras-dizzy-birth-livingstone-c1932–2008/. Both sites accessed March 30, 2014.

101 The 'lion and the lamb' expression is almost certainly an abbreviation that has acquired cultural significance across the centuries. Isa 11:6 links the wolf and the lamb, although a lion is mentioned in the verse. For Ejay Khan's website, see: http://www.khanstu diointernational.com. Accessed March 30, 2014.

2

RASTAFARI LITERARY ART

Introduction

Although observers of Rastafari often concentrate on reggae music, and not without good reason, many do so at the expense of examining the movement's growing
presence in literary art.[1] Here I correct this oversight by tackling two early novels
and then by taking up several modern stories. First, I consider how Roger Mais
(Brother Man; 1954) and Orlando Patterson *(The Children of Sisyphus;* 1964) locate
locksmen at the center of their fictions.[2] In Mais's story, Bra' Man stands out as a
Christ-figure, the agent of 'peace an' love' in an unfriendly world, and in Patterson's
story, Brother Solomon comes across as a poignant, heart-rending soothsayer. Contrasts in characterization notwithstanding, both novels come together to help situate Rastafari on the world's cultural map. Second, I build on the work of Mais and
Patterson by surveying selected fiction from the past three decades, focusing on two
genres, drama and the novel, which jointly explore what we might call the varieties
of Rastafari religious experience. Authors in this part of the chapter include Edgar
Nkosi White; Barbara Makeda Blake Hannah, who also looks back on her life and
art in an interview; Masani Montague; N.D. Williams; Jean Goulbourne; and, Geoffrey Philp. A brief, religious reading of Philp's *Benjamin, My Son* (2003) shows how
the story blends literary artistry with sociological acumen to create a laudable textual successor to *Brother Man* and *The Children of Sisyphus.* Throughout the chapter I
explain these novels' social and political context and thus trace change over time in
Rastafari. To that end, an interview with Philp concludes the chapter.

The UWI *Report* (1960)

His Imperial Majesty Emperor Haile Selassie I was crowned in November 1930,
as the last chapter notes, and in the first twenty or so years that followed his

ascension to the throne, Jamaican Rastafari began to develop the religious dimensions that became the movement's identity markers—Selassie's divinity; Ethiopianism; personal and communal black somebodiness; dreadlocks; ganja smoking; and an enthusiastic hope for an imminent repatriation to Africa. Generally, Rastafari of the 1940s and 1950s were pugnacious. Hundreds of them marched through Kingston, annexed public property, staged protests, defied social convention, and some militant Rastas broke the law.[3] For their part, the Jamaican authorities hurriedly sought to repress the movement—Rasta reasoning sessions were often broken up by the police, for example, and several collective efforts to repatriate ended in fighting and failure. As Hélène Lee's biography of Leonard P. Howell testifies, the police raids (1941, 1954) on Howell's Rastafari commune epitomized mounting tensions.[4] By the late 1950s, the Jamaican people had had enough, as Ennis B. Edmonds reports:

> Rastas were no longer regarded as curious misfits or belonging to a lunatic fringe. Many people seriously believed that they were a credible threat to national security, and they were treated that way by politicians and law enforcement. The then premier, Norman Manley, used the country's newspapers to castigate the Rastas as dangerous enemies of Jamaica and a serious threat to its push for independence. He appealed to the public to monitor and report on the movements and activities of Rastas.[5]

Mortimer Planno, whom Lee calls "the most powerful chief and theorist of the Rasta movement" since Howell, eventually took matters into his own hands. He urged academics associated with the University College of the West Indies (now University of the West Indies [UWI]) to research Rastafari.[6] Three scholars issued their trailblazing *Report on the Rastafari Movement in Kingston, Jamaica*, in 1960, and in it they pressed the public to "recognize that the great majority of Ras Tafari brethren are peaceful citizens, willing to do an honest day's work."[7]

The UWI *Report* highlights the movement's many religious dimensions. In charting Rastafari's historical development, for example, it affords prophetic status to Marcus Garvey, and it isolates him as the most significant of the faith's early leaders. Howell stands out as another early, energetic symbol of Rastafari's organizational and social dimension.[8] And a third driving force, King Emmanuel Charles Edwards VII (in the *Report*, Prince Edward C. Edwards), eventual leader of the Bobo Shanti mansion, is credited by the *Report*'s writers with holding the first Rastafari "convention" in Kingston's Back-O-Wall settlement, in early 1958. This agitated assembly, which lasted three weeks and attracted three thousand brethren and sistren,

> marks the decisive point in the deterioration of relations between the Government and the public on the one hand, and the Ras Tafari movement on the other. The anti-social elements so heavily emphasised during those three weeks were perhaps irrevocable. During the latter part of 1958 two

cases occurred at Trench Town, Kingston in which Ras Tafari men were said to have thrown children into the fire as sacrifices.[9]

A little later, in 1963, violence erupted between Rastas and housing developers in Coral Gardens, Montego Bay; this hostile event led to several deaths and numerous arrests, and Rastafari to this day memorialize the event annually.[10]

In explaining the movement's doctrinal dimension, the *Report* notes that most Rastafari make two faith claims, and ones I discussed in the last chapter. First, they declare Selassie's divinity:

> All brethren agree that the Emperor Haile Selassie is the Living God, the Returned Messiah and the Representative of God the Father. The name 'Selassie' means 'Power of the Trinity'; Ras was the Emperor's title before his coronation in 1930; Tafari is a personal name of the Emperor Haile Selassie before his coronation. Many brethren nowadays refer to the Emperor only as Haile Selassie, arguing that after his elevation to the throne, the use of his former title would be incorrect. Proverbs 22, Isaiah 43 and John 16 ('For I am in the Father and the Father is in me') shows that Ras Tafari is the Living God, the Old Alpha, the Lion of Judah—invincible and visible, the Redeemer of Israel, who are the black race. A full-length photograph in the *Illustrated London News* of Saturday 11th January 1936 shows the Emperor standing with his right foot on an unexploded Italian bomb. This illustrated his invincibility. Photographs of the Emperor defending Ethiopia against the Italians, and such publications as *The March of Black Men—Ethiopia Leads*, support his role as champion of the black race.[11]

A second element of Rastafari religiosity, one that has changed over the past fifty years, is the belief that salvation involves going back to Africa, the Black Person's Vine and Fig Tree (Mic 4:4). On this view, Ethiopia is the true home for every black woman, man, and child currently trapped in diaspora:

> Zion is "on the side of the North, the City of the Great King" (Psalm 48). It is known to the uninstructed as Addis Ababa. Ethiopia is the prepared place for Israel, the heaven of the black man, just as Europe is the heaven of the white man and China is the heaven for the yellow man ... The only thing which will satisfy the true brethren is repatriation to Ethiopia.[12]

Jamaica is evil, then, and it may best be seen as a modern-day Babylon.[13] Beyond such twin affirmations, the *Report* acknowledges that doctrinal differences exist among Rastafari, because no two or more Rastas think and act alike, which guarantees the movement's heterogenous or diverse character.[14] The UWI professors encountered Rastas who questioned Selassie's divinity, even as other devotees upheld it; and, the scholars discovered Rastas who favored marijuana smoking, even as other brethren and sistren dismissed ganja—one of the ritual or practical dimensions of the movement—as an "evil" that "befuddles the brain."[15] Finally, the *Report* identifies considerable difference of opinion among Rastafari concerning dreadlocks, or the treatment of the hair, and the UWI academics tie this particular dispute to diverse interpretations of the Bible as well as to competing views of how devotees should relate to their wider society.[16]

In time, the UWI *Report* proved instructive. It "became a kind of public policy document that provided the impetus for a thawing in the conflictual relationship between Rastafari and the rest of Jamaica," Edmonds observes.[17] And Leonard E. Barrett declares:

> The work of the university professors, issuing from the most prestigious institution of the island, gave high visibility to the Rastafarians in the public eye, and people of the community began to take the movement more seriously, many seeing the cultists as the vanguard of social transformation. Their ideology was soon to affect the economy, politics, social relations, and the educational system, but their struggle had only just begun.[18]

Mais and Patterson are part of this attitudinal adjustment toward Rastafari. Even if it is difficult to calibrate the exact nature of their contribution, their novels push Rastafari onto the world's cultural stage and implore their readers—a more educated, Western elite—to take the movement seriously. The UWI *Report*, then, gives a historical context to the fiction of Mais and Patterson, and the tremendous challenge they confront.

Roger Mais's *Brother Man* (1954)

Roger Mais was a leading Jamaican social activist and writer who ventured to reflect Rastafari in the three novels for which he will be best remembered. In its context, *Brother Man* is a remarkably radical tome. This is because the Kingston Rastas in the 1940s and 1950s were an ostracized community, as noted; and yet, in the words of Edward Brathwaite, in Mais we find an author

> making a Rasta the centre of his novel … Brother Man did not represent violence, drug abuse or criminal mentality, as John Public then thought; but rather, as the Rastas themselves had always averred, Peace and Love.[19]

Such "Peace and Love" signifies Rastafari's ethical dimension—far from serving as a simple salutation, or a greeting between brethren and sistren, "Peace and Love" represents the religion's most basic moral imperative, as we will see.

The novel's setting is Orange Lane, a slum in the heart of the Jamaican capital, and the story centers around Bra' Man (John Power/Brother Man) and his community standing. While most of the Lane inhabitants are openly hostile to

Rastafari, some admire the quiet, dignified way in which Bra' Man enacts his faith:

> Brother Man belonged to that cult known as the Rastafarites, and some people said he was mad. Others again thought he was a holy man and healer, and many came to him, secretly, because they feared gossip, to heal their sick, and for advice and encouragement when things were going wrong.
>
> Sometimes when they heard other people abusing and traducing Brother Man, they stood up in his defence, the people whom he had helped in times of trouble and sickness, but at other times they thought better of it, because they feared what their neighbors might have to say about them behind their backs, lacking the courage of their convictions. Sometimes they forgot, some of these people, that he had helped and comforted them, and healed their wounds. Sometimes they secretly despised him that he cared so little for himself, and so much for others, that he would give what little he had to succour another whose need he thought greater than his.[20]

This initial description telegraphs Bra' Man's specialness. He "show de gospel way," as the chorus of the people in the Lane chant.[21] Such allusions to the New Testament only build and intensify as the novel unfurls. And in time we sense that Mais's characterization of Bra' Man resembles Jesus of Nazareth's basic portrait in the canonical Gospels. Like Jesus, Bra' Man works wonders by healing the aged as well as the sick, and for such 'miracles' he is eagerly sought and much revered, as was Jesus. Brother Man even experiences a symbolic crucifixion and resurrection, actions that prompt me to categorize the novel as "postfigurative," because its general plot and action is prefigured in the mythic pattern associated with Christianity's founder.[22]

Edward Brathwaite problematizes such Christic allusions. "For the contemporary reader," he reflects, "Brother Man is perhaps too Christ-like to be always 'true'; unlike the ideal of the Rastas, he is not fully enough grounded in reality."[23] In his foreword to the novel's fiftieth anniversary edition, however, Kwame Dawes seems more sanguine. In *Brother Man*, Mais "saw quite easily a rich opportunity for the telling of the classic narrative of Christ in the slums of Kingston," he announces.[24] I suspect that Mais saturated *Brother Man* with Christic allusions so that his novel would inspire his implied readers—Jamaican Christians who held Rastafari in contempt—to emerge from the text somewhat modified or moved by the narrator's obvious sympathy for Bra' Man's Christ-like livity or behavior.[25] Consider how Bra' Man's greeting anchors Mais's fictional re-presentation of Christ in the Kingston tenements:

> He looked at her [Minette] gravely and said: "Peace an' Love."
>
> "Why you always say that?" she asked, half closing one eye, as though the better to study his face.

"It is the salutation. It is the way the brothers should greet each other. It is like sayin' good morning, howdydo. But it is more than that too, it is the affirmation of our faith, the Jesus-talk, what you call the way."

She didn't understand a word of all this. It showed in her face.

"Did Jesus talk it that way, that what you mean, Bra' Man?"

He nodded his head, gravely. "He give us that word, sister: peace an' love."[26]

Mais uses this act of welcoming or addressing somebody, so indicative of Rasta livity, as a bridge between the messy verities of human existence and the ideal to which we often find ourselves aspiring. In Mais's view, worked through in Bra' Man's characterization, there is a broad ditch between what we are and what we ought to be. Time after time we appear crippled by principalities and powers of our own creation as we succumb to the evils of bitterness, jealousy, and hatred, represented in this novel by Bra' Ambro, Papacita, and Cordy, failing to realize that poverty pains, stains, and even kills us. Through Bra' Man, Mais suggests that what we might call 'the saving activity of God' becomes real whenever and wherever people work through their adversity with dignity and integrity.

Bra' Man's own salvation lies in his struggle to vault his own frightening chasm. His abiding concern for humanity and nature is tested toward the novel's end, for example, when he, like Jesus, finds himself betrayed and turned over to the authorities. Bra' Man is falsely accused of forgery but the very fact that he, a Rasta trusted and revered by his community, is initially charged proves enough for others to place him into the category that most, if not all, Rastafari of the time were required to endure—the label of being unkempt, dishonest, good-for-nothing drop-outs. Released on bail, Bra' Man walks straight into some unpleasant anti-Rastafari feeling. And his figurative crucifixion occurs when, during an evening stroll, he becomes the victim of crowd violence. Mais's image of the Rasta as a spiritual frontiersman, crying out as his assailants descend upon him like vultures around a carcass, shocks us, yet solicits our sympathy:

Others joined the little knot of people who followed him; jeering, jibing, they moved in closer on him.

He would stop and speak with them, try and reason with them. He turned and faced them, lifted up his hands, said, in salutation: "Peace an' love."

The eyes of the men right out in front wavered, their gaze fell to the ground before them.

A woman at the back of the crowd shouted: "Oonu 'fraid o'him?"

Another laughed. Those at the back of the crowd pressed forward a little, those in front shifted uneasily on their feet.

"Down de ole Ras Taferite! Murderers dem—"

"Nutt'n but chop man, an' rape woman, an' scuffle an' pass bad money, an' t'ief."

> 'Way wid dem, lick dem down, kill dem!"
> "Ole Ras Tafarite dem!"
> The clamour and the shouting grew louder, coarser, shriller, women and children mostly.
> He said, "Only hear me a little, hear me out—"
> But his voice was drowned in the shrieks and curses of the mob.[27]

Bra' Man is eventually rescued, bruised as well as battered, and the novel closes on an Easter Sunday-like note with Bra' Man's ambiguously stated "vision of certitude."[28] Here, Bra' Man's integrity is intensified rather than forfeited by his conflict with the twin demonic forces that control Orange Lane—that is, Bra' Man surmounts the loathing of others, and he overcomes the difficult, crippling environment of life in the Jamaican projects. He manages such Christ-like progress by exemplifying 'peace an' love,' modeling a way of being religious that Mais hoped would challenge readers given over to anti-Rastafari invective. Kwame Dawes summarizes Mais's contribution:

> Rastafarianism, and its emergence in the Sixties, Seventies and Eighties, represents one of the most significant developments to impact on Jamaica in the last fifty years. It is not likely that many people would have felt this way in 1954. Mais did, and for this he became a visionary who was in fact predicting the arrival of reggae, of Bob Marley, of Peter Tosh, of Don Drummond, of the Twelve Tribes of Israel, of Itse Green and Gold and of the current commercial marketing of the Jamaican society on Jamaican Tourist Board ads that sing in canned melodious notes the music of Bob Marley. But what Mais has preserved for us is the purer version of Rasta—Rasta as a devotional force, Rasta as the voice of peace and love, Rasta as the force that makes Jamaicans see Africa with hope, Rasta as Christ-like, Rasta as something deeply rooted in the Jamaican capacity for survival. This dignity, this grace, this beauty of language is what makes it fitting that we celebrate what can now be quite safely termed a Jamaican classic.[29]

In 1954, Mais saw his story as less of a classic and more of a radical challenge, one that Patterson assumes exactly one decade later.

Orlando Patterson's *The Children of Sisyphus* (1964)

Strongly influenced by the Algerian-born French existentialist philosopher Albert Camus, especially *The Myth of Sisyphus* (1955), Orlando Patterson tells the frightening tale of one Rasta's relentless desire to leave his destitute urban home, the Dungle, and make pilgrimage to Ethiopia. Although the Dungle houses an assortment of characters, it is Brother Solomon who commands our attention, for he serves as Patterson's spokesman for the novel's Rastology. Brother Solomon stands apart from others: a brooding, intensely private figure driven by fidgety ambition and an edgy intellect. Here Sammy the garbage man reflects on Brother Solomon's appeal and, in doing so, Sammy embodies the *tremendum et fascinans* (terrified attraction) of the entire island for Solomon:

> A fairly tall, well-built Rastafarian cultist came out of the little shop beside him and walked up to the cart. Sammy watched him with unwilling awe as he approached. He began to feel afraid. What was it? What was it this man had that he dreaded so much, that everybody else feared so much? The unaffected gracefulness of his walk, the calmness, the slowness? His beard? Like Moses he used to read about. His eyes which saw everything but did not seem to see? Everybody feared him. Everybody respected him. Only the most privileged of the cultists dared to address him as Brother Solomon; to everybody else he was Mr. Solomon. Yet, as far as the garbage-man knew he never did anything bad to anybody to fear him. He never cut up anybody, he never murdered anybody. For all he knew he had not even the distinction of having spat at an American tourist. Still, everybody feared and respected him.[30]

A man of strange powers, at least from the perspective of his fellow Dungle-dwellers, Brother Solomon is at turns taken for a prophet; Garvey's reincarnation; a channel for Selassie's spirit; and, a modern mystic. These perceptions reflect the numerous dimensions of Rastafari religiosity that appear to coalesce in this one, beleaguered soul.

For their part, the people of the Dungle are poverty-stricken as well as uneducated. As they all wish to escape the confines of their urban hell, and to improve their sad lot in life, we are left to ponder the powerful spell the Dungle casts over its inhabitants. Dinah, for instance, is a prostitute and a fifteen-year veteran of the Dungle, who experiences one tragedy after another. Living off the profits of Dinah's whoring, Cyrus is the failed fisherman and fresh convert to Rastafari. An intriguing symbol of the movement's experiential or emotional dimension, Cyrus becomes nothing short of a mad-eyed zealot when he learns that Dinah has left him. In addition, the characters of Mary and Rossetta as well as Mabel and Rachael, who all attempt to flee the Dungle, complete Patterson's extraordinary meditation on melancholic fatalism, that dark, strange, and futilistic force shaping their lives. In contrast, minor characters such as Mrs. Watkins and Seymore Nathaniel Montsaviour illustrate the indifference of middle-class black Jamaicans, whose social privilege is their escape.

Trapped in a web of despondency, the poor and illiterate Dungle-dwellers approach Brother Solomon for hope, an optimistic theology, and he speaks to them of Ethiopian ships bound for Kingston. Unsurprisingly, the indigent savor every encouraging word that drops from his lips. Here Brother Solomon tries to comfort Cyrus after Dinah's sudden departure:

> "I should say to you, be patient, me Brother, and leave it at that. But you will still not be satisfied in your heart even if you told me you was. I'll tell you

what I know, Brother. The delegates we sent to the Holy Emperor to make final arrangements for our return just write us. Their answer show promise. They said that they don't speak to the Holy Emperor yet, but that arrangement is being made by his holy servants on our behalf. So when we hear from them the next time we will hear the good news and know just when we'll be leaving this land of Babylon."[31]

Brother Solomon's promise of speedy repatriation is combined with his belief in the immanence of Jah, or God, in humankind. "Man is God," he tells Cyrus, "the spirit of Rastafari is invested in every one of us"; and it is but mental slavery that prevents every black person from internalizing or, in dread talk, 'overstanding' this important truth.[32] Here, Brother Solomon symbolizes key features of early Rastafari's doctrinal and philosophical dimension. Indeed, an ardent belief in an imminent return to Africa as well as in humankind's divinization grounds Brother Solomon's Rastology of hope—an insightful wisdom that, on reflection, many Dungle-dwellers use to connect him to his counterpart in ancient Israel.[33]

One night the Dungle-based Rastafari assemble and, for his part, Brother Solomon reads from a letter he says he has received from the Jamaican delegates to Ethiopia. This letter announces that repatriation day fast approaches, he says, and that all true believers will soon defeat Babylon. The gathered community is ecstatic, of course, but little do they know that the letter's contents have been embellished. Brother Solomon is lying. Defrocked from the Church of England on the grounds of his "insanity," this anguished soothsayer realizes that "to perceive the truth of existence is to perceive an unutterable tragedy."[34] His tragic wisdom involves knowing that the Dungle-dwellers' hope for repatriation is like a rocking horse—it keeps them moving but it takes them nowhere. Characters such as Brother Brisco, Cyrus, and Emmanuel know that indigent people resemble tiny pieces of rubbish discarded by their worlds, but they also know that such folk derive strength from hope, especially the hope of leaving Jamaica for the African Motherland. The "truth of existence," though, is that the Ethiopian ships will not sail, that the Jamaican delegates will not be returning to the island, and that Babylon will secure yet another victory over the Dungle's apparently godforsaken Rastafari enclave. Brother Solomon knows all this to be true; however, he continues to spin his yarns of hope for the hopeless. He knows his brethren and sistren need the future's power to get by, even if this power is an imaginary power:

> So now all was happiness. All was the release of pain and the anticipation
> of more release. All was joy. All except Brother Solomon. He was the last to
> leave the meeting. He sucked the last fumes from the chillum pipe, wrapped
> it in the flag and placed the bundle under his arms. Then he got up slowly
> and walked to his hut. His head was bowed under the low ceiling of the sky.

His eyes never left the ground, they stared vacantly, in rheumy distraction. He locked himself inside his hut.[35]

Brother Solomon succeeds for the greater part of Patterson's novel. On the strength of the letter the Dungle Rastas, together with their rustic counterparts, experience a new buoyancy, an energy burst of fresh meaning in their otherwise harsh as well as absurd world:

> The ship would come. They talked. They laughed. The ship of the great Emperor would show itself in the morning with the glory of the sun. No, it would come in the evening-time, bursting through the molten fire of the eastern hemisphere, a conquering vessel of joy. Oh, but what did it matter? It would come. Sure as the holy land of Zion that waited now for them, it would come.
>
> In the meantime they talked and laughed at what was past and dreamt of what was soon to be.[36]

But the ship is not coming, as Brother Solomon knows, and when others confront him, on the night before the ship's supposed arrival, he confesses his deceit, and he begs them to understand that he models sincerity despite his duplicity. Brother Ezekiel protests:

> "Listen, Brother, you can't build up a man's hopes an' then shatter them an' expec' them to listen to argument, even if it come from the divine. Those poor wretched people outside there been thinking of heaven fo' the past two weeks. I sugges' dat we arrange to tell them right now that the day of repatriation is put off. We can find some reason. But we mustn't delay any longer or hell goin' break loose tomorrow."[37]

Brother Solomon disagrees:

> "They are not just poor an' wretched people, Brothers. How you could say a thing as simple as that?"
>
> "Then what else them is?" Brother John's voice broke in impatiently.
>
> "They are gods. You can't see? Every wretched one of them is an archetype of the clown-man, playing their part upon the comic stage so well they are no longer conscious of playing. You can't see, Brothers? Every one of them is a living symbol full of meaning and revelation. Look! They have before them one hour, two hours, five, no twelve, before the ship come. Twelve hours of unreality. Twelve hours of happiness. Who else but the gods could enjoy such happiness? For the moment they are conquerors. For the moment they have cheated the dreary circle. And it's only the moment that counts."[38]

In keeping with the conclusion of the ancient Greek myth that enthralled Camus, the rock rolls back down the mountain and Brother Solomon, Patterson's prophet of hope, takes his life, mocking the absurd predicament that always threatened to consume him, and the novel closes on a note of doom. Unlike Camus's sense of spiritual futility, Patterson's is one wrought by political injustice, and so Patterson's depiction has a physical element that Camus's lacks.

Because of the way in which Patterson links the physical and the spiritual, critics praise Patterson's work. Victor Chang treats *The Children of Sisyphus* as a landmark text, for instance, and he quotes Patterson's gloss on his own text approvingly. "His novel, he [Patterson] says 'took the Rastafarians and the urban slums seriously, long before it became fashionable to be concerned about them.'"[39] Other scholars, like David Dabydeen and Nana Wilson-Tagore, are more fulsome. They celebrate the way Patterson's novel depicts how the movement maintains an identity "through its very rejection of the imitative, bastardised version of 'British' society which most middle-class West Indians consider the norm for their own lives."[40] Furthermore:

> In Mais's *The Hills Were Joyful Together* and *Brother Man*, their [Rasta] humane philosophy of peace and brotherhood is explored as a positive unifying force in the pinched and deprived world of the slum. For Orlando Patterson, writing in 1964, however, the Rastafarians signified the very futility of transcending the depression and depravity of the 'dungle'. Although in *The Children of Sisyphus*, the fantasy about escape to Africa is obviously born of the Rastafarian's rejection of his conditions and of the struggle to transcend them, Patterson presents it as part of the general absurdity of man's condition in the West Indies. But the very passion embodied in the Rastafarian's dream of escape is motivated by an awareness of his squalid surroundings and of the deficiencies of the larger social world around him … For behind the Rasta man's illusion of escape, behind the dreadness and the labyrinth in which his perceptions are finally trapped, there is a clear sense of self and a true assessment of society.[41]

Such pronounced black somebodiness—or Rastafari's reclamation of personal and collective agency in the face of Babylon's tyranny—pulsates at the heart of the movement's doctrinal dimension; and in this novel, we find Afrocentrism artfully displayed. Kwame Dawes agrees. And in doing so, he underlines a basic point in this chapter—the early Rastafari novels, penned by sympathetic outsiders, favorably publicized an emerging-yet-reviled faith:

> His [Patterson's] detailed descriptions of the Rastafarians, their rituals, their patterns of reasoning, their language, and their analysis of their social position are striking because this novel appeared years before Rasta speech and Rasta idioms had become a part of the Jamaican imagination through reggae music. Patterson writes about Rastafarian philosophy with the best kind

of reporter's discourse—allowing the Rastas to speak for themselves. It is a smart approach and the effect is to retain a tremendous level of respect for the Rastafarians in the work, despite Patterson's equally clear perception that this is a faith based on a singularly fragile myth.

In 1964, when the book was published, Selassie had not yet arrived in Jamaica, but the novel helps explain why he received such a tumultuous reception as he did in 1966. Thousands thronged the airport to see him and to witness his presence. Many reports expressed shock at the number of Rastafarians on the island.[42]

I have noted how the UWI *Report* was the first in-depth inquiry into the myths, rituals, symbols, and aspirations of the Rastafari religious movement. The *Report* was timely; it satisfied intense public curiosity, and it advocated sympathy toward Rastafari brethren and sistren. This said, the UWI *Report* was not alone in providing national and international readers with an understanding of the beliefs and behaviors of a hitherto unknown and feared religious group. At a time when Rastafari suffered societal disapproval, Mais and Patterson offered sensitive, and hence unprecedented, portrayals of Rastafari as spiritual vanguards and cultural critics. In whatever modest manner, their novels showcased Rastafari at an important turning-point in the history of this still-evolving religion.

Although Mais and Patterson are frequently feted for their fictional creativity and ideological sympathy towards Rastafari, they are, like their readers, outsiders to the movement. And outsiders continue to craft literary art featuring Rastafari, as we will see. Insider writers have emerged in recent years, however, and here I turn to address some of them. Such an amalgamation of outsider/insider perspective(s) promises a balanced assessment of the movement.

Edgar Nkosi White's *Lament for Rastafari* (1983)

Born in Montserrat, the West Indian dramatist Edgar Nkosi White has lived in the United States and England, and his many plays, especially *Lament for Rastafari and Other Plays* (1983), chronicle how blacks in North America, the Caribbean, and Great Britain grapple with modern life's opportunities and challenges.[43] His protagonists often seem restive, and in more ways than one, because their mental migration across different territories of thought and value tends to mirror their physical travels from, say, island enclaves to big city European life. *Lament for Rastafari* maps a West Indian extended family's spiritual and physical pilgrimage from Jamaica to London and finally New York City. The play's several settings and various voices create multiple layers of meaning but it is Lindsay, the Rasta poet, who stands out, because international travel appears to solidify as well as complicate his self-understanding. In Jamaica, for instance, many see Lindsay as an indolent rebel or a rude boy, good for "loud talk about poems and what not else. Babylon go burn. Cho, he a rasta yes—and he does tief too."[44] Then one night, midway through a reggae concert, Lindsay bids farewell to Barrett, a fellow Rasta, and quietly departs for London. Upon his arrival, Lindsay settles into digs near Holland Park and then visits family in Notting Hill Gate. Almost immediately his uncle, Peter Barzy, presses Lindsay on his job status and, with a wisdom forged on the hard anvil of immigrant experience, Barzy urges the newly arrived Rastaman to abandon poetry and take up some kind of trade. By the time Barrett joins him, Lindsay lives an exile's life of deficiency and disenchantment.

In "The Gospel of Rastafari," which focalizes Act II, Scene VII of *Lament for Rastafari*, Lindsay takes his leave of London, "this same land where [Marcus] Garvey died in his exile" and where "[Kwame] Nkrumah [the first president of Ghana] had to search dustbin for food."[45] In abandoning the capital, Lindsay appeals to the movement's organizational and ethical dimensions. He invokes the spiritual founder and moral leader of the Bobo Shanti mansion, for example, and he alludes to the Rod of Correction (Prov 29:15), the Bible's arresting symbol for the believer's wisdom and Babylon's reproof, which Michael Manley, People's National Party (PNP) leader, used in Jamaica's 1972 general election campaign. Lindsay thus rails against Great Britain, the modern-day Babylon, and he laments her slick city streets, "where black men walk with heel mash down and soul mash down."[46]

Strangely fortified by such nitty-gritty Rastafari consciousness, Lindsay heads for New York City. In America he encounters cousin Clayton, who acts surprised and then irritated with Lindsay's Rasta livity, before running into Uncle Harrold, an old Garveyite who recalls Howell's "Pinnacle" commune. Lindsay finally finds his stride, religiously speaking, as evinced by the discussion he conducts with La Puta (aka Lilly), Barrett's sister, concerning Haile Selassie's royal line. Once more, the movement's doctrinal dimension surfaces: "Is not the man I believe in. Is the presence of the man. He can trace his ancestry to black Solomon. We need a past so we can know our future," Lindsay proclaims, and one senses, as the play draws to a close, that memory and visions, or religion as a chain of memory and visions, will liberate as well as buttress the brethren and sistren.[47] Theo Witvliet summarizes this general outlook:

> When Rastafari is called a liberation movement it is not because it has a clearly articulated political and economic programme for social action but because it creates room alongside the existing system for people to experience mental and physical liberation from a slave's existence (and that in itself is powerful enough) … In the sound of reggae and the reading of Rasta poetry this last reality, Jah (God), is evoked and experienced. Africa lives in language and music—a world is yet to come. The Africa/Ethiopia which the Rasta celebrates is an imaginary continent, the product of an anticipatory imagination which refuses to accept Babylon as the ultimate reality.[48]

Interestingly, then, salvation is cultivated through artistic expression. But throughout its early history, that expression was male-centered. A shift can be seen in the works of the two following female novelists, Barbara Makeda Blake Hannah and Masani Montague. This shift parallels Rasta's globalization as well as its growing internal tensions.

Barbara Makeda Blake Hannah's
Joseph: A Rasta Reggae Fable (1991)

An award-winning Jamaican author, social activist, and public intellectual, Barbara Makeda Blake Hannah has spent the last fifty years promoting Caribbean culture and furthering the causes of Rastafari. In the late 1960s, for example, she was the first black journalist to appear on British television, working for several stations and corporations.[49] Hannah returned from the United Kingdom in the early 1970s and almost immediately turned to writing, often publishing thoughtful newspaper

FIGURE 9 Barbara Makeda Blake Hannah (n.d.). Photo: Barbara Makeda Blake Hannah.

articles. One such Op-Ed led to *Rastafari—The New Creation* (1981), the first emic or insider's account of the movement; recently, Hannah placed the seventh edition online as an eBook.[50] She served her people as an Independent Opposition senator in the Jamaican Parliament in the mid-1980s and, since leaving office, she has lectured throughout the Caribbean as well as the United States, often speaking to the several documentaries and two feature films she has produced and/or directed. In 1991 she released *Joseph: A Rasta Reggae Fable*, which her MySpace site describes as "a novel about a reggae superstar based loosely on the life of Bob Marley (whom she knew) but mainly to give an insight into what life was like in the 1970s when reggae and Rasta started going international."[51] Recently re-republished, *Joseph* is being made into a feature film, starring Makonnen David, Hannah's son. In October 2011, Hannah received the Female Lifetime Achievement Award from the Black Entertainment Film, Fashion, Television, and Arts.[52]

Largely narrated by Ashanti (aka Sister Shanty), a Rasta roots daughter, *Joseph* chronicles the fortunes and misfortunes of Joseph Planter, an acclaimed reggae singer who, from the story's outset, symbolizes the edifying elements of "the religious-cultural movement for which Jamaica was famous."[53] Vivid, detailed descriptions of Kingston projects and hilltop Rasta communes abound, adding to the novel's matter-of-fact realism, and Hannah, with the insider's touch, clarifies Rasta livity without once succumbing to didacticism, the creative writer's cardinal sin. When Hannah's narrator describes the Nyabingi ritual, for example, she does not instruct for instruction's sake; rather, Sister Shanty conveys nuances that an outsider can often overlook, and such sentiments combine to conscientize us, offering hope for sympathetic understanding.[54] The novel's other wide-ranging characters, from dirt-poor Jamaican opportunists, like Zuleika, to respected elder locksmen, like Ras Jama, also educate us, especially with their approach to the Bible, Marcus Garvey, Ethiopia, and the 'peace and love' ethic that both Mais and Patterson also emphasize. Here, 'peace and love' signify Joseph Planter's highest ideal, just as it does for Bra' Man, Mais's protagonist, and such remarks are among the first words that Joseph shares with Sister Shanty when they first meet on Eastern Kingston's Wareika Hill, circa 1970, forty years after Haile Selassie's coronation, and on the cusp of Rastafari's globalization.[55] In due course, and with the aid of the man called Busha, who resembles Island Records' Chris Blackwell, Joseph contributes to his faith's international fame, recording Rasta riddims that act like a neutron in a chain reaction of social as well as religious change, as evinced by Joseph's peace concert, which resembles Marley's own, the famous "One Love" attempt to reconcile warring political factions, which occurred at the National Stadium in Kingston, Jamaica, on April 22, 1978. Marley was shot and wounded two years before this concert, as is well-known, and, for his part, Joseph is hurt during his own performance.[56] Sister Shanty and Peter, her husband, flee the chaotic scene, travel to Florida as well as Cuba, and then, at the novel's end, they make pilgrimage to Africa and reunite with Joseph in Shashemene, which lies south of Ethiopia's capital.[57]

This plot summary notwithstanding, three points are relevant here, and I hope what is said will illumine our grasp of Rastafari, not only in the context of the novel but also in the wider milieu of the movement's global spread. To begin with, *Joseph* locates Rastafari's influence beyond Jamaica. Set in the early 1970s, the novel shows us Rastas in Florida, Cuba, the United Kingdom, and Ethiopia; here, the artistic dimension of reggae acts as the main mechanism for the faith's transnational transmission. "Joseph's name travelled the world, and the philosophy of Rastafari began spreading beyond the ghettos and the Nyabingis, to the hearts and mind of a music-loving people," Ashanti announces.[58]

In the second place, Hannah's novel illustrates the range of Rastafari livity in the 1970s. We witness white Rastas in Miami qualifying Selassie's status; socialist or revolutionary Rastas in Havana; and, Rastas in London subverting Babylon. Whatever the location, though, many mansions flourish. And such symbols of the movement's organizational dimension react to mainline Christian churches with ambivalence. Gender relations appear unresolved. Ideological and ethical commitments—from black somebodiness to cultivating locks—seem unstable, open to debate. Even when Joseph becomes confessional, he speaks for himself, and one senses that Rastafari celebrate as well as encourage diversity of opinion in matters of faith and devotion.[59] We also witness contrasting soteriologies, or theories of salvation, with some devotees seeing Rastafari as an antidote to colonialism's poison and other believers viewing Rastafari as promising heightened god-consciousness:

> Joseph, still testing Peter, looked at his short, still-growing locks, and asked whether the locks were a sign of faith or just simply a mark of badness.
>
> "Well, Peter is Fari," I said, "but he is the kind of Rasta who believes that the System won't change unless we ourselves take steps to liberate ourselves."
>
> Joseph, as you know, believed that faith, prayer and righteousness were the weapons that would make change. Joseph could see that he and Peter thought differently about life, but I could see that he was interested in reasoning with a man who held such different views from himself.[60]

Finally, Hannah upholds the wonders of the African world, offering sensitive as well as colorful descriptions of Ethiopia, but she does not romanticize its peoples and places. Capturing sentiments that one may find in documentary films like *The Emperor's Birthday* (1992), as well as in more recent press reports, one official in Addis Ababa distinguishes between the Selassie of history and the Selassie of faith. "The Selassie of your myth was very different in reality. The people of Ethiopia are glad he is gone. They have seen a better life since," he declares.[61] Furthermore, sites like Shashemene, which is "not at all what you would expect," are not necessarily the Black Person's Vine and Fig Tree.[62] "It was lovely to be at Shashemane," Ashanti says, "but after a few days the realities of how hard life there was, made us all a little depressed."[63] Still, Hannah underscores Rasta's earthbound adaptability—the way its adherents modify their livity to ensure their faith's survival, and the following admission illustrates Ninian Smart's observation that religions, once they are transplanted onto foreign soil, must acclimatize themselves to new environments:

> The Shashemane people were peaceful and nice, but there was one thing that we all noticed, and Peter asked the man, "Why don't any of you carry locks? Aren't you Rasta?"
>
> "Body lice," was his simple answer. "When we came here, we realised we could only deal with what was essential. We discover that locks was not essential."[64]

Joseph's epiphany occurs in Lalibela, not Shashemene, and his new illumination involves a realization that the Ethiopian Orthodox Church, especially its evocative liturgy, holds the promised key to his salvation. He also hints that belonging to the Church will enable Rastas to avoid a future without a presiding authority, and he holds out hope that the Church will pursue repatriation as well as reparations.[65] By the novel's end, Joseph embodies political ardor as well as spiritual verve, and one emerges from his transnational story with the conclusion that Hannah treats both traits as vital and necessary concomitants for Rastafari's future.

To test such observations, among other things, I contacted Hannah, who maintains an active Facebook account, and she agreed to an e-mail interview. Like Philp, whom I interview later in this chapter, Hannah peppers her discourse with dread talk, the language of Rastafari. Velma Pollard has done much to describe the religious as well as social origins for such language use; I direct the reader to her unparalled work for additional details, though I take this opportunity to note once more that this hybridized or blended mix of Jamaican Creole and Standard English illustrates Rastafari's ritual or practical dimension.[66]

An Interview with Barbara Makeda Blake Hannah

DJNM: Rastas I have encountered in Jamaica, the United Kingdom, and in Africa frequently describe themselves as being on a quest, a pilgrimage, and I wonder if this vocabulary of faith holds true for you? If so, could you say a little bit about the *three* most important turning-points or stages in your own spiritual journey?

BMBH: The Rastafari Faith is a true pilgrimage. The pilgrim usually starts the journey in Christianity, and then travels questioningly into an abyss of religious, racial, and spiritual knowledge that is so unusual, unexpected, and astonishing that only Faith in its Truth and Goodness can enable the pilgrim to continue the journey to the end. The pilgrimage has its 'Mecca' in

Ethiopia, its holy cities of Lalibela, Axum, Gondar, and even the Rastafari settlement in Shashemene.

The first and most important turning point in my own spiritual journey to Rastafari was seeing the film *The Harder They Come* in the early '70s when I was invited by Island Records to become its PR representative.[67] I was amazed at my first view of the Rasta culture depicted in the film. The view of Jamaica and the Rastafari culture struck deep in my heart, soul, and spirit and immediately made me decide to leave London, England, where I had been living and enduring its racism for eight years, and return to Jamaica to learn more about the Rasta-reggae culture displayed in the film.

Another important moment was hearing Mrs. Amy Jacques Garvey speak about her late husband, Marcus, at a 1972 meeting in Kingston, Jamaica, not long before she died. I had never heard of Garvey before, but the energy and dynamism with which this fiery old lady spoke about him and his beliefs in the African race, fuelled my knowledge and educated my Rastafari journey, of which Garvey was an important philosophical milestone.

And finally, a major awakening came when I first overstood the full meaning of *love* not as a romantic emotion shared between two people, but as a Godly emotion embracing *all* people. It was in Rastafari that I discovered the true meaning of 'peace and love' and found peace and love within myself. I learned this while spending many hours observing how Rastas related to each other, and to the world.

DJNM: Those same Rastas, in different global contexts, often seem ambivalent about politics or political engagement. Not you. Many know you as an Independent Opposition senator in the Jamaican Parliament, where you served during the mid-to-late 1980s, and I am curious: How did Rasta-consciousness, or being Rasta, inspire you politically? Put differently: How did it, and how does it, help you confront the moral and social issues that arise out of the cut and thrust of everyday living?

BMBH: Rastafari is my religion. Jamaica is my home and that deals with a different reality of my life. As a Jamaican resident, I keep hoping to see it become the true Paradise it could so easily be. But a lot needs changing to achieve this. Looking at how the world works and how governments operate, I see clearly that trying to change 'the system' by the bullet only causes death and bloodshed, anger, recriminations, revenge, and the same-old same-old. The only way is to use the so-called democratic system to try to create change legally, using strong arguments to persuade 'the people' to back up your desired change *because* it will benefit them.

When I was invited to serve as an Independent Opposition senator, it happened because I was known as a writer of independent views on topics of all kinds. I had already been expressing my views widely and frequently in the media, so for me to be given a chance to express my views in Parliament seemed like a natural progression.

I think more Rastas should offer themselves as representatives, because Parliament needs more independent voices of all kinds to break the two-Party stranglehold. I am glad to see that after all this time some of the very people who used to oppose 'politriks' are now seeking election to Parliament. I hope that more do so, for only a few Independent MPs would hold the balance of power between the PNP [People's National Party]/JLP [Jamaica Labour Party] rivalry and eventually bring about change in the entrenched system.[68]

DJNM: You are a roots daughter with an insider's keen eye for informed empathy. Using your skills as a broadcaster and journalist, for example, you authored the first text on Rastafari by a practicing member of the faith, *Rastafari—The New Creation*, which has seen multiple reissues since it first appeared in 1981. What, for you, is the most instructive feature of your book—the one teaching point you wish to get across to those seeking to understand the Rastafari?

BMBH: In writing the book, I wanted to explain Rastafari in very simple terms for everyone to overstand. It was first a five-part series in the *Star* newspaper, a very down-market Jamaican publication, so I wrote it simply and found it made the series very popular, so I kept that style when I expanded it into a book. I also wanted to show that Rastafari is a CHRISTIAN religion, a new update on the Bible, a new interpretation of the religious history of the world from a Black perspective.

When I first stepped into Rastafari, the faith was very much Bible-based and Christian. Rastafari is a perfect twentieth-century evolution of Christianity, coming to our African roots through Jamaica. The evolution of Rastafari moves Christianity from a focus on a dead and bleeding Jesus on the Cross, to the Resurrection of *Iyesos Krystos*—a new look at Christ's life through the life of Emperor Haile Selassie I, known as The Perfect Man, bearing the titles of King of Kings, Lord of Lords, Conquering Lion of the Tribe of Judah, Defender of the Orthodox Christian Faith. Here in the twentieth century, as Western Christianity collapses under sexual immorality, a new Christian King comes to be worshipped by a new CHRISTian people whose view of the Bible is "through Ethiopian spectacles," as Garvey instructed. That a 'resurrection' of Christ should emerge in a Black African country and people, may be shocking to those for whom Christ and God are irrevocably 'white blue-eyed blondes.' But surprisingly, many blue-eyed whites locksed their blond hair through the CHRISTly inspiration of this unique Man.

People want to say Rasta is 'heathen,' 'blasphemous,' and 'anti-Christian.' But in fact Rastafari Christianity is the natural evolution of the world since the birth of Jesus of Nazareth two thousand years ago. Since then his perfect example has been clouded by the actions of his followers, until today Christianity hangs its head in shame as wars, corruption, and sexual depravity are approved and practiced by its believers. The faith of Emperor Haile Selassie I in Ethiopian CHRISTianity gave I&I a window into an ancient, holy, spiritual history of our own origins and gave us the key to re-interpret the Bible with African eyes. For showing us this pathway by example, Emperor Selassie has been called 'Christ' and 'God,' as was Jesus of Nazareth who first set the example.

DJNM: Scholars of Rastafari, like Ennis B. Edmonds, marvel at the way brethren and sistren have, in less than eighty years, moved from outcasts to culture bearers—to what do you credit this significant transition, and how do you feel about this new status?

BMBH: New status? I&I have not changed, but there have now been new generations born living more modern lives with knowledge built on the lives of I&I Elders. What has changed is that 'society' has found that despite all its efforts to suppress, discredit, and obliterate Rastafari, the *world* has accepted Rastafari. In fact, through Rastafari, Jamaica has become a world nation, and Rastafari culture has given Jamaica an 'irie' reputation as a vacation destination. But while they will use us to advertise their products, they won't change their laws about our Sacrament, which everyone knows is a major part of what makes Rastafari what it is. It's like they can't live with us, but they can't live without us. The 'new status' is a grudging but inevitable evolutionary growth of something *good*, and a sign of the Victory of *good* over *evil* globally, not just in Jamaica.

DJNM: Your novel, *Joseph: A Rasta Reggae Fable*, was published in 1991, was reissued a few years ago, and was inspired by the life and musical art of Bob Marley, who did so much to place Rastafari on the world's cultural map. Among other things you accomplish in this pilgrimage story, you illustrate the broad, transnational range of Rastafari livity in the 1970s. What was your own experience of the global spread of Rastafari in the latter part of the last century, and how does this experience compare to the present day?

BMBH: All these types of Rastas were actual people I met and know. Rastafari has become a global belief shared by all the world's people with good hearts. The fact that you can identify so many types of Rastas in my book (I wasn't even aware I had done that!) means that Rastafari is well on the way to becoming a powerful instrument on the minds of millions. The global spread increases exponentially as 'the system' continues to crumble through economic decline, wars, and political corruption.

The world seeks something *good* and Rastafari offers this in a package of *peace and love* of all mankind; no racial, social, economic, or geographic boundaries—just a commitment to *right*eousness. Isn't this the "heaven on earth" we ask for in the Lord's Prayer? Who among us does not hope this will happen in their lifetime? Rastafari are all actively working for it to be so *now*. I pray and hope the work I&I are doing to heal and unite the world will bear fruit in my lifetime. In fact, I am actively working for that to happen.

DJNM: Allow me to build on my last question. Some of my research into Rastafari's internationalization has turned up some intriguing occurrences, like sound system operators in the Slovak republic who do not consider themselves 'real

Rastafarians' but who are committed to spreading Rastafari's 'cultural vibes' where they are located. What's your verdict on such happenings?

BMBH: It's what I said above: the world is waiting for the one person who will unite us all for *good*. Jesus of Nazareth has tried, and created Christianity to do the work. Emperor Haile Selassie I has tried and Rastafari is the outgrowth of H.I.M. doing the work. People don't have to be Buddhist to praise the life and work of the Dalai Lama.

DJNM: Returning to your novel: I think one emerges from Joseph's story with the sense that you see spiritual verve as well as political ardor as vital and necessary concomitants for Rastafari's future. Is this a fair observation?

BMBH: I always describe my novel as 'what could have been, what should have been.' I didn't write this book, it was written by unseen hands guiding mine, because it was begun just after my son's birth when I needed glasses and had neither electricity nor typewriter, writing by lamplight with a pencil. It's like I am just a puppet being used by JAH to bring forth words because I have been given the talent and experiences.

I definitely see my Rastafari mission emphasizing the necessity for baptism and membership in the Ethiopian Orthodox Church. It was the faith of the Emperor; he was the Defender of the Faith, and he prayed each day in front of an altar with an icon of the Black Madonna and Child. His selection as Emperor was endorsed, as it had to be, by the Patriarch and Priests of the Ethiopian Orthodox Church and his coronation was a church ritual and ceremony.

My famous "No More Rasta" (1983) article was saying that defining 'Rasta' had become so clouded by the unrighteous actions of some claiming to be Rasta, that the only way I wished to be defined was as an Ethiopian Orthodox Christian Rastafari. Most people read only the headline of this article, not the message.[69]

I am confident that Bob Marley achieved his 'eternal life' because he allowed himself to be baptized in the faith by Archbishop Mandefro before he died, when he received the Ethiopian name Berhane Selassie. So I definitely wanted the novel to take a Hero's Journey along that Orthodox path and illuminate it in a way that had not been done before. It's interesting that after I wrote about the Ethiopian journey, I showed the passage to an Ethiopian friend and asked him if I had described the country accurately. He smiled and said: "I thought you had been there!"

I wanted to show how after Joseph's healing baptism in the holy waters, he was revived to challenge the world from a new perspective. I hope I showed that by coming close to death, Joseph was fearless to speak the truth as he saw it about Rastafari's role and ambitions. I hoped to inspire Rastafari to follow Joseph's 'dream.' It's a dream we all had when we first became Rasta in the 1970s, with classic Wailers songs like "Dreamland." The dream can still be realized, but it would need united and revolutionary focus. I am just a writer, so I can dream with words.

DJNM: Have you read any recent Rastafari literary art? If so, how would you assess it or them?

BMBH: The only literary representation of Rastafari I have read was Roger Mais's *Brother Man*. Written fifty years ago and re-published recently, it is set in West Kingston when the Dungle was a real place, and it is a very accurate description of a time and place in Rasta history. I'd love you to recommend some titles to me.

DJNM: In your opinion, what does the future hold for Rastas? What do you think we will be saying about them in, say, fifty or eighty years?

BMBH: I am not a prophetess, so I cannot predict. However, as a priestess I am confident in the victory of *good over evil*. The strength that Rastafari has gathered over the past decades will continue to grow, as Rastafari advances to influence decisions in Jamaica and the world. I sincerely hope the voice of the Rastafari nation will grow stronger and louder, using all media to speak to the world and stop the culture of war, greed, and depravity and bring JAH Kingdom come on earth, so as it is in ZION.

DJNM: And finally, what about your own future plans? What's next?

BMBH: I just celebrated JAH gift of 'three score and ten' years of life and that is quite an achievement. My plans include slowing down a little to rest and write more. I have an unfinished novel. Plus, I want to publish a collection of my newspaper articles since 1972 that document a lot of Rastafari history. I am also the organizer of an annual Reggae Film Festival. Yes, I plan to rest a little!

Masani Montague's *Dread Culture: A Rastawoman's Story* (1994)

While Hannah largely focuses on male characters, veteran playwright and community organizer, Jamaican-Canadian Masani Montague released *Dread Culture: A Rastawoman's Story*, an insider's fictional treatment of Rastafari women, or roots daughters, in 1994. Today, her novel serves as the basis for a much-admired reggae musical.[70] Set within a Jamaican black and Rastafari community in Toronto, Canada, in the 1970s, *Dread Culture* explores the untidy verities of Rastafari identity formation amidst the daily challenges of the immigrant experience. Thick descriptions of such challenges abound in this novel—police brutality; racial discrimination; religious intolerance; violence during soundclash or reggae music competitions; and wrongful incarceration. Life in diaspora is messy, and it is diverse. Ideological multiformity among the expatriate Rastas—evinced by male elders, like Wolde and Big Dread, who gather in an ital shop to spar vigorously on the merits and demerits of Rastafari versus Christianity—is a case in point. And although such lively exchanges occur within the confines of a *fictional* shop, they nonetheless reflect enduring, *factual* tensions within the movement, both outside and inside Jamaica, as Anna Kasafi Perkins's work shows.[71]

Dread Culture is not about Rastafari men; and it does not follow the narrative arc of earlier fictional treatments of the movement. Montague's novel focuses on Sheba, who spends the story's greater part keen to prize open a space in her frenetic, browbeaten life to where she can pause and reflect on Rastafari's meaning and purpose for her existence. Conflict, suffering, struggle, and sacrifice dog her footsteps. Yet through it all she rises above the novel's other characters and, to a degree, the racist sociocultural context that holds them in thrall, becoming a 'Jah Dawta,' one who weathers the fragility of relationships, even abuse, and cultivates her own Rasta-inspired, gendered subjectivity. Here, Sheba asserts her independence and difference from her mother, Doris, whose parental power seems restrictive and intolerant:

> "Sheba?" Doris sucked her teeth. "Me christen dis girl Vinette Caroline Smith, and all of a sudden she become Sheba Tafari. Yuh tink anybody want Rasta fi look after dem pickney inna daycare?"
>
> "Mama, yuh should get used to me being a Rasta. Nuh matter what yuh seh, ah is a Rasta and ah gwine mek it as a Rasta. Nutten gwine change mi mind. Mi is proud to be a Rasta and determined fi graduate from college and own my own daycare centre."[72]

This is not the only time that Doris—like Esther, her own mother—castigates Rastafari.[73] And in reading Montague's novel, we become alert to other folk, both without and within the Jamaican immigrant community, who display contempt for the small-but-growing movement congregating around Iration Dread's ital shop on Eglington Avenue—a store or space that illustrates Rastafari's ethical and organizational dimensions.

Married with seven children, Iration Dread is Sheba's King man, a man of special status, and the novel's salient symbol for Rastafari's patriarchalism, which Montague only partially tolerates. She helps us understand that Rastas like Iration Dread think the way they do because they read the Bible though male-centered spectacles, but Montague will not condone women being denied full human subjectivity by the male-controlled ordering of the movement.[74] Through Sheba, her symbol of the intrepid woman who insists on access to the process of forming Rasta identity, Montague enunciates a post-patriarchal Rasta vision, one where a new discourse is being created and a fresh sense of self is being shaped, the initial signs for which include Sheba's disavowal of Iration Dread's domestic abuse; Sheba's setting up Jah Children's Daycare; Sheba's act of mentoring her imprisoned brother, Johnny/Menelik, in the way of the Black Messiah as well as in Rasta livity; and, in Sheba's welcoming, non-judgmental response when Akilah, her abused Rasta sister and coworker, comes out as a lesbian.

It is certainly possible to overstate Sheba's reaction to Akilah's sexuality. "One problem with the text, not stated but implied, is that Akilah's choice to 'be lesbian' seems to be a result of her negative experiences with men rather than a natural and positive life choice," Loretta Collins Klobah suggests.[75] At the same time, Sheba's sympathetic imagination seems telling; indeed, her stance, while limited, accentuates the Rasta woman's struggle for self-determination, and it actually frees some space for other voices, especially for those previously silenced, muffled, or unheard by traditional, heterosexual Rastafari men and women. The crucial conversation reads:

> "Mi [Akilah] understand how difficult it is fi yuh, an mi nuh blame yuh. Many of di brethren and sistren have mi up because mi get divorce and cut off mi locks. Dem nuh understand dat sometimes yuh haffi tek certain steps fi yuh own survival and happiness. Haile Selassie still in I heart, but dere were certain tings I had to reconcile fi I self."
>
> "Akilah, ah could never blame yuh for yuh decision. Sometimes—although is only yuh di I can seh dis to—I an I feel dat being a good Rastafarian is harder for us sistren dan fi di brethren. Mi just haffi keep asking Jah fi guidance."[76]

Obiagele Lake's ethnographic work, *RastafarI Women: Subordination in the Midst of Liberation Theology* (1998), supports Sheba's feeling, revealing that Rasta women are, for the most part, politically and culturally marginalized because Rasta men, both outside and inside Jamaica, utilize biblical literalism to render Rasta women secondary or inferior.[77] Yet such women do not seem to experience the despair of being forever marginalized. Times are changing. Documentaries, such as *Roots Daughters: The Women of Rastafari* (1992), *Omega Rising: Women in Rastafari* (1995), and *Rastafari Women Today: The Anthology* (2010), feature Rastafari elder women—Judy Mowatt, Empress Baby-I, Nana Farika Berhane, Barbara Blake Makeda Hannah, as well as others—and they help to uphold their stories of struggle as well as to support their redemption songs. Prominent Rasta women are challenging strict dress codes. And the Inaugural Rastafari Studies Conference, which took place at The University of West Indies, Mona, Jamaica, in August 2010, suggests that women are rising phoenix-like from the ashes of traditional Rastafari patriarchy.[78]

Today, Rastafari women are leaven for change within the movement. And female Rasta literary artists, like Montague, were among the first to suggest the importance of naming oneself out of the depths of patriarchal oppression, to call other Rasta women to agency, and to push 'peace and love' to include women's personal and political liberation. As Montague and, previously, Hannah show, gender relations have been a primary challenge and change within more contemporary Rastafari. So too have the realities of diasporic life and its resulting globalization and appropriation of Rastafari by white outsiders, which N.D. Williams addresses in *My Planet of Ras*.

N. D. Williams's *My Planet of Ras* (1997)

Born in Guyana in 1942, Williams studied at the University of West Indies, Mona, Jamaica, in 1968; here, he witnessed the (Walter) Rodney riots, an experience that he folded into his first novel, *Ikael Torass*, which appeared in 1976, winning the Casas de las Americas prize. His early work focuses on the prophetic function of indigenous art forms, such as reggae and yard theatre; on the way higher education promotes social division; and, on the origins as well as effects of repressive forces in Jamaican society. Williams has lived in Antigua; however, he now lives in New York, and his literary art throughout the 1990s and early 2000s—short stories (*The Crying of Rainbirds* [1992]), novels (*The Silence of Islands* [1994] and *Julie Mango* [2003]), and two novellas (*My Planet of Ras* and *What Happening There, Prash* in *Prash and Ras* [1997])—grapples with the contrast between island and diasporic life. In *My Planet of Ras*, Williams uses fiction to explore German appropriations of Jamaican culture, and thus he opens an entirely new window onto Rastafari's global appeal.[79]

Williams's novella tells the story of Kristal Marie Braun, an anxious but adventurous young German woman, who travels to Jamaica—the "Planet of Ras"—to flee her failed romance, to abandon her dysfunctional family, and to work through the effects of a botched drug overdose.[80] The travel trope is not incidental. Kristal is one of life's many walking wounded, keen to escape her own personal Babylon, and when she encounters three Rastas shortly after arriving at the airport in Kingston, she purchases some petrol in exchange for a lift in their car to Jamaica's north coast. Her new friends—Selassie [not to be confused with His Imperial Majesty], Ikael, and Kilmanjaro—belong to the Twelve Tribes of Israel mansion and, in short order, Kristal feels drawn to their rustic spirituality. "There was a gentle feeling about them, an ancient ease; I was charmed by their lean bearded angular hardened looks, the Bible-based language of their planet."[81] Stirred by Kristal's disgruntled, questing soul, the brethren encourage her to stay in their commune. She accepts their hospitality and, in time, comes to overstand or grasp how Rastafari live and breathe through their religion's ritual dimension, especially those rituals involving "the herbal bond that joined me in spirit to the Ras," and she reconstructs her fragmented identity.[82]

In her journey to overstand, Kristal learns from Selassie, "a diminutive man, with a lion tamer's voice," a reader, a healer with herbs.[83] He teaches two specific lessons, which coalesce to illustrate Rastafari's mythical, experiential, and ethical dimensions. First, he tells extraordinary narratives about His Imperial Majesty, sacred myths whose truths seem beyond question, and we witness how such stories become internalized over time, how they lodge themselves deep into the very pit of Selassie's entrails, and thus provide intense, experiential meaning:

> I read the [newspaper] article [about the Emperor's visit to Jamaica in 1966]
> again, focusing on the words he'd [Selassie] underlined, the phrases he drew
> my attention to, which hinted that somehow the event, a ghostly yellowed

thing of the past, had taken root inside him, had spread thick vines on his stomach's soft walls; and was at moments like this—what moment like this?—a floating shard in the eye of his memory.

"An *attraction* at once physical and spiritual, repeated through the centuries: the shaman and the tribe," he said. "Yet when his His Imperial Majesty step forward here, *tears roll down from his eyes*. For whom did he cry?"

"Were you there? Did you see him?" I asked.

"The crowd surging forward as he stepped off that cabin in the sky. I man feel that surge like some huge ocean swell uplifting I vessel, sweeping I forward. I never tell this to a soul but when I sight him there, I man was shaking like a leaf, weeping like a child."[84]

If religion is a chain of memory, as Danièle Hervieu-Léger claims, then Selassie's emotional confessionalism links him, and us as readers, to His Imperial Majesty's centrality in the worldview of Rastafari.[85]

Second, Selassie's nature mysticism presents Kristal with an alternative vision, a way to chant down her own personal Babylon or, to switch the trope, an antidote to her toxic, urban European life. The chapter-a-day imperative associated with the Twelve Tribes mansion means Rastas like Selassie brood over the Bible; also, biblical literacy fosters an overlay that resembles the worldview of the Psalms, which celebrate God's handiwork (Ps 8, 104):

"Hail up!" Selassie shouts to me, waving me to join him. "I man thought you would sleep forever. Welcome to our window to the universe. The planetarium, you might call it. But I man see it differently."

"What a marvellous view," I said.

"More than a *view*, daughter. And in time you might marvel at the many things you see. *Selassie I Rastafari!*"

He shouted those last words with defiance and praise and wild jubilation. Such an arrangement of syllables and sibilants I had not heard before.

"Call to the sea and sky. Fill up your lungs; empty your soul of dead matter, dead habit. You stand before the miracle of creation. You watching a process that began millions of years before. Call to the sea and sky. Give thanks to the miracle of your creation. *Selassie I Rastafari*."

"Selassie I Rastafari," I said laughing.

"No, daughter! Call like a child just born; scream like the mother pushing that child; shout like the midwife giving comfort to that miracle."

"Selassie-i-ras-tafari!" I cried.

"*Irie!*" he said, gently, approvingly.[86]

Here, Jamaica is Jah-maica: a verdant, spiritually revivifying place; and Selassie, the voice of Rastafari, assuages Kristal, offering her an overlay that aids her self-shaping or soul-searching.

In his recent anthropological study, Marvin D. Sterling surveys a similar "search for actualized selfhood through the international."[87] He consults Japanese non-fiction and fiction about travel to Jamaica, and he addresses Japanese appropriations of Jamaican culture, including Rastafari culture, noting that "the lone, global self-searchers of the present day often leave Japan to escape the restrictiveness of a powerful nation in decline. The third world is often represented as a space in which this sense of restrictiveness can be overcome."[88] Kristal's Germany is not in decline, not in 1969, the novella's setting, but *she* is worsening, "smelling of stillborn love," and her family's stoicism in the face of her failed suicide attempt puts fetters on her.[89] Jamaica represents a new space, at least for Kristal, marked by beguiling otherness, and her story, which she narrates in a series of journal entries, shows how she writes her self onto the pages of Rasta-inspired, postcolonial Jamaican society—"the other end of everything I had always known."[90] The novella's final words hint at two truisms—one, that a Rasta-identifying German and a Jamaican Rasta can come together, and in such a way that Kristal and Selassie speak "from one heart"; and two, that *My Planet of Ras* telegraphs Rastafari's transcultural appeal—themes now dominant in these later Rastafari novels.[91]

Jean Goulbourne's *Excavation* (1997)

Born in rural Jamaica, Jean Goulbourne follows this trajectory. She studied history at the University of West Indies, Mona, Jamaica, and then, in 1971, equipped with a Diploma in Education, she began teaching in St. Catherine's penurious Ginger Ridge district. Poetry was her first love. And Goulbourne's initial, rather vituperative verse captures her fury with what she witnessed during her educational tour of duty. Her first collection, *Actors in the Arena*, appeared in 1977. A second volume, *Under the Sun*, was released in 1988. In addition to writing poetry, Goulbourne has secured several fellowships and prizes, and in 1997 she published a novel, *Excavation*, which combines her high regard for the past with deep, probing questions about postcolonial identity formation in modern-day Jamaica. Set on the island's north coast, Goulbourne's story explores interactions among several archaeologists conducting a dig on a former plantation site. Each character works tropologically. Carla, the novel's protagonist, has mixed ancestry; and, her love triangle with David (a white American) and Professor Milton (a black Jamaican) symbolizes Jamaica's fraught past—two men tussling for the attention of one woman, two ideological forces contending for the island's heart and soul. Other characters include Kwame, the dig's supervisor, whose Akan day-name reveals his Ghanaian roots; Martin, the businessman's son from America's Deep South; and, Akete, the black Jamaican Rasta, whose name not only evokes the highest-pitched Ashanti drum used in Rasta rituals but also suggests a person both blessed with a sensitivity to the problems faced by others and cursed to become too involved in their affairs, often to the point of acute anxiety. As these six characters sift and unearth the past, both social and personal, they come to cultivate contrasting overlays, different ways of looking at the world.[92] Shortly after finding the bones of a run-away slave, for example, Akete proceeds out from as well as enters into his race's troubled history and, among other things, bristles when David makes romantic advances toward Carla.

"Akete guarded his religion like a beloved woman," Goulbourne's narrator declares, and Akete's quest to internalize as well as mine African heritage represents an essential yet anxious feature of his Rastafari religiosity.[93] There are times when his desire to honor and reclaim his connection to the Motherland clashes with his distaste for Jamaica's Babylonian poli-trickery, its widespread inequity, causing internal strife:

> Kwame heard the agony in Akete's voice. His plight was one he thought he understood. As a western-trained Ghanaian he had known something of the same divisions, though he had a language, a tribe and a proud past to sustain him. Here was Akete trying to find a route back in a society which denied its African roots. The road back was potholed and still strewn with the rubble of the past.[94]

In other moments, though, Akete reflects closely on the ties that bind him to his ancestral kinsmen and kinswomen, and he—to borrow Charles Price's description of second-generation Rastafari—instantiates "a positive purchase on a stigmatized identity."[95] After attending Kwame's illustrated lecture on Ghana, for example, Akete exhibits his own brand of religiously informed mental migration:

> The night was ink black by the time Akete went down to the beach for a swim. He walked carefully along the sand with his towel in his hands, his bare feet touching the ground lightly. He had seen a glimpse of the Africa he idealised. The huts and the stove were not new to him; he had seen them before in books, but the slides had brought them closer and he wanted to know more. He had to go there, to learn more about his homeland and feel the welcome that he was sure would come to him, to go there and swing his locks low and feel that he had, at last, come home.[96]

For the novel's greater part, then, Akete reconfigures his moral identity, as Price would say, and Akete espouses a "durable set of ideas about Blackness, justice, and redemption," manifest in the disavowal of his middle-class upbringing; in his appeal to Garveyism and other forms of black nationalism; in his consumption of ital food; in his twofold attack on black mimicry of the west and western mimicry of blackness; in his preference for rural forms of Rasta livity; in his fondness for reggae, which he recognizes as the reason for Rastafari's global presence; and, in his yearning for Africa.[97] This said, we should not think that Akete's morally configured black identity is atomistic; he connects with others and, on at least two occasions, he inspires Carla to consult her "Zion self."[98] Proceeding out from

Mircea Eliade's oft-cited work, though, we might theorize Akete's Afrocentrism by saying that he displays an "ontological thirst" to live as near as possible to the *axis* or *imago mundi*, the spiritual Center of the World, and that his "religious nostalgia" for Africa keeps him craving the continent's "cosmicized space."[99] Expressed in more basic terms, Akete's very being yearns for Mother Africa. But as our final novelist suggests, Rastafari and, by implication, the Motherland eventually transcends any one geographic place, emerging in twenty-first-century postcolonial literature more as a psychological, political, and spiritual state of being.

Geoffrey Philp's *Benjamin, My Son* (2003)

The author of *Florida Bound* (1985) *Hurricane Center* (1998), *Uncle Obadiah and the Alien* (1997), *Xango Music* (2001) and other creative writings, some of which have recently appeared as eBooks, Geoffrey Philp enjoys a textual friendship with Dante Alighieri, the Tuscan theologian-in-verse.[100] We see it, for example, in the way Philp takes the poet's moral topography of Hell and applies it to contemporary Jamaica in *Benjamin, My Son*, turning this novel into an adroit fictional transfiguration of *The Inferno*. Within Rastafari literary art, this strategy of fictional transfiguration has proved effective. Roger Mais transfigured the Gospel story in *Brother Man*, as I noted earlier, and Orlando Patterson transfigured an ancient Greek myth in *The Children of Sisyphus*. Both texts were success stories, and perhaps in more ways than one. For those of us who are keen to find new narratives on recent Rastafari, though, Philp's novel repays our close interest.

First published in Great Britain in 2003, and then nominated for the IMPAC Dublin Literary Prize, *Benjamin, My Son* uses the politics of postcolonial Jamaica as a backstory to an intriguing narrative about a Jamaican expatriate, Jason Stewart (also known by his Rasta name, Benjamin), who returns to the island from Florida after his father's ("Dada") inexplicable death. Why did Dada die? This is the question that Jason wants answered. And all initial clues point to David Carmichael, PNP politician for the Standpipe constituency, even though he eventually fades away toward the novel's end.[101] Yet Jason cannot hope to solve this mystery alone. He has a brother, Chris, but Jason feels lost, like Dante before him, and in need of a Virgil-figure, someone to guide him through a life he no longer recognizes. Here, in this captivating tale, Virgil wears dreads and his name is Papa Legba. This symbolic name—Papa Legba—invites links to the Caribbean religions of Vodou and Santería, where Legba (aka: Eleguá or Esú-Eleguá) is the crossroads deity, a trickster figure who presides over the future, and an enthusiastic messenger god who closes and opens the pathways people attempt to take.

Jason's appearance at Dada's funeral stimulates many memories, especially in the form of personalities and issues from Jason's past. Seeing his friend, Trevor, smoking marijuana, causes Jason to think of the times he hung out with his Rastafari friends, Reuben (former name Adrian) and Papa Legba, as well as his involvement with the Twelve Tribes of Israel mansion, salient symbol of Rastafari's

organizational dimension. As we soon discover, Philp's characters help to elucidate Rastafari's other religious dimensions. We hear about Marcus Garvey; Haile
Selassie; the 'groundation' ritual, which sees Rastafari congregate to smoke ganja
as well as to parse scripture and culture; dreadlocks and dread talk; Babylon; and,
the religion's use of reggae music to transmit its message of peace and love.[102]

We learn much about Rastafari's later evolution from Philp and for this reason
he complicates earlier portrayals of the movement's nascent stage. In Philp's hands,
for instance, the Rastas seem neither overtly Christic, as they might have with
Mais, nor woefully tragic, as we saw with Patterson. Now, Rastafari has become a
dense and sometimes ambiguous example of anticolonial resistance. When Jason
visits Standpipe, for example, he laments the way it stands out as a modern-
day Hades, a hellish existence marked by poor sanitation, malnutrition, violence,
prostitution, drugs, and sexism. But socially conscious roots reggae music fills the
tenement air. And Jason thinks the Standpipe Rastafari work best when they use
dread talk to call the practitioners of institutional sin—corrupt politicians, the
black petty bourgeoise, and others—to account for their Babylonian downpression. He puts it this way:

> Rasta gave us pride, made us proud to be young Jamaicans. We could live
> without the sinking feeling of never measuring up to British standards—
> that always began and ended with colour, class, or religion—of what it
> means to be civilized gentlemen. Or just human.[103]

Note the emphasis here, and elsewhere, on Rastafari's part in providing ordinary
Jamaicans with a sense of personal and collective identity. An ardent rejection of
white privilege pulsates at the religion's heart, Jason implies, and the divinity of a
black man upholds African-Caribbean self-esteem in face of racial prejudice and
subjugation. Expressed succinctly: Rastafari is a reclamation of a self and cultural
identity denied by Babylon. When Jason's former art teacher, Basil Cunningham,
dismisses Jason's Rastafari sympathies, Jason accentuates this sense that Rastafari
helps people learn dignity and pride:

> Although I could never accept Haile Selassie as the reincarnated Christ,
> it [Rastafari] helped me overcome my woundedness over my wealth, my
> colour, and my class. I saw the oneness in things—like the light the Impres-
> sionists said suffused all things. You taught us that.[104]

Academics are often fond of addressing religion's role in personal and communal identity construction. Clinton Hutton and Nathaniel Samuel Murrell, for
example, say this about Rastafari in Jamaica and beyond:

> In a real sense, Rastafari has given Jamaica a way to its neglected soul.
> This movement has engendered the kind of psychology the island needs

to deal with important aspects of its colonial legacy and usher in national development. By identifying with African heroes and with folklorist and ancestor stories, by adopting cultural and religious symbols of Africa, by carrying a nonconformist and non-Western persona or physical appearance, and by affirming and reclaiming the beauty and dignity of Africa, Rastas help Blacks fill a cultural and ethnic void in their inner being. By forcing the issue of identity on national consciousness, Rastafari seeks to overturn certain assumptions of the ideology of racism among the middle class in Jamaica and throughout the black diaspora.[105]

For his part, Philp seems aware of recent studies surrounding Rastafari. He uses Jason, for instance, to show us that Rastafari's sense of "somebodiness"—to use a term coined by Hutton and Murrell—appeals to people who occupy several layers of the Caribbean social pyramid.[106] In *Benjamin, My Son*, Rastafari recruit from all classes, not simply from the indigent; and thus Philp augments Mais as well as Patterson, moving beyond their portrayal of Rastafari as a poor man's religion to capture an important transitional shift in the movement's development in Jamaica. Yet *Benjamin, My Son* also reveals that not all social classes look upon Rastafari favorably. The novel's wider Jamaican society responds to brethren and sistren with considerable apprehension, as evinced by Cunningham, and sometimes, as the case of the police sergeant makes clear, with horrifying disgust.[107]

Various Rastafari, admittedly minor characters but not unimportant to the story's overall trajectory, surface throughout *Benjamin, My Son*. We meet Verna, for example, Jason's former maid, whose Rasta roots daughter shuns the church: "She wore flowing white robes and a red tam. Her face was round and her eyes were deep set. The plainness of her dress against the ebony hue of her skin made her all the more beautiful—a true Rasta queen."[108] And we encounter Doris, the woman whose flowing locks and feisty attitude convince Jason that she "had entered their [Rastafari] world and was holding her own with them, at their own game."[109] Yet it is Reuben and Papa Legba who stand out. Both are larger-than-life characters, and Philp's novel turns on their actions.

Thrown into jail after being caught with marijuana, Jason eventually meets with Reuben, also in custody, and learns of Chris's part in Dada's murder. For his part, Papa Legba—true to his role as ruler of the roads—advises Jason to shun Babylon, to challenge his disloyal brother, and to trust Jah Rastafari. Faith in Jah illustrates Rastafari's experiential dimension; here, in the novel's final few pages, Jason embodies such faith and he personifies this religious dimension. Guns finally fire when Jason faces off with Chris, Papa Legba dies, and Philp's fictional transfiguration draws to a close. Just as Virgil is unable to accompany Dante beyond the inferno and into purgatory and then on to paradise, so Papa Legba travels only so far on Jason's journey of self-discovery, leaving Jason to find within himself—and from the Beatrice-like figure of Nicole—the resources he needs to face the perils and possibilities that lie ahead. Because of

Papa Legba, and others like him, Jason arrives at the novel's end having recovered his own voice. "There was no need to run any more," Jason says, "I was home."[110] And "home," at least in *Benjamin, My Son*, captures Jason's Rastafari-refreshed sense of identity and belonging, which persuades him that he is no longer at the mercy of the image of blacks in the white, colonial mind; rather, he is free. Similarly, Rastafari is no longer tied to any one particular place as well as people or class. But, as I will explore in future chapters and Philp signals in his interview below, this transition also comes at some cost—both literally and figuratively.

An Interview with Geoffrey Philp

DJNM: Could you say a few words about how you came to be a writer?

GP: I started off writing poetry so I could impress the girl next door. Her sister was an English major at the University of the West Indies, so she quickly saw through my fake Khalil Gibran poems. I had to step up. I bought a copy of Dennis Scott's *Uncle Time* [1973] (he was my literature teacher at Jamaica College) and he autographed it for me. I gave her the book and started imitating Dennis, but no one can write like Dennis. So I tried to write like Tony McNeill, but that didn't work either. Then, I discovered *Another Life* by Derek Walcott (1973), and I said, "Yes, this is possible." When several ideas came to me and I realized that they could not be handled by poetry and that I had to learn how to write prose, I began re-reading V.S. Naipaul, Orlando Patterson, Roger Mais, and Edgar Mittelholzer.

DJNM: Who are some of your literary influences? And whom do you read these days?

GP: I would say: Matthew Arnold; Kamau Brathwaite; Albert Camus; Flannery O'Connor; Dante; William Faulkner; Robert Lowell; King James Bible; George Lamming; Bob Marley; Anthony McNeill; Gabriel García Marquéz; Edgar Mittelholzer; Mervyn Morris; V.S. Naipaul; Pablo Neruda; Orlando Patterson; Dennis Scott; Shakespeare; Derek Walcott; and, last but not least, Robert Penn Warren. As for your question about whom I am reading now: Marcus Borg; Adrian Castro; Junot Diaz; Elaine Pagels; Philip Roth; Shunryu Suzuki and, finally, Quincy Troupe.

DJNM: Since your writing has a lyrical or song-like quality, perhaps I should also ask: whom do you listen to these days?

GP: I'm listening to RAI. My daughter introduced me to it. She also introduced me to System of a Down and GodSmack. My son introduced me to Outkast, Biggie, 2Pac, and Sean Paul. When I'm by myself, I listen to Miles Davis, Sting, Gypsy Kings, Carlos Vives, Maroon 5, Marvin Gaye, Anita Baker, Spinners, and Bob Marley.

DJNM: You have addressed [http://geoffreyphilp.blogspot.com/] the need for Caribbean writers and artists to develop a "reggae aesthetic." Please elaborate.

GP: The term "reggae aesthetic" was coined by Kwame Dawes and it refers to reggae's ability to combine the personal, religious/prophetic, political and the erotic—sometimes in a single lyric.[111] Consider "Is This Love" by Bob Marley. Poverty, love, sex, and God all in one song. Which other art form can do that? Reggae speaks to what the Jesuits called the 'whole person.' It represents an alternative to the binary, Cartesian mode of thinking that I find uncomfortable and which results in the fragmentation of the self. I'm not saying that kind of thinking is not valuable. What I'm saying is that given our history of fragmentation in the Caribbean we should be aiming for wholeness.

DJNM: Rastafari often speak of such 'wholeness'—as much is implied in their 'InI' relational theology. When did you first encounter Rastafari?

GP: I first encountered Rastafari in the early seventies and by the time I was in fifth form at Jamaica College, it seemed as if all of my friends had become Rasta. My contacts also deepened because I used to play soccer for several teams and I met people like Seeco Patterson and Gilly Dread. Micky Mowatt of JahLove Musik lived right behind me and idren like Fred Locks or Bob Marley would pass through every now and then. What I loved about Rastafari was the reasoning. Man and man haffi reason. Rastafari employed the 'Socratic method' in the yard so that anyone could come to an understanding of a subject and him/herself through reasoning.

DJNM: It sounds like your knowledge of Rastafari has been forged on the hard anvil of lived experience. Are you Rasta? If not, how would you characterize your own approach to the religion?

GP: First, I am a Christian belonging to the Methodist tradition, so I could not accept the divinity of Haile Selassie as God Incarnate. By 'God' I mean unfathomable existence, the possibility of all possibilities who is as remote as the furthest universe, but as near and dear as a loving father/mother. I really think Rastafari have discovered a means of experiencing God personally when they say, "The I haffi start with the I to know InI." If we can begin with that self-scrutiny, then all kinds of areas for spiritual discovery begin to take place. I am very interested in the idea of InI because of the closeness to the Jesus that we meet in the Gnostic gospels. The I AM that is part of everything—the consciousness that pervades all I-ration.

DJNM: What kind of contribution do you think Rastafari have made to Jamaica?

GP: Rastafari has a great deal to teach us about ourselves. It's our homegrown wisdom that teaches us, especially with the idea of I-man, that I am responsible for my misery and depressions and also my happiness and joy. It is our ideas about ourselves that either liberate us or keep us in slavedom. All that we say we are or what we are not is really a matter of consciousness. Our consciousness determines our heavens and hells. The choice is ours. Rastafari also sensitized many in my generation to race and class. It broadened our perspective about the work that had to be done in emancipating ourselves from mental slavery. It's a great line, but are we really committed to it?

DJNM: I have lived among and studied Rastafari in England, Jamaica, Texas and, most recently, West Africa; and scholars are now beginning to say some interesting things about Rastafari in global contexts. Here's a two-part question. First, what thoughts come to mind when you hear the phrase 'the internationalization of Rastafari'? And second, to what or to whom would you credit Rastafari's place on the world's cultural map?

GP: Reggae and Rastafari go hand in hand. Reggae is an auditory representation of the experience of Rastafari. Reggae is also music of rebellion which is always attractive to the young, and Rastafari encourages reliance on individual experience. When you have that potent mixture, then the message will be spread far and wide, "like the waters cover the sea." Rastafari's place on the world's cultural map rests largely on the shoulders of Bob Marley. Of course, there are others such as Peter Tosh, Freddie McGregor, Burning Spear, Aswad, Culture, Dennis Brown, and Morgan Heritage, but Bob's song-writing ability and charisma made Rastafari sexy and popular. And let's not forget ganja. Most religions followed trade routes, so if you followed the ganja trade routes, you will also find Rasta. So put them all together: sex, ganja, and reggae. That's a winning combination any way you look at it.

DJNM: Do you have experience with Rastafari outside of the Caribbean and North America?

GP: Not a lot. I mainly read articles about them. But I don't have the physical, hand-shaking, "Wha guwane, idren?" contact that I had in Jamaica.

DJNM: Obviously, many Rastafari have returned to Africa, some to Ethiopia, and several to Senegal as well Ghana. What do you make of this *apparent* reversal of the journey through the Middle Passage?

GP: But is this a conscious reversal? Has this reversal shown up in the communal consciousness of Jamaicans and people of the Caribbean? This is where the role of art/writing can take us. Unless an action is registered consciously, then what's the point?

DJNM: As Rastafari have become more and more global, how do you perceive their transcultural tensions? I have noticed that expatriate Rastafari struggle to find an identity and a sense of acceptance when they return to Africa, for example, but what are your thoughts?

GP: All religions face a dilemma once they go outside the tribe. The early Christians faced the problem of Gentile converts. Rastafari will face several issues regarding Africa and the identity of Haile Selassie.

DJNM: What "issues" do you have in mind?

GP: The first that comes to mind regarding Africa is that Rastafari is a foreign religion—non-indigenous, so in places like Ghana and Nigeria, it may not be welcome. Also, non-African views of Haile Selassie seem quite different from those of Africans, especially those in Ethiopia. Was Selassie God incarnate or was he God expressed in a kingly form? I'm thinking along the lines of was Jesus *the* Christ or was Jesus a man who realized the Christhood that is inherent in all human beings? In other words, was Selassie God or an expression of God (as I think we all are). If he was an expression of God, then Rastafari may have a way forward.

DJNM: How would you assess the role of Caribbean letters, especially novels and dub poetry, in serving as *part* of the mechanism of transmission for the global spread of Rastafari?

GP: That's a very difficult question. Most of the artists/writers are not proselytizers of Rastafari. But Rastafari could not/cannot be ignored. Reggae and Bob Marley could not be ignored. So, in writing about myself, family, and community, Rastafari was bound to emerge. But art/writing has its own tyranny. And if you are going to write a novel or short story with a beginning, middle, and end, then the background information that the reader needs to understand the characters' motivations will include the histories/biographies. And if you are writing about contemporary Jamaica, then Rastafari will have to be part of the narrative.

DJNM: What effect, if any, did some of the early novels about Rastafari, such as Roger Mais's *Brother Man* and Orlando Patterson's *The Children of Sisyphus*, have on your literary and/or religious imagination? Did Mais and Patterson fill you with an anxiety of influence, for example, or did their work invite you to become part of a Rastafari literary art tradition, as it were?

GP: I read both stories long before I even thought I would write a novel. But these things prepare you. I guess I was doing my homework and didn't know it. When I started to write, however, and found that I wanted to write about Rastafari, they fascinated me. *Brother Man* and *The Children of Sisyphus* gave me the courage. It had been done before. But Mais and Patterson didn't fill me with an anxiety of influence. The writers who filled me with anxiety were Walcott, Brathwaite, Scott, and McNeill. I wasn't trying to become part of the 'Rasta Lit.' tradition. I wrote stories because I knew the characters and they knew me. They wouldn't leave me alone and I wasn't going to leave them. Rastafari was part of the larger questions that I was asking myself: Who am I? What are the things in my past that shaped me? What's happening to me right now? Of course, these things move outward from individual, to family, to community, country, region and as I added another circle, I picked up a larger identity.

DJNM: Turning to your novel, *Benjamin, My Son*, what kind of research did you conduct for its writing?

GP: I drew on the memory of people from my adolescence and fused them. But to write the novel, I had to learn how to write. As I envisioned the novel, it would be a Caribbean coming-of-age novel (George Lamming's *In the Castle of My Skin* [1953]) with elements from James Joyce's *Portrait of the Artist as a Young Man* (1916), Robert Penn Warren's *All the King's Men* (1946), Dante's *Inferno* (1314), Shakespeare's *Hamlet* (1603), and the mystery novels of Miami writer, James Hall.

DJNM: And what of Dante's influence?

GP: Dante's *Inferno* and his life were gold mines. I could creatively misread his life and the *Inferno*. He was in love. He was exiled because of conflicts between the Whites and the Blacks. He saw through the corruption in his homeland. He was trying to make sense of everything in the middle of life's journey. The parallels could go on and on. But I wanted to write about a contemporary hell.

DJNM: Earl Lovelace, the Trinidadian writer, laments the false sense of security that Independence has given to Caribbean peoples. In his view, there is still much work to do, work that he calls "reparation," not 'reparations,' where victim and victimizer welcome each other and set about repairing their souls through mutual grace.[112] I wonder if you share some of Lovelace's sentiments?

GP: I do. If there is one thing that Christianity has taught me, it's the need for forgiveness. It is only through forgiveness that we can heal ourselves. Again, this is what Rastafari has taught me. If I am in hell, it's because I have put myself there. Some of us have put ourselves in hell because of fear and we won't let anyone else out. Maya Angelou (quoting a Roman philosopher I can't remember right now) once said that courage is not the only virtue, but it's the only virtue without which all the others are meaningless. It takes courage to love and to forgive, especially when you are the victim and you didn't do anything 'wrong.' But once you come to realize what has happened, do you continue in the abusive relationship or do you find a way out? The will to power exists in all humans. Once the British left, other downpressors stepped in. This was Frantz Fanon's message (on the psychopathology of colonization). And it was largely ignored. That was why Jason read all those banned books, so he could be schooled in the West Indies of the past and Rastafari of the present. So, yes, there is much to be done in terms of reparation(s). Yet the reparation(s)—and I'm not letting anyone off the hook—begin with InI.

DJNM: Your novel references the Twelve Tribes of Israel, one of the largest Rastafari mansions in the world. How would you describe their appeal?

GP: The Twelve Tribes of Israel modified Rastafari and made it palatable to uptown or middle-class Jamaicans. They helped Rastafari to lose some of its social stigma because it didn't have the militancy of other forms of Rastafari. It was a nice, comfortable compromise. Like how some people choose to be Methodists rather than Church of God or Anglicans.

DJNM: There are moments when Jason (aka Benjamin, his Rastafari name) comes across as a liminal figure. He signifies part of colonial Jamaica, being an 'old boy' of Jamaica College, and yet seems connected to working-class Rastafari. He is linked to Florida, moreover, but he appears disillusioned with North America. Is he a symbol of transculturation, intended to embody the existential tensions that occur when one straddles two or more cultures?

GP: Jason is part of the Jamaican diaspora (a Jah-Merican) and is from that generation of privileged young men who attended Jamaica College when poor and middle class students were integrated into the student body. Jason is also part of the 'creative class' that has fled the Caribbean and is asking questions such as: Who am I? Where have I been? Where am I going? He is one of those figures like Matthew Arnold (aren't we all?) who is caught in the teeth of monumental, overwhelming change—where nothing fits. The trope of the exile (which is why Origen taught that the Bible should be read metaphorically) dramatizes the existential crisis (and this is where Camus is helpful) of all humans. The past is an illusion and the future a dream. Our identity is not determined by either pole of that equation. It's determined by the eternal present where InI stand.

DJNM: Jason/Benjamin celebrates Rastafari for their anticolonial religiosity. How would you assess their role as instruments in the task of decolonizing theology and religion throughout the Caribbean and beyond?[113]

GP: Rastafari is but one important part of the 'decolonization of the mind' that is necessary for the liberation of the Americas. The central concept of Rastafari, InI, if it is grasped, contains the seeds of personal responsibility and by extension, community, and national responsibility. If InI could overstand the political, economic, sociological, and ecological implications of this concept, then can you imagine the change this would bring about in the Americas?

DJNM: Besides Jason/Benjamin, there is Papa Legba. He is a Rasta, of course, but his name evokes the 'master of the crossroads' in Haitian/Benin (Dahomey) Vodou. In Haiti, he is sometimes called 'Papa Legba of the Old Bones.' Quite aged, he lives bearing the enormous weight of other people's suffering. Above all, Papa Legba opens the way to memory. He is also connected to Santería—in the form of Eleguá or Esú-Eleguá. Here he is linked to the future, the hereafter. So, you are using a name with more than one meaning, a name that gestures toward not one but three Caribbean religions. Is it fair to say that with Papa Legba you uphold the value of religious syncretism or inclusivism? Or is something else at work in this name symbolism?

GP: Papa Legba is all that and he is also a Rastaman. He points to syncretism, but he remains solid in his knowledge of Haile Selassie as Jah Rastafari. Figures like Papa Legba are often unaware of their significance. They do things that they know they should do, but are unaware of the full import. Remember Papa Legba is a man, like Marcus Garvey, who has traveled through the Caribbean. He renamed himself Papa Legba knowing about the connection to Africa and these other Yoruba-based religions. I can imagine if he was challenged by some 'righteous' Rastaman about his name who would ask him, "How can you, as Rastaman, have a name like Papa Legba? I-man hear say, the name mix-up, mix-up with obeah." And Papa Legba after sucking on his spliff and drawing in the dirt would answer, "The name come from Africa. And is just Jah, you know. Just Jah."

DJNM: Looking back, are you happy with your portrayal of Papa Legba? Do you feel you did justice to his Rastafari faith?

GP: I feel I did justice to Papa Legba's faith. Again in creating the scenes, I interrogated Papa Legba before I wrote any chapter that he was in to find out what he was thinking. So when I put him in the scene, I knew what he was thinking. But sometimes he surprised me. For example, it wasn't until I was writing the novel that I realized how much he hated Chris. I had figured he disliked Chris because of his love for Jason. I was using Jason's and Chris's rivalry as a familiar trope from the Bible of the younger son usurping the older brother. But as I wrote the novel, I discovered that Papa Legba hated Chris because of what he was doing. Papa Legba kept his hatred under wraps because he was trying to demonstrate love. That was a revelation.

DJNM: And what of Reuben and Doris?

GP: I tried to show in Reuben and Doris that they were decent honest people who made mistakes and lived life as they see fit. In writing novels, I've learned to become much more tolerant than I was in the past. We don't like to think that we are evil. We make rationalizations. Before I write any story, I put myself in the character's life and I ask them this question: Why are you doing this? I answer the question as if I were the character. That's when you really learn, 'Judge not.' So, yeah, I feel and hope that I did justice to their faith.

DJNM: The discussion of women and Jamaica College fascinates me. Like the College authorities, Papa Legba seems to see little or no place for women in society. Is this a fair representation of his views? Rastafari theology, as you know, once stipulated male headship in all things; intriguingly, as the religion has evolved, spreading out from its Caribbean base, more and more women have taken up positions of leadership within the movement. Comments?

GP: Papa Legba is a prophet and a man of his times. He has views about women that a man of his generation would have. It's the same way that I view 1 Tim 2:12. Could Paul have said such things about women? Probably. But he was also the Jewish mystic who wrote of love's patience (1 Cor 13:4).

DJNM: Doc's discussion of western art's importance for westerners, even if they are of African descent, makes me wonder how you, the author and not your character(s), view art's purpose. Is it to tell us who we are? To transport us to the Other, in a form of mental migration, or is it a bit of both?

GP: I believe that art connects us to the right here, right now and makes us realize that we are always standing on holy ground. It should also entertain, challenge, and sometimes hurt us because in hurting us, it may be forcing us to part with identities that are no longer useful. Ultimately, however, I believe art to be a tool for liberation—setting the spirit free. This is what Jesus in the Gospel of Thomas seems to be saying to me.

DJNM: What's your assessment of the Jamaican public's perception of Rastafari? Are most people like Basil Cunningham, who rejects the movement as a phase in its devotees' disenfranchised lives? Or should we, at least these days, speak of the social legitimacy of Rastafari? If the latter, what accounts for such social legitimacy?

GP: There are still people in Jamaica who dismiss Rastafari as irrelevant. In fact, they don't even think about the meaning of Rastafari within the continuum of Jamaican experience. Whenever I go to Jamaica, I listen to the talk shows and the ones here in Florida. There are some people who don't want to hear about or even talk about Rastafari. Some don't talk about Rastafari on religious grounds. I can respect that. But there are some people who because of classism or racism think that Rastafari was the worst thing that could have happened to Jamaica. I disagree with them. Regarding social legitimacy, I would say this: In those places where Rastafari is accepted—Rastafari doctors, lawyers, et cetera—it's usually because these are socially accepted professions. Twelve Tribes may also have something to do with the social legitimating of Rastafari in Jamaica because once Rastafari moved uptown, it gained a patina of respect.

DJNM: My own research convinces me that Rastafari, especially those in Africa, are revising their doctrinal dimension(s) these days, in that they either downplay or deny Haile Selassie's divinity. Jason/Benjamin certainly seems to symbolize this trend, no? At one point, he champions Rastafari for its moral dimension—unity and oneness—and not for its doctrine. Thoughts?

GP: Jason is what I would call a secular Rasta—he accepts the unity and oneness, but not the divinity of Haile Selassie. All religions adapt and change, but in changing they face the issue of remaining true to their core ideas. If Rastafari can perhaps come to a compromise—Haile Selassie represented the kingly aspect of the Christ nature and preserve InI, the indwelling god connected to God, they could survive.

DJNM: Jason/Benjamin's Dada hates marijuana, the weed of wisdom, and he acts tough on drug crime. And yet he defends Papa Legba's use of ganja on ritual grounds. Does this aspect of your novel either reflect or call for some modicum of acceptance of Rastafari from high-placed non-Rastafari in Jamaica, possibly beyond?

GP: Jason's father, Dada, belongs to that class of enlightened Caribbean politicians (of which there are so few now) who were committed, bone, blood, and marrow, to the cause of liberation—the process of freeing the children of Plantation America from the legacy of slavery and the colonization of the hearts and mind which resulted in inferiority complexes and other forms of spiritual insults. Dada loves what Papa Legba represents. Dada also comes out of that tradition that we inherited from the English of defending an individual's right to be wrong. It's that sense of British decency. Dada is also influenced by the Maroons who will fight down to the last woman for freedom. But, again, I see these characters as characters. I have no wider agenda. I think about characters, put them in untenable situations, and then ask them, so what are you going to do now? I don't see it as a call or anything like that. Dada because of who he is will do one thing, and Carmichael will do another.

DJNM: Papa Legba helps Jason/Benjamin recover his own voice at the novel's end, and Rastafari clearly provides Jason/Benjamin with an intense sense of identity. Is such identity formation, for want of a better term, Rastafari's first function in the world? And as Rastafari go global, as it were, do you expect their sense of identity to change as it finds itself in different environments?

GP: Rastafari's use of the term, InI, means that everything begins and ends with I. Therefore, I must know I. Jason goes through this transformation or ordeal and sheds those unwanted parts of himself that are not true. He goes through hell to discover his identity. Rastafari will change and it will be interesting to see how it changes as it moves to other places. Jamaicans are fiercely individualistic, so it will also be interesting to see what happens when Rastafari meets cultures that readily acquiesce to authority. How will InI survive?

DJNM: Does it feel strange to you that Rastafari are the subject of seminars around the world and that people are teaching your novelistic treatment of them, or do you feel thankful for that?

GP: Rastafari is the most interesting religious movement in the Americas because of the concept of InI. We haven't even begun to scratch the surface of the political, social, and economic implications of this idea. I give thanks when *Benjamin, My Son* or *Uncle Obadiah and the Alien* are taught in seminars or used in schools. But I'm also asking larger questions of identity in terms of gender and community. And then, what about the diaspora? How will that change our sense of ourselves?

DJNM: You are part of a movement to exonerate Marcus Garvey.[114] Why is this important to you?

GP: Marcus Garvey represents the root of Black liberation. There were other Black leaders before him who fought against slavery, colonialism, imperialism, and other forms of downpression of peoples of African descent, but he was the first to create a coherent universal philosophy for the redemption of Black people. Garvey's exoneration would be tantamount to an apology for the historic injustice and would be a historically redemptive act for the government of the United States in recognizing their culpability in the persecution of an innocent man.

DJNM: Finally, what are your future plans? What can we expect next?

GP: I'm enjoying myself with a blog I've created. I'm writing a few short stories and poems. I'm trying not to think about novels because I'm beginning to get frustrated with the rejections and the commercial aspects of writing. But rejections will never stop me from writing because ultimately, as Rastafari teaches, it's how I define myself. What do I want to be? How do I want to be remembered by InI? That's what matters. I am a writer. It's what I do. I'll keep on building and building and then, one of these days when I think I have enough short stories or poems for a book, I'll publish the collections. Like the song I learned in Sunday school goes, "This little light of mine, I'm gonna let it shine." It's all I can do. Say a prayer for me.

Conclusion

Ending his study of doctrinal diversity among Rastafari, Michael Barnett claims:

> the Rastafari movement is a multi-faceted one, and not the uniform, homogenous movement many people conceive it to be. Because of the polycephalous, decentralized, and multi-mansional structure of the movement there is little consensus on many things, but there does remain a common core, that of Haile Selassie I and Ethiopia as an important place on the globe. An additional note should also be made of Marcus Garvey who although not as revered to the same extent as Haile Selassie I by the various mansions of the movement, save for the Boboshante mansion, is still held undoubtedly in high esteem (even by the Coptic mansion). For this author [Barnett] a central driving force that runs through the whole Rastafari movement and effectively binds it together, is the desire or need to reconnect or stay connected to that African essence that lies within all of us.[115]

Art imitates life. Reading Rastafari literary art alongside modern ethnographies, like Janet L. DeCosmo's fieldwork among Bahian Rastafari in Brazil and Neil J. Savishinsky's research into Muslim Rastas in Senegambia, we discover that the literary Rasta mirrors his or her real-world counterpart—both have evolved over the last several decades, often by negotiating an identity for themselves outside and inside the movement, and we learn that the variety of Rastafari religious experience, in fact as in fiction, renders talk of the normativity of Rastafari belief and behavior decidedly problematic.[116] To move beyond a superficial understanding of Rastafari, which is often reduced to reggae, scholars would do well to first plunge the depth and richness of these Rastafari novels. Reading chronologically from Mais to Philp, we observe the evolution of Rastafari—its diversification and internationalization, and ultimately how Rastafari construct and reconstruct themselves in disparate and distinctive ways.[117] Now turning in the next two chapters to Rastafari reggae, especially in the mode of dub or performance poetry, we engage these changes firsthand, both in artistic form and primarily from insiders.

Notes

1 I recognize that the term 'literary art' could also refer to performance poetry and song lyrics but I am using it in the more traditional sense to signify written novels, stories, and plays. Relatedly, then, the audience for this literary art is quite different from that of the reggae musicians and dub poets I later consider. The latter play as much for insiders as outsiders. The audience for the fiction I address here is primarily a more educated, Western elite, making the goal of these authors a different one as well.

2 Roger Mais, *Brother Man*, special fiftieth anniversary edition, with a foreword by Kwame Dawes (Oxford: Macmillan Caribbean, 2004). Also see Orlando Patterson,

The Children of Sisyphus, with an introduction by Kwame Dawes (Leeds, England: Peepal Tree Press Ltd., 2012).

3 On such militant Rastas, see Michael Hoenisch, "Symbolic Politics: Perceptions of the Early Rastafari Movement," *Massachusetts Review* 29 (1989): 432–449; Sheila Kitzinger, "Protest and Mysticism: The Rastafarian Cult in Jamaica," *Journal for the Scientific Study of Religion* 8.2 (1969): 240–262; Joseph Owens, "Ras Tafari: Cult of Outcasts," *New Society* 4.111 (Nov. 12, 1964): 15–17; and George Eaton Simpson, "Political Cultism in Western Kingston," *Social and Economic Studies* 5 (1955): 133–149.

4 Hélène Lee, *The First Rasta: Leonard Howell and the Rise of Rastafarianism* (Chicago: Lawrence Hill Books, 2003), 145–159, 189–200. Also see Robert A. Hill, "Leonard P. Howell and Millenarian Visions in Early Rastafari," *Jamaica Journal* 16.1 (1983): 24–39. Howell wrote an early treatise on the Rastafari, *The Promised Key*, and work by William David Spencer both reproduces the long-lost text in full and comments on its main features. See Spencer, "The First Chant: Leonard Howell's *The Promised Key*, with Commentary by William David Spencer," in Nathaniel Samuel Murrell, William David Spencer, and Adrian Anthony McFarlane, editors, *Chanting Down Babylon: The Rastafari Reader* (Philadelphia: Temple University Press, 1998), 361–389. Among other things, Spencer compares "Howell's early recorded vision with today's global adaptation of Rastafari" (362). For additional details on early social responses to Rastafari, see Leonard E. Barrett, *The Rastafarians*, with a new afterword (Boston: Beacon, 1997; 1988), 84–102.

5 Ennis B. Edmonds, *Rastafari: A Very Short Introduction* (Oxford and New York: Oxford University Press, 2013), 20.

6 Lee, *The First Rasta*, 200. Best known as Bob Marley's mentor, Planno transitioned in March 2006, aged seventy-six. On Planno's influence over Marley, see Colin Grant, *The Natural Mystics: Marley, Tosh, and Wailer* (New York and London: St. Martin's Press, 2011), 134–153. Also see Murrell *et al.*, *Chanting Down Babylon*, 63, 152, 243–248, 256–257, 361, 423, 439.

7 See M.G. Smith, Roy Augier, and Rex Nettleford, *Report on the Rastafari Movement in Kingston, Jamaica* (Mona, Jamaica: University College of the West Indies, Institute of Social and Economic Research, 1960), 38. Here, Sir Augier comments on the Report: http://www.youtube.com/watch?v=RznJr07F284. Accessed March 30, 2014. Today, UWI's Institute of Caribbean Studies offers numerous courses on Rastafari and reggae.

8 Smith *et al.*, 4–10.

9 *Ibid.*, 15.

10 For an eye-witness account of the Coral Gardens incident, see Prince Williams with Michael Kuelker, *Book of Memory: A Rastafari Testimony* (St. Louis: CaribSound Ltd., 2004). Also see Deborah A. Thomas's recent documentary film, *Bad Friday: Rastafari after Coral Gardens* (New York: Third World Newsreel, 2011). The 2013 Inaugural Rastafari Studies Conference marked the incident's fiftieth anniversary with several scholarly presentations. Finally, see Edmonds, *Rastafari*, 21–22.

11 Smith *et al.*, *Report on the Rastafari Movement*, 18.

12 *Ibid.*, 20, 21. A 1961 Mission to Africa, ostensibly to discuss the possibility of repatriation, included Mortimer Planno. Back in Jamaica in 1966, Planno calmed the overly enthusiastic crowd that greeted His Imperial Majesty on his only visit to Jamaica. See Grant, *The Natural Mystics*, 46, 126–129, 132–152. Lambros Comitas, a Columbia University professor, has done much to promote Planno's significance: http://rastaites.com/Videos/Planno.htm. Accessed March 30, 2014.

13 Smith *et al.*, *Report on the Rastafari Movement*, 18–22.
14 *Ibid.*, 23–29.
15 *Ibid.*, 23.
16 *Ibid.*, 25–26.
17 Edmonds, *Rastafari*, 20.
18 Barrett, *The Rastafarians*, 101.
19 Edward Brathwaite, "Introduction," in Roger Mais, *Brother Man* (Oxford: Heinemann, 1985), xi. When I cite from the novel proper, I use the Macmillan Caribbean publication. Mais's characterization of Bra' Man draws on his positive portrayal of the Rasta character, Ras, in *The Hills Were Joyful Together*, first published in 1953. See Mais, *The Hills Were Joyful Together* (Leeds, England: Peepal Tree Press Ltd., 2012).
20 Mais, *Brother Man*, 26. For the open hostility toward Bra' Man, see 169.
21 *Ibid.*, 12.
22 I owe this terminology to Theodore Ziolkowski. See his *Fictional Transfigurations of Jesus* (Princeton, NJ: Princeton University Press, 1972), 6–7.
23 Brathwaite, "Introduction," xii.
24 Kwame Dawes, "Foreword," in Mais, *Brother Man*, special fiftieth anniversary edition, 5. An accomplished artist in his own right, Dawes adapted Mais's novel into *One Love*, a musical play or 'dubaretta,' which was performed in the UK in 2001. "The play, which was later published by Methuen, sought to bring together everything we have learned from the impact of Rasta on Jamaican life since the publication of *Brother Man* with the spirit of Mais' novel" (3).
25 Robert Beckford and William David Spencer have sought to cement this connection between Jesus and Rastafari. See Beckford, *Jesus is Dread: Black Theology and Black Culture in Britain* (London: Darton, Longman & Todd, Ltd., 1998) and Spencer, *Dread Jesus* (London: SPCK, 1999).
26 Mais, *Brother Man*, 27.
27 *Ibid.*, 178–179.
28 *Ibid.*, 183–184.
29 Dawes, "Foreword," 9–10.
30 Patterson, *The Children of Sisyphus*, 32–33. When I cite from the novel proper, I use the Peepal Tree Press Ltd. publication. Patterson serves on the faculty of Harvard University, where he teaches courses on the history and sociology of slavery. For details, see: http://scholar.harvard.edu/patterson/. Accessed March 30, 2014.
31 *Ibid.*, 58.
32 *Ibid.*, 58, 59.
33 *Ibid.*, 61.
34 *Ibid.*, 70, 73.
35 *Ibid.*, 129.
36 *Ibid.*, 198.
37 *Ibid.*, 210.
38 *Ibid.*, 210–211.
39 Victor Chang, "Introduction," in Orlando Patterson, *The Children of Sisyphus* (New York: Longman, 1994), x.
40 David Dabydeen and Nana Wilson-Tagore, "Selected Themes in West Indian Literature: An Annotated Bibliography," *Third World Quarterly* 9.3 (July 1987): 945.
41 *Ibid.*, 945–946.
42 Kwame Dawes, "Introduction," in Patterson, *The Children of Sisyphus*, 20.

43 Edgar White, *Lament for Rastafari*, in William B. Branch, editor, *Crosswinds: An Anthology of Black Dramatists in the Diaspora* (Bloomington and Indianapolis: Indiana University Press, 1993), 162–202. The play was first performed at the Billie Holiday Theatre, New York, USA, 1971, and the play was first published in 1983.

44 *Ibid.*, 179.

45 *Ibid.*, 189.

46 *Ibid.*, 189.

47 *Ibid.*, 196.

48 Theo Witvliet, *A Place in the Sun: An Introduction to Liberation Theology in the Third World* (London: SCM Press, 1985), 116.

49 Hannah made a film—*Race, Rhetoric, Rastafari*—in 1983 for the start of Britain's Channel 4-TV. It is now available, in four parts, on YouTube. For details, see: https://www.youtube.com/watch?v=kzWDZrsvHp8. Accessed March 30, 2014.

50 The eBook version, also known as the seventh or 'Gold Medal Edition,' is published by CreateSpace Independent Publishing Platform, available through most online booksellers. For the print version, see Barbara Makeda Blake Hannah, *Rastafari: The New Creation*, sixth edition (Kingston, Jamaica: Jamaica Media Productions, 2006; 1981).

51 See: http://www.myspace.com/barbaramakeda. Accessed March 30, 2014.

52 Barbara Makeda Blake Hannah, *Joseph: A Rasta Reggae Fable* (Oxford: Macmillan Caribbean, 2006). This text was first published as Barbara Blake Hannah (Makeda Levi), *Joseph: A Rasta Reggae Fable* (Kingston, Jamaica: Jamaica Media Productions, 1991). I cite the 2006 Macmillan Caribbean edition, the more readily available of the two texts. For the film's trailer, see: http://www.youtube.com/watch?v=-xuncb6mUP0&NR=1. Accessed March 30, 2014.

53 Hannah, *Joseph*, 1.

54 *Ibid.*, 39–47.

55 *Ibid.*, 10.

56 *Ibid.*, 78. Also see Grant, *The Natural Mystics*, 245–249.

57 Hannah, *Joseph*, 80, 96, 115. On Rastas in today's Shashemene, see: http://www.guardian.co.uk/world/video/2010/jul/23/rastafarians-shashamane-ethiopia and http://www.guardian.co.uk/music/2005/feb/07/popandrock.ethiopia. Both accessed March 30, 2014. Also see essays by Jahlani Niaah and Erin C. MacLeod in Michael Barnett, editor, *Rastafari in the New Millennium: A Rastafarian Reader* (Syracuse: Syracuse University Press, 2012), 66–103.

58 Hannah, *Joseph*, 38.

59 *Ibid.*, 8–9, 23, 25, 40–43, 49, 51–59, 89, 93, 96–97, 128–129, 138–139, 147, 153, 171–172.

60 *Ibid.*, 68.

61 *Ibid.*, 115; also see 125, 134–135, 143, 149, 173.

62 *Ibid.*, 125.

63 *Ibid.*, 130.

64 *Ibid.*, 128.

65 *Ibid.*, 171–172, 175, 177, 179–182, 184, 191.

66 Velma Pollard, *Dread Talk: The Language of Rastafari*, revised edition (Montreal: McGill-Queen's University Press, 2000). Also see Edmonds, *Rastafari*, 45–47.

67 On this film, and other feature films featuring Rastafari, see Kevin J. Aylmer's "Towering Babble and Glimpses of Zion: Recent Depictions of Rastafari in Cinema," in Murrell *et al.*, *Chanting Down Babylon*, 284–307.

68 The People's National Party and the Jamaica Labour Party represent the two main political groups within Jamaican society.

69 Barbara Blake Hannah, "No More Rasta for-I," *Gleaner Sunday Magazine*, September 11, 1983, 2–4.

70 Masani Montague, *Dread Culture: A Rastawoman's Story* (Toronto: Sister Vision Press, 1994). In Toronto, Montague has organized numerous workshops, Bible studies, film events, reggae concerts, and intra-faith dialogues. See Loretta Collins, "Daughters of Jah: The Impact of Rastafarian Womanhood in the Caribbean, the United States, Britain, and Canada," in Hemchand Gossai and Nathaniel Samuel Murrell, editors, *Religion, Culture and Tradition in the Caribbean* (New York: St. Martin's Press), 233. Written by Montague, directed by Luther Hansraj and starring David Smith, *Soundclash* enables attendees to sense the Jamaican immigrant experience alongside various moments in the evolution of Jamaican popular song—ska, rock steady, and roots reggae. Brian Meeks adopts a similar strategy in his *Paint the Town Red* (2003) novel. On Masani's projects, see: http://masaniproductions.com/main-set.html. Accessed March 30, 2014.

71 Montague, *Dread Culture*, 73. Also see Anna Kasafi Perkins, "The Wages of (Sin) Is Babylon: Rastafari versus Christian Religious Perspectives of Sin," in Barnett, editor, *Rastafari in the New Millennium*, 239–252.

72 Montague, *Dread Culture*, 50.

73 *Ibid.*, 12, 15–16, 42, 49, 55, 58–59, 68, 76, 78, 82, 85, 94, 99.

74 *Ibid.*, 51–52, 65.

75 Loretta Collins Klobah, "Journeying Towards Mount Zion: Changing Representations of Womanhood in Popular Music, Performance Poetry, and Novels by Rastafarian Women," *IDEAZ* 7 (2008): 188. Also see Zindika, *A Daughter's Grace* (London: Karnak House, 1992).

76 Montague, *Dread Culture*, 140.

77 See Obiagele Lake, *RastafarI Women: Subordination in the Midst of Liberation Theology* (Durham, NC: Carolina Academic Press, 1998), 93–102. For a succinct summary of the traditional expectations surrounding women in the movement, see: http://www.bbc.co.uk/religion/religions/rastafari/beliefs/women.shtml. Accessed March 30, 2014.

78 Some such documentaries are freely available. See: http://vimeo.com/10653070 and http://www.youtube.com/watch?v=-VRBMRebh_Y. On 'disrobing,' see: http://jamaica-gleaner.com/gleaner/20080309/ent/ent3.html. On the conference, see: http://jamaica-gleaner.com/gleaner/20100704/lead/lead8.html. All sites accessed March 30, 2014.

79 N.D. Williams, *Prash and Ras* (Leeds, England: Peepal Tree Press Ltd., 1997).

80 *Ibid.*, 9–13.

81 *Ibid.*, 15.

82 *Ibid.*, 29.

83 *Ibid.*, 14.

84 *Ibid.*, 66. Rita Marley experienced similar feelings, as noted previously.

85 Danièle Hervieu-Léger, *Religion as a Chain of Memory* (New Brunswick, NJ: Rutgers University Press, 2000).

86 Williams, *Prash and Ras*, 28–29.

87 Marvin D. Sterling, *Babylon East: Performing Dancehall, Roots Reggae, and Rastafari in Japan* (Durham, NC: Duke University Press, 2010), 203.

88 *Ibid.*, 197.

89 Williams, *Prash and Ras*, 12.

90 *Ibid.*, 11.

91 *Ibid.*, 74.

92 Jean Goulbourne, *Excavation* (Leeds, England: Peepal Tree Press Ltd., 1997), 35, 41.

93 *Ibid.*, 67.

94 *Ibid.*, 30.

95 Charles Price, *Becoming Rasta: Origins of Rastafari Identity in Jamaica* (New York: New York University Press, 2009), 231.

96 Goulbourne, *Excavation*, 61.

97 Price, *Becoming Rasta*, 230. Also see Goulbourne, *Excavation*, 8, 13, 19–20, 27, 31, 33, 41–42, 52–53, 64–65, 85–86.

98 Goulbourne, *Excavation*, 42, 53.

99 Mircea Eliade, *The Sacred and the Profane: The Nature of Religion* (New York: Harcourt, Brace and Company, 1959), 63–65.

100 For a BBC radio interview, see: http://www.bbc.co.uk/programmes/p00bqsdk. In addition, I address Philp's work in a Podcast series on Rastafari, now available through Philp's blogspot: http://geoffreyphilp.blogspot.com/2009/05/all-you-ever-wanted-to-know-about.html. Both sites accessed March 30, 2014.

101 Geoffrey Philp, *Benjamin, My Son* (Leeds, England: Peepal Tree Press Ltd., 2003), 8–9, 33, 40, 151.

102 *Ibid.*, 13, 30–32, 37, 124, 127, 136–142, 177–179.

103 *Ibid.*, 102; also see 71, 85, 90–91, 107–109.

104 *Ibid.*, 124.

105 See Clinton Hutton and Nathaniel Samuel Murrell, "Rastas' Psychology of Blackness, Resistance, and Somebodiness," in Murrell *et al.*, editors, *The Rastafari Reader*, 51. For a more generic discussion, see Carl Olson, editor, *Theory and Method in the Study of Religion: A Selection of Critical Readings* (Belmont, CA: Wadsworth, 2003), especially chapter seven. On religion and identity construction in the Caribbean, see J.W. Pulis, editor, *Religion, Diaspora and Cultural Identity: A Reader in the Anglophone Caribbean* (New York: Routledge, 1999). For details on identity construction and Rastafari, see Noel Leo Erskine, *From Garvey to Marley: Rastafari Theology* (Gainesville, FL: The University Press of Florida, 2005), 189–198. Finally, see Barry Chevannes, editor, *Rastafari and Other African-Caribbean Worldviews* (New Brunswick, NJ: Rutgers University Press, 1998).

106 Hutton and Murrell, "Rastas Psychology," 36–54. Also see Barry Chevannes, "Rastafari and the Exorcism of the Ideology of Racism and Classism in Jamaica," in Murrell *et al.*, editors, *The Rastafari Reader*, 55–71.

107 Philp, *Benjamin, My Son*, 124, 163.

108 *Ibid*, 90.

109 *Ibid.*, 137.

110 *Ibid.*, 185.

111 Kwame Dawes, *Natural Mysticism: Towards a New Reggae Aesthetic in Caribbean Writing* (Leeds, England: Peepal Tree Press Ltd., 1999).

112 On Lovelace's reparation theory, see Darren J.N. Middleton, *Theology After Reading: Christian Imagination and the Power of Fiction* (Waco, TX: Baylor University Press, 2008), 117–120.

113 On Rastafari and decolonizing theology, see Erskine, *From Garvey to Marley*, xi, xiii, xv, 3–5, 113–115, 124, 184, 178. Also see J. Richard Middleton, "Identity and Subversion in Babylon: Strategies for 'Resisting Against the System' in the Music of Bob Marley and the Wailers," in Gossai and Murrell, editors, *Religion, Culture and Tradition in the Caribbean*, 181–205.

114 For details, see: http://www.mdc.edu/main/thereporter/archive/vol03–13/news/
mdcprofessor_campaigning_to_exonerate_bl.aspx. Accessed March 30, 2014.
115 Michael Barnett, "The Many Faces of Rasta: Doctrinal Diversity within the Rastafari
Movement," *Caribbean Quarterly* 51.2 (2005): 77.
116 Janet L. DeCosmo, "'A New Christianity for the Modern World': Rastafari Fundamentalism in Salvador, Bahia, Brazil," in Barnett, editor, *Rastafari in the New Millennium*, 104–122. Also see Neil J. Savishinsky, "The Baye Faal of Senegambia: Muslim
Rastas in the Promised Land?" *Africa: Journal of the International African Institute* 64.2
(1994): 211–219. Other case studies of global Rastafari are featured in my book's
bibliography.
117 For a general discussion of the literary Rasta as part of the broad tradition of Jamaican
storytelling, see Hugh Hodges, *Soon Come: Jamaican Spirituality, Jamaican Poetics* (Charlottesville and London: University of Virginia Press, 2008), especially 128–172.

3

RASTAFARI'S RIGHTEOUS WAIL

From Reggae to Dub Poetry

Introduction

Fortified by an arsenal of word and sound, Bob Marley used his Rastafari faith in a bitter, protracted campaign against Christian missionary propaganda and capitalist imperialism. He chanted down Babylon. And over time songs like "Africa Unite," "Get Up, Stand Up," and "Blackman Redemption" not only served to accentuate the Rastafari religious movement's devotion to social change through protest music, they also helped to place its livity on the world's cultural stage.[1] "Marley's reggae burrowed so deep that its rhythms and words erased barriers of language and culture, so that even the globe's most marginalized citizens embraced the Rastaman's vibration," Klive Walker states, referencing Marley's popularity throughout the 1960s and 1970s.[2] Unlike the literary art previously explored, this early reggae was an insider artistic expression, produced by and intended for Rastafari themselves. Since then, reggae music has catapulted to the status of popular art form, and nowadays it serves as the main mechanism of the Rastafari religion's transcultural transmission. Its more recent forms (dancehall, ragga, reggaeton) stand in contrast to roots reggae, the socially conscious music that Marley pioneered, making contemporary reggae a complicated affair. Non-Rastafari and Rastafari currently produce it, for example, and non-Rastafari frequently employ the dread talk that Rastafari first introduced to the world, often blurring the line between the two groups. Insiders and outsiders thus shape Rastafari, which means I must attend to both perspectives as well as their overlap.

This chapter outlines reggae music's history, pausing to feature interviews with insiders like Asante Amen, a Rasta singer-songwriter from Jamaica, and with outsiders like Reggae Rajahs, India's first reggae sound system and one of the latest symbols of the genre's globalization, before concentrating on three Rastafari performance or dub poets: Mikey Smith, Mutabaruka, and Jean 'Binta' Breeze. Prophets of an Afrocentric theology of hope and liberation crafted in defiant as well as satirical verse, dub poets shun the moral leniency ('slackness') associated with dancehall reggae and, instead, use roots reggae's repeating riffs to express their ardent, lyrical uprightness and to carry the torch of social justice that they believe Marley passed on to them when he transitioned in 1981.

A Short History of Reggae

Reggae is a distinctive form of Caribbean music, developed in the 1960s by art-ists interested in blending Jamaican folk music and African American rhythm and blues (R&B).[3] However, deeper sources of reggae lie in numerous Jamaican musi-cal styles, such as mento, ska, and rock steady, which are united, for the most part, by the use of complex percussive arrangements, recurring guitar plucks, pounding bass effects, and song lyrics that are often political.[4] Popular in the 1940s, mento performers fused African musical traditions with calypso music from the island of Trinidad, creating a hybrid sound that remained fashionable well into the 1950s, when it was replaced by ska, a more upbeat genre. Ska represented a musical merger of mento, American R&B, and New Orleans jazz. Jamaicans, including musicians, had become aware of R&B and jazz by means of shortwave radio broadcasts from Florida. Early ska was largely instrumental and emphasized the first and third beats in a four-beat musical measure.

Pioneered by artists such as Prince Buster, Coxsone (also known as Downbeat), Don Drummond, Jackie Mitto, and Rico Rodriguez, ska was very popular in Jamaica in the early 1960s, partly because vans equipped with record turntables, so-called sound systems, would travel to various parts of the island, spinning the latest tunes. Ska's more melodious vocal form, rock steady, became popular in the mid-1960s. Rock steady also reflected a new era in Jamaican musical history, since rock steady groups, including Justin Hines and the Dominoes, seemed more concerned than their musical forebears with confronting, by means of their music, what they perceived to be societal and political injustice. Emphasizing both drum and basslines, rock steady eventually evolved into reggae, which first appeared in 1968 as a hybrid of rock steady and ska. Count Ossie, a Jamaican jazz percussionist who had performed on numerous ska recordings, was one of many artists who facilitated this evolution. Here the narrator of *Paint the Town Red* (2003), Brian Meeks's Rastafari-inspired novel, describes reggae's transcultural traits:

> She [Caroline Barnett, the novel's female protagonist] played the homeric triple album by the Mystic Revelation of Rastafari and he [Mikey Johnson, the novel's male protagonist] caught her enthusiasm at the merger of the akette drums with avant-garde jazz horns. She explained how in "Bongo man a come" saxophonist Cedric Brooks merged jazz ensemble playing with drums and the New World African tradition of improvisation.

"It's like Harlem meets Kingston somewhere over Lagos, y'know. It's the same message as the Congoes; us Africans staking out our place in the modern world."[5]

Reggae's first 45rpm single promoting Rastafari spirituality, Little Roy's "Bongo Man," hit the top of the Jamaican song charts in 1969. In addition, reggae's evolution was accelerated by Jimmy Cliff ("Wonderful World, Beautiful People"), who became an international star in 1972 for his part in the reggae-inspired movie *The Harder They Come*. Other reggae artists included the group Toots and the Maytals, whose song "Do the Reggay" solidified the genre's name.

In the late 1960s Bob Marley teamed up with Peter Tosh, Bunny Wailer, and session musicians, the Wailers, to craft a lyrically potent sound that captured the doctrinal and philosophical dimension of Rastafari, the belief that God or Jah is a living black man, His Imperial Majesty Emperor Haile Selassie I. By 1975, Marley and the Wailers were global recording stars, admired for albums such as *Catch a Fire* (1973), *Natty Dread* (1974), *Rastaman Vibration* (1976), as well as *Exodus* (1977), and Rastafari, Marley's faith, became more internationally visible.[6] In New Zealand many well-known reggae artists, particularly Tigilau Ness (also known as Unity Pacific), credit Marley's 1979 Western Springs Stadium concert with fostering reggae's countrywide growth.[7] Cultural critics refer to Cui Jian as China's Marley, because he uses reggae to address the plight of everyday Chinese.[8] Monica Haim's documentary film, *Awake Zion* (2006), also addresses the connections between Marley's reggae culture and Judaism, which one can view at the Official Israeli Reggae Site.[9] In other words, all roads lead to Marley, so that one cannot overstate his global influence. Roger Steffens declares:

> Today, the Havasupai Indians who live at the bottom of the Grand Canyon regard Bob as one of their own, a man of the soil who revered Mother Earth and Father Sky as they do. In Nepal, Bob is worshipped by many people who regard him as an incarnation of the Hindu deity, Vishnu. In Addis Ababa he is thought of as a modern reincarnation of the ancient Ethiopian church composer the Holy Yared. On a mountainside above Lima, Peru, carved in huge letters, is the legend "Bob Marley is King." Maori, Tongan, and Samoan islanders join together in a band called Herbs to sing Bob's 'songs of freedom.' Rebels of every stripe march to battle singing Marley's anthems. Says Jack Healy, head of Amnesty International, "Everywhere I go in the world today, Bob Marley is the symbol of freedom." Thus the music and lyrics continue in the hearts of Jah's people as they chant down Babylon on their way to freedom.[10]

Anthony Bogues concurs. He acknowledges that even though today's agents of Marley's worldwide commodification "work overtime to make the Rastaman who 'chanted down Babylon' into a fangless musician, a symbol of exotic

FIGURE 10 Lois Cordelia, "Bob in Blue" (2011).

difference, trapped and captured in an illusionary rainbow world of dreamers," there is no escaping Marley's universality.[11] Bogues continues:

> In the end, whenever I think of Marley, I cannot help recalling my arrival in Mexico City in the mid-1980s, seating myself in a cab with a driver who

spoke only Spanish and who, after I finally communicated my destination, wondered if I was a Jamaican. Receiving an affirmative answer, he stopped the car, searched under the seat for a set of tapes, placed one in the cassette player of the car, and proclaimed with joy on his face, "Jah! Jah lives!" He was not a Rastafarian, and did not seem to have profound understanding of the doctrine, but somehow he had heard the voice of prophetic criticism, and it was that which he was celebrating. Surely the time has come for us to chant down Babylon one more time.[12]

Still, during this period, there were others. Besides Marley, the Abyssinians ("Satta Massagana"), Big Youth ("I Pray Thee"), The Congos ("Ark of the Covenant"), Misty-in-Roots ("True Rasta"), Prince Far I ("Wisdom"), Ijahman Levi ("Jah is No Secret"), and Ras Michael and the Sons of Negus ("Truth and Right") also dispersed the movement's message internationally.

Nevertheless, throughout the 1970s, the 'internal' remained as important as the 'international'; or one could even argue that the internal dynamics usurped the significant process of internationalization, and this echoes our novels' depiction of Rastafari and its evolution as well. In his investigation of over 100 reggae songs, recorded and released between 1968 and 1981, Stephen A. King argues that the music galvanized Rastafari internally, meeting the "in-group goals" of creating and sustaining "a healthy and positive self-image of 'blackness' while, at the same time, intensifying cohesion and 'groupness' within the movement."[13] In words that echo Ninian Smart, we might say that Rastafari's material or artistic dimension here served the needs of the movement's organizational or social dimension. As King notes, songs such as the Abyssinians's "Declaration of Rights" and The Mighty Diamonds's "Natural Natty" admonished Rastafari to transcend a slave mentality and to reach for an ideal type, the figure of the noble African herbsman or the vibrant, defiant locksman. Such reggae strengthened the Rastafari from within, for the music's militant denunciation of Babylon bolstered "the Rastafarian's ego or self as distinctly superior to its evil counterpart."[14] By the late 1970s, however, the boundaries or demographics were being stretched. Reggae had reached the ears of countless middle-class Jamaicans, and it moved many of them to identify with Rastafari responsible for making and performing it, which conferred cultural legitimacy on an otherwise outcast group.[15] This fresh sense of social acceptability soon paved the way for the global spread of the movement and its music.

The genre known as dub reggae came into its own in the mid-to-late 1970s, pioneered by eccentric record producers such as Lee 'Scratch' Perry ("Rasta Dub") and King Tubby ("Natty Dub"), and their inventive work soon moved beyond Jamaica to Europe, as Christopher H. Partridge's work reveals.[16] Faced with the need to avoid the expense of recording a new song for the B side of a band's or singer's single, Perry and Tubby stripped the A side of its vocals and added echo, distortion, drop-outs, equalization, and additional ambient soundscapes, thereby creating a 'dub plate' (acetate disc) of the original cut. Following such producers, various Jamaican sound system operators and disc jockeys, such as U-Roy ("Babylon Burning") and I-Roy ("Step On the Dragon"), began adding their own lyrics, sometimes impulsively or spontaneously. This development led to what Kwame Dawes and Klive Walker identify as the art of toasting, which, after it was heard in Los Angeles and New York City in the early 1980s, inspired both hip-hop and rap music.[17]

Connected to dub reggae, a second wave appeared in the 1980s. Artists such as Aswad ("African Children"), Burning Spear ("Calling Rastafari"), Israel Vibration ("We a de Rasta"), and Third World ("Reggae Ambassador") emphasized Selassie's divinity, stressed Africa's preeminence, and underscored black solidarity—themes we also saw in the novels from this period. The Grammy-winning albums associated with some of these performers, such as Black Uhuru's *Anthem* (1984) and Steel Pulse's *Babylon the Bandit* (1986), reached as well as inspired audiences far and wide. In Greece, for example, bands like Locomondo, who fuse Caribbean rhythms with Greek lyrics, cite such albums favorably.[18] Second-wave Rastafari reggae combines the deeply evocative appeal of biblical tropes with a strident, inventive denunciation of the socioeconomic injustices perpetrated by those in Babylon who are seen to control and sanction society's status quo—colonial power, the state, the police, and the church.[19]

FIGURE 11 Lois Cordelia, "Black Uhuru" (2010).

Stephen Foehr traces Rastafari reggae's visionary and prophetic function to those who settled in Kingston's depressed neighborhoods after the police raided Leonard P. Howell's Rasta commune at "Pinnacle" in 1954:

> They had an off-beat, Old Testament flair, with their long matted dread-locks swirling about their heads as they shouted out passages from the Bible. Their voices hot with the flame of righteousness, they called down destruc-tion on the Babylon around them, which is on everyone else. They were weird. Outside the box. Over the top. A disquieting and threatening pres-ence among people still caught up in the colonial pattern that might lead to bourgeois respectability. They were madmen, and the aspiring middle classes didn't want to hear their madness, didn't want to witness it, didn't want to be baited by it. They were crazy boogiemen. Out of their foxy insanity emerged classical reggae, an art form that has steadily marched around the world as a flag bearer confronting injustice and oppression.[20]

Other scholars find Foehr's Old Testament allusion felicitous. Nathaniel Samuel Murrell hears an echo of the Hebrew Psalms in Rastafari reggae, for example, and he celebrates the way Rastas draw on this dimension of the Bible not only for their self-definition but also to oppose capitalism's unfair economic and social matrix:

> By taking over the Hebrew Psalms and using them as munitions to resist the Babylon culture, Rastas' unorthodox Bible reading has created a new politi-cal theology of the Psalter. The adoration, enthronement, sovereignty, and power of Yahweh—who Rastas view as distant and removed from human disaster like African slavery and the Jewish Holocaust—are returned to a theology of 'JAH Rastafor-I,' God with humans and humans with God. The theology of personal piety, on which Hugh Olds says classical Protestantism has thrived since the days of Martin Luther, is lived out in a political theol-ogy of liberation, equality, and justice for the people of God. The theol-ogy of lamentation as a means of quietism and refuge in self pity from the 'troubles of the world' and oppression by the enemies of 'Israel' is returned to the theology of revolution in peaceful protest against the oppressors.[21]

I-Roy's "Sufferer's Psalm," which uses dread talk to recast Psalm 23 as an anti-capitalist lament, characterizes Murrell's thesis that Rastafari use their faith's material or artistic dimension to explore its mythic or narrative dimension. Fur-thermore, this link between reggae and scripture is not lost on British-based visual artist Lois Cordelia, who maintains "Words of Wisdom," an instructive website that matches reggae song lyrics to biblical quotations.[22]

Building upon the work of Cordelia, Foehr, and Murrell, I present Rastafari reggae singers and musicians as modern prophets with two special tasks. First, they seek to expose and condemn those inadequacies that society's poor and dispossessed are socialized into merely enduring. Like Amos and Isaiah, that is, Rastafari reggae musicians and singers challenge both personal and institutional sin. Various albums by Black Uhuru, especially *Red* (1981), stress this desire to advance individual as well as social change through music ("Youth of Eglington" and "Utterance"). Second, Rastafari reggae singers and musicians strive to raise the awareness of others, freeing them from mental slavery, just as Jeremiah and Ezekiel did in their time. Having released several albums promoting Marcus Garvey's philosophy of self-determination and pan-Africanism, Burning Spear models this conscientization task adroitly ("Slavery Days" and "Marcus Children Suffer"). These tasks, however, have been questioned, starting in the late 1980s.

At this point, Jamaican reggae took on a more synthesized feel, leading to electronic subgenres of reggae such as dancehall, ragga, and reggaeton. Music from this period features not only punched-up techno rhythms but sexual boasting, drug references, and anti-feminist as well as homophobic themes, made famous by artists such as Buju Banton ("Boom Bye Bye"), Mad Cobra ("Flex"), and Shabba Ranks ("Trailer Load A Girls"). The departure from Marley's message is incontrovertible. This said, reggae's potent motifs of black unification and emancipation were never entirely forgotten. Some of the era's prominent Rasta-inspired musicians include Anthony B ("None a Jah Jah Children"), Capleton ("Bible Fe Dem"), Dahweh Congo ("Seek Jah First"), Garnett Silk ("Every Knee Shall Bow"), Luciano ("It's Me Again Jah"), and Richie Spice ("Motherland Calling"). Crafted and performed by artists such as Linton Kwesi Johnson ("Dread Beat and Blood"), Mutabaruka ("Great Kings of Africa"), and Benjamin Zephaniah ("Roots and Culture"), dub poetry, as we will see, also emphasized reggae's social and religious message. In addition, the roots reggae tradition, in some ways traceable to Bob Marley, was specifically taken up by Ziggy Marley ("Conscious Party"), the eldest son of Rita Marley and Bob, as well as by numerous 'reggae sistas,' often as a critique of dancehall's *perceived* ethical slackness or carelessness.[23]

The critiques and rebuttals continue today, also invoking a particular commodification.[24] In his review of Kevin Macdonald's documentary film, *Marley* (2012), Anthony Lane bemoans: "If you visit the West Indies, get ready to be mortified, beyond shame, by the sound of those spiky and militant compositions being smoothed down into wallpaper, as a background for badly dancing tourists. *Marley*, by reminding us of the longing and the indignation from which the music leaped, does a grand job of turning the volume back up."[25] But as our study of the novels indicated, contemporary Rastafari, and its musical expression in reggae, has surely become far too global and diverse for any one, final assessment. All is not lost. Today, artists such as Chronixx ("Thanks and Praise"), Protoje ("Dread"), and Tarrus Riley ("King Selassie H.I.M.") take reggae's liberative torch from Bob Marley and the Wailers.[26] Speaking to America's National Public Radio, Ragin Fyah's vocalist Kumar Bent ("Nah Look Back") thinks "new-school roots" reggae supercedes dancehall. "This movement now that's happening is a revival of consciousness," he asserts. "It's not about singing about a girl's skirt anymore; it's about upliftment of the mind."[27]

And as Allan Bernard's study shows, Sizzla Kalonji ("Rastafari Teach I Everything") is a leading influence on a new generation of Rastafari youth.[28] Indeed, Sizzla's involvement with the Reggae Compassionate Act, which decries sexism and homophobia, among other things, may be a case in point.[29]

In a recent interview Edward Seaga, former Jamaican prime minister, recognizes that reggae, in all of its historic manifestations and forms, pulsates at the heart of world culture.[30] Besides Locomondo in Greece, reggae's success has inspired Ireland's Sinéad O'Connor, who has recorded two albums that are suffused with Rastafari sentiments, as Adam John Waterman's work demonstrates.[31] Germany's Basic Channel dub music label continues to release tracks that highlight the movement's message positively.[32] Great Britain's *Guardian* newspaper marked the thirtieth anniversary of Bob Marley's passing with an account of his music's global afterlife—an intriguing playlist of international hits, rarities, and unforeseen tribute songs.[33] Menelik Shabazz's documentary film, *The Story of Lover's Rock* (2011), shows how this sub-genre, reggae's Motown, gave voice to many women, like Janet Kay ("You Bring the Sun Out"), when it first appeared in London in the mid-to-late 1970s. These days, singers such as Sandeii, Machaco and Iria illustrate the success of lover's rock in Tokyo.[34] Furthermore, Japan's annual Yokohama Reggae Festival features young, homegrown talent like Mighty Crown, who craft their own brand of Japa-reggae around dancehall-inspired tunes laced with Japanese lyrics.[35] In South Africa Nkulee Dube, the daughter of the late Lucky Dube, the so-called African Peter Tosh, has released a debut album, *My Way* (2013), to acclaim.[36] Reggae has had considerable impact on North American popular culture as well.[37] Reissues of Bob Marley's earlier work sell very well in the United States, established as well as upcoming reggae artists perform regularly in concerts in major American cities, and Grammy Awards are given to reggae artists annually. Reggae is also popular over the airwaves and in the cinema, as evidenced by the soundtracks of Hollywood movies such as *Heartland Reggae* (1972), *Countryman* (1982), *Club Paradise* (1986), *New Jack City* (1991), *Cool Runnings* (1993), and *Dancehall Queen* (1997). Critics like Andrew Ross have also explored connections between reggae, rap, and African American performance poetry.[38] The story of reggae in Canada is ongoing, with new and intriguing chapters added with each passing year, as Klive Walker shows.[39] From Warieka Hill to Zimbabwe, then, Rastafari has popularized Jamaican music across the world.[40] Over time, such reggae has become indigenized, and local languages now articulate Rastology, which anyone with internet access can hear and assess for themselves. Indeed, today's reggae creates an exciting arena for polyvocal, cross-cultural dialogue, according to the essayists in Carolyn Cooper's edited volume, *Global Reggae* (2012).[41] This said, Sarah Daynes claims that the music's many routes and roots has created concerns, which look like being unresolved for the foreseeable future:

> Today, reggae music is listened to and played on the five continents, travelling in a double movement: (1) the international diffusion of Jamaican reggae,

through recordings as well as through the concerts given by Jamaican artists; and (2) the emergence of 'local' reggae, as well as the influence reggae can have on other musical styles. The simultaneity of these two movements can be seen as a paradoxical tension between the local and the global: on one hand Jamaican reggae is following the routes of the diaspora—becoming global; on the other hand, reggae music is settling in various places, where it develops its own sound and themes—becoming local. The circulation of reggae music between all the places of the diaspora—and out of the diaspora— is made of these multiple interconnections between the local and the global, and is highly dependent on the various meanings attributed to it by both performers and listeners.[42]

To illustrate reggae's localization and internationalization, I interview two contemporary reggae artists. Asante Amen, a Rasta singer-songwriter who works from Kingston, Jamaica, is featured in my first interview. A baptized member of Priest Dermot Fagan's School of Vision, one of the most recent Rastafari mansions, Asante Amen represents the emic or insider perspective and, as we will see, his broad-minded convictions typify the diversity observable within the faith. The second interview is with India's first reggae sound system, Reggae Rajahs, who do not consider themselves Rasta, even though they identify with the movement's general spiritual vibe. The Reggae Rajahs signify the etic or outsider approach to this topic.

FIGURE 12 Asante Amen in concert (2012). Photo: el Puru Photography.

An Interview with Asante Amen

Born Gavin Walters, the artist Asante Amen symbolizes a new generation of Jamaican Rastafari reggae musicians, having surfaced in 2011 with songs such as "Wipe Your Tears" and "Beating."[43] He added harmonies to the music of others for several years before embarking upon a solo career, and he has performed with many artists both throughout the Caribbean and across the United States. Asante's inaugural album, *Over The Years: The Underground Project* (2011), secured some time on California's KDVS 90.3 FM Reggae/African Top 25 album chart and, at the time of writing, his compositions are experiencing major rotation across Europe and Africa. Recent partnerships with Lutan Fayah ("Nuh Fraid"), JAH Thundah ("More Fyah"), and Karamanti ("So High") are cementing his already robust reputation. And now that he has secured a distribution deal with a European company, various new and unreleased tracks are scheduled to appear on a revised version (*Over the Years: The Europe Edition*) of Asante's debut release, thus making it possible for a genuinely global audience to value this fresh voice.

DJNM: Your star is on the rise, Asante, because reviewers believe you represent a future/retro roots reggae with a dubstyle infrastructure. Your songs are being heard in countries such as Italy and Kenya. How did it all come to this? How would you describe your personal and musical journey (to date)?

AA: Where I am in music today is as a result of hard work, determination, faith in YHWH/JAH and listening more keenly to when the Master speaks to me. I have been singing JAH's praise for a decade now and if you listen keenly to my music over the years, you will hear the changes not only in my voice but in the musical messages I send out. But my sense is that now is the time for those defending YHWH to rise and YHWH has been preparing His children for this time. So my ears were pricked many years ago and I answered the call and offered my life to Him and to preaching His truth, and He has been molding me ever since. And now it feels like YHWH is ready for me to move to the next level and so I submit to His will and pray that if this is indeed my time that I remain focused on the mission and bring glory to my God and King.

My musical journey to date has not been an easy one. I have been a part of various groups and companies in the business, hoping that one of them would have been my musical home or musical family. That wasn't to be. And so in July 2011, I launched my own record company, High Priest Records, and released my first album called *Over the Years: The Underground Project*. Since the album, I have been networking with musical people both locally [Jamaica] and globally to establish Asante Amen, as a reggae artist, both nationally and internationally.

DJNM: And then there's Rastafari: Where or how does Rasta livity fit into your life and art? A song like "Praises" strikes me as an excellent introit to your lyrical thinking, for instance, because it emphasizes how Haile Selassie, as the Earth's rightful ruler, is the ground and grammar of your own righteousness, your own spiritual pilgrimage. Might you elaborate? Do you belong to a certain Rastafari mansion, for example, and how do your convictions about everything from cooking ital food to smoking ganja shape your work?

AA: InI is Rastafari. Rastafari is my life; it is the vehicle through which I choose to experience earth. And so every aspect of my livity is shaped or influenced by the livitical consciousness of Rastafari. Therefore my art (musical expression) is also molded and packaged by consciousness. Now, onto the song "Praises."

Let me first make a clarification: JAH/YHWH is not His Imperial Majesty (H.I.M.) Emperor Haile Selassie I in my eyes. As I have grown in Rastafari and taken on the study of H.I.M., I have come to see that H.I.M. is not God Almighty as one school of thought in Rastafari teaches, but rather the fulfillment of the Davidic covenant that we, the scattered Children of Israel/Africa, needed to see in order to reconnect with our divine root. So as a result of this enlightenment, when I speak of YHWH/JAH I am referring to that Divine Essence that permeates *all* life and sustains all things; and when I speak of H.I.M. Emperor Haile Selassie I or Ras Tafari, I speak of the one who JAH sent to remind us that He (JAH) has not forsaken us and that we must return to worshipping Him (JAH). Therefore the song "Praises" is all about lifting up the name of YHWH/JAH to the fullest, and taking the time to thank Him for His mercies and blessings.

In terms of being an official member of a mansion of Rastafari, I am a baptized member of "His Imperial Majesty, Haile Selassie I School of Vision, Bible Studies, Prophecies & Sabbath Worship"—simply called the School of Vision, headed by Priest Dermot Fagan. My views on H.I.M. do not concur with the teachings of the School, however, as it [the School] sees H.I.M. as the second advent of Yahshua Ha-Mashiach (God the Son; Jesus the Christ), and I don't. That aside, there is no denying the cosmic pull of the Priest and after walking with him for a while, I felt compelled to go through the initiation of baptism, which is a fundamental aspect of his teaching. It was important that I do it on three levels: (i) it operates as a public declaration of one's love for YHWH/JAH and acts as a seal/covenant between you and JAH; (ii) the ritual of baptism or water initiation can be found in a number of African cultural practices, including the Hebrew culture, so to see Priest Fagan retaining this traditional African practice is very important as it reflects an aspect of our spiritual understanding as Israelite/Africans; and, (iii) this process of initiation was undertaken by no higher personalities than Yahshua Ha-Mashiach and H.I.M. Emperor Haile Selassie I, so why not I?

In terms of my livity, I eat healthy and prepare my meals healthily as well. It is imperative that one sustains one's physical temple with the right foods and juices, along with exercise, meditation, and thanksgiving. Thanks to the livity of Rastafari, living this way is made easy because you're not alone in the trod or journey and you get guidance from others on how you can improve yourself regularly. It is truly a great institution to be a part of. My meals are not ital in the sense that I do use salt, but I am vegetarian. On the next side, I don't smoke marijuana much anymore. I much prefer to have it in tea form now as this is a healthier way of partaking of the holy herb.

My convictions shape my work and my approach to it tremendously. As I observe and learn from the things happening around me, contemplate my role/calling in life and my understanding of JAH and how everything fits together, I put these understandings/meditations/inspirations to music. So just as a tree that is planted by the rivers of water, so too do my tunes reflect the fruits that I bear as my roots (mind/spirit) are watered by JAH.

DJNM: Allow me to ask about the School of Vision, especially Priest Fagan's famous rhetoric concerning microchips and UFOs. I am fascinated by this side of the mansion. What do you think? What is your sense of what others think?

AA: Yes, Priest Fagan believes in "circular ships that produce rings of fire," which he says are what people call UFOs; and, he connects such ships to scripture, especially words about "chariots of fire" in 2 Kings 2:11 and 6:17. I don't believe it. I think he is reaching on that point, but he believes it to be so and so I let it be. When I first heard it, I was shocked and disbelieving; now I am just disbelieving as I have heard him teach that lesson about a hundred times. If anything it still puzzles me that he believes that; but I guess some teachings of the Bible can do that to you. History is replete with many groups having bizarre beliefs, which they claim they can support through some passage in the Bible. So Priest Fagan is not the first and he certainly won't be the last.

As for how outside people receive it, the best example I can give is when he was on Mutabaruka's radio program a few years ago and this UFO issue came up. When he told Muta what UFOs—in his mind—really were, Muta had to ask him to repeat what he said about three times; and even after that he had to ask him where he got that from, and then a long debate about biblical interpretation followed. A similar reaction came from others. For the average Rasta folk that came around during the time I walked with Priest Fagan, I think the teaching for some was hard to figure out while others believed it wholesale; such is life. But for the regular folk who I have been around and who had heard about that teaching, they would ask me if he was mad, if I believed him, or if I just found him amusing. I know this: One can't take away his passion; he speaks with real sincerity and total conviction. Yes, Priest Fagan is a special one indeed!

DJNM: You've worked with some high-profile Rastafari reggae singers, so you know that artists such as Anthony B and Luciano see themselves as a 'teacher' and a 'messenger' respectively. What lies at the heart and soul of your vocational self-understanding—how do you see yourself? And what artists, if any, have mentored you to this point in your life, where you stand poised to take up your place as part of the next generation of Rastafari vocalists?

AA: I see myself as a being trying to come into the full understanding of who JAH/YHWH/God is and living by the teachings of that Supreme Being the best I can as I learn them. I acknowledge that I falter sometimes during this mission and that I get a little stiff necked from time to time but I am doing better as I get older. So I see myself as a work in progress, with my destination being salvation.

My primary musical mentor up to this day is Garnett Silk. He was an awesome artist, a pure spirit, and he displayed a genuine desire to seek JAH and all His glory. His life was cut short, but he has left an indelible mark on me and so he is my main musical guide. The works and lives of Dennis Brown, Jacob Miller, Bob Marley, Peter Tosh, and Gregory Isaacs also serve as great teaching tools for me. As for artists in the flesh now, I have learnt a lot from persons such as Tony Rebel and Luciano. I have spent a lot of time around these brethren and they have showed me a lot about the business and life in general.

DJNM: Could you say a few words about how you approach the writing and recording process? Are there rituals or routines that you engage in preparation for composing and/or singing, for instance, and what song, from your discography, makes you most proud or summarizes your life vision?

AA: The first thing I have to do is be in a space all by myself. I don't do well with other energies around me when I am writing my songs, so I much prefer when it is just me, the music, and JAH in the room. Dependent on the riddim I am listening to or the original piece I am creating, it can take me anywhere between ten to twenty minutes to write a song or a couple weeks to a month to complete a song. I try to make the writing process as natural as possible, so when I have competing demands on my time or things on my brain, I don't write. But if at three in the morning or noon I feel an inspiration to write, a song or two will be written in an hour or so. There are times when I get the inspiration, but it's only for the hook/punch line of the song. If that is the case I will revisit the song at a later date or when the energy is right.

I don't have any rituals I perform other than praying to JAH to allow the words from my mouth to be acceptable to Him and to anoint my voice so that the recording touches whoever hears it. And also I ask JAH to write the message I have communicated in my music, upon the table of the listener's heart. Otherwise, my routine is vocal warm-ups and listening to the demo version of the song repeatedly before I record.

The song I am most proud of—from a vocal delivery standpoint—is "Wipe Your Tears." The song that summarizes my life vision is "Mek Mi Rich."

DJNM: "Only Ras Tafari" is an anthem to Selassie's unconditional love for His brethren and sistren—does this song reflect your desire to "Tell Out King Rasta Doctrine," to cite Mortimer Planno, the late Rasta elder, who saw reggae as an opportunity to spread the good news of Rastafari?[44] Or is something else going on in this song?

AA: Something else is going on in this song. In fact, many things are going on. For a start, I wrote "Only Ras Tafari" during one of my stiff-necked periods, and at that time the song could be taken as—and it was certainly intended at that time to be—a straight ode to H.I.M. as God and King (this was a few years ago). However, by the time my manager and I agreed to actively promote and officially release it as a single, in early 2013, I was in a different place spiritually, so I had to review the lyrics to see if the song was consistent with my revised theology. It was while I was doing this that YHWH/JAH opened my eyes to the song's real meaning. Let's look at the lyrics first, then I will offer an analysis:

Intro
Whooohhh Ooohh oooohhh
Oh Yes
Ooohhhhhhh Lord
Ras Tafari, lives and rules and reigns
Ooohh Lord

Punch
Only Ras Tafari,
Keeps me firm
Only Ras Tafari.
Yes only Ras Tafari
Keeps me firm
Only Ras Tafari

Verse 1
Yes there's no other King I can depend on
To save my soul
He's the only conquering lion,
In full control
So don't hesitate, don't be too late, for JAH call
Cause you don't, realize JAH was by your side all along; So

Punch
Verse 2
So if you know seh a true me a talk
Raise one hand and put di next pon yuh heart
Cause this is no time to be joking, we got to be working,
cause JAH JAH is calling
Us home; So

Punch
Repeat Verse 1

When I say "Only Ras Tafari," I am speaking not just to the strength and guidance I get from the teachings of H.I.M., but also the power and identity that Rastafari culture gives me. So the title of the song carries a dual meaning. In the first half of the first verse I am speaking to the sublime wisdom of H.I.M. and how his teachings have led me onto the path to salvation (salvation being YHWH). In the second part of the first verse, I am speaking to the unconditional love of JAH/YHWH (our salvation). So, just as Yahshua Ha-Mashiach has been the way, the truth, and the light to many, so too has H.I.M. been the way and a guiding light in my life. For if it was not for H.I.M., I might have never revisited the teachings of Yahshua and received the greater understanding that I feel I now have. But because YHWH knew from the beginning that all of us—the lost Children of Israel/Africa—would not have received the teachings of Yahshua, or listened to the prophets or recalled the countless blessings He has bestowed upon us, He made sure to set a perpetual covenant with David. And this covenant has manifested itself in my time, because through the Royal lineage of Ethiopia, the Lion of Judah has prevailed in the personality of H.I.M. and his heirs and successors. H.I.M.'s exemplary life has been a refuge for me over the years, and if anyone takes the time to read the words of H.I.M., one will see that Yahshua was a great source of inspiration to him. Since Yahshua was an example unto H.I.M., it was only right that I took the time to understand why H.I.M. revered Yahshua so much. This meant therefore that I had to remove as many of the biases and negative perspectives I had about Yahshua, the Bible, and Christianity from my mind as I could, and read the Bible (as H.I.M. had asked us to) with a clear conscience. As a result, I began to look more keenly at Yahshua's many pronouncements and found that, like H.I.M., YHWH had called him [Yahshua] to be a refuge unto those that can 'see' him.

There are three key teachings of Yahshua that have helped me to arrive at the spiritual place I am at today. They are: (i) greater works than he [Yahshua] we can do; (ii) nothing that he [Yahshua] says or does he does of himself; and, (iii) none is perfect except YHWH. So after reading the words of H.I.M. and Yahshua Ha-Mashiach, with a clear conscience and doctrinal rhetoric aside, it became clear to me that ultimately our lives should be lived in service to YHWH/JAH and no one else. So when I say "Only Ras Tafari" now, it is with this frame of mind that I say it; and these days, I experience an inner peace that I never had before this fuller understanding came to me.

Now, this interpretation of the first verse brings the second verse into play expertly, because if my evolved Rastafari and/or theological perspective has merit and resonates with your spirit (as it does mine) then there is no time to waste, and we must do the will of JAH while we are fit and able to do so. For time lost can never be regained and when JAH calls us home our time for work would have passed. So basically, what I am saying is, if it wasn't for the trod of Rastafari—the livity and/or the movement—I would not possess understanding today, so it is indeed "Only Ras Tafari [that] keeps me firm."

I know that many will take this song to mean what I originally intended it to, at the time that I wrote it; and many have confirmed this already. However, I am heartened by those who have approached me and said that they think the song has a deeper meaning than it seems to be saying on the surface. This has showed me that YHWH was indeed behind this song from the beginning and its true meaning will shine through. Notwithstanding my belief, I will use opportunities such as this interview to let others know what the song means, at least to me, with the full understanding that they may either choose to accept it or opt to work with the meaning the song gives them when they listen to it. Either way, I know there is a blessing to be gained by those who listen to and receive the message contained in "Only Ras Tafari."

DJNM: A reference to the Organization of African Unity, which Selassie helped to establish in 1963, appears in "Keep Holding On," a song that serves as your theo-musical resistance to Babylon's many attempts to downpress brethren and sistren. The song also alludes to Selassie's famous speech before the United Nations, also in 1963. What is Africa to you?

AA: "Keep Holding On" serves as a rallying cry to my brothers and sisters who see JAH, whether metaphysically or through the personality of H.I.M. Emperor Haile Selassie I, to not give up on their faith and beliefs, but also it is a testament to the indelible contributions of the Emperor during his time here with us on earth. If we look through history closely—especially after His Majesty transitioned—much was done to discredit him; and this was done most certainly in an attempt to throw cold water on the faith of Rastafari brethren and sistren. So when I was asked to write a song about H.I.M., I opted to write the song in such a way that people might learn of some of the King's good deeds, while at the same time give strength to those in the faith before me and since my time, because this journey is not an easy one and we all need encouragement from time to time. Allow me to quote the lyrics.

Intro
Oooohhhhh
Ras Tafari lives and reigns
Yeah, yes, ooh Lord

Punch
Victory is near my brother
Salvation is close,
So keep holding on, keep holding on, keep holding on
To JAH Love [x2]

Verse 1
Your sticks and stones, cannot break my bones [no]
'Cause I'm made of 100% Rastafari steel [hmmmmhhh]

Moulded by His Divine Wisdom, and by His Grace and Glory,
Every nation shall bow before H.I.M [Lawd]
Yes understand that, he's the man who, formed the African Unity;
And gave a speech that, still can save the world from destruction.
So don't you ever try to compromise the worth of H.I.M.,
For he's the truth and he's the way forever
[Forever and ever x2]
Forever, yes

Punch
Verse 2

Sometimes I feel like, the battle has been won and good has overcome [yes]
Over all its obstacles, [lawd]
And give thanks Selassie I, cause you always a guide over InI [Oh yes].
'Cause I understand that you're the man who formed the African Unity,
And gave a speech that still can save the world from destruction
So I won't ever try to compromise the worth of your Majesty,
Cause you're the way and you're the truth forever
[Forever and ever x2]
Forever
Punch

Africa is a state of mind. I don't need to live in Africa to be African and feel authentic. To me, it is more important to have an African state of mind than anything else—Rastafari theology brings you face to face with your African heritage and culture and cultivates within you that desire to want to know the motherland on a personal level. As a result, I don't think I will feel complete in myself as a person until I travel to Africa. So I don't have to live in Africa or repatriate physically as Rastafari teaches, but I must at least behold the continent—or as much of it as I can visit—with my two eyes; that would be sufficient.

DJNM: Righteous works and conscious lyrics coalesce in "Never Stop," a song that urges Rastafari—and perhaps anyone trying to live faithfully in seemingly faithless times—to cultivate goodness and devotion. Is it hard professing Rasta today, eighty years into the movement's history? If so, why? If not, why not?

AA: "Never Stop" was written for all people, irrespective of race, creed, or nationality. In today's world it seems much easier and you're looked at as more 'cool' if you are a deviant or out-of-the-box, so to speak. Singing about truths and rights and love for God, or trying to be an upstanding citizen who observes common courtesies such as 'good morning' or 'excuse me' is no longer the 'in thing.' Through "Never Stop" I want to implore persons who in fact know better, to do better. I want to encourage them to resist peer pressure or the emerging societal norms that seem to deviate from the basic wholesome teachings they received—if they indeed received them, as I did. I find—and it has been said in different ways by many great thinkers—that the hardest things to do are the simple things or the ones that are right, and since I know all too well about the internal conflict that one can have in deciding to do the right thing, I had to write a song that encourages and reassures persons to do good, no matter what.

The mission of Rastafari is not an easy one, especially from an artist's point of view, if you have to repeatedly explain why he/she hails H.I.M. as God or the source of their being or their spiritual leader/teacher, knowing that this is not a new teaching. Also, in my humble estimation, a lot of the Rasta reggae artists are under pressure to stay popular and current—from a Jamaican perspective—so singing about H.I.M. all day won't get you prime billing or airtime in this country. So many have opted to tone it down or sing the kind of music everybody else is singing. Except for a select few, the Rasta chanters do seem hard-pressed to stick with the message music that was so captivating in times gone by.

As for me, I am not fazed by the 'noise' of today, so my messages will remain the same. It is a spiritual war that I fight, so from where I sit, if I begin to dilute my music and push God to the background for fear of offending someone or because it might affect my chances of stardom, then Babylon would have won. I cannot afford that, so I will press on, in spite of all the 'noise' around me, to put out songs that uplift, inspire, and hopefully save souls. But I would be lying if I said it is easy doing this work. It isn't. And for me specifically there is an added challenge as I want to use some of my music to challenge the Rasta community to reassess how they look at H.I.M. So thus for me I face a more localized challenge in delivering the message I have inside me.

I must say that I am particularly inspired by the reggae revival that is taking place in Jamaica today. Although reggae music never went anywhere and many like myself were here making this music during the lull period of the last decade, there has undoubtedly been more focus and a renewed interest in roots reggae music in more recent times. One must acknowledge the likes of Raging Fyah, Protoje, Iba Mahr, and Chronixx as the leaders in this new wave we see in Jamaica at this time. This new wave has given me renewed strength and represents, in my mind, a beacon of light from YHWH/JAH to those of us who have been on this musical mission for a while now to keep going.

DJNM: "What is This?" is an uncompromising Rasta-infused lament of current politics in Africa and the Caribbean. You speak of how we are living in the age of 'the political terrorist.' And you caution your hearer(s) to be aware of the "dragon" in the "big Great house." The "big Great house" might be an allusion to the White House/United States, yet your dragon imagery intrigues me, because it is a customary image for China and, as my book shows, African reggae singers, like Blakk Rasta, are critical of China, especially Chinese economic involvement in Africa. So, allow me to put this question out there: Has China become, for you, the new Babylon, as it has for someone like Blakk Rasta?

AA: "What is This?" is my most politically released song to date. I have written and recorded a couple others before this one, but "What is This?" has seen the light of day and so we are thankful for that. It is indeed an uncompromising Rasta-infused lament of the current political landscape, but from a global perspective. I cite the United States of Africa and the Caribbean as examples of territories that have fallen victim to this political terrorism, but my lament doesn't apply to these territories alone. Just look across the world right now and see which other territories/countries have a big stick being waved over their heads and by whom and you will see quite clearly which countries—on both sides of the fence—I am referring to.

As for the portion of my song that you refer to, the full line actually says, "Every Nation now is willing to be a slave / to the dragon in the big Great house / weh a seh dem brave." That line wasn't for China at all, but as in the case of Blakk Rasta as you say, based on his world view, he might see this line as best fitting China. And isn't that a beautiful thing? That this line in the song will resonate with the oppressed wherever they are, because the oppressed always has an oppressor/dragon; but we all don't share the same oppressor—though many of us do. So basically, the nation I refer to doesn't hold China in high esteem and China is certainly not a part of the gang of seven! And this nation is. But as my brother Bob said, "Who the cap fit, let them wear it."

DJNM: Jahlani Bongo Niaah thinks a lot of contemporary reggae falls into a category he calls "redemption serenading."[45] This arresting term refers to the art of composing and performing music with the dual purpose of elevating the Jah-consciousness of others, especially those trapped in the African diaspora, and of equipping them to fight for liberation (African repatriation or Babylon's rehabilitation). How do you react to Niaah's term? Does it capture or reflect a lot of the reggae you hear these days? If so, how? If not, why not? And ultimately, would you be content if someone applied this term to your own work?

AA: I think Bro. Jahlani has identified in what he calls "redemption serenading" two key pillars to reggae music, which were certainly an overtone in the music historically and that can still be found in the art form today. I probably wouldn't have used his label, but he is accurate in his assessment, even if I would broaden the reach of the category to look at the issue from two standpoints—local (Jamaica) and overseas (world).

In my honest estimation of the local scene, I see clearly the two pillars Bro. Jahlani notes, but I also see a third—the affairs of the heart compositions. There are plenty of love songs around today, they are coming from every reggae artist in Jamaica. And from my assessment of the local scene, it is the love songs from reggae artists generally that are leading the way, in terms of popularity/chart success, etc. When I look farther afield, however, I see more militant messages and praise music tunes being gobbled up by the overseas market. When one takes into consideration, the continued success that reggae greats such as the Abyssinians, The Congos, Israel Vibration, Burning Spear, Max Romeo, just to name a few, are still having internationally (knowing that these reggae acts are serious freedom fighters and spiritual liberators), there can be no doubt that the category Bro. Jahlani has created fits better when placed in a global context.

My music certainly fits in with Bro. Jahlani's operational term and I wouldn't have a problem, necessarily, with someone using it to describe my music, as I am aware of what the term means. However, personally, I think the use of the word "serenading" softens the impact of what it is I am dealing with in my music. My music is liberation music—spiritually, mentally, and physically. My music is redemptive as well as a mental and physical relaxant. My music appeals to the individual on three levels: psycho-physical, psycho-social, and psycho-spiritual. I thus consider my music and certainly try to steer it on a level that Bro. Jahlani's terminology does not capture on a holistic level.

DJNM: Here we are, at the dawn of what many Rastafari scholars believe is a new epoch for the movement, marked as it appears to be by outpourings of Rastafari creativity in many, far-flung places of our world. These days, Rastafari show up in India, Japan, the Slovak Republic, New Zealand, the list goes on; and without a doubt, art has globalized Rastafari. Do you have a sense of yourself, and your music, as part of this ongoing trend or development?

AA: In the ocean that is reggae music, my works are but mere pebbles. But within this ocean, I have been fortunate to see my music make ripples upon it. My music is indeed caught up in the international wave taking place at this time and the periodic feedback I get from people in countries like the Netherlands, Germany, UK, USA, and Tanzania confirm this fact.

As long as human beings exist, we are certain that these things will exist as well: inequality; injustice; marginalization; discrimination; segregation; and spiritual as well as material impoverishment. By virtue of this reality, Rastafari and music such as mine will always have a place in this world. My mandate therefore is to stick to delivering messages of truths and rights, and to continue to let JAH and the things around me inspire and provoke me to write the kind of songs that can make a difference—no matter how small. This is how I see myself in this ongoing international trend or development. I just pray that JAH gives me the strength to continue playing a part in this most vital work, and that He broadens my reach/impact, so that I can bring more souls into the Kingdom. For it is without doubt that JAH works shall and *must* be done.

DJNM: You strike me as the kind of artist who wants to create the kind of sound paintings that people will continue to address and ponder in the future. So, what would you like fans to be saying about you in, say, twenty years?

AA: I would love my fans, reggae enthusiasts, and musicologists to be able to look at my work twenty or thirty years from now and still find it relevant to their lives. I would want my catalog of work to be referred to as one of substance, depth, and having done justice to the foundation set by all the great ones that came before me. I would love my fans to be able to give testimony upon testimony of how my music improved their lives or enlightened their consciousness.

DJNM: And finally, what do you think the future holds for Rastafari? What do you think we will be saying about the brethren and sistren in, say, fifty or eighty years?

AA: I think the Rastafari movement will be around for as long as the earth keeps spinning. However, I think that the future of Rastafari, in terms of its relevance, potency, or continued vibrancy, will be determined by its willingness to tackle three basic issues. First, Rastafari need to address birth, marriage, and death. At present no structure or protocol exists across the breadth and depth of the movement to handle these significant life factors and I think the movement will have to revise its outlook on these issues if it hopes to appeal to an even wider cross-section of people. Second, Rastafari need to periodically review and revise its teachings or dogma so that as new understandings and truths arise, they can be incorporated into the livity. The individual Rasta man or woman, or a mansion of Rastafari, should not be afraid to reframe the structure of the beliefs they hold if the new understanding they have received genuinely warrants it. A case in point is the fundamental shift that Prophet Gad, founder of the Twelve Tribes of Israel, made in the late 1990s as it relates to the nature of H.I.M. and whether or not he was Christ in his Kingly character. Third, Rastafari in Jamaica and outside of Jamaica needs to be officially recognized as a way of life by the powers that be across the world, so that the level of discrimination and prejudice being experienced by its members might be lessened. With an official status, the members should have the right to use the holy sacrament without fear of persecution, for example, or be able to worship openly and freely and enjoy whatever benefits those jurisdictions have for such groups or classification of people. The movement then needs its own schools, hospitals, and political machinery, to allow for greater stability and advancement of the movement.

I think in another fifty to eighty years' time, the world at large will be commending Rastafari for the positive global impact it has had on international affairs, dietary practices, and social/spiritual awareness generally. Also I think people will still want to ingest the type of reggae music that liberates the mind and soul and tears down the walls of oppression and segregation. I think message music will always be relevant and I know that there will be many more people like me in the days and years to come to provide that brand of reggae to those that need it. And finally, I sincerely hope that in another fifty years the significance of H.I.M. Emperor Haile Selassie I to

FIGURE 13 Reggae Rajahs (2012). Photo: arnaumacia.com.

Rastafari—in the various ways that he is—would have become common knowledge and no more a mystery or a puzzle to those outside of the livity.

An Interview with Reggae Rajahs

Comprising Diggy Dang, Mr. Herbalist, and DJ MoCity (often dubbed Iraq's first soundboy), the Reggae Rajahs currently proceed out from New Delhi, India, working with a familiar Jamaican sound system style (one DJ and two MCs).[46] This trio originated in early 2009 and, since this time, they have dedicated themselves to showcasing an extensive mix of reggae, dub, lovers rock, ska, and dancehall to audiences in Mumbai, Pune, Bangalore, Chennai, Goa, and Manali. Outside India, the Reggae Rajahs have performed in Peru, Panama, and New York City. Along the way they have collaborated with artists such as Brother Culture (UK), Deadly Dragon Sound System (USA), Blessed Love Sound System (Germany), Heartical Sound (France), Steppa Style (Russia), and Supa Bassie & Sargento Garcia (Spain). Nominated for the 2012 Best International Group award at the British Reggae Industry Awards, Reggae Rajahs performed in *OnePeople, The Celebration* (2012), a documentary film that features people around the world celebrating Jamaica's global reach fifty years after independence.[47] For this interview, I spoke with Diggy Dang (Raghav Dang).

DJNM: Tell us how you guys came together.

DD: It was in 2009. I had just returned to Delhi after many years of living in London. I was always fascinated by reggae music from an early age, but when I moved back to my hometown, I realized not many people were familiar with the music. I met fellow reggae music lovers Mohammed and Zorawar, and we collectively decided to start a sound system and promote reggae music.[48]

DJNM: How would you describe reggae consciousness in India?

DD: Reggae music and consciousness is very new to Indians. The music scene itself is in its infancy. Most know about Bob Marley, but beyond that not much else. Interestingly, I think Hindu and Rastafari culture are very similar: Indian Sadhus have been living in forests and the wilderness for centuries, for example, and they grow their dreadlocks, smoke charras in chillums, meditate, and chant in a manner that resembles the Maroons in Jamaica, who left their slave masters to live in forests and chant about repatriation. As Reggae Rajahs started out in New Delhi, the scene is here quite vibrant. More and more people turn out to our gigs, and many are becoming quite familiar with the music we play. Since we started, a few bands have emerged including a ska/rocksteady band called The Ska Vengers. I handle guitar duties for the band, and the vocalist is ragamuffin MC Delhi Sultanate. He is known for socially conscious lyrics that touch on various topics. People have a choice between enjoying catchy rhythms or thought-provoking lyrics, or both!

DJNM: Reggae's so diverse, coming in Rastafari and non-Rastafari forms, and so what place, if any, does Rastafari livity have in your life and art?

DD: I do believe in the principles of Rastafari, which I take to be similar to any philosophy or religion—peace, love, and unity. The positive and uplifting message in reggae music attracts me to it as much as the slick basslines and choppy chord progressions. It's absolutely amazing to see reggae music touch people's lives all over the world, even places such as Russia, Indonesia, and Sri Lanka.

DJNM: I imagine the sound system sub-genre means you lean more to dancehall reggae than to roots reggae, or am I mistaken?

DD: As we are keen on introducing all styles of reggae, from early ska and rocksteady to the digital era of dub and dancehall, we mix it up. We have a weekly night every Thursday in Delhi called Simmer Down. Here we play strictly roots, ska, rocksteady, and early dancehall. We of course run a ram jam dancehall night once a month, where we invite DJs, Selectas and sound systems from all over the world.

DJNM: What's your reaction to being nominated for the Best International Band/Group Award at the 2012 British Reggae Industry Awards, and what do you hope this kind of international recognition will mean for you in the coming months and years?

DD: It makes us immensely proud that reggae in Asia, and India specifically, is being put on the world map. There is massive potential for reggae music in this country and we are doing all we can to keep the flag flying. We hope to have our own Reggae festival one day, yet our immediate plan for the next few months is to release more of our own music, shoot a video, and tour outside of India.

DJNM: And finally, what do you think the future holds for Rastas?

DD: Much like reggae music, Rasta is timeless. I do think just as reggae music spreads to more parts of the world, more and more will be inspired to learn about Jamaican culture and Rasta beliefs. In the future, I think everyone will finally believe that Africa is the mother of all creation, and actually the Rastafari, especially the dub poets, were right all along.

Dub Poetry, or, On Not Being Shakespeare

Jamaica's native tongue is a unique form of Creole patois. This is an elusive, hybrid dialect of English that owes a great deal to traditional African vernacular and to the colonial plantation owners of the eighteenth and nineteenth centuries. In terms of performance, one person stands out as the pioneer of poetry written in patois: Louise Bennett, also known as 'Miss Lou.' Klive Walker writes:

> The politics of poetic social commentary, the use of Jamaican language, and the use of the once-despised rhythms of mento and roots reggae in the metre of Caribbean poetry live an active and healthy life today because the legacies of Bob Marley and Louise Bennett remain important components within them.[49]

Originally educated at London's Royal Academy of Dramatic Arts in the last century's early decades, Bennett is credited with introducing a language often considered by colonial educators as too uncouth for so-called genuine writing. She defends her use of patois, however, with the claim that it signifies the everyday discourse of the influential oral storytellers of her youth. It represents the life-blood of a people run down by centuries of systemic oppression or, better put, the natural linguistic mode for women and men who feel the liberating power of parable and story in harsh times.[50] Bennett's work often employs mother-tongue discourse to craft an indigenous poetics marked by political bite. For example, the poem "Is Me" chastens then-newly elected black officials in post-independence Jamaica, politicians who either see themselves as above the fray or else far too important to listen to the quotidian concerns of the general public:

> Is who dat a-sey 'who dat'?
> Wat a piece o' libaty,
> Gal yuh know is who yuh talkin to?
> Teck a good look, is Me![51]

A similar reverence for the oral tradition or dread talk—with its special lexicon, strange spelling, unfamiliar idiom, and social invective—continues to be the chosen and preferred form of Rastafari poets today. As a corollary, dub lyricists seldom pay attention to standard rules of sound and sense. There are some, like the poet U-Roy, who possess a keen eye for grammatical correctness, but for the most part it proves difficult to find a Rastafari poem written in traditional meter (in English, the ten-syllable unrhymed iambic line of five beats). There are at least two basic reasons for this decision *not* to imitate Shakespeare. First, the so-called educated concern for correct language use in creative writing is viewed as far too stylized, restrictive, and oppressively Eurocentric. By contrast, Jamaican dialect is seen as vibrant, alive, and unable to sustain an interest in conventional poetics; it is the dub lyricists who have always known how best to create strong messages out of patois' powerful word stock. Second, Rastafari dub poets consider social conscience to be a more pressing concern than any zeal for so-called acceptable literary form, and they have worked hard to keep the conflagration of social resistance and community rebellion burning. Rastafari dub poetry is not a refined, classically aesthetic product; rather, it is an evolving as well as dynamic grasping and re-grasping of the theological significance of current events. Christian Habekost declares it "a distinctive brew of Black Power rhetoric, Old Testament Rasta imagery, and ghetto talk, forged into word chains with furious rhymes and fired by exploding reggae rhythms."[52] Kwame Dawes agrees:

> The reggae lyric, then, with its connection to Rastafarian ideology, is rooted in an ethos and aesthetic space which encourages dialogue between the temporal and the eternal, between politics, issues of current social interest, sexuality and spirituality. Most critically for the region's writers, this dialogue in the reggae lyric was conducted in Jamaica's vernacular, suddenly enhancing the status of that language and allowing it to be the basis of literary innovations. Ultimately, however, the fundamental dialogue in reggae is that between the artist and the Jamaican people. This is perhaps what has been most inspirational for Caribbean writers over the past thirty years.[53]

Mikey Smith, the dub or reggae lyricist whose work I examine in the next section, puts it this way:

> We haffi really look into the whole thing of the language thing, because sometime it is used in a negative sense as a hindrance to your progress, and people think seh, "Boy, why don't you communicate in Standard English?" Standard English is good to be communicated, but you must also communicate in what you also comfortable in. And what is widely being used by your own people from which you draw these source. So that's why me communicate da way deh. And if me can really spend some time fi try to learn the Englishman language and so, the Englishman can spend some time fi learn wha me seh too, you know.[54]

Mikey Smith: Word Sound 'Ave Power

A 1980 graduate of the Jamaican School of Drama, Michael 'Mikey' Smith was born on September 14, 1954, and died on August 17, 1983. Until his murder— he was stoned by an angry mob in Stony Hill, St. Andrew, following a minor altercation—Smith was one of the more recognized and provocative dub poets in Jamaica. His performances, using reggae rhythm as a canvas on which to paint his social message pictures, are still talked about with enthusiasm. Here he explains how his fascination with dub poetry arose. Notice how eager he is to draw from the many uses to which patois dialect can be put by everyday folk:

> I was fascinated first by the storeman dem down at Orange Street. The man used to say, "Come een, come een, come buy up, buy up. But no come een, come een, come tief up, tief up, cause we wi beat up, beat up!" A so them used to advertise them little thing, and me did just fascinated by that little rhythms, you know. And then me just feel seh me coulda do one too and do it better. So, you know, the whole thing start, and you just start to find a different analogy. But dub poetry? Dub going to be the future, you know, a reggae music. A deh so it a go go. It a go dub-wise. It haffi go dub-wise.[55]

In a 1981 interview with Mervyn Morris, Smith underscores this chapter's basic thesis—Rastafari dub poetry is an important pedagogical tool; its purpose is to conscientize the hearer, to alert those whose senses have been dulled to the inequalities and rigors of Babylonian capitalism and imperialism:

> I have fi really try fi educate a lot of people out inna earth, because Jamaica how can it rest ya know, a whole heap of we can't read and write, you know. And we seem to rally round the spoken word very nice … Poetry as a vehicle of giving hope. As a means of building them awareness as such. Poetry is part of the whole process of the whole liberation of the people.[56]

"Me Cyaan Believe It" is Smith's most celebrated poem, not least because it takes up Bennett's question—"Ah who dat?"—in "Is Me" and creates a remarkable piece of intertextuality, a blending of stories, which shifts the focus away from indifferent politicians and toward the people they serve:

> Sittin on de corner wid me frien
> talkin bout tings and time
> me hear one voice seh
> 'Who dat'?
> Me seh 'A who dat?'
> 'A who seh who dat
> when me a seh who dat?'

> When yuh teck a stock
> dem lick we dung flat
> teet start fly
> an big man start cry
> me seh me cyaan believe it
> me seh me cyaan believe it.[57]

Close reading shows that "Me Cyaan Believe It" addresses hard-scrabble Jamaican life. And it honors the struggles of those whose spirit has been forged on life's tough anvil. Written in a blues mood reminiscent of the African American poet Langston Hughes, Smith details the squalor of the western Kingston projects, together with the all-pervasive stench of hopelessness:

> Lawd
> me see some black bud
> livin inna one buildin
> but no rent no pay
> so dem cyaan stay
> Lawd
> de oppress and de dispossess
> cyaan get no res.[58]

Smith balances such gritty realism with artful playfulness, though, as evinced by an ironic twist on one of the many English nursery rhymes that the colonialists taught the slaves when they arrived from Africa:

> Room dem a rent
> me apply widin
> but as me go in
> cockroach rat an scorpion
> also come in
> … me naw go stdung pan igh wall
> like Humpty Dumpty
> me a face me reality.[59]

Possessed with all the righteous indignation of some modern-day Job, Smith hurls his fury at a seemingly dispassionate God. In the following lines, for example, we detect a note of heroic pessimism in Smith's theodicy. It is present, I think, in his honest supplication to Jah's Transcendent Mystery ("Lawwwwwwwwd"):

> Me seh me cyaan believe it
> me seh me cyaan believe it
> Yuh believe it?

How yu fi believe it
when yu laugh
An yuh blind yuh eye to it?
But me know yuh believe it
Lawwwwwwwwwd
me know yuh believe it.[60]

Although "Me Cyaan Believe It" makes no explicit reference to Rastafari, other poems do, and Rastology may profitably be extrapolated from some of the comments in the aforementioned Morris interview: "Me is very close to Rasta, you know. Very, very close. In that a lot of things inna Rasta me can understand, and me can identify with. A that really make me very close," Smith declares.[61]

The dub poetry community was robbed when Smith was murdered in 1983, coincidentally on Marcus Garvey's birthday, and two years later Benjamin Zephaniah, the British dub poet whom I address in the next chapter, published "Dem People, Stone Poets," which summarizes the numbing, needless sense of loss that followed in the wake of Smith's untimely death:

You have heard of Luther, and Garvey
dis ting happened in 1983
Lord is what this poet has said
and the words of this dread will never dead,
see when you tell de youth de truth
dem threaten you with gun and shoot
with all manner of tings dem find
justice get left behind.
Dem people eliminate poets,
dem people, day stone poets.

Artist culture and culture rebel
the words of the rant shall burn like hell
de earth had a gift called Michael Smith
wicked see good and stoning it,
Lord is what the poet has said
and the audience start feel red
but those who stoned shall get pay
now it's arts for justice here I say.
Jamaicans here at home and abroad
struggle for some justice hard.

These happenings may seem out of date
but these tings happen in a modern state
be it gone or be it stone, know it now as modern Rome.

> Don't get fooled by dis free speech
> dem stone you for the words you speak,
> dem people eliminate poets
> dem people, day stone poets.[62]

Today, Smith ranks as the first poet laureate of the Rastafari dub poetry movement, a highly decorated general in reggae music's worldwide campaign for moral and spiritual revolution.

Mutabaruka: Poet of Dread

The biting social themes covered by Smith in his verse were taken up by other performers along the way. By late 1983, critics in Jamaica began to say that the hour for the dub poet had arrived and that opportunities to effect social change were there for the taking. This was partly due to the turn by some reggae musicians to invoke messages of sexism, homophobia, and other themes contrary to early Rastafari. Performers such as Oku Onuora and Linton Kwesi Johnson were among the first of a new batch of rebel dub poets, yet it is to Mutabaruka that I now turn.[63]

An accomplished actor and talk show host, Mutabaruka is a Jamaican writer driven by the concern to promote poetry as the instrument of social liberation and black consciousness-raising. In "Nursery Rhyme Lament," for example, he adopts Mikey Smith's ironic use of colonial nursery rhymes to drive home his perceptive social observations concerning life under Empire rule:

> first time
> jack & jill
> used to run up de hill everyday
> now dem get pipe ... an
> water rate increase.[64]

And later:

> jack sprat ... ah, yes, jack sprat
> who couldn't stand fat; im start eat it now ... but
> im son a vegetarian ... 'cause
> meat scarce.
> little bo-peep who lost 'ar sheep ... went out
> to look fe dem
> an find instead a politician ... an
> is now livin in beverly hills.[65]

The poem closes with a chilling reminder to the colonialists that long gone are the days when people could delight in teaching these and other famous verses to the so-called uneducated masses. Human existence is far from the sugary sweet images of life made popular in nursery rhymes and Hallmark cards. In Mutabaruka's vision, everyday existence in the Jamaican tenements is excessively brutal. The brethren and sistren struggle unceasingly. Against the antirealism of colonial nursery rhymes, then, he issues his own lyrical call to arms: "dis is not de time fe dem/cause/dem deh days done/an wi write."[66]

Mutabaruka writes about Rastafari. And his theological understanding is perhaps best expressed through "Say (for ODUN)." This is a brief poem. Yet it provides an instructive example of how the Rastafari dub poet seeks to transform the mind of the reader with its Afrocentric pedagogy. In twenty lines, Mutabaruka equates Rasta consciousness with four ideological convictions: (i) the belief in Ethiopia as the promised land for all Africans temporarily trapped in diaspora; (ii) the importance of education in the fight to loosen the shackles of mental slavery; (iii) the need willfully to help topple all of Babylon's corrupt leaders from power; and, finally, (iv) the notion that humanity is divine. Here Mutabaruka's rhythmic verse recalls the intense Nyabingi drums of traditional African communities:

> when you remember home
> say: ETHIOPIA
>
> when you remember slaves
> say: BLACK
>
> when you shout revolution
> say: FREEMAN
>
> when you shout babylon
> say: DEATH
>
> when you speak of education
> say: GET IT
>
> when you speak of unity
> say: WADADA
>
> when you speak of God
> say: MAN
>
> when you see culture
> say: RELATIVE TO
>
> when you read all this
> say: MADNESSSSSS
>
> when you think like I
> say: RASTAFARI.[67]

The anti-Babylon diatribe of "Say (for ODUN)" is given a new twist in "The Outcry." Here Mutabaruka impresses on the reader a genuine sense of the utter futility of life in the West for the black man: "leave west/east best/unite and fight/sight/JAH light/it right/mighty might."[68] With these lines, moreover, he links himself to one of the main ideas in Rastafari's doctrinal dimension, namely, the hope for repatriation to Africa. In their formative years, as noted earlier, Rastafari resisted all forms of high-profile social involvement in Jamaican or Caribbean life. For this initial refusal to integrate, however, the early Rastas were criticized by the media and religious authorities. Even today, with knowledge that Africa is not the promised land of initial Rastafari preachment, numerous Rastas hold tenaciously to the hope of return to the Motherland. With "The Outcry" poem, Mutabaruka locates himself at the heart of such Afrocentric theology.

Yet "The Outcry" implies much more than this hope for spiritual renewal away from Western societies. In other lines, for example, Mutabaruka leaves open the chance of moral transformation, an Africanization of Babylon, and the option of religious rejuvenation, even in the most corrupt of Western political and social organizations:

> to walk the streets paved with blood
> mud
> mixed with sweat and tears
> years
> of dreams to materialize
> wise
> man
> seekin new plan
> upsettin
> babylon
> gone above babylon infinity
> new martyrs found among so-called madness
> of the city
> pity.[69]

It is hard to know the identity of such "new martyrs." Perhaps this phrase refers to how the emphasis of early Rastafari on 'salvation as repatriation' has become less of an issue for today's generation, who now appear focused on emancipating the disenfranchised in their social location. Ennis B. Edmonds notes that over eighty short years Rastafari has become routinized; that is, Rastas have evolved from outcasts to culture-bearers.[70] Today, Rastafari is an arresting, effective form of Caribbean liberation theology, and its compelling message of African identity within an island context ministers to the poor, the marginalized, and the voiceless, who always have to be seen as the human material for the creation of new and just social orders.[71] Mutabaruka's "new martyrs" work in the madness of a decaying civilization, and it is they who teach to transform those whose senses are dulled to the inequalities and rigors of life in Babylon.

One of the shapers of dub poetry in the 1980s and 1990s, both as a singer and as a producer, Mutabaruka does not crave the publicity that is commonly associated with the music industry. Typical of dub poets, he favors small festivals and intimate workshops. And in 2007, he served as guest artist-in-residence at California's Merritt College, where he taught classes on "Black Poetry: Revolution with Words."[72] Disillusioned with society's fragmented and unjust character, he crafts words that relate Rastafari to social engagement as well as spiritual formation, with the result that his work serves as a pedagogy for the liberation of black consciousness.[73]

Jean 'Binta' Breeze: Bridging Dub Poetry's Gender Gap

Although Rastafari women did not play a leading part in the religion's organizational and doctrinal direction in its inception, the last twenty years have witnessed a major transitional phase in the movement's history: the Daughters of Zion are now voicing their hopes and fears.[74] Bianca Nyavingi Brynda's documentary film, *Roots Daughters: The Women of Rastafari* (1992), ranks as one of the first accounts of such change, filming various Rasta women from Jamaica, Guyana, South America, and Canada, fighting for equality within Rastafari's largely patriarchal world. More recently, the Empress of Zion Incorporated, an organization created to help women in the Rasta community self-identify and uplift one another, commissioned an anthology of writings penned by the sistren and released it during the fifth annual Empress of Zion Conference held at the University of West Indies, Jamaica, March 2007.[75] Concerned to facilitate a renaissance of respect for Rastafari women, symbols of Mother Africa and Mother Nature both, this volume shows how women mitigate Rastafari's male-centeredness by claiming political as well as personal space, one of the dominant themes in the work of Jean 'Binta' Breeze, Jamaican-born artist.[76]

Growing up in Hanover, Breeze moved to Kingston in 1978. Here she attended the Jamaican School of Drama, where she encountered Mikey Smith, and in an interview with Jenny Sharpe, she explains how she came to her calling as the first female dub poet:

> One day I turned on the radio, and it was playing, 'Sitting on the Dock of a Bay.' Now the bay near us is Montego Bay, so I got on a bus fifteen miles to Montego Bay and sat out on the pier, waiting to see who was waiting for me on the dock of the bay. And I was sitting there writing, when a Rastafarian man came up to me and said—"So! The daughter is a poet!" And I said—"Yes!" And he said: "Would you like to perform at a concert for His Majesty's 90th birthday?" And I said—"Yes!" This was 1980 or 1981, and the next week my name was in the papers as one of the artists in the show.

So I saw him again, two nights before the show, and he said, "We're having a rehearsal with the band." I said, "Wow, with a band!" So I went to the rehearsal and Mutabaruka, who was already quite a well-known dub poet who had recorded in Jamaica, was a guest artist and was there rehearsing with the band. He liked my poem and he told the band what to do with it musically. He was so interested in the work that he recorded me a couple of weeks later. I was elated. And that's how I became the first female dub poet.[77]

Breeze shared the stage with Mutabaruka at the 1981 Reggae Sunsplash, her first live performance, and she eventually recorded several songs, some of which caught Linton Kwesi Johnson's ear. In time, Johnson introduced her to audiences across Europe. Celebrated for the way she combines diverse musical styles (mento, blues, jazz, reggae) with poignant lyrics about ordinary Caribbean women, Breeze now tours the world frequently, and has made London her home since 1985. Queen Elizabeth II awarded Breeze an MBE (Member of the British Empire) in 2013.[78]

Some of Breeze's literary art displays openly political messages. "Third World Blues" rails against the 1983 U.S. invasion of Grenada, for example, and "Anthem for Black Britain" states how the big-city, ethnically diverse strongholds of London, the Midlands, and the Northwest must celebrate as well as promote multiple expressions of national identity.[79] Also consider "Aid Travels With a Bomb," which begins by linking the plantation whip with globalization's grip, and then issues an unbending, forceful rejection of the International Monetary Fund's (IMF) advice for restructuring Third World economies.[80] Black women and men need to look to themselves, not external agencies like the IMF, for the means to flourish. In "To Plant," for example, she laments the depopulation of rural Jamaica, and urges a return to agrarian livity, which signifies black culture's primary solution to many of the problems in Jamaica.[81]

Breeze complements her edgy, political voice by writing and publishing "women's domestic dub."[82] Her "Ordinary Mawning" poem discovers something treasurable in sending children off to school or doing the laundry, life's quotidian details and duties.[83] Also ponder "simple tings," which fuses Breeze's interests in land cultivation, gendered agency, and the need for sistren to articulate a sense of themselves through narration:

> de simple tings of life, mi dear
> de simple tings of life
>
> she rocked the rhythms in her chair
> brushed a hand across her hair
> miles of travel in her stare
>
> de simple tings of life

ah hoe mi corn
an de backache gone
plant di peas
arthritis ease

de simple tings of life

leaning back
she wiped an eye
read the rain signs
in the sky
evening's ashes
in a fireside

de simple tings of life.[84]

"The arrival of Brighteye" poem moves away from life's ordinariness to think through big picture issues of migration affecting postwar Caribbean women. Breeze seems sensitive to the pain that trails in mobility's wake. Riffing on an old nursery rhyme, like the other poets in this chapter, she adopts a child's voice to communicate the effects of transculturalism on family life:

My mommy gone over de ocean
My mommy gone over de sea
she gawn dere to work for some money
an den she gawn sen back for me

one year
two year
tree year gawn

four year
five year
soon six year come

granny seh it don't matter
but supposin I forget her
Blinky Blinky, one two three
Blinky Blinky, remember me.[85]

Brighteye eventually travels to England but, like many Commonwealth migrants, she struggles with racism and rising unemployment. She bears children, who will one day see themselves as Black British, maybe Rasta, and yet Brighteye's own mother, aged and infirm by the poem's close, takes her leave of Brighteye again. Her mother wants to die in Jamaica. And thus the immigrant woman's wisdom is forged on life's tough anvil, Breeze implies:

> An de children, ah jus can't leave de children, but mamma leaving me, she bring mi here an tell mi is home but now she leaving me to go home, an she was mi home, from de day she meet mi off de train in Waterloo, by dat time ah was crying so much ah wasn't looking out fah mi madda face again … an suddenly ah hear a voice shout 'Brighteye' an is she, an she lif mi up an squeeze mi in her bosom, ah never see her face but ah remember de smell, rub up wid Vicks, an how her bosom feel, an now she leaving mi here wid de children and grandchildren, but how ah going to hole up everyting, how I going to hole dem up, and she going home tomorrow, she say her work is over an she going home tomorrow, but ah just want to be Brighteye again, as hard as it was it was easier dan dis burden, an where ah going to put my head now, when all de others resting theirs on me, where ah going to rest mine.[86]

Globalization dis-members us, Breeze says, but memory redeems. Nostalgia for country higglers prevails in "Riddym Ravings (the mad woman's poem)." Here, an indigent woman roams Kingston's streets, hears dancehall reggae everywhere she goes, and finds relief from her tragedy when she learns how to link her own labyrinthine ways with thoughts of how her grandmother often walked to town to sell fruit.[87]

Critics frequently view dancehall reggae culture as demeaning to women. Mutabaruka finds little or nothing redemptive in it, for example, but others, like Carolyn Cooper and Jenny Sharpe disagree. Here is not the place to rehearse their nuanced arguments.[88] Suffice it to say, Breeze's poetry captures both sides of the discussion, provoking the reader to arbitrate the debate. Whilst "Get Back" grabs and holds DJ slackness in a poetic headlock, for example, "Dubwise" identifies a dancehall diva's dirty dancing as an attempt not simply to control the floor, or even her male partner, but to legislate life itself; in short, slackness serves as the soundtrack to female self-determination.[89]

Like the other artists throughout my book Breeze celebrates reggae, not just dancehall but all forms, and her "Tongue Your Funky Rhythms in My Ear" poem rhapsodizes reggae's "special" adeptness in spanning the globe to articulate its "songs of freedom," crafting melodies that impart "living power" on hearers.[90] For Breeze, moreoever, the Rastafari reggae artist embodies the ancient trinity of prophet, priest, and king (Deut 18:14–22; Ps 110:1–4; Ps 2):

> Locksman coming from the mountain
> Bringing Jah prophecy
> To all the rainbow children

To all who'll listen and hear
Bringing words of our salvation
Calling time on sufferation
Giving power to the nation
Come closer now he'll say

He's borrowing from the bible
From the proverbs
From old people
From the songs of Solomon
From the patience of a man called Job
From country and from western
From jazz and souls and blues
From all the choirs angels
Even from the morning news

He's the griot, the storyteller
He brings a warning for the killer
He chants for unity
Brings a vision of the free
Love poems for you and me
Open your eyes and see.[91]

Other, enthralling stanzas follow these words, creating the effect of a versified reggae Hall of Fame. Breeze heralds Rasta genii such as Toots and the Maytals, Desmond Dekker and the Aces, Burning Spear, and Culture, before pausing to switch genders:

The three sisters came on after
Rita Marley, Marcia Griffith, Judy Mowatt
With harmonies straight from heaven
Singing for women and the children
Remembering the African nation.[92]

The I-Threes were formed in 1974, as vocal support for Marley when the original Wailers left the band, and Marley dominates the poem's final lines. We hear "the echoes of his song" around the world, Breeze says, and in a move that forestalls an essential part of Kevin Macdonald's *Marley* (2012) documentary film, Breeze describes how Marley's music functions as an international auxilliary language:

I travelled to Korea
I show immigration my passport
They say, oh, Bob Marley country
You come from Bob Marley country

Few days later into Johannesburg
Show them my travelling documents
They say, oh, Bob Marley country
You come from Bob Marley country

I headed east and into Japan
Customs say 'sing for me redemption song'
Because you come from Bob Marley country
Oh, Bob Marley country.

South west I travelled down to Brazil
On the streets I see pure red, gold and green
They say try this smoke
Tell me if it's really good
Because you come from Bob Marley country
Oh, Bob Marley country.

I wander in a record shop in Barcelona
A young Spaniard with locks down to his shoulder
He says 'you're the dub poet from Jamaica
Tell me all about Bob Marley country
Because you come from Bob Marley country'

In a pirate station in London
Reggae kicking out all over the town
Three little birds sitting on the window
The DJ giving me the history of the man
Because he come from Bob Marley country
He come from Bob Marley country[93]

Marley's international stardom helps explain, at least in part, Rastafari's presence on the world's cultural map, a theme I revisit in later chapters. For now, though, it is enough to declare that in Breeze's poetry we hear an echo of her song—a song of women's power to reclaim and reshape their lives.

Conclusion

Although the recent flourishing of self-published, insider accounts of the Rastafari appear to be democratizing and transforming the literary landscape, at present the Rastafari community does not possess anything that resembles the systematic tomes of Christian theologians such as John Calvin or Karl Rahner.[94] This absence need not prove to be a threat to the movement's flourishing, though, since some might say that a vibrant, evolving religion inevitably declines when believers busy themselves with the so-called central tenets of their faith, and with the task of recording such doctrines or worldviews in architechtonic manuscripts and books. Against the propositionally oriented tradition of Christian theology, then, Rastafari has the advantage of keeping what it believes fairly fluid, using reggae to intone spirited contextual wordscapes, to chant imagistic litanies, and to sing a sense of the holy eternally renewed in the common. When it acts in concert with reggae's drum-and-bassline, moreover, dread talk sustains and then advances Rastafari beyond Jamaican and Caribbean boundaries to the rest of the world; and in reggae music, Rastafari find the sprightly resources both to artfully remember their past and to restate their communal as well as personal identity. Jahlani Bongo Niaah puts it this way:

> In Rastafari music there is discernible grafting and inscription of African diaspora memory and experiences, connecting to a longer framework of African history. This elaboration and popular articulation of Pan African ideals places the Rastafari movement in the forefront of global emancipation, as it expounds itself through a system of sounds expressing a new articulation of the African Presence in documenting 'Our' collective 'Black My Story.'[95]

As noted earlier, non-Rastafari frequently feel moved by Rastafari's energy for "global emancipation," couched as it so often is in reggae's repeating riffs and poetry's sound and sense. Denouncing social injustice and urging wide-ranging rural as well as urban renewal, Rastafari dub or performance poets—especially the three I have examined in this chapter and the one I analyze in the next—are religious prophets, like Marley before them, striding through what they take to be an unredeemed world, producing politically charged compositions in service of Rastafari's righteous wail against Babylon.[96]

I now turn to Benjamin Zephaniah, the United Kingdom's premier dub poet, who pounds out his iron-willed irreverence toward his nation's social and political authorities on roots reggae riffs, emerging with Rastological sound paintings for Britain's post-imperial age.

Notes

1 For a recent book-length assessment of Marley, see Colin Grant, *The Natural Mystics: Marley, Tosh, and Wailer* (New York and London: St. Martin's Press, 2011). Also see Noel Leo Erskine, *From Garvey to Marley: Rastafari Theology* (Gainesville, FL: University Press of Florida, 2007). For an introduction to Marley, see Roger Steffens, "Bob Marley: Rasta Warrior," in Nathaniel Samuel Murrell, William D. Spencer, and Adrian A. McFarlane, editors, *Chanting Down Babylon: The Rastafari Reader* (Philadelphia: Temple University Press, 1998), 253–265. For Marley's official website, see: http://www.bobmarley.com/. Accessed March 30, 2014.

2 Klive Walker, *Dubwise: Reasoning from the Reggae Underground* (Toronto: Insomniac Press, 2005), 43. Other texts advance this thesis about reggae's global reach and Rastafari's international appeal. For the most recent work, see Carolyn Cooper, editor, *Global Reggae* (Kingston, Jamaica: Canoe Press, 2012). In addition, see Barry Chevannes, *Rastafari: Roots and Ideology* (Syracuse: Syracuse University Press, 1994), 269–273; Sebastian Clarke, *Jah Music: The Evolution of the Popular Jamaican Song* (London: Heinemann, 1980); Ennis B. Edmonds, *Rastafari: From Outcasts to Culture Bearers* (Oxford and New York: Oxford University Press, 2003), 97–115; Christian Habekost, *Verbal Riddim: The Politics and Aesthetics of African-Caribbean Dub Poetry* (Amsterdam; Atlanta, GA: Rodopi, 1993); and, finally, William David Spencer, "Chanting Change around the World through Rasta Ridim and Art," in Murrell *et al.*, editors, *Chanting Down Babylon*, 266–283.

3 Sources for this sketch include: Heather Augustyn, *Ska: An Oral History* (Jefferson, NC; London: McFarland and Company, Inc., 2010); Steve Barrow and Peter Dalton, *The Rough Guide to Reggae* (London: Penguin, 2004); Kevin O'Brien Chang and Wayne Chen, *Reggae Routes: The Story of Jamaican Music* (Philadelphia: Temple University Press, 1998); Clarke, *Jah Music*; Chuck Foster, *Roots, Rock, Reggae: An Oral History of Reggae Music from Ska to Dancehall* (New York: Billboard Books, 1999); Peter Manuel with Kenneth Bilby and Michael Largey, *Caribbean Currents: Caribbean Music from Rumba to Reggae* (Philadelphia: Temple University Press, 1995), 143–182; and, finally, Chris Salewicz and Adrian Boot, *Reggae Explosion: The Story of Jamaican Music* (New York: Mango Records, 1993).

4 Andrew Kaslow, "The Roots of Reggae," *Sing Out!: The Folk Song Magazine* 23.6 (1975): 12–13.

5 Brian Meeks, *Paint the Town Red* (Leeds, England: Peepal Tree Press Ltd., 2003), 88. While this novel charts personal and political changes within late twentieth-century Jamaican life, it also shows how such changes are mirrored, more or less, by changes in musical styles—rock steady (28), roots reggae (47), dub (59), and dancehall reggae (114–115).

6 On Marley's life and work, especially his global significance, see the following sources: Stephen Davis, *Bob Marley* (New York: Doubleday, 1985); Christopher John Farley, *Before the Legend: The Rise of Bob Marley* (New York: Amistad, 2007); Rita Marley with Hettie Johns, *No Woman, No Cry: My Life with Bob Marley* (New York: Hyperion, 2005); and Timothy White, *Catch a Fire: The Life of Bob Marley* (New York: Owl Books, 1998).

7 For details, see: http://www.stuff.co.nz/southland-times/features/48735. Accessed March 30, 2014.

8 For details, see: http://www.npr.org/templates/story/story.php?storyId=7489307. Accessed March 30, 2014.

9 For details, see: http://www.irielion.com/israel/. On Haim's documentary, see: http://www.awakezion.net/home.php. Both sites accessed March 30, 2014.

10 Steffens, "Bob Marley: Rasta Warrior," 264. There is no questioning Marley's significance, as Steffens and others note, though Carolyn Cooper laments the way "the revolutionary Tuff Gong Rastaman has been commodified and repackaged as our 'One Love' apologist for the Jamaican tourist industry." For the way she questions such politics of (mis)appropriation, see Cooper, "'More Fire': Chanting Down Babylon From Bob Marley to Capleton," in Timothy J. Weiss, editor, *Music, Writing, and Cultural Unity in the Caribbean* (Trenton, NJ: Africa World Press, 2005), 215.

11 Anthony Bogues, *Black Heretics, Black Prophets: Radical Political Intellectuals* (New York and London: Routledge, 2003), 187.

12 *Ibid.*, 205. The most recent example of Marley's internationalization, and thus of Rastafari's global spread, is the Marley statue, erected in Serbia, August 2008: http://www. guardian.co.uk/music/2008/aug/25/bob.marley.statue.serbia. Accessed March 30, 2014.

13 Stephen A. King, "Protest Music as 'ego-enhancement': Reggae Music, the Rastafarian Movement and the Re-Examination of Race and Identity in Jamaica," in Ian Peddie, editor, *The Resisting Muse: Popular Music and Social Protest* (Aldershot, England; Burlington, VT: Ashgate, 2006), 117.

14 *Ibid.*, 117.

15 *Ibid.*, 117. In addition, this 'coming in from the cold' thesis may be found in Edmonds, *Rastafari*, 79–96.

16 In advertisements for Guinness, Perry displays one of his characteristically eccentric wordplays on dub and Dublin (Ireland, home of the Guinness brewery), and also exemplifies dub music's internationalization. For details, see: http://www.youtube.com/ watch?v=mnE0rc_sTS4. Accessed March 30, 2014.

17 Kwame Dawes, *Natural Mysticism: Towards a New Reggae Aesthetic* (Leeds, England: Peepal Tree Press Ltd., 2008), 259–265. Also see Walker, *Dubwise*, 233–256.

18 Locomondo's official site is: http://www.locomondo.gr/. Accessed March 30, 2014.

19 Derek O'Brien and Vaughn Carter, scholars invested in what happens at the intersection of law and religion, show that Rastafari's assessment of the majority culture ('Babylon') offers an illuminating way to safeguard minority interests, evinced by the case of Forsythe v. Director of Public Prosecution (Commonwealth law) and Employment Division v. Smith (written by Justice Scalia, critique by Michael McConnell). See O'Brien and Carter, "Chant Down Babylon: Freedom of Religion and the Rastafarian Challenge to Majoritarianism," *Journal of Law and Religion* 18.1 (2002): 219–248.

20 Stephen Foehr, *Jamaican Warriors: Reggae, Roots, and Culture* (London: Sanctuary Publishing, 2000), 45–46. Howellite Rastafari persist. For an account of how, in May 1989, a group of them based in the parish of Clarendon created a new-yet-ancient sound—a Rasta *kumina ina raggamuffin* sound—see Manuel *et al.*, *Caribbean Currents*, 180–182.

21 Nathaniel Samuel Murrell, "Tuning Hebrew Psalms to Reggae Rhythms: Rastas' Revolutionary Lamentations for Social Change," *CrossCurrents* 50.4 (Winter 2000–2001): 537. For how this allusion fits into the wider context of Caribbean biblical hermeneutics, see Nathaniel S. Murrell, "Wresting the Message from the Messenger: The Rastafari as a Case Study in the Caribbean Indigenization of the Bible," in Vincent L. Wimbush, editor, *African Americans and the Bible: Sacred Texts and Social Textures* (New York and London: Continuum, 2000), 558–575.

22 On "Words of Wisdom," see: http://homepage.ntlworld.com/davebulow/wow/. Accessed March 30, 2014.

23 Walker, *Dubwise*, 79–103. I emphasize 'perceived' because, as Carolyn Cooper declares, dancehall music may be viewed as "a radical, underground confrontation with the patriarchal gender ideology and the pious morality of fundamentalist Jamaican society." See Cooper, *Noises in the Blood: Orality, Gender and the 'Vulgar' Body of Jamaican Popular Culture* (Durham, NC: Duke University Press, 1985), 141. On Cooper's view, slackness symbolizes a black feminist or womanist politics of subversion. For additional details on the controversy surrounding dancehall music, see Natasha Barnes, "Dancehall Lyricism," in Weiss, editor, *Music, Writing, and Cultural Unity in the Caribbean*, 287–305. Also see Tim Chin, "'Bullers' and 'Battymen': Contesting Homophobia in Black Popular Culture and Contemporary Caribbean Literature," *Callaloo* 20.1 (1997): 127–141.

24 See Stephen King and Richard J. Jensen, "Bob Marley's 'Redemption Song': The Rhetoric of Reggae and Rastafari," *Journal of Popular Culture* 29.3 (Winter 1995): 17–36.

25 Anthony Lane, "Jammin'," *The New Yorker*, April 23, 2012: 82.

26 2012 marked the fiftieth anniversary of Jamaica's independence from Great Britain. Tarrus Riley and Protoje feature in an article celebrating this moment and Jamaica's musical heritage. In the eyes of the article's writer, Marvin Sparks, both performers represent the immediate, socially conscious future of Rastafari reggae. And perhaps it is telling that both performers are famous for songs that encourage women to exercise their power of self-determination. For additional details, see: http://www.guardian. co.uk/music/2012/jun/28/jamaica-at-50-the-hot-dancehall-stars. Accessed March 30, 2014.

27 For details, see http://www.npr.org/2013/12/29/256116848/jamaica-s-hottest-new-school-reggae-artists-return-to-roots?utm_medium=Email&utm_source=share& utm_campaign. Accessed March 30, 2014.

28 Allan Bernard, "A Focus on Sizzla Kalonji: A Leading Influence on a New Generation of Rastafari Youth," in Michael Barnett, editor, *Rastafari in the New Millennium: A Rastafari Reader* (Syracuse: Syracuse University Press, 2012), 278–288.

29 See: http://www.soulrebels.org/dancehall/w_compassionate_001.htm. Accessed March 30, 2014.

30 On Seaga's interview, see: http://www.npr.org/2012/12/27/168141811/former-pm-edward-seaga-heralds-jamaicas-music. Accessed March 30, 2014.

31 On Rocky Dawuni, see: http://www.rockydawuni.com/. Articles and interviews with Sinéad O'Connor concerning her Rasta albums are housed at her personal website: http://www.sinead-oconnor.com/home/. Both sites accessed March 30, 2014. Finally, see Adam John Waterman, "I and Ireland: Reggae and Rastafari in the Work of Sinéad O'Connor," in Ifeona Fulani, editor, *Archipelagos of Sound: Transnational Caribbeanites, Women and Music* (Kingston, Jamaica: University of West Indies Press, 2012), 321–339.

32 For details on this label, see: http://www.basicchannel.com/. Accessed March 30, 2014.

33 On Bob Marley's musical afterlife, which illustrates his and reggae's global brand status, see: http://www.guardian.co.uk/music/musicblog/2011/may/11/bob-marley-playlist. Accessed March 30, 2014.

34 On lover's rock's London genesis and later success in the Far East, see: http://www. guardian.co.uk/music/2011/sep/22/lovers-rock-story-reggae. Accessed March 30, 2014.

35 On reggae in Japan, see: http://www.houseofreggae.de/news/3976-reggae-in-japan-the-rock-a-shacka-story.html. Accessed March 30, 2014.

36 See: http://www.npr.org/2013/03/30/175583890/in-south-africa-a-reggae-legacy-lives-on. Accessed March 30, 2014.

37 Kenneth Bilby, "The Impact of Reggae in the United States," *Popular Music and Society* 5.5 (1977): 17–23. Also see Manuel *et al.*, *Caribbean Currents*, 232–246.

38 For details, see Andrew Ross, *Real Love: In Pursuit of Cultural Justice* (New York: New York University Press, 1998).

39 Walker, *Dubwise*, 155–176.

40 Michael Barnett, "From Warieka Hill to Zimbabwe: Exploring the Role of Rastafari in Popularizing Reggae Music," in Barnett, editor, *Rastafari in the New Millennium*, 270–277.

41 See the essays in Cooper, editor, *Global Reggae*.

42 Sarah Daynes, "The Musical Construction of the Diaspora: The Case of Reggae and Rastafari," in Sheila Whiteley, Andy Bennett, and Stan Hawkins, editors, *Music, Space*

and Place: Popular Music and Cultural Identity (Burlington, VT; Aldershot, Hampshire, UK: Ashgate Publishing Company, 2004), 33.

43 See: https://soundcloud.com/asante-amen. Accessed March 30, 2014.

44 Jahlani Bongo Niaah, "Grafting a New History: Rastafari Memory Gems Articulating a 'Hermeneutics of Babylon,'" in Naana Opoku-Agyemang, Paul E. Lovejoy, and David V. Trotman, editors, *Africa and Trans-Atlantic Memories: Literary and Aesthetic Manifestations of Diaspora and History* (Trenton, NJ: Africa World Press, 2008), 353.

45 *Ibid.*, 362.

46 See: http://reggaerajahs.tumblr.com/. Accessed March 30, 2014.

47 See: http://www.youtube.com/watch?v=3rQKFB6qD2Y. Accessed March 30, 2014.

48 For Reggae Rajahs on SoundCloud, see: http://soundcloud.com/reggaerajahs. Accessed March 30, 2014.

49 Walker, *Dubwise*, 78.

50 On Bennett's life and literary art, especially the way her verse both challenges and complements Jamaican male protest poetry of the 1960s and 1970s, see Denise deCaires Narain, *Contemporary Caribbean Women's Poetry: Making Style* (London and New York: Routledge, 2002), 51–88. For links between Bennett and Bob Marley, see Walker, *Dubwise*, 67–78. Also see http://louisebennett.com/. Accessed March 30, 2014.

51 Louise Bennett, *Jamaica Labrish* (Kingston, Jamaica: Sangster's, 1966), 140.

52 Habekost, *Verbal Riddim*, 159.

53 Dawes, *Natural Mysticism*, 141.

54 These remarks were made in an interview with Mervyn Morris. See Mervyn Morris, "Mikey Smith: Dub Poet," *Jamaican Journal* 18 (1985): 42. Enormous controversy surrounds Smith's untimely death.

55 *Ibid.*, 42.

56 *Ibid.*, 40.

57 *Ibid.*, 45.

58 *Ibid.*, 45.

59 *Ibid.*, 45.

60 *Ibid.*, 45.

61 *Ibid.*, 45. For an extended analysis of this poem, see Habekost, *Verbal Riddim*, 124–135.

62 Benjamin Zephaniah, *The Dread Affair: Collected Poems* (London: Arena Books, 1985), 9.

63 For Mutabaruka's own website, see: http://www.mutabaruka.com/. Accessed March 30, 2014.

64 Mutabaruka, *The First Poems (1970–1979)* (Kingston, Jamaica: Paul Issa Publications, 1980), 26.

65 *Ibid.*, 26.

66 *Ibid.*, 27. For an analysis of how Mutabaruka views the relationship between dub poetry, political purpose, and entertainment, see Habekost, *Verbal Riddim*, 185–200.

67 Mutabaruka, *The First Poems*, 25.

68 *Ibid.*, 28.

69 *Ibid.*, 28.

70 Edmonds, *Rastafari*, 117–126.

71 On Rastafari as a form of Caribbean liberation theology, see the following selected texts: Barry Chevannes, *Rastafari: Roots and Ideology*, 1–43; Obiagele Lake, *RastafarI Women: Subordination in the Midst of Liberation Theology* (Durham, NC: Carolina Academic Press, 1998); William F. Lewis, *Soul Rebels: The Rastafari* (Prospect Heights, IL: Waveland Press, 1993), 127–135; and Theo Witvliet, *A Place in the Sun: An Introduction to Liberation Theology in the Third World* (London: SCM Press, 1985), 104–117.

72 For details, see: http://www.mutabaruka.com/merritt.htm. Accessed March 30, 2014.

73 Adwoa Ntozake Onuora, "Exploring RastafarI's Pedagogic, Communicative, and Instructional Potential in the Caribbean: The Life and Works of Mutabaruka as Case Study," in Barnett, editor, *Rastafari in the New Millennium*, 142–158. As Linton Kwesi Johnson notes, Mutabaruka represents "the cutting edge of dub." See: http://www.guardian.co.uk/music/2005/aug/27/popandrock.poetry. Accessed March 30, 2014.

74 On women and the Rastafari movement, see Jeanne Christensen, *Rastafari Reasoning and the RastaWoman: Gender Constructions in the Shaping of Rastafari Livity* (Lanham, MD: Lexington Books, 2014). Also see John P. Homiak, "Dub History: Soundings on Rastafari Livity and Language," in Barry Chevannes, editor, *Rastafari and Other African-Caribbean Worldviews* (New Brunswick, NJ: Rutgers University Press, 1998), 140–142; Nathaniel Samuel Murrell, "Woman as Source of Evil and Containment in Rastafarianism: Championing Hebrew Patriarchy and Oppression with Lev 12," *Proceedings of the Eastern Great Lakes and Midwestern Bible Society* (1994): 191–209; Maureen Rowe, "Gender and Family Relations in RastafarI: A Personal Perspective," in Murrell *et al.*, editors, *Chanting Down Babylon*, 72–88; Lake, *RastafarI Women*; and Imani M. Tafari-Ama, "Rastawoman as Rebel: Case Studies in Jamaica," in Murrell *et al.*, editors, *Chanting Down Babylon*, 89–106.

75 See:http://www.jamaicaobserver.com/magazines/allwoman/121807_Empress-of-Zion-giving-voice-to-Rastafarian-women-Launches-an-anthology-o. Accessed March 30, 2014.

76 An outline of women dub poets in Jamaica and elsewhere may be found in Habekost, *Verbal Riddim*, 201–208.

77 Cited in Jenny Sharpe, "Dub and Difference: A Conversation with Jean 'Binta' Breeze," *Callaloo* 26.3 (2003): 608.

78 For details, see Jean 'Binta' Breeze, "Can a Dub Poet be a Woman?" *Woman: A Cultural Review* 1 (1990): 47–49. On Breeze's MBE, see: http://www.huffingtonpost.co.uk/2013/02/08/jean-breeze-binta-mbe_n_2646051.html. Accessed March 30, 2014.

79 Jean 'Binta' Breeze, *Third World Girl: Selected Poems, with Live Readings DVD* (Northumberland, England: Bloodaxe Books, 2011), 28, 169–171.

80 *Ibid.*, 136–137.

81 Jean 'Binta' Breeze, "To Plant," in *Word Sound 'Ave Power: Dub Poets and Dub* (Cambridge, MA: Heartbeat Records, 1994).

82 Sharpe, "Dub and Difference," 611.

83 Breeze, *Third World Girl*, 34–35.

84 *Ibid.*, 25.

85 *Ibid.*, 124.

86 *Ibid.*, 127.

87 *Ibid.*, 37–40.

88 For details, see Jenny Sharpe, "Cartographies of Globalisation, Technologies of Gendered Subjectivities: The Dub Poetry of Jean 'Binta' Breeze," *Gender and History* 15.3 (2003): 450–459. Also see Carolyn Cooper, *Noises in the Blood*, 136–173.

89 Jean 'Binta' Breeze, *Riddym Ravings and Other Poems*, editor Mervyn Morris (London: Race Today Publications, 1988), 28.

90 Breeze, *Third World Girl*, 148.

91 *Ibid.*, 149–150.

92 *Ibid.*, 152.

93 *Ibid.*, 154–155.

94 A routine search through any of the mainline online booksellers reveals an explosion of such insider accounts. Empress Yuajah seems to be especially prolific. Many texts are short treatments, made possible by print-on-demand technologies. Other, self-published authors include: Jahson Atiba I Alemu, Nigel Daring, Prince Ermias, Kelleyana Junique, Tracy Nicholson, and a publishing collective known as Rastafari Group. For more classic, systematic treatments of the movement, see Jah Bones, *One Love: Rastafari: History, Doctrine and Livity* (London: Voice of Rasta Publishing House, 1985) and Mihlawhdh Faristzaddi, *Itations of Jamaica and I Rastafari*, three volumes (Miami: Judah Ambesa Ihntanahshinahl, 1991–1997). For an overview of other writers of literature on the Rastafari, especially those working from within, see Edmonds, *Rastafari*, 127–139.

95 Niaah, "Grafting a New History," 365. Also see Velma Pollard, "Sound and Power: The Language of the Rastafari," in Sinfree Makoni, Geneva Smitherman, Arnetha F. Ball, and Arthur K. Spears, editors, *Black Linguistics: Language, Society, and Politics in Africa and the Americas* (London and New York: Routledge, 2003), 60–79.

96 Likening Rastafarian dub poets to liberation theologians enables scholars like Robert Beckford to facilitate a dialogue between Rastafari and those invested in black Christian theology in Britain. Ecumenism may prove to be an important part of the Rastafari's future. See Beckford, *Jesus Dub: Theology, Music, and Social Change* (London and New York: Routledge, 2006), 11, 19–20, 23, 68–80, 101–112, 145–150.

4

BENJAMIN ZEPHANIAH

Postcolonial Performance Poet

Introduction

In Great Britain, where literary and cultural critics have often prioritized the white and written poetic tradition, black oral or dub/performance poets, currently hold sway. They seldom work with the printed page in mind, and many are penetratingly political, keen to use the sound and power of words, especially in public settings, to lobby for social justice, and therefore resisting some of the weakening of Rastafari's message for which certain forms of reggae have been attacked.[1] Often funny, their work nonetheless displays serious attention to the black struggle for survival. Benjamin Zephaniah is the nation's premier black performance poet; he is also a celebrated novelist, playwright, musician, and radio as well as television presenter. Labeled a "streetwise, post-criminalized artist," he has been crafting verse for over thirty years, and this chapter catches a spark from his poetic fire, as fanned by Rastafari.[2] After delineating Zephaniah's life and literary art, I address the Rastological and biblical background to two poems, before closing with a recent, brief interview.

From the Margins to the Center

The son of a post office manager and a nurse, Zephaniah was born on April 15, 1958 in Handsworth, a working-class, inner-city area of Birmingham.[3] On July 10, 1981, frustrated with the Conservative government's apparent indifference toward poor blacks, many residents of Handsworth took part in a community uprising. An early Zephaniah poem, "Nice One Handsworth," captures the scarcity and tyranny that, in his view, caused his hometown to go up in smoke.[4] Not surprisingly, this race- and class-motivated insurgency, which spread to cities such

FIGURE 14 Benjamin Zephaniah (2011). Photo: Benjamin Zephaniah.

as Bristol, Manchester, and Nottingham, left an indelible mark on Zephaniah's vocational self-understanding. Now, as then, he forges his work on the hard anvil of black experience, and he labors to make his art accessible to the people he describes, not just to the middle class or the academic elite, the usually assumed audience for poetry, as well as Rastafari novels. To this end, Zephaniah performs anywhere—in pubs, prisons, or refugee camps, wherever people provide him with a stage on which to stride, quite literally, back and forth, addressing the poor's plight in what he sees as a hard-bitten, tasteless world of racism, classism, consumerism, and neo-imperialism.

Even though Zephaniah spent some of his childhood in Jamaica, where he absorbed the Caribbean cultural ethos that he celebrates, he was schooled in Great Britain. He was, by his own admission, a poor student, though he later discovered that he was dyslexic. Deemed incorrigible, he was removed from his comprehensive school at the age of twelve and placed at Boreatton Park, an approved (reform) school in the Shropshire countryside. Zephaniah would mine this experience many years later in his novel about a troubled teen who finds solace in music, *Gangsta Rap* (2004). Ironically, Zephaniah now takes poetry into schools, youth clubs, and teacher-training centers, and beginning in the 1990s he published a steady stream of poetry for children—from *Funky Chickens* (1997) to *School's Out* (1997) and from *Wicked World* (2000) to *When I Grow Up* (2011). Some of this poetry, like *Talking Turkeys* (1995), reflects his commitment to veganism, which Zephaniah recommends to children as an alternative to unhealthy 'fast food' lives. Today, Zephaniah's vegan livity also inspires the social as well as political groups he supports, such is the distinct ethical dimension of his Rasta-fari faith. Other poems of these collections are more generic, simply upholding the wonders of being young and filled with hope for the future. *We Are Britain!* (2002), for example, consists of twelve poems celebrating British children from many cultural backgrounds. In both speaking to and writing for children, Zepha-niah shows himself to be part of an emerging generation of British poets who believe that art's primary function is social engagement, especially in the form of giving back to one's community.

Zephaniah served time in Birmingham's Winson Green prison shortly after leaving Boreatton Park, and this captivity changed him dramatically: it convinced him that he could take some of his energy, not to mention his raw talent, and use it more constructively. In prison he read books on spirituality and black con-sciousness, emerging with the conviction that it would be through Rastafari that he would discover and utilize his voice. As soon as Zephaniah left Winson Green and arrived in London at age twenty-two, he set about performing his poetry in pubs and clubs across England's capital city. A collection of socially conscious verse that tackles working-class issues such as urban deprivation and unemploy-ment, *Pen Rhythm* (1980) appeared the same year. It was an immediate success in London's Caribbean and Asian expatriate communities. Zephaniah then spent some time performing with a band before releasing *The Dread Affair* (1985), his second book of poems.

Dedicated to "true Rastafarians who seek God and revolution within them-selves," Zephaniah's *The Dread Affair* takes two of the movement's most significant doctrines—belief in the divinity of His Imperial Majesty Emperor Haile Selassie I as well as an imminent return to Africa—and recasts them in the form of a Rastology of hope for disenfranchised black British youth.[5] As with the later Ras-tafari novels and music, Africa emerges figuratively, not as a physical location but as a particular state of being or psychological overlay. "Can't Keep a Good Dread Down" explains, in five short stanzas, how the biblical Abraham is connected to Selassie, how ancient Hebrew prophecies point to the emergence of Rastafari, and how traditional Christianity, with its belief in a transhistorical deity, is of little use to blacks, who need an immanent or hands-on God as the ground and grammar of an authentic this-worldly spirituality.[6] Other poems, such as "I Dwell Here" and "Dread Eyesight," treat Africa as the antidote to Babylon's (or the West's) poison.[7] Even more verse(s) illustrate Zephaniah's interest in the Africanization of the West, which involves tackling racism, unfastening the shackles of mental slavery, and affirming black family as well as community life. "Nature's Politics" calls for a nuclear-free environment; "Ganja Rock" appeals for marijuana's legal-ization; "Modern Slavery" laments how military expenditure is bankrupting the country; and, "Dreadie High-Rise Farm" chronicles the black struggle to survive in the tall tenement blocks that dotted England's council housing estates in the 1970s and 1980s.[8] *The Dread Affair* thus portrays the gritty realism of black British life. Beneath this unsettling vision of wrongful arrests and dole queue doldrums, though, we witness a Rasta-stimulated social action, which Zephaniah uses both to challenge and chant down Babylon. "Keep Cool Dreadie Cool," this collection's penultimate poem, is a case in point:

> Some say rastaman is waging war
> dreadlocks know sey dat nar get him far
> some say rastaman is robbing bank
> but rastaman is in a higher rank.
> Some say rastaman is doing crime
> but rastaman do better with him time
> they say rastaman is running racket
> when rastaman play reggae in high attic.
>
> People always try to keep us down
> but they're false kings and they all wear false crowns
> always trying to say that we are bad
> trying to forget that bad times that we had.
> People are controlled by what they read
> that's why they fight my people and their seed
> still we have come to set your wisdom higher
> and let the pirates burn in hotter fire.
>
> Equal rights and justice stands for all
> we won't be here when weakhearts start to fall
> he who lives by gun must die by gun
> we won't be here when weakhearts start to run.
> Silhouettes hide and firm things move about
> we won't give up and we will not sell out
> colour has no meaning in our places
> we live far away from this rat race.
>
> Policeman always pull us by our locks
> they want us to live in prison blocks
> Selassie I has give us what we need
> and now we understand we need no greed.
> Peace is what is written upon graves
> give us equal rights and mek we rave
> Genesis is only part the truth
> we come with a message for the youths.
>
> Over there and round there
> rasta love is everywhere
> from the future to the past

weak false gods will never last.
From the drum roll to the bass
dread don't eat their nuclear waste
we don't care if you're black or white
eye and high and I want unite.
Keep cool, natty cool
keep cool, dreadie cool.[9]

The Dread Affair exposed Zephaniah to a wider audience, and his extensive touring, sometimes alone and sometimes with a band, cemented his reputation. Despite his growing fame, many commentators viewed him suspiciously, partly because of his reform-school background and partly because of his controversial views on white privilege. His supporters believe the media has treated him unfairly, however, especially when he was shortlisted for the position of Creative Artist in Residence at the University of Cambridge in the mid-1980s. At this point, for example, *The Sun* tabloid newspaper asked its readers: "Would you let your daughter near this man?" Frustrated but far from discouraged by this smear campaign, Zephaniah did not take up the Cambridge position but, instead, accepted an offer from the city of Liverpool to spend one year as its writer-in-residence. This opportunity to work with young people and students led to *Inna Liverpool* (1992), which captures his varied experiences in this working-class city. The media also questioned Zephaniah's credentials when he was shortlisted for the post of Regius Professor of Poetry at the University of Oxford in 1989.

At the end of April 1988, Zephaniah journeyed to Palestine and Israel, where he set himself the difficult task of understanding not only the Palestinian struggle for self-government but also the Israeli opinion. He interviewed countless individuals and discovered that every person, Palestinian and Israeli, had a story to tell. The result was *Rasta Time in Palestine* (1990), his first non-fiction text. Equal parts travelogue, political commentary, and poetry, this book records his experiences with, and impressions of, the people of the Gaza Strip and the West Bank. Zephaniah does not pull any punches; he repudiates Zionism and, in Rastafari's name, equates Zion with Ethiopia and not the state of Israel. Poems such as "Mosquitoes in Jerusalem" and "Know Your City" lament European involvement in setting up the state of Israel, enjoin Palestinians to fight for their freedom, and call for unity in struggle.[10]

The focus of one of the first documentaries screened on British Channel 4 TV, Zephaniah has since appeared on numerous talk shows, music specials, and poetry programs, as well as in political debates. He was the first singer to record with The Wailers after Bob Marley transitioned in 1981. In addition, he has penned a steady stream of plays since 1985, including *Job Rocking* (1987), *Mickey Tekka* (1991), and *De Botty Business* (2008). At the close of 1991, the British Broadcasting Corporation (BBC) aired his first television play, *Dread Poets Society*. In it an engagingly imaginative Zephaniah debates past and present poetry with Mary Shelley, Percy

Bysshe Shelley, Lord Byron, and John Keats. In 1993 he also wrote and produced *Crossing the Tracks*, a BBC documentary about black and Asian culture in Britain. A radio presentation on "Rasta History," for BBC Radio 4, aired in 2003. This zeal for television and radio work never got in the way of touring and recording, however. Between 1990 and 2000 Zephaniah traveled the globe and released numerous audio recordings, both CDs and spoken-word cassettes. *Us and Dem* (1990), *Back to Roots* (1995), and *Belly of De Beast* (1996) are among his most renowned recordings.

City Psalms (1992) accentuates a Rastology that sponsors practical change, both locally and globally.[11] Here, Zephaniah searches for an identity, which Laurenz Volkmann interprets as "a testing of human and ethnic interstices, of the 'spaces in-between,' which as Homi Bhabha has phrased it so admirably, might help us to 'emerge as others of our selves.'"[12] Put differently, Zephaniah shows himself capable of an astonishing amount of mental migration—capable, that is, of assembling and bringing his thoughts to bear on various problems of oppression throughout the world. He addresses miners in Wales, socialists in Nicaragua, student protestors in China, World Bank members, peace negotiators in the Middle East, neo-Nazis in West London, and troops in Northern Ireland. Given this subject matter, it seems fair to view *City Psalms* as an eclectic, secular liturgy, evoking through arresting words and sounds an ecology of place as well as a topography of shared struggle. In "Black Politics of Today," for example, Zephaniah declares that he has studied much philosophy and religion and found, to his great interest, something common to each worldview—a desire to "check tings politically," to order human affairs so that all people live together hospitably and justly. As a "modern-day Rasta," moreover, Zephaniah wants the "Black people situation" to improve.[13] He craves black flourishing. And poetry facilitates such flourishing, for it helps to awaken conscience and raise awareness of the rigors and inequalities of lives lived under oppression. The final poem in this collection, "The Old Truth," hints at religious inclusivism with its bold claim that all the world's spiritual heroes and heroines appeared on earth to show us that "our destinies are all (rumour has it) de same."[14] What emerges as a hint in *City Psalms* appears throughout Zephaniah's later work, especially *Propa Propaganda* (1996). Indeed, he now promotes the idea that all the world's religions—including Rastafari—may best be understood as different expressions of one common experience and future. This conviction now seems to be more typical of many global Rastafari.

In 1999 Zephaniah published his first novel. Another text written with children (particularly teenagers) in mind, *Face* engages the theme of prejudice in narrative rather than lyrical form, a new departure for Zephaniah but one that many critics favored; *Face* was shortlisted for the Children's Book Award 2000. Set within London's 'new East End' with its blend of African, Asian, Caribbean, and traditional Anglo working-class families, this story focuses on Martin Turner and his 'gang of three.' After an evening of nightclub revelry, Martin and his friends become involved in a joy-riding accident. Martin's face is disfigured, and the rest of the novel is given over to how he transcends the many prejudices he faces, both literally and symbolically. Underneath this tale of pain, even cruel rejection, lies the hope that the East End is changing, that its time-worn racism is giving way to a new inclusivism.

Zephaniah also aimed *Refugee Boy* (2001) at his growing teenage audience. It tells the story of an Ethiopian boy, Alem. Barely a few days into his first visit out of Africa with his father, Alem wakes up in a London bed-and-breakfast and discovers that his father has left him. In the letter he writes and leaves behind, Alem's father explains that both he and Alem's mother believe Ethiopia's political problems are too much for a little boy to endure. Feeling Alem would be safer in London, they forsake him with little more than directions to the social services and the Refugee Council. Grounded in Zephaniah's own work with asylum seekers, the novel's central thrust concerns Alem's struggle, the way he lives for the letters from Ethiopia, and his new life in England. Zephaniah's most recent novel, *Teacher's Dead* (2007), is a detective thriller that focuses on a playground crime scene. Zephaniah's novels engage the challenge of diasporic life, in ways that resemble the postcolonial literature I discussed previously.

The tribulations that affect all asylum seekers are one small but not unimportant aspect of black life in modern Britain. *Too Black, Too Strong* (2001) addresses some of the other aspects. This collection of poetry, drama, and criticism includes verse written during the time Zephaniah spent with the prosecutor Michael Mansfield working on the high-profile, racially motivated killing of Stephen Lawrence.[15] Zephaniah's personal website indicates that he intends this book to be a tribute to Great Britain, a testimony to the fact that he loves it so much that he is prepared to fight for his rights there, and for the rights of black people to move from society's margins to its center—a general journey that parallels Rastafari's particular movement from outcasts to culture bearers.

In 2005 Zephaniah returned to recording, though he continued with many of the same themes in his novels and poems. The eleven tracks on *Naked* indicate that he has not lost any sense of the oral or performance poet's belief that 'word sound 'ave power.' Here he covers subjects such as climate change and globalization—issues rooted in his sustained commitment to grassroots organizations such as Blackliners (a black and Asian AIDS and HIV network), the Chinese Women's Refugee Group, SHOP (Self-Help Organization for ex-Prisoners), and SARI (Soccer Against Racism in Ireland). Radio DJ and hip hop pioneer Rodney P eventually remixed four of the album's tracks, and Zephaniah released the album in a limited edition form, *Naked and Mixed Up* (2006).

To show how far he has moved from his days in an approved school, and thus from the margins to the center, we can look to the ways Great Britain's most prestigious academic and cultural institutions have showered Zephaniah with awards. He won the BBC's Young Playwrights Festival Award in 1988, and the universities of North London and the West of England awarded him honorary doctorates in 1988 and 1999, respectively; he has been presented with thirteen additional doctorates since, the most recent of which was from the University of Glamorgan. He was nominated for the post of British poet laureate in 1999; he lost to Andrew Motion. And yet, he resists this cultural positioning. In 2003, for example, he found himself at the center of a political uproar after he refused to become an Officer of the Order of the British Empire (OBE), an honor that Queen Elizabeth II confers on her subjects upon the prime minister's recommendation. Zephaniah declined the OBE because, as he put it, the title evoked the "thousands of years of brutality" inflicted on his African forebears by British colonizers.[16] And in an interview that appears in Barbara Baker's *The Way We Write* (2006), he elaborates:

> There is a whole legacy of white supremacy that tells young black kids in school today that they will never be as good as the white man, so they don't want to do academic stuff, they want to be a rapper or a boxer. We talk about this all the time, but we say, "White people are so proud of their Empire, don't say anything in front of them. Tell them they gave us cricket, and roads and the civil service." I thought, "No". There is no doubt that there are some good remnants of the Empire, but why couldn't we get that without all the rape and pillage? So there is the historical aspect, and also the modern-day one.[17]

To be sure, in life as in his art, Zephaniah remains an ardent, Rasta-inspired critic of imperialism; in his view, empire sucks the life out of others.[18] Everything about him protests injustice, especially structural injustice, and like the ancient Hebrew prophets with whom he is frequently compared, Zephaniah is unafraid to use his performance skills to speak truth to power—to chant down Babylon. Writing in "Benjamin Zephaniah, the Black British Griot" (2005), Eric Doumerc describes him thus:

> Whether we like his poetry or not, it has to be admitted that Benjamin Zephaniah is a major player on the British literary and cultural scene and has made his mark in a significant way. It could be said that his poetry is characterised by its stereoscopic nature and presents us with a double vision of British society. This 'double consciousness' appears in both the thematic concerns and forms that Zephaniah uses in his poetry and which make his art truly 'Black British'. His poetry transcends racial and cultural boundaries as it is steeped in the very British tradition of doggerel and nonsense while paying homage to the Caribbean oral tradition in its various forms and guises. His poetry is a hybrid, creolised product of the meeting of two cultures and is characterised by the coexistence of several voices which correspond to various roles or functions assumed by the poet: the wordsmith, the broadcaster/griot, and the satirist.[19]

Doumerc's description comes to mind when one views Zephaniah's 2013 release, *To Do Wid Me: Benjamin Zephaniah Filmed Live and Direct*; captured by Pamela Robertson-Pearce; the footage for this DVD-book offers a striking portrait of the artist through interviews and concerts. Today, Zephaniah holds a chair in Creative Writing at London's Brunel University. In the end, he is a critic of the forces and institutions that have propelled both him and Rastafari to stardom.

Riddim Wise and Scripture Smart

When seen across the last thirty years, Zephaniah's verse illustrates what postcolonial religion and global Rastafari looks like on the streets of secular Great Britain. And in this section I ponder two poems, which not only reveal his historic Rastological roots and activism, they help us grasp his sense of the mythical or narrative dimension of his faith, or what we might call the biblical background to Rastafari's behaviors and beliefs. Despite the global and postcolonial trajectory of Zephaniah's art and Rastafari's message, these poems reflect many of the early concerns and convictions of the movement.

A. Can't Keep a Good Dread Down …

> The seed of Abraham grows
> it will not stop
> and he who sees it knows
> Rastafari is on top,
> great schools and churches have been built
> to hide us from the real,
> but those who built burn in their guilt
> as prophecies reveal.
>
> Sympathizers come
> to dance to rasta sound
> we can't live in the atmosphere
> we must live on the ground,
> businessmen are some
> they buying rasta sound,
> they have no love for riddim
> their interest is the pound.
>
> The Lion of Judah has prevailed
> the Seven Seals is I
> no living in the grave no more
> King Fari will not die,

no brainwashed education
for wisdom must top rank,
if you want riches
you must check Selassie I bank.

The root of David grows
weakheart get on your toes
And check the dread go sight JAH head
'cause he who sees HIM knows,
the Bible did not end the seed won't disappear
the only difference is that now
the rastaman is here, and,

Selassie I keeps on coming
can't keep a good dread down
those that stood start running
when JAH JAH comes to town,
greater love keeps coming
Alpha is here wid us,
so stop praying to polluted air
and give rasta your trust.[20]

B. Dread John Counsel …

Here I scribe just doing what comes to me naturally
everything I write is my account of history
just like an ambassador without an embassy
in my manifesto there is dread democracy,
I am here to take the good and throw the bad away
I represent a kingdom that has lived from time I say
in the counsel there are wise men with no mind to betray
in this kingdom there is love for all for love will not decay,
and this is me in exile so far away from home
no labour or conservative can give me what I own.

In this land my brothers and some sisters fight me down
therefore in the dark place and the jailhouse I am found
but I have a weapon that shall burn the enemy
and it has a fallout that shall rule equality,
the court is revolutionary the righteous ones shall stand
and in the tabernacle there doth play a reggae band
there is no House of Commons and everyone is high
and this kingdom is governed by a upfull one called I,

but I am here in exile so far away from home
still in this sick captivity I will not use their comb.

Tafari is my partner and Hannah is my tool.
David is my tuning key, Isaiah is my school,
dread John is my thinking, Obadiah is my aim,
Ezekiel is part of me I would like to make this plain,
in no case will we sit here in this democracy
believing what they tell us 'bout black equality,
when flies are caught in spiders' webs the spider must return
so if a one should stay here with them that one will with them burn,
we are not too fussy 'bout being British free
the kingdom's international a kingdom we can see,
they will never give us what we really earn
come our liberation and see the table turn,
still this is me in exile so far away from home
still recruiting soldiers to break this modern Rome.[21]

What follows involves accentuating, by brief commentary, some of the scriptural references in Zephaniah's two poems. In several places he refers to biblical books, themes, and personalities. By discussing those references, I show how Zephaniah reads the Hebrew Bible and the Christian New Testament—significant symbols of his religion's narrative or mythical dimension—through Rastafari's spectacles.

The first stanza of "Can't Keep a Good Dread Down" calls to mind the Abraham Saga, which takes up thirteen chapters of Genesis. Zephaniah says that "the seed of Abraham grows/it will not stop/and he who sees it knows/Rastafari is on top." This reference points to Abraham, son of Terah (Gen 11:26–29), the so-called 'friend of God' who probably lived around 1800 BCE (Isa 41:8; 2 Chr 20:7). Originally called Abram, his name was changed to Abraham, which was understood to signify "father of a multitude"; Abraham was the father of the people who were later called the Jews (Gen 17:5). Thus, Zephaniah takes us right back to God's promise to Abraham that he would be the father of many people, to show that Rastafari (God, for Zephaniah) was guiding all true devotees from the dawn of time and shaping their future. Furthermore, Zephaniah believes that Rastafari are the People of Jah (and Jah, as we have seen, is the Rastafari rendering of Jehovah, the English rendering of the Hebrew tetragrammaton YHWH, the unpronounceable name of the God of Israel), through whom Jah will benefit the rest of creation.

Allusions to the Christian New Testament book of Revelation can be found in the third stanza of "Can't Keep a Good Dread Down." Here Zephaniah declares that, "The Lion of Judah has prevailed/the Seven Seals is I/no living in the grave no more/King Fari will not die." Also, in the fourth stanza, he asserts that "The root of David grows." Now, the text of Revelation 5:1–5 lies behind both remarks. First, this passage speaks of a kingly messiah ("the Conquering Lion") who will come from the royal tribe of Judah (Rev 5:5). While traditional Christian preaching associates the lion trope with Jesus of Nazareth, Zephaniah connects it to Selassie, who took the title "Lion of Judah" at his coronation, and who, to Rastafari, is a direct descendent of King Solomon and Queen Sheba and thus of the stock or "root" of David. Second, the idea of the "Seven Seals" is a reference to the apocalyptic scroll fastened with seven emblems (Rev 5:1). It would not be far wrong to suggest that the number of seals means that it is difficult for an unworthy soul to gain access to this unique papyrus roll. In Zephaniah's view, Selassie ("King Fari") is authorized to open and read the sacred document. Such worthiness is linked to the emperor's Davidic ancestry. Moreover, every Rasta is worthy ("the Seven Seals is I") by virtue of his/her association with Selassie; indeed, the divine spirit of King Fari is invested in every devotee of the King of Kings, the Lord of Lords, the Conquering Lion of the Tribe of Judah. Thus, for Zephaniah, all Rastafari play a part in Jah's final plan for the world's destiny.

"Can't Keep a Good Dread Down" closes with a line inspired by Revelation 1:8; 21:6; and 22:13: "Alpha is here wid us/so stop praying to polluted air/and give rasta your trust." A title of Christ, Alpha is the first letter of the Greek alphabet—Omega is the last—and, when taken together, the Alpha and the Omega, the beginning and the end, the first and the last, is a phrase that expresses the divine power over all creation. Selassie is Christ's second coming. And notice how Zephaniah appears to use his own theological immanentalism to counter the traditional Christian belief in theological supernaturalism. Indeed, he seems to regard the Christian belief that God, or Alpha, lives in the sky, up there in heaven, as little more than white man 'trickery,' a 'kind o' nonsense' used to pacify marginalized black people. Thus, Zephaniah enjoins us to "stop praying to polluted air," that is, to abandon theological supernaturalism, to believe that the true Alpha is Rastafari, who resides inside rather than outside one's soul, and to trust that the greatest embodiment of Rastafari is found in the Holy Emperor. Similar themes surface throughout Rastafari art, in everything from Bob Marley and the Wailers' "Get Up, Stand Up" to Tarrus Riley's "Love Created I."

A similar reverence for the Holy Emperor is set within the framework of "Dread John Counsel …" Here Zephaniah describes himself as a scribe in a kingdom characterized by deathless love. Notice how he uses "kingdom" five times in this poem; it signifies the absolute rule of Jah Rastafari revealed in Selassie to vanquish Jah's enemies, creating a community over whom Jah reigns, the whole mass of creation, and issuing in a sphere in which the authority of Jah is experienced. Although I should be careful not to make the parallel between Zephaniah's verse and the Christian New Testament too close, perhaps I can say that the Gospel picture of the 'kingdom of God/heaven,' like that of Zephaniah's "kingdom" of Jah, is chiefly one in which the believer voluntarily submits to the divine rule (Jn 3:3–5; Mt 19:23–24; Mk 10:23–25; Lk 18:24–30). Of course, Zephaniah does not share the Johannine view of an other-worldly kingdom (Jn 18:36); indeed, his kingdom theology is this-worldly, secular, and Afrocentric.

"Dread John Counsel …" closes by invoking the names of several heroes and heroines of the Hebrew Bible. In doing so, Zephaniah takes us to the heart of his Rastology: "Tafari is my partner and Hannah is my tool/David is my tuning key, Isaiah is my school/dread John is my thinking, Obadiah is my aim/Ezekiel is part of me I would like to make this plain." At least five items of theological interest surface at this point. First, I have said that Zephaniah versifies Rasta's sense of oneness with the spirit of Rastafari; thus, to refer to Tafari as a "partner" is once again to express the idea that life's secret is found through the Holy Emperor's divine inspiration.

Second, it seems that Zephaniah references Hannah, the gracious mother of Samuel, in order to highlight his own Nazarite heritage. The Nazarite was an Israelite who sanctified himself and took a vow of isolation and self-imposed discipline for the purpose of some higher mission. He refused to consume wine, to use a razor, and to touch dead bodies. There are at least three Nazarites in scripture, namely, Samson (Jude 13:5–7), Samuel (1 Sam 1:11), and John the Baptist (Mt 11:18; Lk 1:15). In 1 Samuel 1:11 Hannah promises God that Samuel "shall not drink neither wine nor intoxicants, and no razor shall touch his head." The last clause in the last sentence is especially noteworthy; indeed, dreadlocked Rastafari often claim that the Nazarite vow not to use a razor and/or comb is an ancient sign of moral holiness, an emblem of purity that upholds the ethical and ritual dimension of their faith (Lev 19:27–28; Num 6). Since the penultimate stanza of "Dread John Counsel …" ends with a defiant refusal to use "their comb" in "this sick captivity" (the non-African world, Babylon), it seems that Zephaniah uses Hannah as his "tool" to uphold his spiritual status as a contemporary, consecrated Nazarite.

Third, the writer of 1 Samuel 16:21–23 describes David as a skillful soldier who was appointed to play the lyre to Saul, Israel's first king, requested by popular demand against Samuel's wishes, when he (Saul) was depressed. Thus, Zephaniah's claim that David is his "tuning key" is almost certainly a reflection of Zephaniah's belief that he, like David, is being chosen for great things. The connection is clear: just as David was the musician chosen to slay the feared Philistine, Goliath of Gath (1 Sam 17), so Zephaniah is favored to use music and poetry in his fight against "this modern Rome," the non-African world, Babylon.

Fourth, Zephaniah claims that he belongs to the "school" of Isaiah. Now, the prophet of Isaiah 1–39 is known as First Isaiah, or Isaiah of Jerusalem, and his task in the southern Kingdom of Judah was to condemn social and religious evils. In particular, this eighth-century BCE prophet told the leaders of Judah that they were heading for disaster unless they changed their ways. Preaching against Assyria's foreign gods, Isaiah of Jerusalem advised Judah to put their trust in God alone, whose power extended over all nations. Finally, during one political crisis, Isaiah of Jerusalem used symbolic actions—he wore sackcloth and walked barefoot—to stress his message that Judah would be stripped of her special status if she trusted Egypt to assist her in the campaign against Assyria (Isa 20:2–3). In short, Isaiah of Jerusalem is a prophet-statesman. And Zephaniah sees himself as a Rasta prophet-statesman; if one glances through his work, one will notice that much of it addresses social and religious evils. "Dread John Counsel ..." is an excellent example. Here Zephaniah asserts that British black people are blind to the truth about themselves as African sons and daughters of Jah, because of their false trust in Britain's political process ("no labour or conservative can give me what I own"). Like Isaiah, who advised Judah to trust in God alone, Zephaniah preaches—in this poem at least—single-minded devotion to Rastafari.

Fifth, Zephaniah supplements his interest in Isaiah by associating himself with two other prophets, namely, Obadiah, the fourth of the Minor Prophets, whose concern was for the destruction of Edom, one of Israel's archenemies and, with Ezekiel, the last of the Major Prophets. The aim of the short book of Obadiah is clear: the writer pronounces judgment on Edom and declares an imminent restoration for Israel. Thus, when Zephaniah says that "Obadiah is my aim," we can perhaps interpret this as a sign of Zephaniah's own mission, that is, to pronounce judgment on Britain, the modern Edom, and to declare a restoration for all sincere Rastafari, the true Israelites, in the day of the Holy Emperor.

Ezekiel's early message was one of doom and gloom (Ezek 7) until Jerusalem was destroyed in 586 BCE. After the worst happens, Ezekiel begins to sing a new song: the same God who brought the two Israelite kingdoms to their knees is the same God who will raise them up once more. The famous vision of the valley of dry bones represents Ezekiel's theology of hope (Ezek 37:1–10). For Ezekiel, the bones represent the Israelite kingdom, in ruins but able to be restored by God's mighty power. The last nine chapters of the book of Ezekiel record the prophet's vision of the restoration of the holy temple, the holy city of Jerusalem, and the holy land of Israel. Like Ezekiel, Zephaniah views himself as a performance prophet, that is, a man blessed with words he feels in his body, which he cannot hold in, and as a man who sees fantastic visions and has experiences of being beside himself with emotion. Christian Habekost puts it this way:

> Dub poetry is performance poetry with or without Reggae music. When Benjamin Zephaniah recites his famous "Dis Policeman" on stage, then one can see what is meant by the 'power'. Of course, it is possible to get the meaning of the poem when reading it, the black experience of "law and order" inside the ghettos of democratic England. Listening to the recording of the poem one can even get an oral impression too, the provocative rhythm and the different shades of the voice come across. But these are not the poet on stage with flying dreadlocks, an angry expression on his black face, murderously kicking into the air with his motorbike-boots just as the police boots kicked him. Only then does one realize what is really going on.[22]

"Dread John Counsel ..." foretells doom and gloom for those British blacks who place their trust in 'democracy'; and yet Zephaniah writes his poem to rally the dispirited and the downtrodden. Indeed, he preaches that Jah will one day liberate Jah's people, illustrated in the Ezekiel-like vision of a new tabernacle (the second stanza). Elements of this vision emerge from the following recent interview with Zephaniah.

An Interview with Benjamin Zephaniah.

DJNM: In an Op-Ed for *the Guardian* newspaper in Great Britain, you comment on Snoop Dogg/Lion's conversion to Rastafari: "Snoop Lion wants to spread the message of Rastafari, but does Rastafari need an ambassador? Yes, is my answer, we need as many as we can get. I think we are one of the most misunderstood groups of people in the world."[23] Does the misunderstanding stem from Rastafari's diversity, a symbol for which might be the way different Rastas reacted to Sizzla Kalonji's 2012 inauguration as presiding head of the movement, or does the confusion arise from something else?

BZ: I think it is the diversity that makes it difficult for people to understand Rastafari, along with the lack of visible leaders, but I don't think that is a bad thing. Islam, Christianity, and even Buddhism have a great deal of variation within them, but they do have various kinds of power structures which I would prefer not to have. The only respect that I have to give any Rasta is the respect I have to give any other human being; there is no individual Rasta who can claim to speak for me, and I cannot speak for any other individual. That said, we know who we are; and poets, singers, and intellectuals can speak about the persecution of Rastafari to the world, or encourage Rastafari unity around a cause or a campaign.

DJNM: Rastafari scholar Ennis B. Edmonds ends his recent book with this observation: "Rastafari and reggae have provided Anglophone Caribbean writers with a distinctive voice that has liberated them from mimicking the aesthetics of British literature. Bob Marley is certainly right. The rejected and maligned Rastafari has become the cornerstone of Caribbean cultural production, whether in music, art, or literature."[24] Do you share Edmonds's sentiments? And was there a specific moment in your career, a turning-point in your time as a poet and a Rasta, when *you* 'came in from the cold,' as it were?

BZ: I think Edmonds is absolutely right. I remember as a very young boy wanting to be a writer but feeling that Standard English just couldn't contain me. Rastafari liberated me. It did the same of course for my interpretation of religious scriptures. I can remember hearing Big Youth chanting psalms over reggae music and feeling that they were made for each other; the music and the words blended quite easily and young people began chanting psalms as they walked the streets—something my parents had been trying to get us to do for years. From that point on I decided that I was going to contribute to the 'third testament.'

DJNM: You've created a body of work that personifies what Caribbean poet and cultural critic Kwame Dawes calls "the reggae aesthetic"—verse that sees the body, the emotions, the imagination, and the spirit coalesce in service of an uplifting, challenging, even erotic message.[25] Your reaction? And if you had to highlight one poem or one book from your literary backlist, one that you are most proud of both aesthetically and politically, what would it be, and why?

BZ: I find it very difficult to analyze my poetry, and I don't think of its place in the world as I write. I do feel the need to move people emotionally with my work, share my imaginings, and uplift people spiritually, but when I am creating a poem (or any other piece of art) even those things are far from my mind. When I have something to say the need to say it feels like a powerful urge, a creative scream that I need to let off, or even something beautiful that I want to connect with or express. I am often amused when people review or analyze my work because sometimes they show me things about the piece that I didn't see. Sometimes they say something that I feel is just right, and of course sometimes they say things that are very wrong. I am a creative being who wants to reach as many people as possible, to express as many things as possible.

I think the poem that expresses my spiritual outlook, my politics, and my message best is "Naked," which appears in the book *Too Black, Too Strong*, or on the music album of the same name. Others have said differently, but for me this poem brings so many ideas together—as I try to clarify in a recent video.[26]

DJNM: Scholars of religion are often intrigued by the way religions brand or commodify themselves. And marketing Jah, for want of a better phrase, seems to be a topic of genuine interest—from "Marley's Mellow Mood" [an ital herbal drink] to "Rastamouse" [British TV children's show]. How do you feel about such developments? Are they an inevitable part of the international spread of Rastafari, and/or of globalization in general, or are they misguided attempts to partner with late modern capitalism, Babylon let's say, and thus doomed to trivialize and/or exploit Rasta's artistic/cultural heritage?

BZ: Sometimes I hate having to sell my work, but there is no other way in the world as it is organized now. The important thing for me is not to think about the monetary shitstem [pejorative term: system] as I create. The commodification of any religion or spiritual movement makes me sick. If they need to sell themselves there must be something missing. I am interested in the 'breath' and with how breathing can enlighten you. I can show you some exercises but I have nothing to sell here. I am happy to read any holy book, I am happy to listen to any sermon or music, but when all those things are taken away there must still be something you feel, something you experience. If you can't get the experience without all the other stuff I don't want to know. I have to have a direct connection to God.

DJNM: And finally, how would you describe the Rastafari roots reggae landscape today? And what's in your immediate future?

BZ: There was a period in the 1990s, and early 2000s when there were some aggressively anti-gay, anti-feminist, and tribalistic tendencies in reggae. But I think that, to a great extent, has passed. I do think that much of what happens in reggae is not necessarily reflected in Rastafari. These days, it is uplifting to see how many young Rastas have a more spiritual, holistic, compassionate approach to life. If we want to talk about music and Rastafari, then Tarrus Riley ["I Sight"] and Queen Ifrica ["Lioness on the Rise"] represent a new generation of righteous griots.

Me? I just keep doing what I do. The major change in my life is that I have become a Professor of Poetry, which I could have not foreseen. Fortunately the institution [Brunel University, England] wants me to continue doing what I do, so that helps. I feared losing my creativity as I chased 'targets' and 'outputs' and all that stuff, but it hasn't been like that. I have devised a module, 'Writing Poetry for Performance,' and I am really enjoying passing on my knowledge to a new generation of performance poets.

Conclusion

Whether on the stage or on the page, Zephaniah is an erudite and often traditional Rastaman, as evidenced by his biblical faith and historic interpretations of God and Selassie, and he wastes no time exploring the finer points of politics, veganism, spirituality, music, and the status as well as the nature of poetry today. Rastafari's energetic breath sustains him, giving life to what is also a very postcolonial poetry, rooted as it is in the diasporic experience and concerns. Zephaniah is far more concerned with the state of Britain than any repatriation to Africa. But it is also Jah who takes this black man and bids him sing, inspiring him to flash his locks as he performs as well as writes the empire back. "The British (serves 60 million)" is his winsomely poignant paean to the nation's culturally pluralistic society, one that moves well beyond the simple black and white dualism seen in Mais's novels and Marley's music:

> Take some Picts, Celts and Silures
> And let them settle,
> Then overrun them with Roman conquerors.
> Remove the Romans after approximately 400 years
> Add lots of Norman French to some
> Angles, Saxons, Jutes and Vikings, then stir vigorously.
>
> Mix some hot Chileans, cool Jamaicans, Dominicans,
> Trinidadians and Bajans with some Ethiopians, Chinese,
> Vietnamese and Sudanese.

Then take a blend of Somalians, Sri Lankans, Nigerians
And Pakistanis,
Combine with some Guyanese
And turn up the heat.

Sprinkle some fresh Indians, Malaysians, Bosnians,
Iraqis and Bangladeshis together with some
Afghans, Spanish, Turkish, Kurdish, Japanese
And Palestinians
Then add to the melting pot.

Leave the ingredients to simmer.

As they mix and blend allow their languages to flourish
Binding them together with English.

Allow time to be cool.

Add some unity, understanding, and respect for the future,
Serve with justice
And enjoy.

*Note: All the ingredients are equally important. Treating one ingredient better
than another will leave a bitter unpleasant taste.*

*Warning: An unequal spread of justice will damage the people and cause pain.
Give justice and equality to all.*[27]

Notes

1 For an early history of the British dub poetry scene, see Christian Habekost, *Verbal Rid-dim: The Politics and Aesthetics of African-Caribbean Dub Poetry* (Amsterdam; Atlanta, GA: Rodopi, 1993), 27–33; 219–228. Also see Meryvn Morris, "Dub Poetry?" *Caribbean Quarterly* 43.4 (1997): 1–10.
2 Alison Donnell and Sarah Lawson Welsh, editors, *The Routledge Reader in Caribbean Literature* (London and New York: Routledge, 1996), 349.
3 Sources for this biographical sketch include: Victoria Parker, *Benjamin Zephaniah* (Oxford: Heinemann Library, 2007); Verna Wilkins and Gillian Hunt, *Benjamin Zephaniah: A Profile* (Northwood: Tamarind, 2008); and Benjamin Zephaniah and Victor G. Ambrus, *Benjamin Zephaniah: My Story* (London: Collins Educational, 2011). For details, see: http://benjaminzephaniah.com/ and http://www.youtube.com/channel/HC73eZfZYvsl0. Both sites accessed March 30, 2014.
4 Benjamin Zephaniah, *The Dread Affair: Collected Poems* (London: Arena Books, 1985), 19.
5 *Ibid.*, 7.
6 *Ibid.*, 24–25.

7 *Ibid.*, 47, 79–81.

8 *Ibid.*, 12, 60–61, 73, 94–95.

9 *Ibid.*, 110–111.

10 *Ibid.*, 27–28.

11 Benjamin Zephaniah, *City Psalms* (Newcastle upon Tyne, England: Bloodaxe Books, 1992).

12 Laurenz Volkmann, "The Quest for Identity in Benjamin Zephaniah's Poetry," in Dunja M. Mohr, editor, *Embracing the Other: Addressing Xenophobia in the New Literatures in English* (Amsterdam: Rodopi, 2008), 261.

13 Zephaniah, *City Psalms*, 62–63.

14 *Ibid.*, 64.

15 Benjamin Zephaniah, *Too Black, Too Strong* (Tarset, Northumberland, England: Bloodaxe, 2001).

16 For details, see http://benjaminzephaniah.com/me-i-thought-obe-me-up-yours-i-thought/. Accessed March 30, 2014.

17 Barbara Baker, editor, *The Way We Write: Interviews with Award-Winning Writers* (London: Continuum, 2006), 225. For other recent interviews, see: http://www.independent.co.uk/arts-entertainment/interviews/benjamin-zephaniah-im-just-a-normal-bloke-who-writes-poems-1708406.html;http://www.writersandartists.co.uk/writers/advice/37/a-writers-toolkit/interviews-with-authors/interview-with-benjamin-zephaniah; http://www.guardian.co.uk/books/2009/jan/18/benjamin-zephaniah-interview-poet; and, http://www.youtube.com/watch?v=O5IGvPyma9w. All sites accessed March 30, 2014.

18 "Empire—Bomb the Bass," a song Zephaniah recorded with Sinéad O'Connor, rhymes "empire" with "vampire," for instance, and it serves as an instructive example of how he performs poetry over music to confront and challenge imperialism. See *So Far: The Best of Sinéad O'Connor* (London: Chrysalis Records, 1997).

19 Eric Doumerc, "Benjamin Zephaniah, the Black British Griot," in Kadija George, editor, *Write Black, Write British: From Post Colonial to Black British Literature* (Hertford: Hansib, 2005), 195.

20 Zephaniah, *The Dread Affair*, 24–25.

21 *Ibid.*, 54–55.

22 Christian Habekost, *Dub Poetry: 19 Poets from England and Jamaica* (Neustadt, West Germany: M. Schwinn, 1986), 36.

23 See: http://www.guardian.co.uk/commentisfree/2012/aug/07/snoop-dogg-rastafari. Accessed March 30, 2014.

24 Ennis B. Edmonds, *Rastafari: A Very Short Introduction* (Oxford and New York: Oxford University Press, 2013), 127.

25 Kwame Dawes, *Natural Mysticism: Towards a New Reggae Aesthetic in Caribbean Writing* (Leeds, England: Peepal Tree Press Ltd., 2008), 29–32, 80–83, 95–103, 242.

26 See: http://www.guardian.co.uk/commentisfree/video/2012/oct/01/benjamin-zephaniah-poetry-video. Accessed March 30, 2014.

27 Benjamin Zephaniah and Sarah Symonds, *Wicked World!* (London: Puffin Books, 2000), 38–39.

5

THE REEL RASTA

Selected Documentary Films

Introduction

As the previous chapters have shown, the Rastafari religious movement has had an extraordinary effect on the arts, and the arts have promoted and sometimes consumed, quite literally, Rastafari.[1] In my first chapter, I pointed to examples of Rastafari in consumer culture: Rasta Pasta, Rastananas, and so on. But we could also look to the bob-sledding Jamaicans of the widely popular film *Cool Runnings* (1993). In almost no other medium than film, it seems, is the artistic portrayal of Rastafari as lopsided. How, then, do we begin to grapple with this cinematic history?

Against the direction of most scholars, I argue that we must include motion pictures in this broad definition of art, because movies featuring Rastafari are available and have been for some time now. Over the course of the last century, film grew to become one of, if not the, most popular artistic mediums of the day, and that growth just happened to parallel Rastafari's globalization. To go global, so to speak, means Rastafari appear more regularly in Hollywood productions. And yet because of these lopsided depictions and stereotypes, scholars have simply ignored or dismissed one of the most significant artistic mediums of our age. I will open this chapter, then, by looking at Hollywood, but I will not linger here long, turning instead to answer the aforementioned question of 'how' through documentary films.

As I argue, we can turn to documentary features as a form of cinematic portrayal that straddles both the artistic and the scholarly realms, bringing the two together. The bulk of this chapter then will explore documentaries, which I have chosen for their artistic value and scholarly merit. As to the former, we can connect them most particularly to the evolution of the novelistic portrayals of Rastas—as film, even documentary, rests on narrative plot and a particular ordering of events, selection of characters, and a sense of setting or place. Over the course of my selected documentaries, Rastafari move from Jamaica to Africa, even Israel, become more ethnically and globally diverse, and include prominent women, Jews, and so on. As I will also indicate, documentaries are intended, perhaps even first and foremost, as scholarly studies, and the documentaries that I will discuss not only reflect trends in our academic understanding but influence, shape, and predict the actual scholarship surrounding Rastafari. In my analysis of the documentaries, however, and be forewarned, I will not be so deliberate in distinguishing the artistic from the scholarly, as it is the nature of this specific medium to bring those together, or at least blur the lines of separation. Moreover, for my part, I view documentary films featuring Rastafari as instructive, not simply because they show us how flesh-and-blood brethren and sistren articulate as well as find their voices, however harmonious or inharmonious they sound in the final analysis, but because such documentaries represent thick descriptions of the movement's transcultural presence, bringing all our artistic and scholarly senses together. Finally, by the end of my chapter, I think we find not only Rastafari transformed and reinterpreted but Bob Marley himself reborn and resurrected. Who is 'Bob Marley' becomes a rather complicated question with multiple—and sometimes conflicting—answers.

Cinematic Portrayals: An Overview

One of the few scholars to consider Rastafari in motion pictures is Kevin J. Aylmer.[2] In "Towering Babble and Glimpses of Zion: Recent Depictions of Rastafari in Cinema," Aylmer emphasizes the *varieties* of Rastafari religious experience in eight movies first released in the late twentieth century. Although the Rasta presence in *The Harder They Come* (1972) appears "benign," for example, the musicians featured in *Heartland Reggae* (1982) accent Rasta "as a way of life, as millennial expectation, as non-violence and separation. Their embrace of Rastafari is a psychic sanctuary in a tropical maelstrom of daily struggles to survive."[3] *Countryman's* (1982) Rasta is "a positive force that is energetic and redemptive"; he is "the embodiment of Rasta's interconnectedness with the seamless fabric of life, a lifestyle that confers on a select few glimpses of Zion," Aylmer says.[4] By contrast, Hollywood's comical and clichéd treatment of Rasta surfaces in *Club Paradise* (1986), "where the wildly disheveled Rastafari are inclined toward late-night revels and chanting down Babylon with such sentiments as 'Fire burn in Babylon' while crowding around bonfires or milling about dance halls, thereby adding requisite coolness."[5] One specific scene depicting an important Rasta ritual "borders on parody, its participants caught in the throes of a mysterious Orientalism that speaks in tongues, chants, and shouts jeremiads with blood-curdling ferocity."[6] Two other films, *Marked for Death* (1990) and *New Jack City* (1991), sustain such stereotyping by situating Rastas in dispossessed, urban neighborhoods in the northeastern United States, where they serve as "mere ciphers, communicating in stage patois ('Wait here for de mon!' 'Everybody want to go to heaven, but nobody want dead') and even engaging in the occult."[7] Hollywood eventually revived this formula of false representation with *Cool Runnings*, where the mockery masks an ironic, nefarious connotation:

> The film has been hailed as another *Rocky* on ice, exploring pride, power and dignity. On closer examination of the film, however, the classic Rastafarian themes of racial pride, self-reliance, self-assertion, and cooperation have been co-opted and transformed into a sports success story, where commercialism is the subtext and competition is an indispensable means to a decidedly Babylonian end—Olympic glory.[8]

Appearing after Aylmer's insightful commentary, later films show that they also advance this comedy and commodification motif. Consider *Shark Tale* (2004), a computer-animated motion picture. Here, Ernie and Bernie are dreadlocked marine invertebrae, voiced over by Doug E. Doug and Ziggy Marley, and when they are not sporting tams (Rastafari head coverings) or thrumming to the music's beat, they serve at the pleasure of the puffer fish Sykes, a vicious ganglord, and thus they look like little more than aquatic thugs, brutish and yet oddly endearing.[9]

As stated above, documentaries are a different kettle of fish. Described as "a landmark documentary exploring the Rastaman *in extremis*," *Stepping Razor—Red X* (1992) offers a painstaking account of the philosophy and opinions of Peter Tosh, one-third of the original Wailers music group. Aylmer knew Tosh personally, and although Aylmer has concerns about the film's numerous and inexplicable misunderstandings, he applauds its "sensitive" and "candid" approach to "the life of Jamaica's Bushdoctor."[10] The remainder of this chapter thus examines six documentary films for the way they illumine the religious worlds that Rastafari make and the people who study and render them as both artists (film-makers) and academics. Each film appears different, which is to be expected, and yet they also seem united, at least for the most part, by their ability to serve as an antidote to Hollywood's toxic treatment of Rastafari in cinema as well as to chart the evolution of Rastafari and our understanding of them. We pick our story up, then, in the early 1990s, as documentaries experience a surge in popularity, straddling not only the artistic and the scholarly but the elite world of academia and the popular medium of film. Documentaries featured in this chapter include: *The Emperor's Birthday* (1992); *Roots Daughters: The Women of Rastafari* (1992); *Ras tafari* (2001); *Awake Zion* (2006); *Coping with Babylon: The Proper Rastology* (2007); and *Marley* (2012). Other documentaries exist, and I hope scholars and students will find themselves able and inclined to seek them out and ponder them in turn, yet my sample offers an informative window on the last twenty or so years of the movement.[11]

The Emperor's Birthday (1992)

John Dollar's 1992 documentary film follows those Rastafari from various parts of the world who made pilgrimage to Ethiopia to commemorate Haile Selassie's centenary birthday celebrations (July 23, 1892).[12] As a feature, it investigates Rastas' physical and mental movement from present to past origins, and back to the present. Using archival footage and reggae music (the performers include Houdini, Mighty Terror, Prince Buster, Tilahun Gesesse, and Yared Tefarra), *The Emperor's Birthday* also investigates the genesis of Rastafari myth and ritual. In addition, it combines the testimonies of non-Ethiopian Rastas as well as non-Rasta Ethiopians and, in the process, it illustrates the movement's anxious standing in this part of the Horn of Africa; assuredly, the tension between such groups is as palpable as it is intriguing. An Ethiopian docent in the National Musuem in Addis Ababa shows us Selassie's throne in one scene, for example, and then Dollar asks the man about the Rastafari who visit the Museum. "Many Rastafarians" come to see it, the docent says, and when they do, "they give as, like as a god, you know." He acknowledges that Rastafari "trust" Selassie is still alive, but he, the docent, remains unconvinced. "It could be for them," he concedes, "but we know that he died already, in 1974, by the Derg," a reference to the 1974 Marxist group led by Mengistu Haile Mariam.[13] For their part, several Rastas featured in Dollar's documentary—such as Ras Tekla, recently arrived from the United Kingdom, and Bongo Papa Noel Dyer, who made the lengthy pilgrimage to Ethiopia from his native Jamaica via London in 1961—take issue with such sentiments, and in more than one scene we see them counter the official Ethiopian claim that skeletal remains exhumed from the former royal palace belong to the country's late Emperor.[14]

One of the oldest settlers in Shashemene, until he transitioned in 2000, Dyer serves as Dollar's chief spokesperson, and Dyer's lively account of his own journey into Rasta, including his repatriation to Ethiopia, commands our attention. He tells us about living in Kingston in 1959, at the height of the social unrest I noted in chapter two, and how the Jamaican government eventually came to realize that the Rastafari were far more religious than they were political. He speaks warmly of the Rastafari patriarch Mortimer Planno ("He look like Moses") and, in a mood of spirited confessionalism, Dyer describes hearing Planno's compelling blend of biblical interpretation and African diaspora history, saying, "from that time a different spirit does enter me through that man. Immediately, right away, I was converted." Dyer's own biblical theology means he sees himself as a modern-day Jonah, called by Jah to leave Jamaica, and this belief in his own life as sacred narrative explains why he set sail for England in the early 1960s. Skirmishes with the British police over ganja-related issues forced Dyer to leave London in 1964 and, after hitchhiking through Europe and North Africa, he arrived in Addis Ababa, Ethiopia, in 1965. "You couldn't get Africa out of us," he announces. Others would eventually join Dyer, as Jahlani Niaah and Erin C. MacLeod point out in recent studies; and the Rastafari presence in Ethiopia has, for the last fifty years or so, been relatively steady, if at times fretful, as reflected in community letters to the United Nations as well as in print and video reports in newspapers.[15]

The Emperor's Birthday captures the anxiety that many non-Rasta Ethiopians feel towards non-Ethiopian Rastafari. First, Dollar joins a small but not insignificant group of marchers lobbying for the country's return to a constitutional monarchy, and he speaks with an unidentified Ethiopian man who indicates that "our people" find it difficult to accept the Rastafaris' "belief point of view." Here, the implication seems to be that indigenous folk have a hard time lionizing their rulers, even if they hold their office in high esteem. Second, Dollar interviews Tadela Kibret, an Ethiopian politician, who laments those Rastafari immigrants, like Dyer, who responded to Selassie's call to return to the Motherland but who did not "bring education, technical know-how, nor enough money" with them, thus straining the nation's already delicate infrastructure, Kibret declares. Third, Dollar visits with an Ethiopian Orthodox priest, Abba Michael, who insists that Rastafari are wrong to worship the late Emperor: "Haile Selassie a man, great of Africa, but not God," he says, and the viewer senses that the priest speaks not simply for himself but for other Ethiopians, like the bemused onlookers at a Rastafari reggae concert, whom we see in other, telling scenes.

Seemingly undaunted by the puzzled, tepid, and sporadically hostile response to their presence, the non-Ethiopian Rastafari featured in Dollar's documentary accentuate Zion's glories, and many uphold their African cultural citizenship. We see the aforementioned Ras Tekla reading the Bible "with an Ethiopian perspective," for example, and we hear him describe the country of Ethiopia as "a picture of the Bible itself." We also encounter a Bobo Shanti priest, Harry Karr, quietly as well as patiently explaining his work with the then-transitional government of Ethiopia; priest Karr mobilizes for specific ships, part of a reparation/repatriation package that the Bobo Shanti mansion sees as a moral duty on the part of all who have benefitted from the slave trade. Another British Rasta, Ras Obediah, appears on screen and recounts Rasta's transcultural spread from Jamaica to the United Kingdom in the 1960s; he stresses the importance of elders, the success of reggae music, and the experience of racial prejudice in the British secondary school system as factors that facilitated Rastafari's growth in various British cities in the late 1960s and early 1970s—such things helped "us draw towards our blackness and look to Africa." And finally, we witness Dollar engaging members of the Ethiopian World Federation at the end of their week-long journey to Shashemene. Despite the interview's edginess, prompted by the fact that many did not wish to be filmed, we hear brethren accept and quote the Bible; uphold Selassie's divinity; emphasize African slave history; endorse Rasta's peace and love philosophy; celebrate their faith's promotion of spiritual and moral awareness; and they even walk Dollar through the many ways they are developing Shashemene with small-scale or cottage industries, even housing schemes. The Ethiopian World Federation eventually registered as an NGO, around ten years after Dollar's documentary, and several foreign embassies have applauded their community service in the last decade or so, as Niaah's research shows.[16] Whatever else it is, then, Rastafari represents a religious nostalgia for the Motherland, and *The Emperor's Birthday* evokes such yearning for return.

Dollar recognizes the difficulties that attend such longing. Yet he is not alone in documenting such concerns. As we saw with Barbara Blake Makeda Hannah's protagonist in *Joseph: A Rasta Reggae Fable* (1991), Rastas frequently defer their dreams of a fresh start. Shashemene has "problems," Joseph the devout insider concedes, and later voyagers to this town, inquisitive outsiders like Emily Raboteau, only confirm the Rastafaris' continuing struggle to live a new life in the Promised Land.[17]

"Perhaps the mystery is the idea of a 'true home,' which calls the children of Africa back to her," Dollar concludes, and, in the end, I suspect *The Emperor's Birthday* not only displays an uneasy alliance between Rastafari and Ethiopians, it illustrates what Mircea Eliade would call an "ontological thirst" for meaning on the part of returning Rastafari—a thirst that Rasta quench by treating Shashemene as their *axis mundi*, their world's center:

> In the realm of sacred space which we are now considering, its [the ontological thirst] most striking manifestation is religious man's will to take his stand at the very heart of the real, at the Center of the World—that is, exactly where the cosmos came into existence and began to spread out toward the four horizons, and where, too, there is the possibility of communication with the gods; in short, precisely where he is *closest to the gods*. We have seen that the symbolism of the center is the formative principle not only of countries, cities, temples, and palaces, but also of the humblest human dwelling, be it the tent of a nomad hunter, the shepherd's yurt, or the house of a sedentary cultivator. This is as much to say that every religious man places himself at the Center of the World and by the same token at the very source of absolute reality, as close as possible to the opening that ensures him communication with the gods.[18]

In 1992, Rastafari from across the world were drawn like iron filings to Ethiopia's magnetic force, and Dollar's film features interviews with Rastas united, for the most part, by an Eliadean desire for being. African slave history, nostalgia, and the thirst for meaning are intricately related; nostalgia is a return through memory to one's origins or past experiences for the sake of re-membering or re-ordering cosmic chaos and creating meaning. So, this yearning for return to Ethiopia is not merely physical movement, but journeying in the mind's eye as well. "Simply put, the ancestral return cannot be equated to mere travel or migration," John Homiak writes in a review of Dollar's film. "To the true Rasta, Ethiopia is more than a territorial entity: it is a moral destination."[19] And thus here, in this fifty-two-minute documentary film, the diasporic Rastafari quest for meaning manifests itself in what Eliade calls a "cosmicization" of the continent—an attempt to valorize the world religiously by situating everything, and especially Rastafari, underneath the Black Person's Vine and Fig Tree (Mic 4:4), in Africa or Ethiopia, where the oldest known hominid (Lucy, Berkenesh) was discovered, and where the world first began to unfurl. Unlike some of the fiction and songs I noted in earlier chapters, with the exception of Hannah's *Joseph*, Dollar's documentary represents one of the first attempts to display the uneasiness of life in Zion, and it captures what scholars now recognize as the tension that surfaces whenever Rastas ponder the dialectic of repatriation and rehabilitation.

Roots Daughters: The Women of Rastafari (1992)

Given Rastafari's documented problems with patriarchal practices, it should hardly seem surprising that no women speak in Dollar's film. In contrast, the women of Rastafari featured in Bianca Nyavingi Brynda's *Roots Daughters* break the code of silence, articulating their long struggle for autonomy in a male-dominated culture, like Sheba does in Masani Montague's 1994 novel, which I addressed in chapter two.[20] In *Roots Daughters*, reggae serves as the catalyst for such eloquence and empowerment. This 1992 documentary stars Judy Mowatt, the first woman reggae artist nominated for a Grammy Award, and one-third of the I Threes, the celebrated backing singers for Bob Marley and the Wailers. Here, the lyrics and real-life experiences of artists like Mowatt both enlighten and embolden the Rastawomen that Brynda, a convert to the movement, interviews on location in Jamaica, Guyana, and Canada. *Roots Daughters* thus archives a turning point in Rastafari's history and livity, as Montague's novel does, showing how and why 'conscious' women both subvert habitual models of womanhood and urge *all* Rastafari to usher in a new age of equal rights and justice by embodying Rasta's emancipatory message in the fullest way possible.

This film begins by providing an overview of Rastafari's history, and it sees the movement as one of the many Caribbean creolized religions—the others include Vodou, Santería, Obeah, and Espiritismo—that developed through contact with Christian and European colonization. On Brynda's view, Rastafari represents an anticolonial, spiritual retort to slavery's "deliberate genocide of black identity" or, to invoke the language of this book's other chapters, the movement signifies a reclamation of self and cultural agency denied by Babylon. We learn that in 1992, three main Rastafari mansions or "factions" coexist, united by a shared sense of "black solidarity and black dignity," and Brynda stresses the Nyabinghi mansion. Her focus is gender-based. Tradition explains that Nyabinghi's roots reach back to the eighteenth century, when Queen Kitami ruled over the Bgeishekatwa tribe in East Africa. Several sacred myths came to be associated with Queen Kitami, who was revered and renamed Nyabinghi after her passing, and the most significant story involves her control of a mystical drum. It seems Queen Kitami used this instrument to frustrate her tribal enemies and to establish matriarchal power, which was buttressed by an elaborate system of rituals upheld by an intricate network of Nyabinghi priestesses.

Rhythmic drumming has been the ritualistic life-blood of the Rastafari religion for some time now, especially among brethren who align themselves with the Nyabinghi mansion, and yet, as many of the 'roots daughters' in this film testify, traditional Rastafari men not only prohibit women from drumming, they often display cultural amnesia in face of their faith's matrilineal heritage. Ras Fitz Elliott symbolizes such forgetfulness in this film. He also typifies Rastafari's male dominance, which appears as an ingrained refusal to treat Rasta sistren as equal. Elliott employs dread talk, for example, to claim that whereas men have "overstanding," women have understanding only; the insights and ideologies associated with Rasta women are inferior. All women are evil, he later declares, citing Eve as the first in the Edenic Fall (Gen 3:6), and final blame for every error made by a man lies at the feet of a woman, he holds. Such beliefs are born of anxiety, one Rastawoman in the film reasons; brethren like Ras Elliott are "like the sun that has a fear of the moon, the moon that is woman." Fear only divides people, she implies, and fear is based on ignorance. In contrast, ritual practices of remembering African roots and culture will help the movement take the women dis-membered by gender conflicts and bind them back (*re-ligare*; religion) to the larger group, determined to worship Jah inclusively.

Mowatt upholds the value of studying African roots and culture. And this film presents her as an important link to an illustrious, if derided, past. She appears on camera performing "Warrior Queen," which honors momentous black women from across the centuries, and, in her follow-up interview, she declares that late-twentieth-century Rastafari women are now living in a "new dispensation," where sistren are discovering themselves, voicing their own sense of Rasta womanhood rather than cultivating obsequiousness toward their Kingmen. *Roots Daughters* showcases sixteen such women from three countries. And each "dawta of Jah" tackles topics such as ital food, dreadlocks, head covering or wearing a "tam," menstruation, contraception, polygamy, and the importance of education. Diverse opinions abound. Other chapters in my book reference the varieties of Rastafari religious experience; for its part, Brynda's documentary film reveals that no two Rastawomen act and think alike, even if the Bible's stress on the sovereignty of Jah serves as the common denominator inspiring their ethics and philosophies.

Some sistren appeal to scripture when discussing livity. Running her fingers through her hair, one Guyanese women refers to the locks as "I and I crown, and you got to wear the crown; it's in the Bible." Another woman points to Jesus of Nazareth and Selassie, asserting that both were Nazarites, holy men who disavowed razors (Num 6:1–21). Still more view locks as a symbol, as some kind of supplement, or else as an identity marker, reserved principally for those mature enough to tolerate the "tribulations" and "persecutions" (Mowatt) that frequently follow the person who flashes dreads. A difference of opinion also attends to head covering, since some Rastawomen, like Norma Wilkinson, think the practice is biblically mandated (1 Cor. 11). However, sistren like Petal Roberts treat tams as optional. Moreover, Brynda's documentary reveals that Rastafari women are at odds on the significance of ital food. Some shun meat and instead choose to keep the mind 'pure' by observing a vegetarian or vegan diet. Others, like Lorna Dixon, prefer to self-identify as omnivores. Dixon declares that Marcus Garvey ate meat, for example, and she believes that in doing so he neither polluted his body nor compromised his spirit.

Other gender-based practices, such as women isolating themselves from men during menstruation and what garments women should and should not wear, provoke additional variation in views. Birth control stands out as a delicate topic.

Norma Wilkinson and her daughter, Ingrid, appear circumspect when asked on camera about contraception, although Norma eventually urges sistren to "leave it up to Jah" and, where possible, avoid birth control. Mowatt, who sees herself on a Jah-inspired mission to use reggae music and conscious lyrics to strengthen and console women, addresses the issue from another angle. She holds that all sistren must make themselves women, which is to say "self-sufficient and independent," before they have children. Also, Mowatt stresses male responsibility. She slates absentee Rasta fathers, for example, and she chides those Kingmen who "break up the family" through polygamous or polyamorous behavior, which often leads to children "here and there," running around with little or no moral influence in their lives. Outside this film, Mowatt takes up these and related themes in songs such as "Sisters' Chant," "Only a Woman," and "Hush Baby Mother."

Mowatt sings from a future-retro Rastafari hymnal, as it were, because she reaches back into the past, into the female roots of Nyabinghi ritual, and she urges the movement's next generation to foster the autonomy of women, to listen to the hopes and fears of the 'roots daughters,' and to help women realize collective as well as individual agency. We sense that Mowatt is not alone in her struggle, and we catch a glimpse of what she hopes for, when Brynda documents a multiracial, gender-inclusive Nyabinghi drumming session. Situated towards the close of the film, this scene selection features women assembling, against customary wisdom, to invoke Selassie ("Papa Jah"), to chant down Babylon, and to perform with an instrument made famous by a noble African queen. Music thus helps to create an authoritative platform for Jah's dawtas—a stage upon which to worship freely, to think independently, and to effect the Rastafari movement's self-transformation. In the end, *Roots Daughters* anticipates what we see as the reconfiguration of the Rastawoman by musicians like Queen Ifrica, performance poets like Jean 'Binta' Breeze, novelists like Masani Montague, and painters like Ejay Khan.

Final footage of Rastafari children assembled in their own faith-based school and sitting at the feet of eager tutors, like Ariane Lock and Sister Dawn, underlines Brynda's conclusion: Rastafari's next generation stands poised to take this organic, multidimensioned movement into some spacious directions, away from sexism and towards fairness—into a way of life where women as well as men experience self-determination, not system-determination, and where equal rights and justice pertain to all, not simply a few. The last decade or so has seen some valuable changes in this direction, as earlier chapters recognize, and there is every reason to believe that the sistren's status will improve, especially now that they have increased their visibility and found their voice in the Empress of Zion Inc., and other international Rastafari collectives. These days, scholars like Noel Leo Erskine look to the future for women in Rastafari and, all things considered, they seem sanguine about progress. Erskine writes:

> The challenge for Rastas is not to flee Babylon or merely to interpret Jah's displeasure with Babylon but to work for transformation in Babylon. This would include releasing women from the shackles of subjugation and second-class citizenship within Rastafari. Rastas must begin to understand that their dignity and freedom are tied up with those of women. As they allow the wind of Jah's spirit to blow freely in the community, women will once again be empowered as in the [Jamaican] Revival Church to take their rightful place in Rastafari and in the wider community. Rastas will begin to view the world from a new place, Zion, not Babylon. In Babylon it is fashionable for masters to keep slaves and for men to lord authority over women. In Zion, where women are celebrated as daughters of Jah, there is equality and dignity for all Jah's children.[21]

Ras tafari (2001)

Directed by James Ewart, and released in 2001, *Ras tafari* brings artistic insiders and scholarly outsiders together, united by the desire to offer a structured explanation of the Rastafari movement at the new millennium's dawn.[22] Six sections divide Ewart's documentary, and although no interviewee mentions Ninian Smart, the film's architecture creates an informative, unintended account of the application of his dimensional theory of religion to Rastafari. In the end, we emerge from this fifty-two-minute portrait grasping the biblical as well as spiritual significance of Selassie, Garvey, Jamaica, ganja, reggae, and Rasta's experiential philosophy.

In the film's opening frame the familiar Nyabinghi drumming soundtracks Omaal Wright, an actor, as he reads scripture, his dreadlocks flashing in the bright Jamaican sunshine. Then we encounter Barry Chevannes, the leading-edge academic at work in Rastafari Studies until his passing in 2010, who appears on screen to inform us that devotees have many reasons for finding Rasta appealing, the most important being its "profound wisdom," which often sustains as well as inspires a convert's fresh sense of self. Yasus Afari, Jamaican dub poet, concurs. Using words that uphold Rastafari's experiential or emotional dimension, he announces that the movement represents the "only authentic, holistic, and indigenous response to the crucifixion called colonialism." Rasta is the reclamation of black agency, an ardent hymn to African-derived somebodiness. Furthermore, brethren and sistren serve like warriors in a cosmic combat zone; all Rastas are

Selassie's soldiers, striving to "bring back man in harmony with the Creator," Afari states. Fighting in this theater of war is not a religious endeavor, though, it is a spiritual one. Here, Afari sounds like Mutabaruka, whose unyielding opposition to religion I note in chapter one, because Afari clearly relegates 'religion,' as an organized form of the faith, below "spirituality," which he defines in communitarian terms as a "network that links us all together onto our source, the Creator." Perhaps 'livity' operates as dread talk's synonym for Afari's "network," since livity, as we have seen, signifies the many and varied activities—locks, ganja, reasoning, music, vegetarianism, etc.—that delineate the movement's ritual or practical as well as experiential or emotional dimensions.

Among the Rastafari, livity *is* spirituality. Barbara Blake-Hannah, one of several Rasta novelists I survey in chapter two, agrees. On Ewart's film, she describes Rasta as a "way of life." Rasta is "an Afrocentric style of behavior," a mode of individual and collective meaning-making that not only links blackness with sacred power, it emphasizes the need to act godly—that is, to strive to receive Jah's grace to cultivate livity. Such livity fosters "creational fraternity," Afari continues; put differently, Rasta's rituals or sacred actions heighten humanity's divinely mandated duty as stewards of Selassie's creation.

Ras tafari's first major section, "Growing Up Rasta," introduces us to additional insiders, such as social worker Dawn White and Rasta elder Mortimer Planno, and we learn that although brethren like Afari hold that Rasta is "an inborn concept," society and culture nevertheless accelerate the emergence of Rasta consciousness. White shares that she was initially drawn towards Africa and Selassie because she saw something of her own survival story reflected in the endurance tale of an ancient continent and one of its embattled yet brave, modern rulers. White's grandmother admired Selassie, moreover, and White's father prized Garvey's pan-Africanism. White was part of the crowd that welcomed Selassie to Jamaica in 1966. And she tells us that he was a "magnetic force," a "striking yet meek" figure whom Rastas, herself included, soon came to mythologize and revere as the personification of the returned Messiah. Family and politics helped Dawn White grow into Rasta. For Planno, it was location, family, and music that made the difference. In Trench Town's public housing projects, Jamaican reggae's visceral drum-and-bass mixed with song lyrics that upheld spiritual verities and chanted down colonial untruths, with the result that "the Rastafari sound [eventually] became embedded in me." Garvey's philosophy and opinions formed part of this sound, and Planno's mother was a "staunch Garveyite." When Planno committed to Rasta, she said she was pleased she had "a son who stood in defense of Africa." Planno would later prove crucial to Bob Marley's spiritual formation and musical success, as earlier chapters in my book note.

Garvey, Africa, and Selassie form Rastafari's fundamentals, Chevannes resumes, and this film's insiders concur, thereby offering an etic/emic illustration of at least three of Smart's dimensions: the mythic or narrative, the doctrinal or philosophical, and the social or organizational. Such essentials were part of the "mystique"

that first attracted Afari at the tender age of fourteen. And the biblical background
to the movement's features represents the main reason why Blake-Hannah celebrates Rasta for how, on the one hand, it blends scripture with black history
to counter-read racism and, on the other, for the way it helped to free her from
mental slavery. For his part, Afari recites several familiar Bible verses on film, each
one providing warrant for everything from his doctrine to his ethics.

Ras tafari's second section, "Locks," chronicles the social stigma that surrounds
the characteristic hairstyle associated with brethren and sistren. We learn that
Dawn White has worn dreadlocks for twenty-five years, for example, and that
numerous Jamaicans have spurned her for her actions. Afari remarks on his family's intense pressure to have him trim his beard as well as crop his hair to hold
down a steady job. Although other Rastafari in Ewart's film, such as Trench Town
Community Association Chairman Mikey Beard and TV director Ray Smith,
appear to think that the locks issue is a "fight that don't exist" (Smith) and that
one may be Rasta without flashing dreads (Beard), public disapproval nonetheless
persists, as *The Gleaner*'s May 2013 gloss on the *US International Religious Freedom
Report for 2012* reveals:

> In Jamaica, the State Department says there were reports of societal discrim-
> ination based on religious affiliation, belief, or practice, stating that Rastafar-
> ians alleged the overwhelmingly Christian population discriminated against
> them, "although there were signs of increasing acceptance."
>
> "Rastafarians said that elements of their religion, such as wearing dread-
> locks and smoking marijuana, presented barriers to their ability to find
> employment and achieve professional status in the official economy," the
> report states.[23]

Notwithstanding present and past prejudice towards Rastafari, Ewart's decision to
juxtapose White and Afari with Beard and Smith reveals the diverse, acephalous
nature of the Rastafari movement—an observation that Benjamin Zephaniah and
others make in my book's previous chapters. No two Rastas think and act alike.
Some suppose that locks are part of the "vow," as one unnamed Rasta in this film
voices, yet others, like Planno, think that dreads signify an outward manifestation
of an internal disposition. Such diversity continues into the film's fourth section,
"Sacrament," where we gather that although Dawn White does not smoke ganja,
she does not see herself as "less of a Rastafarian." In contrast, Planno refers to the
holy herb and Rasta as "Siamese brothers." Clearly, the Rasta thread of the global
religious tapestry is made of an intermingled yarn.

The film's third and fifth sections, entitled "Trench Town" and "Music" respectively, celebrate how western Kingston's projects reflect a spiritual ecology of
place and serve as a stage for religio-artistic expression. One of the area's most
famous sons, Planno sees sites like Coronation Market and Government Yards as
"holy ground," a magnet for "mystic" types; "God's people can be in Rome," he

says, "but God's people were in Trench Town, too." Such people include reggae musicians such as Wailing Souls, Toots and The Maytals, Dean Fraser, Alton Ellis, Bongo Herman, Massive Dread, Peter Tosh, and Bunny Wailer. Trench Town is reggae's birthplace, the pounding drums combining with politicized lyrics and the chunking sound of the rhythm guitar to serve as the Rastafari sound, analogous to the way gospel music works for Christians. "You can't disassociate music from Rasta or Rasta from music," Afari declares, "because music is really the tool which helps Ras Tafari to manifest and to fulfill itself." Speaking in *Ras tafari*'s final section, "Philosophy," Blake-Hannah underlines Afari's comment. Art forms are vehicles. And reggae's emotional, physical power works best when it performs Rasta's most basic belief, which is Jah's love for all humankind, made manifest in the livity of Selassie, she claims.

Music acts as a transnational touchstone of human lives, connecting us one to another, to sacred power perhaps, and in Blake-Hannah's opinion, singer-songwriters like Bob Marley have realized for the Rastafari what George Harrison accomplished for the Hare Krishna—global status. Through music, that is, they have caused their religions to grow very rapidly around the world. Today's Rasta reggae artists, such as G Vibes ("Globalization"), Massicker ("New Millennium Rasta"), and Rasta Duke ("Reggae International"), carry Marley's torch across borders and into new regions of the world, establishing intimate, lively reggae scenes, like the one in Israel, which director Monica Haim features in *Awake Zion*, her 2006 documentary about the transcultural coalition between Jews and Rastafari.

Awake Zion (2006)

Ancient Bongo Daniel, an esteemed elder of the Nyabinghi mansion in Scotts Pass, Jamaica, and Nigel the Admore, Jamaica-born white Jew currently living in Israel, symbolize the mesmerizing mashup of faiths that pulsates at the heart of Monica Haim's film; and they illustrate the growing internationalization of the Rastafari movement at the onset of the twenty-first century.[24] But this is not their story alone, valuable though they are, since there are other interviewees in *Awake Zion*, and each of them helps Haim conduct her compelling, cross-cultural visual analysis. Throughout the film, we witness dissimilar people celebrating as well as sharing three religiocultural traits: a devotion to the Hebrew scriptures, an intense desire to connect to one's ancestry, and an appreciation for reggae culture. After exploring such themes, this section concludes with an interview with Haim.

"How is it these African men in the Caribbean were telling me about the lineage of the ancient Jewish kings," Haim asks, midway through her filmed visit to Jamaica. One answer to this question lies in the Rastafari's impressive biblical literacy, which Haim documents extensively. Several scripture passages are cited in this film, and each quotation illustrates the Rastafari religion's ritual as well as narrative dimension. In the parish of St. Catherine, for example, Haim visits Congo

Ashanti Roy's Rasta compound, which he calls "the lion's den" (Dan 6:1–28), and there she discovers she needs to change clothes before she reasons with Roy and other brethren; she puts on a long skirt (Deut 22:5), which reminds Haim of her "Hebrew school days." Satisfied by this gesture, Roy then précises the 1 Kings 10 story of King Solomon and the Queen of Sheba, arguably the central mythic expression of the Rastafari, because it calls out from across the centuries, signaling both Selassie's messianic significance and each African's "true Israelite" status. Sister Cherry, a Rasta from Manchester Jamaica, builds on Roy's hermeneutics, for she appears on film and declares that the Queen of Sheba signifies the "missing" link between Rastafari and Judaism. Eager to explore what she calls this "unsuspecting kinship" between Jews and Rastas, Haim eventually escorts Ancient Bongo Daniel to a local synagogue, where he expresses amiable surprise when he sees the Star of David symbol scattered around the temple. Back in Roy's lion's den, Daniel cites the Hebrew Bible, this time to validate two main traits of Rasta livity, the ritual action(s) of flashing dreadlocks and smoking weed. "I am telling you," he asserts, "Rasta is identity, and you can't go to Zion with no scissor and comb" (Num 6:5). Likewise, marijuana is "a plant of renown" that Jah raised up for "the healing of the nations" (Ezek 34:29; Rev 22:2). Scripture, then, is central to the Rastafari. In fact, the Bible is to Rasta what the Torah is to Jews. And several interviewees appear on screen to agree with this thought. Rabbi Simon Jacobson, who leads a Crown Heights synagogue, admits Africa's standing in the Bible. And Carol Haile Selassie, a white Jew married to an Ethiopian Rasta and living in Los Angeles, values the biblical background to Rastafari's attractive "culture and lifestyle." Other Rastafari, from Trench Town's Bobo Dread to New York's Ras Prince, express similar sentiments. And informed outsiders to Rasta, like Barry Chevannes and reggae historian Roger Steffens, convince Haim that Rastas like those featured in her film are not alone in their exegetical endeavors. Like most Jews, almost all Rastas read their lives scripturally. That is to say, brethren and sistren often pick up and treat the Bible as if it were a mirror reflecting life's easygoing as well as unforgiving truths. This method of internalizing the ancient story recalls the interpretive strategies of African Americans who, after abandoning the South and crossing the Ohio River during the Great Migration, equated their experience to Israel's departure from Egypt. Surely, the Bible helps the Rastafari fathom their captivity in Jamaica, "a land of sad intrigue and human suffering," as Haim puts it, and it assists their search for Zion.

Awake Zion features Rastas and Jews connecting to their respective religion's ancestry or heritage through sacred texts, rituals, and music. Jews consult the Torah, electing to see their lives as making most sense when lived within the fence of the Law. Traditional Rastas also take their ethical and ritual cues—what we might call their livity rules—from various laws in the book of Leviticus. Jews also uphold particular Hebrew Bible stories, such as legends of the quest for Zion, and tales of the greatest kings the Israelites ever had, David and Solomon. Rabbis in Haim's film stress scripture's significance as an account of a pilgrim people following their God toward the promised land. For their part, Rastafari appear on camera to accentuate the value of the Bible and the *Kebra Nagast*. Here, Rastas re-present stories about the Solomonic dynasty, which are included in both texts, and they underline each narrative's basic endorsement of Africa as holy land. Each time Jews and Rastas consult and read their sacred myths, then, they converse with the faith of generations that have gone before them, and thus join with them in a chain of memory. Haim wonders: "If Jews and Rastas identify with the same things, do we not identify with one another?" Eventually, we learn that one answer to this question lies in a shared approach to music (Ps 87:7). Consider Matisyahu, Crown Heights Hasidic Jew and dancehall reggae exemplar, who reveals that he spent his teenage years listening to Bob Marley, noticing the Star of David symbol on album cover art, and smoking the holy herb.[25] Matisyahu ("King Without a Crown") divulges a particular fondness for Marley's use of Wisdom Literature, an observation that later scholars, like Dean MacNeil, have also noted.[26] Such Rastafari reggae helps make Judaism more "attractive—real, whole, complete," Matisyahu declares. To test the other side of this insight, as it were, Haim spends time with Super Dane, a Crown Heights Rasta, who concedes that before listening to Matisyahu, he passed Jews on Brooklyn's streets every day, wondering why he lacked common ground with them. Because of Jews like Matisyahu, who holds "so much spirituality with what he has," Super Dane now celebrates as well as sees the similarities between Jews and Rastas. And all over New York City, "the two cultures are slipping into one another," Haim proclaims.

An appreciation for reggae culture, especially for its role in helping to establish Rastafari internationally, unites the Jews and Rastas featured in Haim's documentary. Rabbi Jacobson underlines David's musical gifts (1 Sam 16:21–23), for example, and fusion artists such as King Django and Alan Eder blend Jewish and Rasta styles, from klezmer to rock steady, to produce their "Passover reggae" riddims and "ska-mitzvah" soundscapes. In the Holy Land, singers like Iyam and combat soldiers like Tuba describe Jamaica and Israel as united, for the most part, by harsh or fraught environments (Babylonian "energies"), which reggae helps to assuage. "Reggae is the language of the people," according to Tony Ray, owner of Tel Aviv's "Rasta Pub" and, on this film, such grassroots tunes and vibes inspire self-identifying modern Israelites, such as Congo Eyal, Daddy G, Fishy, and Ras Amram, to view Rastafari as "serious business." Here, Nigel the Admore serves as Haim's uncomplicated symbol of such seriousness. Originally from Jamaica's St. Ann parish, also home to Ancient Bongo Daniel, Nigel the Admore now lives in Jerusalem, where he performs Jewish reggae to popular applause. He views all Africans in the diaspora as "displaced brothers" and, like many of them, he yearns for Zion, which he sees as a form of self-awakening, not merely as a holy place or a sacred destination.

Awake Zion's three featured topics—the Bible, anciency (or the desire to connect to one's roots), and reggae—offer an instructive window on to Rastafari and Jews "willingly and unwillingly, knowingly and unknowingly, participating in one another's culture," Haim states. On the surface Jews and Rastas revere the Star of David, lament Babylon, and allude to Zion. Here, Haim advances beyond such initial alliances, listening to practitioners of both faiths "to get the truth," to explore as well as to locate deeper connections, and, in the end, she tells a tale of unity-in-diversity, one that is replete with opportunities for spiritual hospitality. The Rastafari religious movement is becoming increasingly globalized, as I note elsewhere, and the challenge for Rastafari's latest generation involves recognizing that people around the world are more alike than different, and that differences need not prevent devotees from conversing—an insight that Haim communicates in the following interview.

An Interview with Monica Haim

DJNM: *Awake Zion* takes a multisited, transnational approach to an amazingly diverse religious movement. Before we delve into your film, please discuss your own spiritual journey, which stretches from Colombia to New York City via California.

MH: I was born in Bogota, Colombia in 1975 to a Jewish family (with half Ashkenazi and half Sephardic roots). We moved to Miami when I was five years old, and I spent a good portion of my life there. At eighteen, I moved to New York City and lived there for fifteen years, with the exception of one year, 2000, that took me to the Bay Area, where my passion for Rastafari was lit.

DJNM: You are a documentary film-maker. What value does the genre have for you and perhaps for other Jews and for Rastafari?

MH: The value of documentary filmmaking for anyone, I believe, is the fact that it invites forth a dialogue. For any cultural group, be they Jews, Rastafari, or anything in between, documentary work opens up the essence of the everyday, allowing the rest of the world to get a closer glimpse of what really goes on with them socially, historically, and spiritually.

DJNM: Relatedly, who do you feel is your most important audience?

MH: As a Jew, it excites me to elucidate for my own people the many common denominators that our culture shares with the rest of the world, though I truly feel that every audience is important because the lesson at the root of my film transcends these types of labels … or at least aims to.

DJNM: As you prepared for *Awake Zion*, were you aware of other documentary films exploring the Rastafari? If so, how would you assess them? Did you ever suffer an anxiety of influence, as it were, or were you convinced, after viewing them, that there were things Rastafari had to say to the world that they had not said in earlier documentaries?

MH: As I worked on the pre-production for *Awake Zion*, I felt there was a shortage of up-to-date information and literature about Rastafari in general. I used whatever material I could find to saturate my own knowledge of Rasta, and spent as much time with Rastas to learn about the lifestyle; so I never really felt an anxiety of influence, as you described, but rather an understanding that I would need to 'be with Rasta' in order to really get it.

DJNM: Please describe the impetus for researching and filming *Awake Zion*?

MH: It's really very simple, and I believe it happens to a lot of young Jews who encounter reggae or Rasta for the first time (usually through the music of Bob Marley). From the moment anyone has an encounter with reggae or Rasta, it becomes readily apparent—through lyrics, on cover art, and in the recurring themes and motifs—that there is some semblance of Jewish presence somehow built into the culture. Be it the word 'Zion,' the idea of repatriation, the association with ancient Israel via the Davidic descendents, and many other examples, it hit me that 'there was something Jewish about Rasta.' And so began the research …

DJNM: How did you decide which voices, Jewish and Rasta, to use in your film? And whose voice did you find most informative, and why?

MH: Besides relying on actual experts in both camps, as well as real Rastas, I also looked for voices who could somehow speak to this idea of cultural convergence through their own choices—Jews, for example, who felt the strength of their own culture through the lens of Rasta. To me, each voice is informative and adds a new dimension of perspective that ultimately celebrates our kinship as a people.

DJNM: With specific regard to your film, but without overlooking your more general experience, how do you find Rastafari ideas about Jewishness beyond the Jewish diaspora's customary limits? Many Rastas view themselves as the 'true Israelites,' for example, and several see Ethiopia as the 'real Zion.' Thoughts?

MH: I only think any of these theories are helpful when they are seen and used as bridge-building tools. When two people from seemingly polar ends of the spiritual spectrum can find a place to meet, that's what I am looking for.

DJNM: In his "Towering Babble and Glimpses of Zion: Recent Depictions of Rastafari in Cinema," Kevin J. Aylmer notes:

> The Jamaican-born, Rasta 'Babylon' metaphor has provided lyrical grist for the social consciousness of singer-songwriters and 'roots' musicians, as well as fascination in Hollywood for exploring perceptions and aspects of Rastafarian culture. Babylon crops up in hundreds of reggae songs and many movies. Within the last two decades, several films have explored this Rasta conception of the Babylon system as an integral part of a worldview and cultural perceptions. Often Babylon suggests a visceral, explicit menace, as in *The Harder They Come*; sometimes it refers to an alien, corrupting materialism run rampant, as in *Club Paradise*; and at other times it shows the subtly implicit nuances of institutional racism, as in the comedy *Cool Runnings*. But in all of these films, songs about Babylon are being sung while the viewer is engaged in a predominantly passive observation of a primarily visual phenomenon.[27]

How would you describe the perception of Babylon that emerges from your documentary? And is there something about the documentary film, as opposed to the Hollywood motion picture, that circumvents or prevents the problems associated with "a predominantly passive observation of a primarily visual phenomenon"?

MH: Given my film's particular area of exploration, the Rastafari's notion of Babylon emerges in parallel to the Jewish context, which historically refers to a place of exile. My intention throughout the whole film is to depict some of these 'shared themes,' and the idea of Babylon is at the top of that list.

DJNM: One might say that 'home,' like 'Zion,' is an antonym for Babylon, especially when one considers the feelings for home that are expressed very strongly in Psalm 137, not to mention your film's soundtrack, and I think your viewers will find themselves struck by the religious nostalgia for home that saturates your documentary. Is this a fair observation? What does home mean for you, a Rasta-identifying Jew?

MH: I should clarify that while I love, respect, honor, celebrate, and believe in Rasta, I am not Rastafari. I simply developed a curiosity and admiration that turned into a project. I also feel that while a sense of home is built in to our collective plight as humans (especially those who have been cast from theirs), it is ultimately our job to make home wherever we are.

DJNM: Some sociologists of religion, like Danièle Hervieu-Léger, note the link between 'memory' and 'religious identity,' which is a connection, however implicit, that you also make in your film.[28] For Hervieu-Léger, collective or group memory forms and endures through elaborate strategies of disremembering, scrutinizing, and concocting. In her view, all religions promote memory and continuity by emphasizing the ancestry of believers and devotees ('my father was a wandering Aramean' among Jews, let's say, and Rasta reverence for the *Kebra Negast*'s account of the Solomonic line of kings, for example). How would you describe the part memory plays in Rastafari as well as Jewish identity? And are Jews and Rastas united, at least in part, in their shared-yet-different attention to elaborate strategies of disremembering, scrutinizing, and concocting?

MH: I think that when it comes to Rasta, memory is elemental, because so much of Rasta's essence has to do with revitalization of the sense of history and identity that was blatantly stripped from the African slaves during their forced captivity. In a way, Rasta *is* the rememberance and glorification of this lost identity.

DJNM: Please describe today's reggae scene in Israel. Is it religious, for example, or is it primarily an urban subcultural force?

MH: The reggae scene in Israel today is not particularly religious, but is instead born from the energy of tension and political strife that prevails in the area.

DJNM: How has your documentary been received in Brooklyn? In Jamaica? In Israel?

MH: Thankfully, because the film ultimately has a positive message about unity, tolerance, and kinship, it is always received well.

DJNM: In your opinion, what does the future hold for Rastas? What do you think we will be saying about them in, say, fifty or eighty years?

MH: That's a tough one. I can only hope that Rasta will continue to develop as a pivotal voice of empowerment for anyone in the world who feels oppressed or marginalized.

Coping with Babylon: The Proper Rastology (2007)

Oliver Hill's film describes how disciplined or 'conscious' livity enables Rastas, as true Israelites, to navigate life in a social system that places profit over personhood and materialism over meaning-making, 'Babylon' in the language of the Rastafari.[29] Sitting outside Kingston's Bob Marley Museum, dreadlocked Paul Kelly scorns late modern capitalism. "Greed, power and wealth is what Babylon seeks," he contends. "I and I seek the preservation of life." Barry Chevannes adds: "Rasta has a critique of the world, and how the world is going." The Rastas in this film equate the United States of America with the world, and they label America's free market system, especially the wealth inequality it fosters, Babylonian. As Hill shows, though, Rastafari reggae speaks truth to such power. An artful, militant analysis of the Bush Doctrine enlivens the music video for "New World Order" by conscious deejay Fire Key. Dub poet Mutabaruka ("Life and Debt") performs in concert, deploring gun violence. And singers like Freddie McGregor ("Jah Love Di Whole a Wi") and Luciano ("Material World") use back-stage or at-home interviews to describe reggae as "message music." In the end, reggae preaches "positive livity," which in this film means that brethren and sistren are able to cope with Babylon when they implement three lifestyle choices. No two Rastas make the same choice, as Hill reveals, and yet practicing "tafari livity," however broadly understood, acts as an antidote to Babylon's toxicity.

First, the act of cultivating livity means upholding "roots and culture," which involves becoming literate in black history, especially the history of the slave trade, and in colonialism's centuries-old denigration of Africa. Without such literacy, confusion abounds. 'Babylon' is code for the "confused self," musician Peter Morgan ("Children of Selassie") declares, which explains why reggae seeks to conscientize the hearer or, in other words, to help Rastafari celebrate as well as know their own culture. Against dancehall reggae's "frivolousness and profanity," Luciano defines roots reggae as "reality music," an attention-grabbing sonic mix of rhythm and lyrics broadcasting black somebodiness and African greatness. All good reggae is "survival music," singer Half Pint states, because it articulates "our liberation, our life, our love, and our heritage." Selassie and Garvey give focus to Rastafari's heritage, Chevannes explains, and although Rastas differently embody their faith in such storied figures, roots reggae propagates their basic importance as the basis of "a revelation that consumes them [Rastafari] and puts them on a different, particular path for wholesomeness and integrity."

Second, ritual paves the way toward Rastafari righteousness. My book describes such rituals, like ganja smoking and flashing dreadlocks, and it notes how and why various Rastafari mansions approach sacred action(s) differently. Hill's film illustrates such in-house variety. Strict clothing and dietary regulations as well as explicit, gendered concepts of purity and pollution govern ritual life in the Bobo Shanti commune, for example, and both insiders and outsiders appear on camera to clarify such austere, patriarchal livity.[30] According to Prince Jesus Emmanuel, a member of the Bull Bay commune, ritual exactitude fosters black self-reliance and self-worth. In contrast to such 'narrow path' isolationism, members of the Twelve Tribes of Israel mansion, like Phyllis Freeman, a nurse from Elmont, New York, integrate themselves wherever they go. And generally, ritual is a picture preference; some Rastas in this mansion see the herb as a sacrament, for example, and some do not. In the end, though, Chevannes claims that the Twelve Tribes mansion promotes a livity that middle-class blacks like Freeman find appealing. Decisions are often left to the individual, which suggests a kind of religious privatism prevails, where one copes with Babylon by oneself yet from within an inclusive community. Some Rastas outside the Twelve Tribes mansion find fault with this middle-class focus. If the Twelve Tribes Rastas tend to think through the Nazarite vow for themselves, for example, then Priest Dermot Fagan, the founder of the School of Vision, a recent Rastafari mansion, proclaims that "the proper Rastology" involves "knowledge [of Selassie's divinity], plus locks and beard." The Christian religion represents another source of in-house debate. Whereas the Bobo Shanti problematize Christianity, members of the Twelve Tribes mansion cement connections between their faith and the faith of Christians. Freeman sees Jesus's spirit in Selassie, for example, and Freddie McGregor believes scripture's salvation history—its broad, narrative sweep from Genesis to Revelation—underlines Jesus's and Selassie's redemptive importance for humankind. Abuna Ammanuel Foxe, the originator of the Church of Haile Selassie I, denounces the Twelve Tribes' religiously inclusive tendencies. Foxe sees Christianity as a "conqueror faith" that privileges the "Caucasian concept of civilization." Also, he distrusts both Bobo Shanti and Twelve Tribes because, in his view, their roots and culture are tied to West Africa rather than to Abyssinia. Like the main Rastafari mansions, though, Foxe favors ritual action, even if other Rastafari sometimes struggle to share his belief in the wisdom of observing *seven* sacraments (Prov 9:1). The website for the Church of Haile Selassie I stipulates regular "temple worship through liturgical chant and rituals dated back to the days of Moses in the Wilderness," and Foxe insists that without such temple worship, Rastafari would not be able to cope with Babylon.[31] Rather than the sinuous robes and tricolor tams of the Bobo Shanti, though, the temple dress code at the Church of Haile Selassie I is "business casual." In Hill's film, Mutabaruka contends that "the beauty of Rastafari" lies in such intra-religious diversity. He may be correct. As Rastas try to live into the new millennium, though, it may not be sufficient to practice ritual action as well as uphold roots and culture; the task of coping with Babylon may require that Rastafari think beyond their mansions and consider centralizing the movement. Hill's film shows that centralization is an important part of the process whereby Rastas work out their understanding of salvation.

Third, Rastafari cope with Babylon by living out their salvation in one of two ways, either through rehabilitation or repatriation, and the effort to centralize the Rastafari, which insiders and outsiders in Hill's film advocate, epitomizes the rehabilitation model, together with a desire to educate Rastafari's next generation.

Foxe favors repatriation. And his followers in the Church of Haile Selassie I, like Junior Anderson and Denton Smith, champion the same cause, content to concur with Foxe's mission to use the "third world as a base" to train people to move to Ethiopia. Priest Fagan also favors repatriation. But he hopes to settle his people in Palestine, not Ethiopia, although he does not appear on camera to offer a fulsome explanation for this venue change. Fagan's effusiveness appears in his attack on "the world's secret order," which he connects to North America, to Free Masonry, and to the Illuminati. Such groups represent Babylon, especially the United States of America ("Under Satanic Authority"), and Fagan believes they are all trying to surreptitiously implant microbiochips in our bodies, in order to control our minds. In Hill's film, which was shot on location in 2006, Fagan announces that he does not intend to live in Jamaica after 2007; and, he declares that "celestial ships" or UFOs (2 Kgs 2:11; 6:17) are coming to expedite repatriation. These days, Fagan leads worshippers at the School of Vision's "Jah Sabbath" (Ex 20:8) gathering on Mount Zion Hill in Kingston, Jamaica's capital. Ras Sydney Da Silva, the elected President of the Rastafarian Centralization Organization, recognizes the appeal of repatriation, but he prefers rehabilitation, which he understands as the unification of the many, diverse houses and mansions of Rastafari. Da Silva believes Rastas will learn to cope with Babylon by coming together to transform it, assembling under an "umbrella" organization that promotes education. Dilpi Champagnie, who teaches at Kingston's Amha Selassie School, agrees. He thinks his brethren and sistren will move forward when they join hands to teach the next generation of Rastafari, and Mutabaruka maintains that Garveyism, "the pan-Africanist part of Rastafari," must pulsate at the heart of this educative process. In sharp contrast to Da Silva and others, though, Foxe insists that such Rastafari ecumenism is an unworkable vision, much too impractical, and he likens it to Daniel's image of a statue with feet partly of iron and partly of clay (Dan 2:32–34). Foxe is alone, if ardent, in this conviction. McGregor claims that centralization is *the* issue facing new millenium Rastas, for example, and Chevannes holds that if the Rastafari desire "political clout," then they will need to unify.

Bob Marley championed such unity. He pushed past petty and multiplied denominationalism to embrace "all houses of Rastafari," Paul Kelly asserts, and Marley did so because he hoped Rastas would help one other to avoid late modern capitalism's corrosive effects. Marley was Rasta's first global ambassador, and he cultivated livity in the lion's den, eventually finding a way to cope with Babylon amid the clamor of his international celebrity. In his afterlife, he continues to be a model who blazes a trail. "The man who can meditate on top of a mountain where no one is, is a great man," Mutabaruka declares, "but the man who can meditate in a market, with noise, is the greater man." Many Rastafari movement insiders and outsiders think Marley symbolizes this "greater man," and *Coping with Babylon* certainly supports this thought, but it is Kevin Macdonald's *Marley* (2012) that validates how this tuneful, spiritual force for change inspired countless, diverse followers of His Imperial Majesty.

Marley (2012)

Africa is a continent of great diversity, and her cultures, traditions, and religions are steeped in ancient wisdom and beauty. But Macdonald's film does not begin here; rather, it opens with a docent taking the crew and us, the viewers, through Ghana's Cape Coast, a fortified castle, which was built to house captured Africans until the arrival of the slave ships.[32] At one point the camera alights on the notorious Door of No Return, through which the slaves passed before setting sail for the feared voyage to the New World, and then the film's gaze turns towards the Caribbean, as an aerial shot en route to Nine Mile, in the parish of St. Ann, transports us to the unassuming, rural Jamaican birthplace of Robert Nesta Marley OM (1945–1981). Macdonald's biopic then proceeds out from this picturesque outpost of the African diaspora, telling Marley's story through concert footage, archival interviews, and several conversations with his friends and family. Most of the signposts along Marley's life-journey are well known, given the numerous books and documentaries that have surfaced since his untimely death in 1981, yet this 145-minute film reveals several insights into reggae's global icon.[33] Some of the key aspects of Marley's personality to emerge are his sense of rejection; his yearning for a father figure; his Afrocentric spirituality of social justice; and his desire to use music to foster solidarity and unity. More challenging matters discussed include his treatment of Rita Marley and other women.

Born to Norval Sinclair Marley and Cedella Booker, Bob Marley held both British-Jamaican and African-Jamaican ancestry, and many in Nine Mile viewed him as bi-racial, multiple heritage or, to invoke the term that surfaces throughout this film, mixed race. Norval provided for his family, but he often spent time away from them, and he suffered a fatal heart attack in 1955, when Bob Marley was ten years old. Being bi-racial bothered Marley. Although he made friends with talented youngsters like Neville Livingston, better known as Bunny Wailer, a frequent interviewee in this film, Marley felt lonely and rejected in Nine Mile. Eventually, he moved with Booker to Trench Town, Kingston, when he was twelve. Bunny holds that Marley's mixed race ancestry made him feel liminal, like he was caught betwixt and between, neither fish nor fowl. Judy Mowatt, one of Marley's backing vocalists, and Rita, Marley's widow, suggest that this troubled psychology explains his global appeal: Marley the outsider wrote and performed songs about outsiders, such as "Corner Stone" and "Small Axe," and now, as then, outsiders thrum to Marley's work.[34]

The move to impoverished Trench Town underlined Marley's outsiderness. When Bunny moved there, however, they joined up with Peter Tosh and explored various musical styles, like ska and rock steady, before deciding on reggae, which soon became the soundtrack to the struggling lives of marginalized misfits drawn to the first soundings of an unconventional theology, Rastafari. This documentary maps Marley's journey to Rasta, an Afrocentric "liberationist religion" preaching self-reliance and self-confidence, and it suggests that Marley's troubled childhood explains, at least in part, why he joined the movement. "In the knowledge of Haile Selassie, Bob found his real father, which he never really knew," Neville Garrick, sometime artistic director of the Wailers, claims. There were other father figures, such as record producers Clement 'Sir Coxsone' Dodd and Lee 'Scratch' Perry, but none rivalled Selassie, and "the deeper Bob got into the Rastafarian faith, the more his music became entwined," Clive Chin, another record producer, states.

By the early 1970s, Marley was using reggae as the primary mechanism for the transmission of his Rastafari self-understanding, and *Catch a Fire*, which he recorded with the aid of Chris Blackwell, the founder and then owner of Island Records, was released to critical acclaim in 1973. It was the first of many albums mixing themes of Rastafari livity, romantic love, and the messy nature of political engagement. Here, Macdonald's film emphasizes how Marley's reggae, "Exodus" and "One Love" particularly, reads the history of downtrodden Jamaicans through the lens of biblical history, a theo-musical strategy that fosters struggle, solidarity, and hope for the future. Recent commentators, like Dean MacNeil, also stress that scripture quotations and allusions in studio albums released on Blackwell's label repay close scrutiny:

> There is much to be gained from listening to Bob Marley. He teaches us to be actively engaged with scripture, to see ourselves in the Bible, to pray unceasingly, and to cherish life. He teaches us to see the world with a wisdom consciousness, that there is often more than meets the eye, and that we are sometimes in the midst of a spiritual war, the solution to which is love. He teaches that God is with us always. He teaches us to stand firm in our convictions, to favor knowledge over belief, to stand up for what is right, and to resist the ways of Babylon. [This said,] … the resistance against Babylon is only part of a process that includes liberating people from Babylon. These are the twin barrels of Marley's musical shotgun.[35]

When Marley took up residence in Blackwell's Kingston property, 56 Hope Road, Marley intended "to bring the ghetto uptown," and so he did, eventually building his own recording space, Tuff Gong Studios, which meant that many musicians appeared at the house to help Marley craft and promulgate his Rastafari message of resistance and redemption. Reggae came alive in this place, Aston 'Family Man'

Barrett declares, with the drums serving as the genre's "heartbeat" and the bass as its "backbone." Other interviewees also reveal that during this period, the early 1970s, 56 Hope Road became a "Rasta camp," because it attracted brethren and sistren from far and wide, expressly those in Kingston's projects, to assemble, sit, and talk about religion, politics, and history.

If 56 Hope Road may best be understood as a Rastafari think tank, a place where pulsating reggae riffs and a melodic call to arms soundtrack ganja-induced reasoning sessions, then it seems to have been a traditional or patriarchal one. We are told that everyone consumed wholesome meals, for example, and that brethren obligated sistren to practice a strict dress code (Gen 1:29; Deut 22:5; 2 Kgs 9:30; Prov 6:25). Rita Marley was not allowed to wear "war paint" (to use cosmetics to beautify the face), she was forbidden to wear pants, and she was advised to ignore her partner's infidelities and, instead, to see him as faithful to Jah if not to her. On screen Rita Marley likens herself to a "guardian angel," commissioned to protect Bob Marley from admirers and hangers-on, and she rationalizes his behaviors by emphasizing his mission, which she compares to "an evangelist's campaign, to bring people closer to Jah," and to one another.[36]

Marley reveals that reggae divides as well as unifies. The Wailers parted ways in 1974, for example, and a new line-up emerged. Peter Tosh railed against "Whitewell," his snarky name for Chris Blackwell, and two days before a free concert ("Smile Jamaica," December 5, 1976) that was designed to respond to growing political dis-ease in the capital, an unknown marksman broke into 56 Hope Road and injured three individuals, including Marley. Relocating to the Bahamas and then to England created the distance Marley needed to write and record new Rastafari hymns, songs like "Jamming," which speaks of bullets being unable to stop the righteous from their journey to Zion. Assuredly, Marley's brush with death inspired fresh creativity, and it inspired him to redouble his efforts in using reggae to bring people together, as evinced by his performance in the 1978 "One Love Peace Concert," during which he worked the audience into a frenzy by bringing two rival politicians up on stage to join hands. Neither People's National Party advocate nor Jamaica Labour Party backer, Marley found himself in the middle, on the platform as in life, and here the film reiterates how his liminality helped him unite others. *Marley* also wants us to realize that the singer had to fly back from exile in London to perform at this concert, and Macdonald's footage of fans greeting Marley at the Kingston airport evokes the mood of joyous bedlam that Selassie found when his plane arrived in April 1966.

Marley flew to Africa in 1980, a decision that made sense in light of three core aspects of his life at the time: his long-standing hope for repatriation to the Motherland; the religiopolitical, pro-Africa message behind albums like *Survival* and *Uprising*; and his basic amity with Africans' anticolonial yearning for black somebodiness and political freedom. Marley journeyed to west central Africa, for example, and besides appearing at a concert in Gabon's capital, Libreville, he met with youths at a local beach and answered searching questions about his Rastafari livity. He also performed at Zimbabwe's Independence Day festivities, April 17, 1980, using his own money to underwrite the event. With this and other concerts, like the one in Milan that attracted 100,000 fans, Marley almost single-handedly situated Rastafari reggae on humankind's cultural map.

Tragedy accompanied Marley's global triumphs. He developed cancer, and although he initially invoked his livity and refused medical advice, Carlton 'Pee Wee' Fraser, a Rasta physician, eventually urged treatment. Chemotherapy rounds caused Marley's locks to fall out, and Macdonald informs us that Marley read the book of Job as the remaining dreads were cut. Marley died in May 1981; he was only thirty-six years old. While not by definition a martyr, he was tragically struck down in his prime. Perhaps because, like many martyrs, he died at the zenith of his professional and personal life, as a young, gallant, athletic, musical black prince, he quickly rose from the dead, and today, his afterlife is well known. Although some scholars disapprove of how commercial products linked with Marley—from lava-lamps to relaxation drinks—serve to mollify the Nine Mile theo-musical activist, they agree that his is the soul of Jah Music.[37] If some Rastafari await Selassie's return, Marley has been resurrected, again and again.

This consensus perhaps appears nowhere more clearly than in *Marley*'s end credits, when the camera shows us different people in various countries jamming to his familiar songs. Such scenes précis a nineteen-minute special feature ("Around the World") on the film's DVD, an extra that reinforces Marley's global superstardom. But if Macdonald explores the question: Who is Bob Marley, the answer, it seems, is that in his resurrection, Marley has surpassed Selassie. From India to Japan and from Kenya to Brazil, reggae fans line up and declare their Marley-love. In his physical absence, these people seem to feel that they have *become* Marley, somehow destined to carry his torch and to stand up for their rights. It is in this sense that *Marley*'s ending recalls a different film, one that tells the story of another black man famous for his international call to action.

Toward the close of the Spike Lee biopic *Malcolm X* (1992), the late Nelson Mandela appears on screen in a classroom, standing in front of Soweto children. The teacher asks, "Who is Malcolm X," with child after child claiming, "I am Malcolm X"; No, "I am Malcolm X"; Ah, yes, "I am Malcolm X." Neither life nor death can contain Malcolm X, as the American Civil Rights movement morphs into the anti-apartheid struggle. The global Marley fans in Macdonald's film exude similar sentiments. They identify with Marley. They sing his songs. And they appeal to his spirit. In rising to greet Marley, to embrace the eternally youthful prince, they embody and become Marley, enmeshed perhaps in different circumstances yet chanting down Babylon, whether it be on the frontlines of Egypt's Arab Spring or at the heart of the Tibetan Buddhist struggle against Chinese occupation. Like Malcolm X, Bob Marley had to die so that he could continue to live, to inspire.

Viewers who watch the "Around the World" extra will find themselves inspired. They also will find themselves returning to Ghana, where Macdonald's documentary first began, to hear local artists both praising Marley and performing reggae in the shadow of the Cape Coast slave fort, which inspires me to think that Marley made music as a way to figuratively walk back through the Door of (No) Return and to help repair ancestral links broken by the transatlantic slave trade. Others have followed in Marley's footsteps, as it were, and some have taken reggae and Rastafari to other parts of Africa and, indeed, to the world. The next chapter explores two of them, Rocky Dawuni and Blakk Rasta.

Conclusion

The six documentary films surveyed in this chapter cover a twenty-year period, 1992–2012, and they uphold the varieties of Rastafari religious experience, giving voice to numerous insiders (and outsiders), who may best be seen as reel or real Rasta, everyday brethren and sistren who provide an expansive context to the movement's history. Different stories emerge in such films, and through different styles of filmmaking, but, taken together, they counterbalance Hollywood's ersatz images of Rasta. And from *The Emperor's Birthday* to *Marley*, the language of art functions as the common denominator, because reggae's sprightly signatures here soundtrack the diverse, wide-ranging livities of women and men eager to reclaim a sense of black somebodiness and cultural agency denied by Babylon.

The Rastafari are internationally well known, in part due to reggae, and my next chapter considers the brethren and sistren who have used Ghana as their gateway to Africa. Interviews with two Ghanaian musicians, Rocky Dawuni and Blakk Rasta, help me to demonstrate how today's artful Africans are indigenizing Marley's Jamaican musical model and then exporting it across the world. The special feature in Macdonald's film also includes an informative segment on Marley's reception in Japan and, to reveal how this reception complicates the usual interpretation of a term like the 'African diaspora,' I review Marvin D. Sterling's work on Japanese Rastafari.[38] A concluding interview with Sterling emphasizes how and why today's Rastafari uphold customized livities and craft hybridized sounds.

Notes

1 On Rastafari visual art, see Wolfgang Bender, editor, *Rastafarian Art* (Kingston, Jamaica; Miami, FL: Ian Randle Publishers, 2005). In addition, see Randall Morris, *Redemption Songs: The Self-Taught Artists of Jamaica* (Winston-Salem, NC: Winston-Salem State University, 1997). On film, reggae, and the branding of the Rastafari religious movement, see: Noel Leo Erskine, *From Garvey to Marley: Rastafari Theology* (Gainesville, FL: The University Press of Florida, 2007); Stephen Foehr, *Jamaican Warriors: Reggae, Roots and Culture* (London: Sanctuary Publishing, 2000); and Ennis B. Edmonds, *Rastafari: From Outcasts to Culture Bearers* (Oxford and New York: Oxford University Press, 2003), 97–115.
2 Kevin J. Aylmer, "Towering Babble and Glimpses of Zion: Recent Depictions of Rastafari in Cinema," in Nathaniel Samuel Murrell, William David Spencer, and Adrian Anthony McFarlane, editors, *Chanting Down Babylon: The Rastafari Reader* (Philadelphia:

Temple University Press, 1998), 284–307. I think Aylmer does for Rastafari in cinema what scholars like Lizabeth Paravisini-Gebert have done for the filmic misrepresentation of Haitian Vodou. See Lizabeth Paravisini-Gebert, "Women Possessed: Eroticism and Exoticism in the Representation of Woman as Zombie," in Margarite Fernández Olmos and Lizabeth Paravisini-Gebert, editors, *Sacred Possessions: Vodou, Santería, Obeah, and the Caribbean* (New Brunswick, NJ: Rutgers University Press, 1999), 37–58.

3 Aylmer, "Towering Babble and Glimpses of Zion," 288.

4 *Ibid.*, 291, 292–293.

5 *Ibid.*, 293.

6 *Ibid.*, 294.

7 *Ibid.*, 302.

8 *Ibid.*, 295. The Babylon trope unites the aforementioned films, even if each movie uses it differently: "Often Babylon suggests a visceral, explicit menace, as in *The Harder They Come*; sometimes it refers to an alien, corrupting materialism run rampant, as in *Club Paradise*; and at other times it shows the subtly implicit nuances of institutional racism, as in the comedy *Cool Runnings*." *Ibid.*, 284.

9 They resemble jellyfish, to the untrained eye, but they are, in fact, Portuguese men-of-war.

10 Aylmer, "Towering Babble and Glimpses of Zion," 297–298.

11 Other documentary films featuring Rastafari include: *Back to My Roots: Living in Zion* (2008); *Bad Friday: Rastafari after Coral Gardens* (2011); *Chant Down Babylon* (2013); *Land of Look Behind* (2006); *Made in Jamaica* (2009); *One Love: Word Sounds & Powah* (2008); *Rastafari Voices* (1979); *Rent a Rasta* (2006); and *The First Rasta* (2011).

12 *The Emperor's Birthday* (New York: Filmakers Library, 1992).

13 Harold G. Marcus, *A History of Ethiopia* (Berkeley, CA: University of California Press, 1994), 181–220.

14 On how this controversy spilled over into the new millennium, see: http://www.telegraph.co.uk/news/worldnews/africaandindianocean/ethiopia/1342650/Quandary-over-funeral-plan-for-Haile-Selassie.html. Accessed March 30, 2014.

15 Jahlani Niaah, "The Rastafari Presence in Ethiopia: A Contemporary Perspective," in Michael Barnett, editor, *Rastafari in the New Millennium: A Rastafari Reader*, with a foreword by Rex Nettleford (Syracuse, NY: Syracuse University Press, 2012), 66–88. Also see Erin C. Macleod, "Water Development Projects and Cultural Citizenship: Rastafari Engagement with the Oromo in Shashemene, Ethiopia," in Barnett, editor, *Rastafari in the New Millennium*, 89–103. In addition, see "Letter from the Rastafari Community of Shashemane to UN Secretary General Kofi Annan, June 27, 2001," in Katherine McKittrick and Clyde Woods, editors, *Black Geographies and the Politics of Place* (Toronto; Cambridge, MA: Between the Lines; South End Press, 2007), 247–248. On some of the difficulties in Shashemene, see Norimitsu Onishi, "Uneasy Bond Inside a Promised Land," *New York Times*, August 4, 2001: A4. For other news, see: http://www.guardian.co.uk/world/video/2010/jul/23/rastafarians-shashamane-ethiopia. Accessed March 30, 2014.

16 Niaah, "The Rastafari Presence in Ethiopia," 84. American Rastafari have been very active in supporting such sustainable development projects. For details, see: http://www.shashamane.org/index.html. Accessed March 30, 2014.

17 Barbara Makeda Blake Hannah, *Joseph: A Rasta Reggae Fable* (Oxford: Macmillan Caribbean, 2006), 173. Also see Emily Raboteau, *Searching for Zion: The Quest for Home in the African Diaspora* (New York: Atlantic Monthly Press, 2013), 109–179.

18 Mircea Eliade, *The Sacred and the Profane: The Nature of Religion*, translated by Willard R. Trask (New York: Harcourt, Brace and Company, 1959), 64–65.

19 John Homiak, "Rastafari Voices Reach Ethiopia: *The Emperor's Birthday* by John Dollar," *American Anthropologist* 96.4 (1994): 961.

20 *Roots Daughters: The Women of Rastafari* (Toronto: Fari International Productions, 1992). Also see Masani Montague, *Dread Culture: A Rastawoman's Story* (Toronto: Sister Vision Press, 1994).

21 Noel Leo Erskine, "Women in Rastafari," in Marcia Y. Riggs and James Samuel Logan, editors, *Ethics That Matters: African, Caribbean, and African American Sources* (Minneapolis: Fortress Press, 2012), 49.

22 *Ras tafari* (New York: Insight Media, 2001).

23 See: http://jamaica-gleaner.com/gleaner/20130528/carib/carib1.html. Accessed March 30, 2014.

24 *Awake Zion: A Documentary* (New York: Cinema Guild, 2006).

25 In recent years, Matisyahu has taken great pains to tamp down his Hasidic or Orthodox sympathies. See http://www.huffingtonpost.com/gabe-crane/matisyahu-spiritual-evolution_b_1153599.html. Accessed March 30, 2014.

26 Dean MacNeil, *The Bible and Bob Marley: Half the Story Has Never Been Told* (Eugene, OR: Cascade Books, 2013), 38–100.

27 Aylmer, "Towering Babble and Glimpses of Zion," 284.

28 Danièle Hervieu-Léger, *Religion as a Chain of Memory*, translated by Simon Lee (New Brunswick, NJ: Rutgers University Press, 2000).

29 *Coping with Babylon: The Proper Rastology* (Oaks, PA: MVD Visual, 2007).

30 Also see: http://www.huckmagazine.com/features/boboshanti/. Accessed March 30, 2014.

31 For the Church's website, see http://www.himchurch.org/. Accessed March 30, 2014.

32 *Marley* (Los Angeles: Magnolia Home Entertainment, 2012).

33 For a selection of such sources, see: Colin Grant, *The Natural Mystics: Marley, Tosh, and Wailer* (New York: W.W. Norton, 2011); Chris Salewicz, *Bob Marley: The Untold Story* (New York: Faber and Faber, 2010); Jason Toynbee, *Bob Marley: Herald of a Postcolonial World?* (Cambridge, England; Malden, MA: Polity, 2007); and Timothy White, *Catch a Fire: The Life of Bob Marley* (New York: Henry Holt, 2006). In addition, see *Bob Marley: Time Will Tell* (Santa Monica, CA: Immortal, 2006) and *Rebel Music: The Bob Marley Story* (New York: Palm Pictures, 2000).

34 Publicity surrounding the documentary's release emphasizes Marley's troubled psychology, brought on by intense reflection on his bi-racial biology. For details, see: http://www.theguardian.com/film/2012/apr/08/bob-marley-life-documentary-macdonald and http://www.pbs.org/newshour/art/ziggy-marley/. Both accessed March 30, 2014.

35 MacNeil, *The Bible and Bob Marley*, 144, 145.

36 One such infidelity involved a former Miss World, Cindy Breakspeare. For additional details, see: http://jamaica-gleaner.com/gleaner/20140220/ent/ent2.html. Accessed March 30, 2014.

37 On the critical side, see Dave Thompson, *Reggae and Caribbean Music* (San Francisco: Backbeat Books, 2002). Also see the essays in Eleanor Wint and Carolyn Cooper, editors, *Bob Marley: The Man and His Music* (Kingston, Jamaica: Arawak Publications, 2003). On today's transcultural reggae, see the essays in Carolyn Cooper, editor, *Global Reggae* (Kingston, Jamaica: Canoe Press, 2012).

38 Marvin D. Sterling, *Babylon East: Performing Dancehall, Roots Reggae, and Rastafari in Japan* (Durham, NC: Duke University Press, 2010).

6

ARTFUL AFRICANS AT HOME AND ABROAD

Ghana and Japan

Introduction

Repatriation pulsates at the heart of Rastafari's doctrinal dimension, as earlier chapters recognize, and even though many contemporary brethren and sistren work for, as well as speak of, rehabilitation, Rastas have always made a point of returning to Africa. Some have made it back to Ethiopia, home of His Imperial Majesty Emperor Haile Selassie I, and Erin C. MacLeod's recent work documents this quest.[1] Other Rastas have taken up residence in Ghana, the first country south of the Sahara to secure freedom from European colonial powers.[2] Ghanaian Rastafari represent the focus of this last chapter's greater part.

A few Ghanaian Rastafari live in small settlements, making money by playing nightly reggae in Akuma Village, not far from historic James Town. Some sell beads and fabrics at the National Cultural Centre, on the 28th February Road in Accra's city center. Still more offer Nyabinghi drum lessons at Kokrobite Beach, location for the Academy of African Music and Arts Ltd, west of the capital. In addition, Rastas can be observed strolling through the campus of the University of Ghana at Legon, pondering political issues, or else reasoning with visitors arriving in Ghana to study and celebrate pan-Africanism at the W.E.B. Du Bois Centre, in Accra's Cantonments area. While the more rural sistren and brethren congregate in Jamaican expatriate neighborhoods up in the Akwapim Mountains around Aburo, some of the more urbane Rastas debate African history and culture in the shadow of the old European forts situated in Cape Coast and Elmina. Even the Muslim region of Northern Ghana hosts several Rastafari communities, especially in the larger towns of Tamale and Bolgatanga. As the close of Kevin Macdonald's *Marley* (2012) documentary implies, Marley-inspired Rastafari have made it back to Africa, passed through the Door of (No) Return and, on top of Mount Zion, they have raised the Red, Gold, and Green standard.[3]

Apart from Neil J. Savishinsky's doctoral dissertation, together with his article, now dated, scholarship on Ghanaian Rastafari has been sparse, although studies by Elom Dovlo, Janice Kerfoot, Claire Stafford, Jonathan Tanis, and Carmen White have appeared in recent years, which suggests academic interest is picking up.[4] Based on a decade's fieldwork, my last chapter corrects this oversight by first discussing Rastafari as a 1970s religious-cultural import to Ghana, focusing on the changing fashions, arts, and message allied to the movement. After this initial scene-setting, I indicate that Ghanaian Rastafari can be best discerned through local Rasta livities, which are shaped and reshaped by both Ghanaian-born and non-Ghanaian Rastafari. Brethren and sistren in assorted Ghanaian communities hold distinct and often conflicting beliefs, in *three areas of Rastafari's doctrinal dimension* especially: their understanding of the character and role of Selassie; their grasp of the Ethiopian-centered aspects of their religion; and their picture of salvation and its political or moral repercussions. An emerging eclecticism with regard to beliefs about Selassie and Ethiopia entails that Ghana accommodates the varieties of Rastafari religious experience.

Ghanaian Rastafari reggae anchors what I do here, and I feature interviews with Rocky Dawuni, an Afro-roots singer-songwriter, and Blakk Rasta, an Accra-based musician and radio presenter.[5] Both artists stress the local as well as global nature of their faith, as we will see. Dawuni, in particular, symbolizes Rastafari's internationalization. After all, he habitually travels over different territories, both literally and figuratively, and he appears to work best when he synthesizes and showcases both African *and* Western influences, earning respect from peoples associated with each realm. In the end, I hold that Ghana is an important country to consider when assessing Rastafari's development because, first, it houses many, different, although integrated, Rastafari communities. And second, the apparent tensions between Ghanaian and non-Ghanaian Rastas illumine the nature and scope of what might be termed the 'Africanization' of Rastafari.

Having examined Rastafari in Africa, or at home, I then travel abroad, in the mind's eye, to briefly ponder the issues featured in Marvin D. Sterling's *Babylon East: Performing Dancehall, Roots Reggae, and Rastafari in Japan*. This 2010 study considers Rastafari beyond the usual boundaries of the African diaspora. Here Sterling charts Afro-Asian cultural exchange, tracing the development of Jamaican dancehall reggae culture through five phases. He discusses dancers like Junko Kudo, musicians like Sawa, and sound systems like Mighty Crown. He maps the Japanese youth who travel to Jamaica in search of self-actualization, he surveys Jamaican attitudes to non-Jamaican appropriation of Jamaican culture, and he describes how "Rasta-identifying Japanese" use dread talk to articulate their rejection of Japan's ties with Western capitalism.[6] I do not treat Sterling's book comprehensively, because it deserves to be studied on its own terms, yet I add to my summary Sterling's own commentary, drawn from an interview he gave to me recently—an exchange confirming how *Babylon East* complicates our sense of what we might call the 'artful African diaspora.' In the last analysis, I argue that whether it be at home or abroad, Rastafari represents a religion of continuing flux and diversity.

Rasta as Religious-Cultural Import to Ghana

Reggae is like 'highlife,' the most popular form of Ghanaian music, which blends both African and Caribbean influences and can be traced to the 1920s and 1930s. While the late South African singer Lucky Dube pioneered reggae in places like Ghana during the 1970s, other imports, such as Don Carlos, Jimmy Cliff, and Marley, not forgetting more recent acts such as Black Uhuru, Steel Pulse, and Luciano, have assembled to create a certain ethos that, from one perspective, may be seen as Rasta. In all likelihood, Rasta as a religious-cultural import influenced a few Ghanaian youth to practice Rastafari in the 1970s and 1980s. Its social message, often wrapped in musical garb, would have been appealing to disenfranchised youth during Ghana's long years of economic mismanagement and domestic privation.[7]

Reggae was, and remains, an important Rasta fashion, and so too is the general look of the Rastafari, particularly the dreadlocks, which carry appeal in Ghana.[8] It is possible that these early Rastas observed the similarity between the appearance of Rasta celebrities like Marley, with his matted hair, and traditional African fetish priests and, thus, perceived Rastafari as an authentically African way of life. Okomfo Anokye is worth noting here as a legendary figure in Ghanaian religion and culture.[9] According to Ashanti mythology, he established the Ashanti Kingdom by calling forth its sacred Golden Stool from the sky. In addition, Ashantis claim that one of the three palm nuts he threw on the ground marks the spot that would later become Kumasi, the capital of the Ashanti kingdom. Furthermore, they link him to a legendary sword, observable today in a small room behind Kumasi's Okomfo Anokye Hospital. Tradition states that this sword was mysteriously placed at the exact spot where Okomfo Anokye called forth the Golden Stool. Royal lore claims that the Ashanti dynasty will suffer unspeakable tragedies should the sword ever be removed. But not only do Ashantis treat Okomfo Anokye as their founder and protector, they hold him as one of their highest fetish priests, mysteriously born as a locksman with fully grown and matted hair. This arresting detail is not lost on current Ghanaian Rastafari. And more than a few non-Rastafari Ghanaians have remarked to me that with the emergence of Rastafari among Ghanaian youth in the mid-to-late 1970s, fetish priests found a wider audience for their words and deeds.

Ras Menelik, for example, is a self-described "Rasta fetish priest" whom I first encountered in the Beach Bay area of Accra, which lies in the shadow of the Mausoleum of Kwame Nkrumah, Ghana's first President. After an initial meeting in a local restaurant, Ras Menelik invited me to his compound. With echoes of Yahweh's instructions to Moses before the burning bush, Ras Menelik instructed me, upon entering, to remove my shoes, for I was on holy ground (Ex 3:5). Inside

FIGURE 15 Okomfo Anokye (2010). Photo: Darren J.N. Middleton.

his sparsely decorated home, he had constructed an eye-catching "fetish shrine." Colorful bottles, incense sticks, ganja spliffs, fresh fruit (which we consumed, scattering the seeds on the shrine "to respect His Imperial Majesty"), a 2000 cedi note (which I learned was an offering to Oba, an abbreviated version of Obatala, the Yoruba orisha, also known as the 'shaper of human forms' and 'maker of babies in the womb'), a cracked mirror, and a bottle of oil containing an Ethiopian Cross together formed Ras Menelik's shrine. When I asked about the shrine, he told me he had dedicated it to the immortal spirit of Selassie, who "lives in every man and every living thing."

Ras Menelik continually referred to himself as an "animist-culture man," a custodian of African history, especially traditional African beliefs and practices. "The Rasta youth of Beach Bay are under my control," he said, meaning that fledgling Rastas come to him for wisdom. This is comparable to the way more rural Ghanaians treat the village diviner as a diagnostician of the soul, a holy man, a mediator between the gods, the ancestors, and all things temporal.[10]

When I inquired about Rasta as a religious-cultural import, Ras Menelik acknowledged that "Rasta is a fashion" for a few individuals; indeed, he conceded that some of the youth of Accra seem attracted to Rasta because of "reggae and weed," or because of "a trend of protest or discovery." But he insisted that such young men were few and far between. "Besides," he said, "every man is a god, every man is a devil, and you must learn to recognize which one of them [god or devil] has the upper hand in each person you meet!"

Grassroots Ghanaian Rasta Livities I: Selassie

Ghanaian Rastafari are tremendously eclectic, prompting me to conclude that there is no such entity as Ghanaian Rastafarianism, only a plethora of *Rasta livities*, which are constantly reconfigured in multiple encounters. In the next three sections I give some attention to this shifting eclecticism, focusing on figures and themes such as Selassie, Ethiopia and West Africa, the presence and impact of non-Ghanaian Rastas, understandings of salvation, and social engagement. I address Selassie first.

A decade's worth of fieldwork in Ghana reveals that Selassie's figure remains shrouded in mystery and ambiguity. Many of the non-Ghanaian Rastas that I encountered—young and old men who have made their way to Ghana from elsewhere in the world—spoke of Selassie as God, as Jah incarnate, citing the by-now familiar verses from scripture to provide warrant for their convictions. Ras Papa, a young man who left London and now spends his days teaching drumming to tourists vacationing on La Beach, is an instructive example. One afternoon, he sat down with me and spoke of Jah's two advents—as Jesus, the dreadlocked Nazarene, and as His Imperial Majesty, King of Kings, Haile Selassie I. However, when I showed Ras Papa, and others, the Sunday, November 5, 2000 BBC news report that the former Emperor had been reburied in Ethiopia, and that Rita Marley, who currently resides in Ghana, had attended the ceremony, many became agitated, even angry, strongly disputing the truth of the report, calling it "Babylon trickery." As one of Ras Papa's friends summarized, "God cannot die, y'know?" In contrast, Ghanaian Rastas took news of Selassie's reburial in their stride. Ras Sly, a former Methodist from Akropong in central Ghana, is a case in point. While steadfastly convinced that Selassie ranks as the 225th descendent of King Solomon and Queen Sheba, he rejected the notion that Selassie is the living God. This rejection came as something of a surprise to me, at least initially, since I had not encountered anything like it in my previous research on the Rastafari. But the more I traveled in Ghana, and the more Ghanaian Rastas I encountered, the more frequent this qualification of Selassie's status was made in my presence. I quickly discovered that Ras Sly was not an anomaly. Whether in Kumasi, Bolgatanga, or Accra, many Ghanaian Rastas spoke to me of the ultimacy of Jah. God, they maintained, is one, not two or three. And so they concluded that Selassie is God's emissary, "like Kwame Nkrumah," a noble man, sent to proclaim liberty, chiefly mental emancipation, but he is not Jah-in-the-flesh.

When asked about the reason for this major difference between Ghanaian and non-Ghanaian Rastas, many noted that Jah moves in mysterious ways among Jah's faithful, inclining different people to believe in different ways. Some interpreted this difference in more negative terms. As Ras Weyori, a Ghanaian Rasta and student based in Bolgatanga, expressed it: "Brethren come to Ghana from Jamaica and the USA and England and they do not know why so many Ghanaian Rastas see Haile Selassie as a good man, not Almighty Jah, but this is because they know so little about the 'real Africa'; they have not seen our leaders up close!" Put differently, Rastas born and raised in Ghana see firsthand that African politics and politicians are or can often be corrupt. Economic mismanagement, kick-backs, "feathering their own nests," summary executions, riots, and general bloodletting—the brutal realities of African political life—make it very difficult for Africans at home, including Ghanaians, to lionize their rulers. They understand their authorities as human, and, in so many words, Ras Weyori accused those Rastas in Ghana who possess an exalted view of Selassie as either ignorant or naïve.

Amidst the divergent views about Selassie, powerful legends about him continue to circulate throughout Ghana, thereby adding to the mystique that surrounds His Imperial Majesty. One story, an echo of Luke's account of the young Jesus teaching the priests in the Jerusalem Temple (Lk 2:41–52), speaks of a twelve-year-old Lij Tafari (an early name for the future Emperor) confounding Orthodox clergymen in the cathedral at the holy city of Axum, Ethiopia. Another story tells of the Emperor's stigmata during his trip to Jamaica on April 21, 1966. A third story, one narrated to me on at least four separate occasions, links the Emperor to both the biblical prophet Daniel and the Christian saint Francis of Assisi, for it heralds Selassie's control over animals. As the story goes, while Selassie, the Conquering Lion of the Tribe of Judah, was alive, two real lions flanked both sides of his throne. One day, when Nkrumah paid Selassie a visit, the lions started to behave strangely, roaring loudly, and pacing around in circles. But the Emperor soon calmed them down, so it is said, by gently raising his hand. The theme of wild animals coming under the control of men is found in many religious stories throughout the world. It symbolizes the moral goodness of the person involved, a basic belief about Selassie, shared by all the Rastas in Ghana that I interviewed.

Grassroots Ghanaian Rasta Livities II: Ethiopia

Understandings of Africa are less basic or commonly held. Research on the Rasta-fari in Great Britain and the Caribbean shows that many devotees long to return to the continent; for them, repatriation equals salvation. Not surprisingly, many Rastas who are able, and it seems there are quite a few, make it back to Ethiopia, the Emperor's home. Such brethren and sistren feature in the films I addressed in the last chapter. Others, however, have returned to Africa via Ghana, at least in more recent years. When I traveled through Ghana and interviewed non-Ghanaian Rastas about their decision to leave London or Kingston and settle in, say, Accra or Tema, not Addis Ababa or Axum, I received replies that cited one or more of three—practical, historical, and ideological—reasons.

First, in practical terms, non-Ghanaian Rastas return to Africa via Ghana because they perceive Ghana to be one of the most affordable, stable, and amiable countries in the continent. Past President Jerry J. Rawlings must take some of the credit for this perception. Assuredly, Rawlings's call for Africans abroad to return to Africa via Ghana has proved effective. And though Rawlings is associated with one of Ghana's bloodiest military coups, not to mention several devaluations of its currency, both of which can cause major instability, Rawlings's Ghana has often been touted, by insiders and outsiders alike, as the ideal African state. Subsequent leaders have cemented this strong reputation. Today, Ghana is much less problem-atic than famine-stricken, war-ravaged Ethiopia.[11]

Second, in historical terms, non-Ghanaian Rastas return to Africa via Ghana because Ghana is perceived to be the locus of origin for so many Afro-Caribbean and African-American women and men; there is some truth to this perception, because many of the colonial castles and forts that dot the West African coastline are in Ghana. As Ras Kofi, a Rastafarian elder who lives and works close to Kok-robite Beach, put it: "For the Rastaman born and raised ina Babylon, who knows his history and his roots, everything points to Ghana and the slave trade." When non-Ghanaian Rastas come to Ghana, then, in order to settle, to "make a go of it," many of them appear to be self-consciously reversing the Middle Passage jour-ney.[12] Jamaican dub poet Mutabaruka writes:

> To me, going into the dungeons was one of my greatest experiences in Ghana: to sit down in the dungeons just by myself for about two hours one night. After all the poetry reading and the various events, I went into this female dungeon and just sat down in there for about two hours. That was really something else. That is an experience which money could never buy. You cannot pay for this particular experience. To know that a lot of these poems that we wrote over the years were leading us to that. It was leading us to that experience. This where we are now. These are the poems that I wrote and this is where they have to stop. This is the fulfillment of this poetry. And to see that I get the opportunity to read these poems in the place where

the poems are relating to. It brought tears to my eyes, you know. I actually cried. Me cry man![13]

Third, for ideological reasons, non-Ghanaian Rastas return to Africa via Ghana because they see Ghana as the home of pan-Africanism—a phenomenon associated with Nkrumah, Du Bois and, to a certain extent, Selassie, as well as revived by Rawlings.[14] Selassie was one of the founding fathers of the Organisation of African Unity (OAU; today, the African Union), an assembly whose headquarters were moved from Accra to Ethiopia after Nkrumah's demise. A docent at the Du Bois Centre in Accra, a university student at work on his own study of the Rastafari in Ghana, met with me on a sunny afternoon and, overlooking Du Bois's final resting place, confirmed my impression that non-Ghanaian Rastas are drawn to pan-Africanist philosophy. "Pan-Africanism is anything that lifts up the image of the black man," he remarked, "and the Rastafari, both those from Ghana and particularly those who have settled here, have played their part in raising African awareness of the beauty of all things African."

Without a doubt, Ghana serves as a very powerful magnet for those diasporic Rastas looking to repatriate. When they arrive and settle, some have the appearance of flourishing. Most, however, struggle in one way or another. Indeed, many appear to become quickly frustrated and/or disillusioned. According to my informants, such disappointment stems from a series of unrealistic expectations. For example, it appears that many non-Ghanaian Rastas come to Ghana and assume, since Ghana is a part of Africa, that the Afrocentric philosophy of the Rastafari will be warmly received. Yet many Ghanaians largely resist or ignore it. Pan-Africanism does not, then, automatically transfer to the Rastafari movement. Indeed, the non-Ghanaian Rastas that I spoke with took little time detailing the price to be paid for practicing Rasta livity in Ghana—social ostracism, negative stereotyping, governmental refusal to assist with Rastafari land development, high fines and lengthy prison time for ganja possession, very few work opportunities, and the list goes on. When I asked several non-Rastafari Ghanaians about the Rastafari in Ghana, almost all of them dismissed the Rastas, home-grown or otherwise, as "drop-outs" and/or "too Western." This second, highly ironic notion requires explanation.

From my research, it appears that many everyday Ghanaians note how the Rastafari extol their African heritage, accentuate their Ethiopian-centered philosophy, and speak longingly of a return to Africa. Yet, to these same everyday Ghanaians, the Rastas, in their speech patterns, their general attire, and their outlook on issues such as family and death, seem noticeably European or Western. On the issue of death, for instance, most Ghanaians follow the traditional African opinion about the hereafter, viewing it as a place linked to the world of the spirits and of ancestors. But these same Ghanaians invariably perceive the Rastafari to be uninterested in the hereafter, especially the very African ceremonies associated with it. As I discovered making my way through Ghana, many Ghanaians believe that the Rastafari, rather ironically, are "not African enough" to warrant serious attention.

This apparent ill-feeling between some Ghanaians and the Rastafari, Ghanaian or non-Ghanaian, appears to be compounded by tensions that exist between Ghanaian and non-Ghanaian Rastas. Ras Sly complained to me, for example, about the "arrogance" of the "Rastas from abroad" who believe "they can tell me all there is to know about my Africa and my God." In my fieldwork, I discovered that Ras Sly's criticism was not uncommon. Several of my informants told of experiences with Rastas who come to live in Ghana and "think and talk and act big" with their "big money." Furthermore, Ras Kofi lamented those "Rastas who arrive from Babylon," who settle in Ghana, and who then suppose they can resolve disputes "Babylon-style" (with guns, knives, and so on). Such "actions are not appropriate in Ghana, are not suitable for the true Rastaman." Non-Ghanaian Rastas, then, have returned to Africa via Ghana, meeting different reactions along the way. They have had to change in light of their encounters with Ghanaian Rastas, as well as wider social criticism of their lifestyle, and disillusionment with Africa itself.

But it is also important to ask after those Ghanaian Rastas, the ones born and raised in this part of West Africa. Do they not also long to make a permanent move to Ethiopia? If yes, what prevents them? If no, then why not? Assuredly, the Ghanaian Rastas I interviewed revere Ethiopia as a holy land. They know, for example, that Christianity is not a new phenomenon in Africa, as a study of the ancient history of the Ethiopian Orthodox Church (fourth century CE) reveals. And they believe that His Imperial Majesty is part of an illustrious biblical lineage, stretching back to King Solomon and Queen Sheba by way of Menelik I, founder of the Ethiopian dynasty. With such knowledge, they connect this storied East African state to God.

Having noted such reverence, I perceive that many Ghanaian Rastas see Ethiopia as spiritually significant but not physically important. In other words, while Ghanaian Rastas think it valuable to visit, say, the rock-cut churches of Lalibela, or to search for the lost Ark of the Covenant, said to reside in the cathedral at Axum erected by Selassie in the 1960s, they do not consider it a necessity to permanently reside in Ethiopia. Practical reasoning accounts for this attitude. Ghanaian Rastas know only too well that recent events in Ethiopia entail that it is a damaged country, too difficult for prospective settlers.

But another reason, one that appears to be more philosophical in focus, is that Ethiopia—as a word and a concept—is synonymous with Africa. According to Ghanaian Rastas, Ghana is Ethiopia and Ethiopia is Ghana. After all, the ancient Greek word for Ethiopia, means, roughly, "the land of the sun-burnt peoples." So, why not speak of Ethiopia as the whole continent, including Ghana, for all Africans are "sun-burnt people"? This rhetorical question formed part of a repeated assertion throughout my travels in Ghana. "I have no need to travel to Ethiopia," Ras Weyori proclaimed to me at a reasoning session in the back streets of

Bolgatana, "not when I'm already in Ethiopia! Seriously, that part of Africa called Ethiopia is a special, sacred place, but the whole of Africa is Ethiopia, y'know, 'cos we are all Ethiopians, we are all sun-burnt people."

Grassroots Ghanaian Rasta Livities III: Salvation

On the subject of salvation, most of my informants, both Ghanaian and non-Ghanaian Rastafari, stressed the importance of Africa, upholding it as the cradle of human civilization or the Black Person's Vine and Fig Tree (Mi 4:4). However, it seems as though each Rasta camp, so to speak, embodies within its own ranks different views on the topic. Some of my informants in both camps treat salvation as a this-worldly reality, manifesting itself in the struggle for equal rights and justice. When prompted to explain this Peter Tosh-like slogan, many spoke of the punishment Rastas incur for practicing Rasta livity in Ghana. Some even dream that the persecution—from shunning to jail time—will one day cease, and many cite the New Testament in support of this dream. For example, Ras Sly hopes that one day the Rastas, like the Christians in the last chapter of the Acts of the Apostles, will live in their society, enacting their message with courage and without obstruction (Acts 28:31). So, for some Rastafari in Ghana, salvation amounts to a time when their distinctive spirituality will be valued the way other religions in Ghana—Islam, Christianity, and traditional African religions—are valued today: as vital, energetic, and legitimate aspects of the social and cultural framework of Ghanaian society.

In contrast to 'this-worldly Rastas,' other 'non-worldly Rastas,' again both Ghanaian and non-Ghanaian, argue that salvation is not secured by lobbying Ghana's leaders and/or stirring up the voting masses. According to Ras Ofori, a Kumasi-based informant who typifies this second, 'non-worldly' perspective, "a politically motivated Rasta is a Rasta who has spent too much time in Babylon."

Such 'non-worldly Rastas' distance themselves from politics. Many opted not to vote in recent and past Presidential elections, arguing that salvation is about livity only, about cultivating a personal virtue that leads to the possibility of life after death, viewed as reincarnation. According to Ras Ragga, a Ghanaian Rasta who lives in Accra, salvation is not connected to social change; its nature and scope are intensely personal, even abstruse, especially to the outsider, and certainly beyond any verbal entrapment: "I can tell you what 'salvation' is, define it for you, y'know, but it's a conscious thing, y'understand? It's a very personal thing, because Rastafari is not a religion with a doctrine and belief and all dem tings; it's a lifestyle, a spiritualism."

Ras Ragga's perspective represents a quite different Rastology from what comes next in my interviews with Blakk Rasta and Rocky Dawuni, two influential Ghanaian reggae artists. Blakk Rasta characterizes a challenging as well as candid voice for socially engaged or 'this-worldly' Ghanaian Rastafari. He rebukes Chinese investment in Africa as neo-colonialism, for example, and he

FIGURE 16 Blakk Rasta in concert (2012). Photo: Blakk Rasta.

urges Africans to cultivate a fresh form of pan-Africanism, two of many political themes that surface in his weekly, Accra-based Hitz 103.9 FM radio show as well as on his albums and in performance. A pronounced need to celebrate as well as practice religious hybridity, which Blakk Rasta models as a self-identifying 'Muslim Rasta,' also forms his hope for the Rastafari movement's future.

An Interview with Blakk Rasta

DJNM: Let me begin by asking you about your spiritual journey. You were born in Northern Ghana to Muslim parents, both educators, in 1974. And your difficult youth, marred as it was by several social injustices, was something you worked through with the aid of art: you wrote plays, penned novels, and you formed a theater company. Am I right in thinking that things started to change for you in 1990, when you first encountered Ras Kimono, a Nigerian reggae performer? If so, are you happy describing this moment as the beginning of your journey towards Rastafari?

BR: Well, I will say that meeting Ras Kimono certainly improved my status as an upcoming, young Rasta. The theater group named after him propelled me to more consciousness and spirituality. It was, truly, the beginning of my Rasta journey.

DJNM: These days, do you align yourself with any particular Rastafari mansion? If so, which one, and why? If not, why not?

BR: Yes, I align myself more with the Nyabinghi mansion. I personally love their teachings of beating the binghi drum, chanting, and black pride advocacy.

DJNM: Your website indicates that you embrace Rastafari, though you remain Muslim, and I wonder why as well as how you blend both spiritualities?

BR: I see Rasta more as a true, original African way of life. In addition, I see Rasta as the mother of all faiths and religion. However, Rasta is not a religion. Rasta is the universal set in which Islam, Christianity, Buddhism, and so on exist as subsets. Practically, I pick bits and pieces of Islam that allow me to still be a Rasta and then I apply them. In most cases, I think it works!—as I think you found it working when you visited Senegal and encountered the Muslim Rastafari known as Baye Faal.[15] To me, Rasta is bigger than religion.

DJNM: You are right about my travels throughout Senegal, and I would dearly love to research the Baye Faal in greater detail! Staying with this theme of religious hybridity: part of me wants to trace the way you harmonize Islam and Rastafari to your childhood in Northern Ghana. But what do you think? I have visited Tamale and Bolgatanga, for example, and I came away impressed by the seemingly peaceful coexistence of traditional African religions, Islam, and Christianity. Would you say that Ghana's most religiously diverse region prepared the way for your later spiritual transformation(s)?

BR: I would. The peaceful coexistence of several religions in my area of upbringing has inspired my religious hybridity and transformation. I also believe that people have found, and will find, Rasta attractive aside other religions. In the future, I think people will synchronize their faith(s) with Rasta so they can belong to both or many spiritualities.

DJNM: Your music has won several awards in Ghana and overseas. Tell me about the intent behind your first album, *Rasta Shrine*, which appeared in 2000. It includes the first lyric you ever wrote, the song "Keep on Rockin' / I & I Rastas," and I'm curious: What message did you hope to communicate with its release?

BR: Honestly, I simply wanted to spread African and Black pride (self-worth) in my music, right from the start, and I still stay focused on that message. I also love to entertain in my songs.

DJNM: Your lyrics reclaim an African, black somebodiness denied by Babylon, and some of your songs reference African leaders, such as Muammar al-Gaddafi, Robert Mugabe, and Nkrumah, and I'm wondering if you see Rasta and reggae as ways to criticize the West, especially its neocolonial tendencies?

BR: OMG! Exactly that! Yet, Rasta is so much more than just an anticolonial tool. Rasta is a tool to fight general injustice—oppression, hatred, prejudice, and so on.

DJNM: OK, allow me to run with this theme of Rastafari reggae music as a political tool. "Our Africa" is a striking song, one that mentions various turning-points in the continent's past, with its allusions to everything from the wonders of the Ashanti world to the tragedy of the transatlantic slave trade, and yet you also pull no punches when you wonder about China's expansive economic influence in Africa. "More Chinese food now than Tuo-bodom plantain" is one line, for example, and "No wonder now, the churches in a Africa / sing Chinese hymns on a higher octave" is another. Is China the New West, as it were, and thus the latest incarnation of Babylon? Or is something else on your mind when you write and sing songs like "Our Africa"?

BR: China is the New West, ready to colonize Africa, and in the same way Europe did, just devoid of physical shackles and chains this time around. I think China has beaten the West to the partition of Africa now. Chinese guys spit into the faces of indigenous Africans—they shoot them, bury them alive in illegal mining pits, and then they go free because they have powerful politicians on their payroll.

DJNM: To me, "Our Africa" also sounds like a powerful hymn to pan-Africanism, which makes sense given that Ghana was the OAU's first home, and yet I wonder how your fellow Ghanaians respond to your message?

BR: Certainly, "Our Africa" is a pan-Africanist hymn. Unfortunately, some Ghanaians have yet to fully comprehend my message, since I delivered it in English for a more international audience. One day, we will get there! I must say, however, a large part of my message is out there, courtesy of radio and reggae, and the youth are navigating their lives towards it. I am so proud to say this!

DJNM: And what of the United States of America and Great Britain? Songs like "Taliban War" and "America (a-Meer-Wrecker)" do not so much lament as excoriate both countries for what you see as their alleged democratic spirit. Like Elijah warning against foreign nations (1 Kgs 18), you rail against Tony Blair and George W. Bush's apparently moralizing attempt to civilize the world. You are not impressed. And once again, we witness Rastafari reggae chanting down Babylon. Tell me about your approach to the aforementioned countries, to the two songs I discuss, and, if possible, say a few words about how you see your brand of reggae in relationship to, say, dancehall reggae, which has come under attack for its seemingly apolitical approach to the world.

BR: Yeah, I believe America is a powerful man and England is his wife. Together they torment their weaker opponents. The war on the Taliban, and the hypocritical wars 'on behalf' of the oppressed do not fool me or us. We know America's and England's ultimate goal: oil.

As for dancehall music, it's purely for dancing, as the name implies, and it is not my focus. It is important. But, I would rather not make or produce it. I think my life on earth would be incomplete if I did dancehall. No disrespect. I was born to preach self-worth, which I do not see in dancehall music.

DJNM: Your music is not all about fiery criticism. You have the honor of being one of the first reggae singers to have written, recorded, and released a song about President Barack Obama.[16] It celebrates his African heritage, of course, and it uses hot and cold imagery in a geo-political sense. The song has appeared around the world, via the BBC and CNN, and I wonder if you might describe why you wrote this song, and what you make of the public reaction to it? But first, allow me to cite some partial lyrics:

Verse 1
Originally stepping out-a Kenya Africa
Adopted into the cold woodlands of America
Trust me Iyah,
Dem youth defy every order an' turn senator
Rat-Rat-Rat-Rat!
De gunshot of hate continue fi echo in-a every corner
How com blackman become president in a money-mecca?
Barack beware! Barack beware! Barack beware!
before dem turn ya name into Barack Osama
In a dis ya time, judgment a com without waata
For legalising abortion in a America, a-fyah! fyah!

Chorus
Mama mama
Com mek wi talk o
Com mek wi talk about Barack Obama
Papa! Papa!
Com make wi talk o
Com make wi talk about Barack Obama
Barack Barack, Barack Obama (2x)

Verse 2
9–11 was de beginning of Satan endtime
Baptising black Americans in a bitter juice of lime
Making sure no black man in a America will see his prime
In a dis ya time a black American president a great sign
Too long dem disrespect blacks and Africans combined
pon black peoples flesh and blood, de kuklax clan love fi dine
Watch out Barack Obama and intensify ya power turbine
Or else breddren Obama, your dark days will never sublime

Verse 3
Yahman! yahman! yahman!
"God bless America" the idiot bwoy always say
When de bombs and weapons fly over innocent people head
Oh Obama, me neva hear you talk 'bout Africa yet

> Or is it a nice way of swerving dem in a ya campaign?
> Mr Obama, bring dis poly-tricks money to Africa and keep de poverty at bay
> Too long black people keep nyaming up horse hay
> Wake up Obama and don't join de band wagon of de gay
> Beware Obama! Watch out Obama! Look around you
> the people dem show you nuff smile
> but dis smile dem a fake! fake! fake! fake smile dem!
> Watch out Obama, a-fake!

BR: "Barack Obama" was a song that Jah sang into my ears! Still, I resisted record-ing a song for a 'politrician.' Like Jonah, though, I was forced to divert to Ninevah (Jonah 3:3), and I am glad that I did. "Barack Obama" is not a political campaign song. I was not trying to endorse Obama. Like you said, the song contrasts heat (Africa) and cold (America). Plus, it urges Obama to always remember his African identity. I am so glad it was the first ever song for President Obama—a song that he himself endorsed over dinner in Ghana! Some people still think it is my best song.

DJNM: Songs like "Ganja Sweet" suggest that the holy herb is important to you. What other dimensions of Rastafari livity shape or govern your life?

BR: I do not smoke anything smokeable. Ganja is medicinal, as studies show, and it is spiritual; it helps with diseases and sicknesses, and it inspires people. Despite such wonderful accolades, it is still illegal, so I do not smoke ganja. I use ganja oil for my hair and skin—it's also helpful as an incense for African mosqui-toes. Since I respect everyting in Jah creation, I am vegan.

DJNM: You must be fairly distinctive among Rastafari reggae artists working today, because you are a reggae FM radio presenter. How did this all start? And if you had to name some Ghanaian, or West African, reggae singers to listen out for, who would they be, and why?

BR: Yes, me on Hitz 103.9 FM radio in Accra has made me unique. I play my own songs and reason on many topics. A lot of Ghanaian radio stations think my music is controversial, so they 'whitelist' my songs. Still, I make music my own way, and I will continue to do so as long as I believe society will benefit. I should say that my radio show is rated the most listened to here. As for sing-ers or artists, I recommend Ras Kimono and Tiken Jah Fakoly, because they are *conscious reggae* musicians.

DJNM: How would you describe the Rastafari presence in Ghana? Do you detect differences between Ghanaian Rastafari and Rastafari you encounter over-seas? If so, what do you think accounts for the differences?

BR: Rasta is growing in Ghana! Yet, to me, Ghanaian Rastas need more education. Most Ghanaian Rastas are uneducated. Rastafari is intellectual and requires some minimal level of education to fully comprehend. Rastas overseas seem to have more insight into Rasta issues than Ghanaians. This situation will change with education.

FIGURE 17 Blakk Rasta with President Barack Obama (2009). Photo: Blakk Rasta.

DJNM: Could you say a few words about *Ancestral Moonsplash*, your most recent album—the significance of the title, for example, and the lessons you wish to impart through its words and sounds?

BR: You seem to know too much about me! Thanks. *Ancestral Moonsplash* is my 'real-me' album, featuring a fusion of reggae with African rhythms and dances heavily touched with African instruments. I have recorded folk songs composed by our ancestors as reggae songs. This style of reggae is named 'moonsplash' by me. Hence, *Ancestral Moonsplash*. You know, I realized after my tours around the world that people gravitated towards my 'moonsplash' reggae songs more than the straight-up reggae ones. And I believe if Bob Marley was alive, he would be doing 'moonsplash,' knowing him for being fond of reggae fusions. On my album, you will hear instruments like the kora, xylophone, talking drum, dondo, gonje, kolgo, to mention a few. You will also hear African animal sounds, jungle sounds, and market sounds. *Ancestral Moonsplash* is an album to watch out for; I believe it is the future for African reggae.

DJNM: And finally, what do you think the future looks like for Rastafari? What do you think insiders and outsiders (to the movement) will be saying about them in, say, 2050?

BR: Rastafari has a very bright future. I believe it will evolve as the years roll by and as more studies happen. I think you will see more religious hybridity because Rasta will be understood more as bigger than any one religion.

An Interview with Rocky Dawuni

In reversing the journey through the Middle Passage, some Rastafari brought their livity to Ghana in the mid-1970s, as I noted earlier, thereby paving the way for young men like Rocky Dawuni to embrace as well as discover an experiential philosophy first forged across the Atlantic but brought 'back to Africa,' so to speak. Over time, Dawuni has contextualized Rastafari, emerging with a form of this religion that reveals itself to have been shaped and reshaped by both African and Western influences. Dawuni has contributed to this process, and continues to do so, as his art has also taken him out of Africa, again reversing the reversal, by crisscrossing the Atlantic, modeling Africa to the West and the West to Africa. For example, many Ghanaian Rastas' recent foray into the political process could be seen as having been swayed by a more politicized North American and Caribbean Rastafari embraced by Dawuni—but again refashioned to fit the Ghanaian context. As the following interview reveals, Dawuni compellingly symbolizes how Rastafari ideas and values are becoming increasingly globalized.

DJNM: Reading interviews with you across the years, I am struck by your eclectic beliefs and practices. How and where did your spiritual journey begin?

FIGURE 18 Rocky Dawuni in concert (2011): Photo: Mike Underwood.

RD: It began when I was around seven years of age and I began to ponder on questions of my relationship to God. We were told that going to church and praying was good so I started searching for God and this journey took me through several religions, from traditional African faith to Buddhism, Christianity, Catholicism, Islam, Eckankar, Krishna consciousness, then Rastafari, and so on. Over the next few years I immersed myself into reading and converting between faiths. This journey gave me an insight into the essence and nature of JAH within my personal spiritual reality.

The most memorable and pivotal moments in this journey were: establishing prayer gathering for all the children in my neighborhood after I got my first bible at age eight, my conversion to Islam while in secondary school, studying the Bhagavad-Gita, discovering reggae music and Rasta consciousness.

DJNM: Would you say your songwriting and performance on stage is the way you best express your spiritual passion?

RD: Yes, songwriting provides me with an uninterrupted and honest medium to commune with myself, my audience, JAH within and JAH without. When I write it usually reflects a certain personal validation of my insights but the stage is the place where the experience takes on a much more physical nature. On stage, the spiritual experience is shared with everyone present and the experience can be transcendental.

DJNM: Do you think Rastafari musicians have a specific mission to the world at large? If not, why not? If so, how would you describe it?

RD: In every period of human history there are certain groups of people who assume the mantle of constantly ringing the bells of righteousness and consciousness regardless of what direction society evolves morally. Rastafari musicians are one of the groups that have assumed this role in this time. A Rasta musician does not necessarily mean someone with dreadlocks but someone who uses word and sound to bring light in this era of darkness.

DJNM: I have journeyed around Ghana a few times in the past decade, either directing study abroad trips or else conducting field work, and Ghanaian people strike me as supremely aware of, as well as positive towards, reggae bands such as Aswad, Culture, and Black Uhuru. Do you think the same can be said of 'home-grown talent' such as yourself?

RD: Definitely, the awareness of "home-grown talent" has been tremendous lately with the radio stations dedicating whole programs to Ghanaian reggae. My annual concerts for Ghanaian Independence Day [March 6] attract over 20,000 people, so I think the awareness is definitely there and growing.

DJNM: You and I first exchanged ideas ten years ago. Looking back across the past decade, what are the turning points for the movement in your part of West Africa, and how would you describe today's reggae scene in Ghana?

RD: In terms of Ghana, Rastafari and reggae music have gained a wider acceptance among the population due to sustained exposure over the years. Beyond the acceptance of its doctrines, the main turning points have been the prominence of Rastafari musicians and personalities in the mainstream and on the national stage. The reggae scene has also kept up its vibrancy with locally grown dancehall and roots reggae stars helping to maintain the movement. Apart from myself and my work on the global stage, artists such as Blakk Rasta, Samini, Iwan, Sheriff Ghale Stoneboy Burniton represent the face of Ghanaian reggae today. Its most significant turning point lies ahead in terms of harnessing its code of morality to champion realistic challenges of addressing poverty, corruption, environmental degradation, and women's issues in Ghana.

DJNM: In recent years many Rastas from the Caribbean, North America, and Great Britain have returned to Africa via Ghana, settling and seeking to make a living in this historic West African state. In your view, why do you think these men and women choose Ghana rather than, say, Ethiopia? And how well do you think these same women and men have fared in Ghana?

RD: Ghana is the current gateway to Africa, the New Jerusalem, and the Western Wall of Ethiopia. The whole continent is one entity and geographical locations created by colonial demarcations are of no relevance in the big picture. It does not matter if it's Ethiopia, Tanzania, or Kenya, as long as it's within the continent. Ghana currently enjoys a stable political environment within the continent and also its historical role as the hub of pan-Africanism makes it the best destination for all Rastas returning home. 'He who feels it knows it' and everyone is feeling Ghana as the place. Also, every situation has its realistic parameters, so all the brothers and sisters coming back to Ghana had to deal with an environment which is different culturally than what they were accustomed to, so there is bound to be uncertainties and challenges but I think generally they have fared well.

DJNM: In their early years, largely through preachers such as Archibald Dunkley and Leonard Howell, Rastafari understood salvation as repatriation. Speaking as an African in Africa, what does salvation mean to you?

RD: Salvation to me is restoration. Dunkley and Howell basically pointed out the other side of the same coin because Africa's restoration depends on the repatriation of its children so it can see itself in its totality. This requires purging the continent of wars, exploitation, corruption, and political and social systems built and perpetuated on a platform of a colonial mentality. This is a big task, which will require input from all quarters. The concept of salvation also changes depending on the requirements of the time period. After the restoration, salvation will eventually take on a new meaning in the new Africa.

DJNM: As you know, Ghanaian Rastafari hold many and different opinions towards Selassie. Many think of him as a god, of course, and yet others qualify this belief, speaking of him as a noble man, rather like Nkrumah, not Jah Himself. Any thoughts on this phenomenon? How would you describe your own convictions about Selassie?

RD: The revelation of the personality of God is like the story of the blind men describing what an elephant is. Those who touched the elephant on its sides said it is like a wall, while those who touched its legs said it is like a pillar. Rastas in Ghana represent these different perspectives in terms of the personality of Selassie. Also, most Ghanaian Rastas grew up Christian, Muslim, or traditionalist so they have to integrate it into their already existing belief framework in order to make it valid for themselves. But in the long run JAH is about totality and endless incarnations so every individual has to see JAH with their hearts and not their eyes. Every man is a reflection of JAH. In terms of my convictions about Selassie, He is the light of the consciousness of Rastafari, the personality around who this powerful movement is built. An illuminated and kingly incarnation of the Christ personality, and a platform upon which we can all strive towards attaining the Christ-like personality and becoming one with JAH. Also, man is one aspect of creation and JAH is all creation, so the truth is a continuing journey rather than a destination.

DJNM: One Accra-based Rasta that I met pointed to Okomfo Anokye, Ghana's most famous fetish priest, and he informed me that there is much to be gained from a conversation between Ghanaian Rastafari and practitioners of traditional African religions. Do you share his view? If so, why? If not, why not?

RD: I definitely share his view. Traditional African religion is based on principles similar to the widely propagated themes of Rastafari such as righteousness, honesty, and service to God through service to man. In traditional religion,

the priest with locks like the legendary Okomfo Anokye are seen as personalities chosen by the creator or the gods to dedicate themselves to the
service of the community. Dreadlocks are a sign of their dedication as it is
in Rastafari. These priests serve as healers, teachers, prophets, arbitrators, and
judges, and their role is in the same line as the dreadlocked Nazarene sect of
the Bible, who dedicated themselves to the service of God (Num 6). These
similarities require further exploration to see where they all intersect.

DJNM: What issues do you think Rastafari in Ghana are likely to face in the coming years?

RD: There is the issue of shaking off the stereotypical assumptions of some Ghanaians in the establishment—that Rastas are lazy, ganja smokers who spew
confusing ecclesiastical rhetoric instead of being messengers of truth working
towards realistic goals. This perspective has changed lately with the increase in
the number of Rasta professionals in different socioeconomic fields and also
Rasta musicians rising to prominence. I am an advocate of a united African
continent in this generation. I'm a part of a growing voice to change the
mindset of the people and the government to focus on self-reliance and self-
appreciation as a stepping stone to breaking the crippling yoke of neocolonial
dependency and mentality. There is also the issue of AIDS and poverty in the
country and the continent as a whole, and I believe our voice and efforts will
be most needed to bring the required sense of urgency to solving the problems caused by both issues.

DJNM: "Solving the problems" makes me think of how some observers think
Rastafari may be seen as a religion of protest. Though this is correct in some
respects, it tends to characterize Rastafari negatively, as Rastafari is much
more than this, because it is also a reclamation of a self and a cultural identity
denied by Babylon—a concept that my book explains. Is this how Rastafari
works for you? Is it a reclamation of agency in naming and defining yourself?

RD: Rastafari represents to me a consciousness rather than a religion with the
aim to preserve, reclaim, and project a true spiritual and cultural identity
based on my being African. The importance of defending these ideals is to
also ensure and cultivate a life of righteousness and goodness for the benefit
of my community and humanity as a whole. This also means that one has to
engage with the reality of everyday life while standing up against injustice
of any kind and promoting a harmonious co-existence among all people. Its
characterization as solely a religion of protest is misleading since protest is
only a means towards this end. Many within Africa and in the diaspora share
this view especially in these times when so many people are struggling to
protect their identity against a Babylonian perpetuation of a spiritually bank-
rupt consumerist global persona. For me, it highlights a supreme path to true
freedom not only from cultural, political, and spiritual slavery, but also a state
of understanding beyond the confines of religious dogma. The universality
of Rasta belief concepts, such as 'oneness,' 'love,' 'peace,' and 'compassion,' are

a way forward as well as a light that can unite many people, religions, and cultures. Music will continue to serve as the instrument for spreading and communicating these universal beliefs.

To me, Rasta is the stone that was cast in Daniel's interpretation of Nebuchadnezzar's dream [to destroy the statue depicting various incarnations of Babylonian power (Dan 2:31–35)]. It's a consciousness that has its roots from the most ancient of days to fight moral and spiritual corruption, and has been gathering momentum through different generations, personalities, names, prophets, and doctrines. Rasta is the last trumpet and advocates a pure expression of the God consciousness in this hour. This has given its message the power to touch the hearts of people worldwide. Most people receive its message through the popular sounds of reggae music, which has made it more accessible to a larger number of people. In the long run its significance will depend on its level of spiritual progressiveness.

DJNM: In an Op-Ed for *the Guardian* newspaper in Great Britain, Rastafari poet Benjamin Zephaniah comments on Snoop Dogg/Lion's public conversion to Rastafari: "Snoop Lion wants to spread the message of Rastafari, but does Rastafari need an ambassador? Yes, is my answer, we need as many as we can get. I think we are one of the most misunderstood groups of people in the world."[17] Do you share Zephaniah's sentiments? If not, why not? If so, do you see yourself as an ambassador for Rastafari, and in what way(s) do you perform this role?

RD: I definitely agree with Zephaniah's point of view. Rastafari needs ambassadors that have an understanding not only of its teachings but the ability to communicate to people of all backgrounds and races with clarity in its message. Snoop's conversion is a personal choice and it's solely up to him as to how he carries out his personal revelation. I see myself as a Rasta ambassador of peace through music. Through my concerts, interviews, and my involvement with social issues I perform these duties. My belief is that Rasta ambassadors have to be articulate modern cultural diplomats emulating Selassie's mastery of diplomacy as their primary means to promote international morality. I like what artists such as Tarrus Riley, Jah Cure, Queen Ifrika, and Protoje are doing to advance the Rastafari message. It's a new time and Rasta rises again! This is the hope I have, moving forward.

The Many Faces of Ghanaian Rasta

With Blakk Rasta and Rocky Dawuni's assistance I have revealed the many faces of Ghanaian Rasta, its plethora of convictions and lifestyles, and its constant change. My study is significant on many levels. First, it is undoubtedly valuable for what it tells us about Ghanaian Rastas. But the multiplicity and change associated with their specific story also points to the internationalization process itself. As seen here, internationalization entails Ghanaian Rastas' increasing dependence upon Western influences but also their independence from Western forms as they reconfigure them to fit their particular African context. Interestingly, this back-and-forth process appears to account for, as well as sustain, an absence of consensus among Ghanaian Rastafari. Perhaps the most compelling example here is the relatively recent changes in their understanding of salvation. Naturally, there are other particular areas—overlooked in my work but important nonetheless—that require attention. How, for example, does African Islam influence Ghanaian Rastafari? What will occur if recent political hopes, expressed by some Ghanaian Rastas, are dashed? How will Western Rastas continue to be challenged as they move into a Ghanaian context? As scholars of the Rastafari explore answers to these and additional questions in Ghana and other settings, like Japan, they will find themselves engaging not only the nature of Rastafari but also the nature of religion itself in an increasingly global world.

No religion is or has ever been static. However, as scholars of religion heighten their awareness of the transcultural nature of encounter in our century, fresh understandings or new models of religious change emerge. Like Marvin D. Sterling's work on Rastafari in Japan, which I address next, my study of Ghanaian Rastafari grapples with the complexity yet richness inherent in such contemporary transformations of religion, and it upholds art's ability to function like a neutron in a chain reaction of religious transformation.

What Has Japan to do with Jamaica?

In 2000, Dean W. Collinwood and Osamu Kusatsu published their trailblazing sociological study of Japanese Rastafari.[18] They argued that a broad, late-twentieth-century internationalism inspired certain Japanese women and men to engage the world at large, especially Jamaican popular culture. Many Japanese soon viewed Jamaican Rastafari's ital or natural livity—the desire to live in a simple fashion and close to the land—as a way to become more authentically Japanese, because traditional or proto-shintō Japan also values existing in spiritual proximity to the earth. Marvin D. Sterling's *Babylon East* (2010) confirms Collinwood and Kusatsu's argument, although Sterling complicates matters by showing that these days such ecological friendliness appears mainstream rather than deviant, as Collinwood and Kusatsu state. Sterling also moves us beyond Collinwood and Kusatsu's study by proving that contemporary Japanese Rastafari both restate and resituate Rasta's many religious dimensions according to local sociopolitical needs.[19] Like Rastafari in other global contexts that I discuss throughout my book, especially the Ghanaian Rastas, Japanese Rastafari favor what we might call situational theologizing or contextual religious thinking. And such local or grassroots livity among Japanese Rastafari inspires the distinction Sterling makes between urban Rasta-identifying Japanese in, say, Tokyo, and rural Rasta-identifying Japanese in, say, Nara prefecture.[20] As the saying goes: location, location, location.

Generally speaking, Sterling's Rasta-identifying Japanese regard Rasta as an experiential overlay, the foremost symbolic as well as philosophical resource for the task of making meaning, and they express this way of looking at the world in regional terms. In the Tokyo metropolitan area, for example, many Rasta-identifying individuals hail from working-class communities, which were hit the hardest when Japan's economic recession began in the early 1990s and several, including the cases Sterling discusses, use the language of 'Babylon' to grasp or overstand their inner-city lives. Speaking as dub reggae artists and informants, Fire and Brother Taffy typify this urban "effort to re-imagine Rasta's black politics in a Japanese context."[21] Fire deploys dread talk, for example, to chant down Japan's perceived Babylonian provincialism or, in other terms, its general social anxiety about cultural otherness. Japanese people do not understand flashing dreads and smoking herb, he says, and thus they spurn their Rasta-identifying compatriots, pushing them out to life's edges.[22] Jah resides in such liminal spaces, Fire hints, and it is here, on society's margins, that Jah inspires outcasts to reason and come to know themselves. Brother Taffy concurs. He also uses dread talk to interpret his troubled past of poverty, educational failure, and *yakuza* gang activity. This past convinces Taffy that he is *burakumin*, an outcast, like those whom Japan's emperor once used for planting rice with meagre reward—and like those African Americans who worked the cotton fields in the antebellum South. Taffy's marginal status thus inclines him to feel solidarity with sidelined blacks throughout the diaspora. A religion that first appealed to Jamaica's ghetto youths, Rasta helps Taffy sense such camaraderie. Sterling continues:

> he [Taffy] also uses Rasta to more generally critique Japan's relationship with the West. Japan, he says, is "mixed up." He thinks Japanese are "kill-ing themselves" by adopting Western-style mass consumption and produc-tion, describing his country as "a money-making factory" that needs to "cool down." "I wanna be spiritual [in] everything," he said, "but I live inna Babylon, inna concrete jungle situation. Now depression in Japan. Soon come inflation. This is Babylon system in Japan." In addition to the uncriti-cal adoption of Western economic values, he sees the spread of signs in English—he points them out as we drive through the city—as evidence of Japanese acceptance of Western cultural imperialism.[23]

As long as there is Babylon, there must be Zion.[24] And reggae influences Taffy's Zionist Rastology. "He sees a universality in Rastafari that helps explains Bob Marley's international popularity: not unlike Marley's, Taffy's blood is 'ghetto blood,'" Sterling declares. "But the same ghetto identification that so powerfully links him to Bob Marley and Rastafari stigmatizes him in Japan."[25] In the end, though, Rasta helps Taffy and Fire to find specific ways of coping with Baby-lon, not unlike those global Rastafari featured in the documentaries I covered earlier.

The Japanese countryside, which includes Mount Yoshino in Nara prefecture, signifies "another space in which Rasta ideology is articulated."[26] Surrounded by autumn's red leaves as well as spring's cherry blossoms, rural Rasta-identifying Japanese imagine Nara's mountainous, forested region as a sanctuary from Tokyo's urban sprawl, and they stand in contrast to Japan's city Rastafari by appearing apolitical, and by practicing holistic communitarianism as well as nature mysticism, especially in their Rasta yards. Sterling traces this rural Japanese fascination for Rasta to the late 1980s, especially to the emergence in Japan of a world culture sensibility, also known as *ensunikku*, which may best be seen in the way the countryside's ethnic shops merchandize all manner of cultural artefacts. Attending a festival that is celebrated once every twelve years (*Inochi no Matsuri*; Festival of Life), Sterling also witnesses this *ensunikku* sensibility firsthand, and he recognizes Rastafari reggae's signal contribution to the ten-day event's cultural mashup.[27]

Not only do rural Japanese identify with Jamaican Rastafari to better connect to nature and to celebrate multiculturalism, they seem to see in Rasta's carefree yet measured livity some kind of antidote to Japan's allegedly poisonous religions of Shintō and Buddhism. Formal faith contaminates one's soul, we read, and roots reggae singers like Ras Seek and Ras Tanaki inform Sterling that they overstand Rasta as something spiritual, but not religious—a theme that appears in my book's earlier chapters. "Rasta revealed for Seek the staidness of the monastic life laid out before him, one he felt compelled to reject. For Tanaki, Rasta gave him a vision of himself as a solitary Japanese Rasta buoyed with a spiritual energy that institutionalized Buddhism lacked," Sterling reports.[28]

Eight Yoshino dreads also teach Sterling about local Japanese Rasta livities. Members of a reggae band, they created and now maintain a ritual space, a Rasta yard, which they style after similar abodes they experienced during their visits to Jamaica. The house belongs to Takuji, the band's lead singer, and the dreads garland it with many religiously and culturally eclectic items, though Rasta focalizes everything, and they intend the yard to instantiate their communal spirit. Hindu religious posters, Japanese *sumi-e* paintings, Ethiopian village life pictures, Selassie photographs, and "the Rasta-colored fliers of the band's performances," are just a few of the many items that show the "easy flow of the many elements of global culture that comprise the residents' international experiences."[29] The yard thus depicts Rastafari's transnational appeal, and it captures the aforementioned *ensunikku* sensibility, which takes root—figuratively as well as literally—in the land. The Yoshino Rasta yard is

> a space in which the men's given identification as Japanese becomes linked to a desired identification with a global that is most specifically Jamaican Rastafarian, but also African, Indian, and potentially, richly, anything else. This given identification as Japanese is given not only because they are Japanese, but also because all these elements are ultimately to be sited in the ground of the Japanese rural.[30]

"Diet, dreadlocks, and medicinal practice are three embodied and interpersonal means of realizing Rastafari" in the yard and, once more, livity appears local.[31] Typically, the wives of the eight band members both cook and serve vegetarian meals, which includes everything from soba noodles to kimchi and miso soup; no alcohol is served. Everything seems ital, as it is in Jamaica, but here, in the Japanese countryside, the piquant theo-politics that often peppers the discourse of Jamaican Rasta yards is absent, and the table talk feels different. "My careful attempts to elicit talk on these matters [Jah Rastafari and current affairs] were met with brief, perfunctory replies, nor did these issues emerge of their own accord," Sterling claims. "This reluctance is part of my sense of Rastafari among some rural individuals as more global cultural than global political."[32] Whatever else they do, the Yoshino dreads do not favor sustained social analysis or intense theological investigation.

Flashing locks forms an integral part of this "global cultural." And among the Yoshino dreads, this ritual action has roots that reach into Japan's history and heritage. For example, inn owner Masato localizes his hairstyle by referencing En no Gyōja, the founder of Yoshino's avowedly syncretic Shugendō Buddhist sect, whom artists often depict as an ascetic with a beard and long, flowing hair. "He is Rasta," Masato declares and, for his part, Sterling suggests: "If this appreciation of Rasta is rooted in the rich soil of Shugendō's past, and if the trunk is Yoshino in the here and now, then Jamaica and Africa are branches that reach more broadly into the global."[33] For me, Masato's appeal to En no Gyōja recalls a similar plea, made by certain Ghanaian Rastafari, to Okomfo Anokye. And I think both entreaties work by striving to retrieve the situational past for the purposes of the contextual present. Put differently: En no Gyōja and Okomfo Anokye are separated by context and culture and yet they appear united, for the most part, by their ability to inspire indigenous Rastas to cultivate a local livity or what might be termed a vernacular religion.

The Yoshino dreads frequently display what Sterling calls "cross-cultural pharmaceutical knowledge," which is to say they often spurn traditional Western forms of medicine and, instead, favor smoking the holy herb and experimenting with natural therapy, also known as *shizen ryōhō*.[34] They apply the leaves and juices of local flora and fauna as pain relievers and fever reducers, and by amalgamating Rastafari approaches to wellness with Japanese holism, the Yoshino dreads prefer an East–West integrative model of health care. Furthermore, this wellness model evokes an essential aspect of the Rastafari religious movement's ethical or legal dimension, especially the imperative that one's everyday routine must be ital in order to fortify oneself as well as to adore and serve Jah. Sterling summarizes: "The enactment of acupunctural and Rastafarian medical techniques upon their bodies, and the resulting marking of the bodies—coupled with dreadlocks and the group's communal consumption of natural food—ground attenuated global selves in local practice."[35] More broadly, Rasta becomes indigenized.

To recap: Japanese engagement with Jamaican popular culture appears in the aforesaid two main forms: Rasta-identifying individuals living in the city and Rasta-identifying individuals residing in the countryside. Sterling addresses other aspects of Afro-Asian cultural interchange, like fictional as well as non-fictional accounts of Japanese journeying to Jamaica in search of existential significance, and explorations of Jamaican attitudes to Japanese adoptions of Jamaican culture, yet I suspect Sterling's work on these two main forms of Rasta consciousness in Japan signifies his shrewd, challenging contribution to the global and academic conversation about the Rastafari's internationalization. Differences between such Japanese urban Rasta and Japanese rural Rasta exist, and Sterling helps us grasp them in turn, but both groups share an almost insatiable appetite for dancehall reggae, roots reggae, and dub music. Art thus explains Rastafari in Japan, as it accounts for Rasta elsewhere in the world.

The Japanese Embrace of Reggae

Sterling chronicles the history of the Japanese embrace of reggae's various forms through five main phases.[36] First, the "birth" occurred from the mid-1970s to the early 1980s, with the 1973 release of Jimmy Cliff's *The Harder They Come* film acting as a cultural midwife, helping to bring a new look and a fresh sound to this island nation in East Asia. A few import record shops helped to boost album sales, and Tokyo's Club 69, which showcased roots reggae, also paved the way for Bob Marley's 1979 performance in Japan. Artists like Freddie McGregor and the Mighty Diamonds, now global Rastafari ambassadors in their own right, arrived later.

Second, the "laying of the foundations" happened from the early 1980s until the mid-1980s. Corporately-funded reggae fanzines first appeared, and small record labels like Overheat journeyed to Jamaica to form business alliances with several Jamaican artists. More and more Japanese attended concerts, especially the world touring Reggae Sunsplash event, which stopped off in Tokyo. Also, home-grown or all-Japanese talent emerged in this period—bands like PJ and Cool Runnings; DJs like Rankin' Taxi; and, sound systems like Brainwash and Earthquake.

Third, the "boom" hit from the mid-1980s to the mid-1990s. The Reggae JapanSplash inaugural concert occurred in 1985, followed by the steady release of books, documentaries, and feature films on Caribbean and Rasta life, among them *Cool Runnings* (1993), and during this time local reggae artists like Nahki started to enjoy high record sales.[37] More and more Japanese visited Jamaica, and many of them returned home to frequent some of the newly opened reggae bars and craft stores, purposely designed to capitalize on the explosive interest in Rastafari and its many, cultural arts.

Fourth, Japanese reggae fans witnessed roots reggae's "contraction" from the mid-1990s to the late 1990s, together with the expansion of dancehall reggae, which Sterling defines as the "patios-based toasting to digitized beats, and the subcultures associated with it."[38] Regional musical tastes became more and more pronounced during this era also, with aesthetic appreciation dividing along city/rural lines, fostering some differences that persist to the present day. Sterling writes:

> Although there are many exceptions, the majority of young, urban dance-hall fans from such cities as Yokohama, Tokyo, and Osaka, though able to appreciate the kinship between roots and dancehall, have comparative difficulty connecting with the former; while in rural areas, where much of the postboom roots scene is now to be found, roots' naturalistic vibe has followers, old and young, who see dancehall as nothing but grating noise and chatter.[39]

Artists like Nahki and Rankin' Taxi soon re-imagined their styles to better blend in with the emerging dominance of dancehall reggae, where creolized Japa-dread talk punctuated single digital percussion arrangements. Sound systems promoted this new music. And female reggae dancers also surfaced during this period, with some of them setting the stage for the major events in the international dancehall community at the new millennium's turn.

Fifth, dancehall reggae music's "rise" has been underway since the late 1990s, and it continues through to the present day. In 1999, as most people prepared for the so-called Y2K disaster, members of the Japanese sound system Mighty Crown traveled to New York City, where they contended with other sound systems as the only non-Jamaican competitor at World Clash 1999; surprisingly, Mighty Crown won the event.[40] Three years later, the Japanese reggae dancer Junko Kudo secured a similar victory, returning home with the honor of being the first non-Jamaican to win Jamaica's National Dancehall Queen Contest.[41] These two victories signified a successful "Japanese excursion into the international," Sterling notes, and the interest in dancehall reggae's potential at home as well as abroad created the phenomenon critics now call "J-reggae," which artists like Fire Ball, Ryo the Skywalker, and Shonan no Kaze have commercialized throughout the last decade.[42] This indigenous form of dancehall music has recently received extensive exposure at places like the Yokohama Reggae Festival, which Mighty Crown's entertainment company now produces and where Rasta's "subcultural imagery" (flags, posters, clothing) both adorns the stage and stirs the spirits of concert-goers.[43]

Sterling's five phases of the Japanese embrace of reggae music and Rastafari underline an important feature of my own book: Rasta and its many artforms are no longer restricted, if they ever were, to a single location. The Rastafari religious movement now thrives in global or multisited contexts, and art explains the situational shape that Rasta takes in any given local or regional sites. My book shows that reggae music's commercial currents have facilitated the Rastafari's internationalization. Assuredly, Rastas have travelled a long way from their early days in Leonard P. Howell's Jamaican commune. Howell's "Pinnacle" Rastas were firm believers in Selassie's divinity, for example, and yet Sterling informs us that he did not meet anyone in Japan who believed that Selassie is God without some qualification.[44] Peel back layer after layer of reggae-influenced Japanese Rasta reasoning, just as I did with Ghanaian Rasta reasoning, and one finds a plurality of Selassies, each one reflecting the face of the one who reasons about H.I.M. As my book reveals, the Rastafari's many religious dimensions are artfully reworked in whatever context they appear, and in the following interview Sterling caringly explores what this observation entails for him.

An Interview with Marvin D. Sterling

DJNM: What are some of the major signposts on your life's journey? You were born and raised in Jamaica, for example, and you self-identify as a non-Rastafarian. Still, I am curious: What's your earliest memory of Rasta in your homeland?

MDS: I can't say that I remember any one moment when I encountered Rastafari or Rastafarians for the first time. It just seemed like, growing up in Jamaica in the 1970s, and going to school in Kingston, the culture was everywhere. You weren't supposed to use dread talk in the classroom, because in the formal educational setting it was considered, and is still considered by a lot of people, to be inappropriate. But even so, it was such a part of the everyday popular culture in the broadest sense of the term that of course young guys adopted it when we were away from those settings.

I immigrated to the U.S. when I was thirteen, to Queens, New York. There wasn't much of a Jamaican community there at all. And as a high school student and as an undergrad, I followed all the curricular steps I needed to take to graduate, but realized only late in the game how little coursework I had taken that was related to where I was from. So there came a point where I really wanted to understand this part of my experience. I made a point near the end of my time as an undergrad to learn more about Caribbean culture and history. So down the line, when I decided as a graduate student to do this research on Rasta in Japan, I really came to feel that it was an important way to stay in contact with my culture.

DJNM: When did you know you were an anthropologist?

MDS: I was a Communications Studies major as an undergrad at NYU, with a specialization in print journalism, and felt pretty sure that I wanted to go to grad school. I got a lot out of my major, and had some great mentors in the program, like Neil Postman, Bill Petkanas, Terrence Moran, and Ed Burns. But I wanted to keep an open mind about what I'd pursue in grad school. I realized at some point that all the Communications Studies courses that I was really into all had some really strong cross-cultural element, and I thought anthropology was the discipline that really went most directly to that interest. So I think I knew that I was an anthropologist when, even though I was coming from a different disciplinary background, I got into the graduate program in anthropology at UCLA!

But I think I really became an anthropologist when I finished writing my dissertation. Dissertation fieldwork is such a major rite of passage in the discipline. And it was for me as well. But if I wasn't able to make some sense of these experiences I had in the field, in a way that I could explain to anthropologists, then I don't think I could say I'm an anthropologist. It was only when I finished the dissertation and thought that it was a good representation of my research experience that I could honestly make that claim.

DJNM: Relatedly, how does being Jamaican constitute a particular perspective in your work?

MDS: With regard to this project on reggae in Japan, I think being Jamaican has made me especially sensitive to wanting to include the Jamaican side of the story. Jamaicans not only have their own investments in reggae, obviously, but also in Japanese investment in the music. I felt a bit of an obligation to capture some of those concerns. More broadly, being Jamaican has made me think about what it means to be a 'native anthropologist,' which my colleague Lanita Jacobs at the University of Southern California, and others, have written about. This includes the expectation that native anthropologists, by definition, write only about their experiences. My research is largely about Japanese people's experiences and largely about my own as a Jamaican. But as a Jamaican who's lived in the U.S. for a really long time, I don't assume to have the same claim to Jamaican culture as a Jamaican who's lived in Jamaica all his life. So I think directly and otherwise my work has been informed by these kinds of questions about native ethnography, cultural ownership, and cultural authenticity.

DJNM: No doubt Japan will strike some observers as the least likely venue for manifestations of African diaspora cultural agency, and for the presence of Rastafari especially, so, what inspired you to travel and research there?

MDS: Before I started grad school in LA, I worked for a year in Skid Row, for an organization that provides social services for homeless kids. Skid Row is right next to Little Tokyo, which had some gift shops for the Japanese tourists passing through. I noticed one day there was a Mammy doll sitting in the window of one of these stores, and this struck me as really surprising. So once I got to grad school and needed to decide on the focus of my research, that moment came back to me. I guess I've been thinking about it ever since.

DJNM: I visited Japan fairly recently and, shortly after my arrival, I found myself most intrigued by scattered signs of Rasta in Tokyo and elsewhere. But I was not sure how to account for it. Thus, I was very pleased to find and read your book, *Babylon East*, after I returned to the U.S. I hope others will join me in finding it instructive, not simply for understanding the internationalization of the Rastafari movement, but because it offers a signal contribution to Global African Diaspora Studies. I wonder: What *one* lesson do you hope your readers will take from *Babylon East's* conceptual braiding of Japanese and Jamaican culture(s)?

MDS: Thanks for your kinds words about my book! Just as a gut response to your question, it's that as unusual as this Jamaican-Japanese encounter around reggae music seems to a lot of people, including, initially, myself, it seems quite normal to the folks involved in it. So I have to wonder what it is about our disciplines that make this empirically very real stuff so hard to imagine, and so hard to understand. I think we've made certain assumptions about who Japanese are, and who Jamaicans are, such that a conversation between them seems unlikely, even as they're actually taking place. So the one thing I want my readers to take from this book is not so much an answer as a question: What kinds of directions can we take our scholarship, and our general thinking about the world and about the people in it, to make these global conversations more comprehensible and less surprising? What kinds of human connections come into view when we remove those discursive blinders?

DJNM: You tell us that one of your book's major concerns involves "thinking about blackness beyond the African diaspora and, more broadly, race in a global context."[45] Why, and how so?

MDS: In answer to the 'Why' part of your question, I've been struck by two things. One is how vivid the imagination of black people can be in places outside the diaspora, and how little research, until recently, has been done on this topic. The other is how much those ideas about blackness are informed by representations and ideologies that originate in the West. So many of the stereotypes about black people that originated in the West are in common circulation all around the world. There are some practical reasons why we should be concerned about these issues. The first is that this imagination of black people in places where there are few black people have a bearing on the experiences of black folks as we travel around the world. Those assumptions about who we are will potentially have a bearing on the relationships between black people in the United States, in Europe, in Latin America and the Caribbean, and non-black people arriving to these areas as immigrants, as diplomats, students, business people and so on. So I think it's worth looking at for these reasons. In terms of how we can think about these ideas about blackness beyond the diaspora, as a cultural anthropologist my most immediate answer to this question is that we can most productively understand blackness in these places by going there, by identifying key social sites within these societies—the reggae club or what have you—that we as researchers can go to, to actually talk with people, to hear how they talk about blackness and to see how they put these ideas into play. So for me, one of the things that I discovered by travelling to Japan was just how separable blackness is for many Japanese people from the bodies of black people, so that it's not so much some property inextricably linked to the bodies of black people. It can be something pretty casually deconstructed and appropriated as an element of style associated with reggae or hip hop or what have you. I value that ethnographic approach because it represents a check, for example, against the assumption that just because so many of the representations of blackness that we see in the West are reproduced in Japan, they mean the same thing. I think in both places they're often ultimately rooted in an assumption about the voicelessness, the subaltern status of black people, this assumption that one can do what one likes with the image of blackness without needing to worry, or even begin to think about what black folks think. But at the same time, I think there needs to be an attentiveness to the local context, including local social history, to really get at some of the nuances in terms of how these images are understood in any particular place.

DJNM: Reggae is the primary mechanism for the global spread of Rastafari, as many scholars, including you, recognize. In terms of accounting for "Rasta-identifying Japanese" today, do you think it is possible to overstate the importance of Mighty Crown and Junko Kudo?[46]

MDS: I'd separate Rasta-identifying Japanese as people who are deeply invested in Rasta from the larger number of fans and practitioners of dancehall reggae music. I think the first group forces us to remember that the popularity of dancehall didn't come out of nowhere, that its success was largely built on the success of roots reggae in the mid-1980s to the late 1990s. For the second group, I do think that the World Clash victory was enormous. Over and over again I asked folks in the scene what they attribute the popularity of dancehall to, and everyone said it was about Mighty Crown's victory in 1999. Mighty Crown was doing really well before that victory: I went to several of their events in fairly large venues and they drew really big crowds. But things went to another level after 1999, because I think for a lot of Japanese fans and practitioners the music was legitimized by that victory over Jamaican competitors. Junko Kudo's victory did something similar. It didn't happen immediately though. It took a couple of years for that escalation to take place. It spread throughout the scene, got a bit of mainstream attention with some big hits and a late-night television show on the scene, and then it took off after that. I also think the popularity of reggae acts like Shaggy and Sean Paul in the United States had an influence, since many Japanese kids are tuned into developments in the U.S.

DJNM: Tell us about today's J-reggae. Is it religious, for example, or is it primarily an urban subcultural force?

MDS: J-reggae is really diverse, as diverse as reggae in Jamaica. For the most part though J-reggae is dancehall driven, so the more spiritual, roots stuff isn't as foregrounded as it was during the first reggae boom beginning in the mid-1980s. It's primarily younger, urban, and subcultural, but a few artists like Miki Dozan and Fireball have had mainstream hits. There are of course a few urban roots reggae artists like Ras Kanto who have that more spiritual vibe, and most of the roots-oriented dub artists I met lived in the city but performed in both urban and rural settings.[47] But for the most part the folks who were most committed to the roots vibe, not just as musicians but as Rastas, were out in the countryside.

DJNM: Who is your favorite contemporary Japanese reggae musician, and why?

MDS: I think there should be creative room for dancehall to be a lot of things, including partying and having a good time. But as someone who recognizes that the music can have a certain amount of progressive political power as well, I tend to like musicians who also use their music to say something important. I like Rankin' Taxi because he does both things.[48] He's an institution in dancehall, partly for being one of the very first Japanese artists to perform in the Japanese language, and so that takes the music in some new creative directions. He's personally a light-hearted guy, and that comes out in much of his music. But he's also used his position to call attention to some important issues, including to criticize the Japanese government and the Tokyo Electric Power Company for their handling of the nuclear crisis in 2011. He does it in a light-hearted way, but also in a way that forces us to think about our own inclination to buy into the illusion of safety. There are a lot of other talented artists out there whose music I appreciate for doing this kind of music in a more sustained way, people like Shandi I and Ras Kanto. I also like H-Man very much as a lyricist. He's a great humorist and storyteller on the stage. Pushim, who is a female singer, has an amazing voice.

DJNM: Carolyn Cooper's analysis of Jamaican dancehall culture problematizes the standard complaint that it is misogynistic and, as recently as 2010, she situates dancehall in the context of West African fertility rituals, and thinks it instantiates a Jamaican womanist politics of subversion.[49] Would you please comment on Cooper's work? Does it display transcultural connection(s) to Japan, as it were, or does Japanese dancehall culture represent itself so differently as to require an alternative reading or interpretation?

MDS: I think Cooper's work is very important for a number of reasons, and the main one might be how consistently she pushes against the tendency among many Jamaicans and others to marginalize dancehall as unworthy of academic inquiry. It's dismissed as misogynistic and vulgar and violent, and the fact that it touches the lives of hundreds of thousands of men and women, in some ways positively, is ignored. It's partly that view of the academy as a space of privileged, esoteric inquiry coming up against the view of the academy as a space for examining all humanity in all of its complexity. As Cooper and Norman Stolzoff and others rightly have pointed out, dancehall in Jamaica really is a metaphor for so much else going on in Jamaican society, including a class divide that gets played out in the academy as this debate about what is considered worth studying. So I appreciate Cooper's work for specifically recognizing the value of studying the lives of the Afro-Jamaican working class who, if it were not for dancehall in all of its good and bad, would that much more easily be ignored.

I don't know enough about the West African fertility rituals that Cooper discusses to make the specific connection that she does to Jamaican dance-hall. Of course it's always tricky to connect two cultural traditions separated over so much space and time. The suggestion is valuable at the very least for foregrounding the Afrocentrisms that do strongly exist in Jamaican culture. By foregrounding them in the way she does in her scholarship, it becomes not something that should be ignored out of some Anglophilic or bourgeois sense of progress, as can be the case in Jamaica, but rather a significant aspect of the Jamaican experience.

As for how her work speaks to transcultural dancehall connections between Jamaica and Japan, I think her explorations of Jamaican society's response to the 'vulgarity' of the dancehall creates some interesting parallels with the Japanese instance. Much of the controversy surrounding reggae dance sexuality in both places has to do with a simultaneously gendered, class-based and racialized expectation that Jamaican women in a sense work preemptively hard to demonstrate their moral worth in a Western-dominated, global moral order that views women of color as backward, promiscuous, and so forth. And I think much the same can be said for Japanese women, whose sexualities are racialized in similar ways. Both in Jamaican and Japanese reggae dance, the performers refuse to play by those rules. I don't see reggae dance as liberatory in quite the same way that Cooper does, because in some ways, as Stolzoff points out, gendered power in the dancehall comes down to male power and male desire in a way that profoundly objectifies women. But I think Cooper's concern with this conjunction of race, gender and class is important in my own thinking about the Japanese instance.

DJNM: Beyond reggae, what else has contributed to the global commodification of Rasta?

MDS: It's hard to think of anything that has had anything like the effect that reggae has had on Rasta's commodification. But a second key way might be tourism. Tourism's a major part of the Jamaican economy, and reggae and Rasta are a major resource that the Jamaican tourism industry rely on to convince people why they should come to Jamaica and not someplace else. So that visual commodification of Rasta in tourist ads and commercials is a significant aspect of that commodification.

DJNM: In Japan, as you show, some Japanese use 'Babylon' to complicate notions of class and race, to problematize Western and Japanese imperialism, and to challenge late modern capitalism's consumerism.[50] Is there anything in this usage that surprises you? Why? Why not?

MDS: In Jamaica, and throughout the African diaspora, the Rasta critique of Babylon is really closely tied into the view of Haile Selassie as that figure who will lead black people out of this corrupted space. Babylon and Zion are deeply opposed ideas and precisely in this way they're deeply intertwined. What's interesting to me is how viable a concept Babylon remains for Japanese

practitioners of Rasta, even without having a clear investment in the idea of
Zion, or in Selassie's divinity. What that says to me is just how compelling the
idea of Babylon itself is to these Japanese practitioners, and of course to many
people around the world.

DJNM: What most intrigues you when you reflect on Rastafari's resituation in
urban and rural parts of Japan?

MDS: Two related questions come to mind when I think about this. The first
is how you answer the question: "How 'authentic' is any religion, or cultural expression generally, when you take it out of its original context?" I
don't know that I've ever come up with a definite answer, except to say that
instead of trying to see Rasta in Japan as fitting or not fitting some standard
of authenticity, it might be more useful analytically to think about how the
dimensions it takes on in the Japanese context reveal something about Japan,
about the dynamics of cultural appropriation generally and so forth. The second question has to do with what it is about Rasta specifically that allows it
to be meaningful not just in Jamaica but also in Japan, and not just in Japan as
a homogenous place, but as a place that can be differentiated in a number of
ways, including in urban and rural terms. I think it's the complexity of Rasta
as a movement that allows it to be so many things to so many people. In the
Jamaican context, it's a religion, a way of protesting oppression, a lifestyle in
the sense of a way of dressing and eating, and more. So it's intriguing to me
how in each place people draw strategically on those aspects of Rasta that
make sense to them, that can be brought together in a coherent way.

DJNM: Could you elaborate on your sense that rural Japanese fascination for
Rasta grew out of frustration with East Asian religions in general?

MDS: I met several people who expressed indifference about Japanese religious
traditions, because these traditions were just so familiar to them. They
described going on a search, exploring religious traditions, so to speak, and
then encountering Rasta, often through reggae music. So in these cases, it's a
sense of disaffection with Japanese religious traditions that comes first.

But most others gave no indication to me of being opposed to local religious traditions, maybe in the general way that most Japanese don't engage
these religions in a faith-based way. They're simply part of their everyday
lives in the way of certain ritual practices, such as those associated with child-
birth, marriage, death, and so on. Sometimes, with the encounter with Rasta,
these individuals might also come to feel the need to criticize Buddhism
and Shintō. I wonder if this rejection is part of a self-conscious effort to
bridge the gap between self-identification as Japanese and Rasta as Jamaican.
In other words, would being able to reject Shintō and Buddhism discreetly
affirm your commitment to Rasta?

But whether in the case of individuals who felt indifference towards
Japanese religious traditions, or in cases where individuals were deeply critical of these traditions, there are these constant returns to Japan, and to

Japaneseness. Rasta becomes a way of vitalizing one's spiritual life in a way that isn't necessarily opposed to Buddhism, or Shintō, or Shugendō. For me, that's the main takeaway, not an oppositionality of religions. Japanese can worship Rasta because a Jamaican Rasta and a Japanese practitioner of Shintō, for instance, are both in awe of a natural divinity that is essentially the same. And so in that way, Japanese can be Rastas. I never sensed that Japanese Rastas were interested in not being Japanese, and to the extent that these local religious traditions are a deep part of Japanese social life, Rasta is really used as something to energize one's spiritual life, including as a Japanese person. That ability to subsume the Jamaican within the Japanese in a way that makes 'Japanese' sense resonates with much of Japanese engagement with foreign culture generally.

DJNM: The Yoshino dreads see the founder of Buddhism's highly syncretic Shugendō sect as a kind of proto-Rasta, because visual art often depicts him as bearded and with long hair, sometimes flowing down to his waist. Something similar happens with Ghanaian Rastas when they discuss Okomfo Anokye, the fetish priest at the center of Ashanti mythology, and I am keen to see if there's anything you'd like to say or add in response to such local or situational theologizing.[51]

MDS: This opinion, in which one Yoshino dread identified the long-haired founder of Shugendō as a kind of Rasta, wasn't necessarily one that the rest of the Yoshino dreads shared. So I don't want to generalize beyond this particular person making this particular remark. But it is really reflective of the almost relentless constancy with which not just the Yoshino dreads but so many of what I call Rasta-identifying Japanese tried to make connections that legitimized and deepened the movement in Japan. There's an element of play in this kind of "situational theologizing," but it's quite serious in the sense that this is the labor that these individuals need to go through to arrive at the point where they can say that Japanese Rasta, or Rastafari in Japan, is definitively such and such. It was really interesting to me to see the creativity and diversity of strategies that went into this, and constancy with which this was being done.

DJNM: *Babylon East* records a trend in Japan that I, working from West Africa, have noticed in places like Ghana: Belief in Haile Selassie's divinity is not an axiomatic feature of Rasta livity in non-Jamaican contexts. What accounts for this 'low Christology,' for want of a better term, and can you foresee this approach to the Emperor shaping Jamaican Rastas in the near future?

MDS: I think in the Japanese context the most straightforward explanation for this "low Christology" has to do with the fact that Christianity hasn't taken root, and so the idea of a Messiah, let alone a black Messiah, doesn't really resonate there. Japan is famous for its 'take the best and leave the rest' approach to cultural adoption, so I don't think there's much issue there about filtering out those elements of Rasta that don't quite work in the Japanese setting.

About whether Jamaican Rastas will adopt a similar approach: I haven't seen enough evidence to believe this will happen any time soon, if ever. There are individual Rastas who don't see Selassie as a divinity, but 'only' as a great man and as an idealized exemplar of black resistance against colonial power. They might see Selassie as divine in the way that all black people are divine, as a perfect manifestation of this black humanity. But I think it's fair to say that this position is in the minority, and that Jamaican Rastas will continue to place Selassie's unqualified divinity at the center of their belief. I feel this way not because I have any profound insight into the future of the movement, but just because of the passion and endurance with which Rastas have insisted on Selassie's divinity.

DJNM: Your last chapter upholds the value of "a postcolonial imagination of blackness."[52] Generally, what *one* thing has Rasta contributed to this way of looking at the world?

MDS: I think the most important thing that Rastas have contributed to this idea of postcolonial blackness is the experiential totality of dissent. Rasta is so many things, all of which in a sense are about recognizing and undermining in everyday life the ideologically complex ways in which black people are marginalized. There's dread talk, the very idea of a black Messiah, the creative re-reading of the Bible in a way that affirms one's racial self-worth, dreadlocks, marijuana consumption, and the recognition that colonialism and capitalism are in many ways the same beast. There's the willingness to separate from Babylon and pursue all of this in a deep way in a Rasta yard or a commune. This is not an exhaustive list, but all of it converges around knowing and feeling and living the worth of black people as deep and complex, in a total, self-contained way, despite some very powerful forces saying otherwise.

DJNM: Many readers will emerge from your book with a sense that Rasta in Japan is not simply a lifestyle—it is a lifestyle with the potential for being a religion.[53] How are you using 'religion' here, and what inclines you to conclude your study in this way? Also, do you think Jamaican Rastas, who often stress 'livity' over 'religion,' would welcome your observation or find it unwelcome?

MDS: 'Religion' is a notoriously difficult concept, so I'll focus on the aspect of it that I think is more directly relevant to this issue of what Rasta is in Japan. I'm using the term religion to speak to a set of ideas and practices that a group of people share as a way of understanding the divine. My skepticism about Japanese Rastafari as a religion, to the extent that we're talking about a Rastafari that's unique to Japan, is that in the course of my research, I haven't heard a consistently articulated theology that's shared by a large group of believers. What's offered in the way of a distinctively Japanese theology is offered in a speculative spirit, rather than in the declarative one that you more commonly find in religion. So for instance, some Japanese practitioners of

Rasta point to some popular writing arguing that the Japanese are the true ancient Israelites. Since Jamaican Rasta identification as such is rooted in the claim that they are the ancient Israelites, for Japanese Rastas, the existence of this literature on Japanese as the ancient Israelites becomes these Rastas' way of claiming that they're real Rastas. But they don't quite say that they buy this literature, since this literature can be stridently antisemitic, and they don't want to be associated with that. So they point to this literature in the spirit of saying, "Hey, what if?", without going so far as saying, "This is so." So I think that a Rasta movement in Japan that's justified as specifically Japanese through this literature doesn't have enough unwavering support to say that such a Rastafari is fully theologically codified.

But I think the potential is there, since even without that theological codification, in the end, you could argue that these practitioners are connecting with the divine, in the form of a profound appreciation of the natural world. The trickiness of this enters the picture when you consider whether that profoundly appreciated natural world is sited in Japan, which would create a possible basis for a 'Japanese' Rastafari. But even if you go with this reading, I'd still return to the absence of a clearly articulated, confidently claimed, widely shared body of ideas that can be considered particularly Japanese. Since that's not there, in my opinion, 'Japanese Rastas' are Rastas if Jamaican diasporic Rastas include them in their community.

Part of the reason I thought this discussion belonged in the final chapter is because I wanted to use this question of diasporic disconnection versus connection, of a Rastafari that was specifically Japanese as opposed to a diasporic Rasta that happened to be in Japan, as a way of thinking about some of the complexity of the Afro-Asian encounter. This was a key concern in this chapter. It leads to the second part of your question, about the question of livity versus religion. I imagine that many Rastas wouldn't appreciate my description of Rasta as a religion, because that positions it as just another theological '-ism.' Rasta for Rastas is simply striving to inhabit uplift and purity and truth in the everyday, in an experientially absolute way. But as an academic, I do feel that I have to engage the term religion if I'm to get at some key distinctions between the Japanese and Jamaican movements.

I describe Rasta as a religion—only from an etic, but non-reductionist point of view—not so much as Rastas take issue with the term, as one-ism among many others. Rather, I'm using the term as many Jamaican Rastas themselves implicitly understand it, and even, in some cases, strategically use it in understanding their movement. This is precisely in the sense that Rasta is *not* arbitrary. Rastas are not just some outcasts whom we can afford to not respect or take seriously. Rather, Rasta is a coherent and generationally sustained movement, which as such entitles Rastas to the human right to freely and openly practice what outsiders like myself, international law and so on might term as their 'religion.' So it's partly in that spirit of acknowledging the need to respect Rasta, and all the rights that come with practicing this 'religion,' in which I'm using the term.

DJNM: In your opinion, what does the future hold for Rastas?

MDS: Of course these things are tough to predict, so I'll answer based on why, eighty years after its birth, we're talking about Rasta right now. The staying power of Rasta is not so much about any one aspect of the belief system but the totality of it, the way that it resonates with people's desire to speak against injustice of all kinds. If Rasta will survive in the future as a global movement, I think it will be largely because of this. But I think when historians fifty years from now or eighty years from now look back to the present moment and before, and to the extent that historians will still be concerned with big picture issues like colonialism as a force that people fought against on the level of ideology, it's really hard not to think about Rastafari. I think that this ideologically coherent resistance against colonialism is likely to be something for which people will remember Rasta for a long time.

As for Jamaican Rastas, I think they'll be around for a long time. As long as some of the issues they address remain with us, as long as they stay outside the system, and as long as they're able to make clear how their beliefs and practices speak to those issues, then they'll be around for a long time. I don't think separatism is necessarily the best way to change things, and being outside the system can sometimes leave you especially vulnerable to it. But I think that it does draw strength from being a lived sign of the possibility of something other than the system.

Conclusion

The Rastafari first appeared in the Caribbean in the 1930s and the movement has steadily spread to many parts of the world ever since due, in part, to Jamaican popular culture's transnational appeal. Today, brethren and sistren are becoming less homogenous, and local livities as well as international diversity are now an integral part of the way Rastas are evolving. Using Ghana and Japan as two case studies of art's role in the Rastafari's global dispersal, this chapter observes that when people around the world embrace the movement's many religious dimensions, they often craft situational Rastafari identities. Recent studies confirm my observation(s).[54] By monitoring the Rastafari's existence and impact in other parts of the African continent as well as in Brazil, Croatia, Cuba, New Zealand, North America and so on, scholars are accentuating the idea that Rasta may best be understood as an artful, vernacular religion in everyday life. Musicians like Mani Kongo ("Rasta from the Kalahari"), Nechi Nech ("Israeli Rasta"), Radio La Chusma ("Rasta Mexico"), The Reggae Bubblers ("St Croix to Shashemene"), and Sydney Salmon ("Shashemene on My Mind") concur. For my part, I suspect that whether they practice their livity at home or abroad, present and future Rastas can expect to have to rise to the recurring challenge to re-imagine their faith to fit their ever-changing world(s).

Coping with Babylon will form an important part of this challenge. Roy Augier agrees. One of the three academics who authored the trailblazing *Report on the Rastafari Movement in Kingston, Jamaica*, in 1960, Augier also gave the opening address of the inaugural Rastafari Studies Conference in 2010. Here, Augier enjoined contemporary Rastafari to follow Bob Marley's example and thus strengthen the movement by taking an imaginative approach to Babylon:

> Those of you who have grasped the true relation of the Rasta to Africa have liberated themselves. They are the ones whose economic condition is several times better than yours. They are the ones who have taken the music, who have taken the culture, who tour, who go to Japan, who make money in Africa, who make money in the United States. Why do they do it? They do it with your culture. If you want a source of economic independence, you have to follow in their footsteps: you have to deal with Babylon.
>
> When you celebrate Bob Marley, when you celebrate the others, are you not celebrating a Rasta who has made his life in acknowledgment of Babylon? You cannot efface Babylon.[55]

Consumerism denotes one small but not insignificant way in which brethren and sistren now 'deal with Babylon,' as it were, and outsiders as well as insiders to the Rastafari movement may be seen playing their various parts in the religion's complex commodification or postmodern branding. In the epilogue that follows this last chapter, I explore the apparent irony behind what Rivke Jaffe calls "Ital Chic," and I consider how the anticapitalist message of earlier Rastafari artists has morphed into more consumer-driven material forms.[56] These days, chanting change around the world occurs through consumer goods, and such goods stand poised to create new possibilities as well as fresh challenges for Rastas, as we will see.

Notes

1 Erin C. MacLeod, *Visions of Zion: Ethiopians and Rastafari in the Search for the Promised Land* (New York: New York University Press, 2014).

2 Henry Louis Gates, Jr., *Wonders of the African World* (New York: Alfred A. Knopf, 1999), 192–215. This book accompanies the PBS television series; for details, see: http://www.pbs.org/wonders/. Accessed March 30, 2014.

3 Research for this article occurred during various visits to Ghana in the first decade of the new millennium. Initial reflection on Ghanaian Rastafari first appeared in Darren J.N. Middleton, "As It Is in Zion: Seeking the Rastafari in Ghana, West Africa," *Black Theology: An International Journal* 4.2 (2006): 151–172. Reproduced with kind permission of Equinox Publishing. The current chapter revises and updates the earlier work.

4 Neil J. Savishinsky, "Rastafari in the Promised Land: The Spread of a Jamaican Socio-religious Movement and its Music and Culture Among the Youth of Ghana and

Senegambia," Columbia University Doctoral Dissertation, Columbia University, Department of Anthropology, 1993. A more condensed summary has been published. See Neil J. Savishinsky, "Rastafari in the Promised Land: The Spread of a Jamaican Socioreligious Movement Among the Youth of West Africa," *African Studies Review* 37.3 (December 1994): 19–50. For more recent studies see: Elom Dovlo, "Rastafari, African Hebrews and Black Muslims: Return 'Home' Movements in Ghana," *Exchange* 31.1 (2002): 2–22; Janice Kerfoot, "Babylon Boys Don't Dance: Music, Meaning, and Young Men in Accra." Thesis (M.A.)—McGill University, 2006: http://digitool.library.McGill. CA:80/R/?func=dbin-jump-full&object_id=99727 (accessed March 30, 2014); Claire Stafford, "Reggae and Rastafari: The Popularity of Reggae Music in Ghana, West Africa." Thesis (M.A.)—National University of Ireland, University College Cork, 2007; Jonathan Tanis, "Babylon by Tro-Tro: The Varieties of Rasta Identity and Practice in Ghana." ISP Collection. Paper 849 (2010): http://digitalcollections.sit.edu/isp_collec tion/849 (accessed March 30, 2014); and Carmen M. White, "Rastafarian Repatriates and the Negotiation of Place in Ghana," *Ethnology: An International Journal of Cultural and Social Anthropology* 49.4 (2010): 303–320.

5 Dawuni prefers the label 'Afro-roots,' because it suggests a blend of traditional roots reggae and Afro-Beat. For details, see: http://www.rockydawuni.com/ and http://www. blakkrasta.com/. Both sites accessed March 30, 2014.

6 Marvin D. Sterling, *Babylon East: Performing Dancehall, Roots Reggae, and Rastafari in Japan* (Durham, NC: Duke University Press, 2010), 155–156, 228–229.

7 For details on Ghana's heritage, and its recent economic as well as political struggles, see Roger Gocking, *The History of Ghana* (Westport, CT: Greenwood Press, 2005).

8 This said, recent studies suggest some stigmatization. Carmen White writes:

> For many Ghanaians, the tattered, scanty clothing, matted hair, and disheveled appearance and regular occupancy of public spaces by the mentally ill signals their lack of care for themselves or care from others, marking their position on the extreme margins of society. This association between locked, matted hair and madness is reflected in the statement of one Ghanaian who pointed out that Rastas with locked hair are spared being labeled as 'mad men' on sight by virtue of their beanies and clothing in Rasta colors. But the connections between locks, Rastas, mad men, and even fetish priests suggest a complex assessment of males with locked hair as a presence beyond the bounds of respectable society. Locked hair is a sign of social disorder in Ghanaian society. Fetish priests, for example, are increasingly condemned as harbingers of paganism and heathenism by the evangelical churches in Ghana.

See White, "Rastafarian Repatriates and Negotiation of Place in Ghana," 310.

9 On Anokye's story, see Gates, *Wonders of the African World*, 209–211. Also see Robert Z. Cohen, *Discovering the Asante Kingdom* (New York: Rosen Publishing Group, 2014). Finally, see T.C. McCaskie, "The Golden Stool at the End of the Nineteenth Century: Setting the Record Straight," *Ghana Studies* 3 (2000): 61–96.

10 On Ghanaian religious specialists, see Robert B. Fisher, *West African Religious Traditions: Focus on the Akan of Ghana* (Maryknoll, NY: Orbis Books, 1998), 105–119.

11 For additional details, see Kevin Shillington, *Ghana and the Rawlings Factor* (New York: Palgrave Macmillan, 1992).

12 On this phenomenon, see Ann Reed, *Pilgrimage Tourism of Diaspora Africans to Ghana* (New York and London: Routledge, 2014). Also see William St. Clair, *The Door of No*

Return: The History of Cape Coast Castle and the Atlantic Slave Trade (New York: Blue-Bridge, 2007).

13 Mutabaruka, "Ghana: Africa from Experience," in Werner Zips, editor, *Rastafari: A Universal Philosophy in the Third Millennium* (Kingston, Jamaica; Miami: Ian Randle Publishers, 2006), 114.

14 Regarding pan-Africanism in Ghana, see Katharina Schramm, *African Homecoming: Pan-African Ideology and Contested Heritage* (Walnut Creek, CA: 2010).

15 Recent fieldwork in Senegal, in cities like Dakar and in fishing villages like Toubab Dialaw, convinces me that Blakk Rasta is not alone in such syncretism. I struck up many conversations with Baye Faal, so-called Muslim Rastafari, who display an intriguing mashup of Sufi Islam and Rastology. Very little has been written about this group's alliance with Rasta. For initial details, see Neil J. Savishinsky, "The Baye Faal of Senegambia: Muslim Rastas in the Promised Land?" *Africa* 64.2 (1994): 211–219.

16 See: http://thecaucus.blogs.nytimes.com/2009/07/12/a-theme-song-for-obamas-ghana-visit/?_php=true&_type=blogs&_r=0. Accessed March 30, 2014.

17 For Zephaniah's commentary, see: http://www.theguardian.com/commentisfree/2012/aug/07/snoop-dogg-rastafari. Accessed March 30, 2014.

18 Dean W. Collinwood and Osamu Kusatsu, "Japanese Rastafarians: Non-Conformity in Modern Japan," *The Study of International Relations* 26 (Tokyo: Tsuda College, 2000): 23–35.

19 Sterling, *Babylon East*, 154–189.

20 *Ibid.*, 143–144, 155–157, 169, 170–171, 179–181, 228–229.

21 *Ibid.*, 156.

22 *Ibid.*, 157–161.

23 *Ibid.*, 162–163.

24 This expression may be traced to Emily Raboteau, *Searching for Zion: The Quest for Home in the African Diaspora* (New York: Atlantic Monthly Press, 2013), 111–181. She traces it to a Shashemene-based Rasta.

25 Sterling, *Babylon East*, 165.

26 *Ibid.*, 166.

27 *Ibid.*, 167–169.

28 *Ibid.*, 173.

29 *Ibid.*, 178. For the complete description of the Rasta yard, see 176–185.

30 *Ibid.*, 178–179.

31 *Ibid.*, 179.

32 *Ibid.*, 181.

33 *Ibid.*, 181, 182.

34 *Ibid.*, 183.

35 *Ibid.*

36 *Ibid.*, 9–19.

37 For Nahki's site, see: http://www.nahki.com/. Accessed March 30, 2014.

38 Sterling, *Babylon East*, 8.

39 *Ibid.*, 13.

40 For Mighty Crown's history and projects, see http://www.mightycrown.com/e/index.php. Accessed March 30, 2014.

41 For Kudo's moves, see: http://www.youtube.com/watch?v=rZsCEL7itig. Accessed March 30, 2014.

42 Sterling, *Babylon East*, 15.

43 *Ibid.*, 17.

44 *Ibid.*, 228–229.

45 *Ibid.*, 5.

46 Ibid., 84–99, 126–133, 155.

47 On Ras Kanto, see: https://soundcloud.com/ras-kanto and https://myspace.com/raskanto. Both sites accessed March 30, 2014.

48 For Rankin' Taxi's site, see: http://rankintaxi.com/. Accessed March 30, 2014.

49 Carolyn Cooper, *Sound Clash: Jamaican Dancehall Culture at Large* (New York: Palgrave Macmillan, 2004). Also see Carolyn Cooper, "African Diaspora Studies in the Creole-Anglophone Caribbean," in Tejumola Olaniyan and James H. Sweet, editors, *The African Diaspora and the Disciplines* (Bloomington and Indianapolis: Indiana University Press, 2010), 279–297. Also see Sterling, *Babylon East*, 61–142. Finally, see Marvin D. Sterling, "Gender, Class and Race in Japanese Dancehall Culture," in Carolyn Cooper, editor, *Global Reggae* (Kingston, Jamaica: Canoe Press, 2012), 241–261.

50 Sterling, *Babylon* East, 143–189.

51 *Ibid.*, 181–182.

52 *Ibid.*, 255.

53 *Ibid.*, 154, 223–255.

54 See the Selected Bibliography, which appears at my book's close, for details of various studies of Rastafari in global contexts. Sarah Borchert (South Africa); Ian Boxhill (New Zealand); K. Gandhar Chakravarty (Canada); Midas Chawane (South Africa); Cheikh Ahmadou Dieng (West Africa); Samuel Furé Davis (Cuba); Jan DeCosmo (Brazil); Katrin Hansing (Cuba); Claudette Hauiti (New Zealand); Randal L. Hepner (USA); Mtendeweka Owen Mhango (Malawi and Zimbabwe); Eileen Moyer (Tanzania); Gerhadus C. Oosthuizen (South Africa); Benjamin Perasovic (Croatia); Lisa Erin Philander (South Africa); and Benjamin Soares (West Africa).

55 Roy Augier, "You Must Be Willing to Reason Together," in Jahlani Niaah and Erin MacLeod, *Let Us Start with Africa: Foundations of Rastafari Scholarship* (Jamaica: The University of West Indies Press, 2013), 54.

56 Rivke Jaffe, "Ital Chic: Rastafari, Resistance, and the Politics of Consumption in Jamaica," *Small Axe* 31 (2010): 30–45.

EPILOGUE

Commodifying Rastafari

Introduction

My book has established that Rastafari may be seen as a religion, at least in a formal sense, because it displays many examples of Ninian Smart's theory of religion's seven dimensions. Insiders are skeptical of this observation. And I have tried to do justice to their disquiet concerning the term 'religion.' Yet, I hope that movement outsiders, and maybe a few insiders, will concede that this book shows how and why Rastafari *is* what brethren and sistren *do*. Rastas eat ital food (ritual dimension); uphold Ethiopianism and revere Selassie (doctrinal dimension); read the *Kebra Nagast* and the Bible (mythic dimension); reclaim cultural identity and feel black somebodiness (experiential dimension); flash dreadlocks and struggle for improved gender relations (ethical dimension); belong to mansions and follow their leaders (organizational dimension); and, many Rastas perform reggae, write novels, craft poetry, direct films, and paint their convictions on a canvas (material dimension). Rastafari is an organic religion, one that is becoming increasingly global, because it lives and breathes through such multidimensionality, which is often re-imagined to fit local contexts and needs.

Rastafari also lives and breathes through our commercial world's cultural products. And in this brief epilogue, I offer some reflections on the branding of Rastafari—the so-called merchandizing of Jah. I describe selected images, which are freely available online, some of which I have organized and now house at my personal website (www.darrenjnmiddleton.com).[1] Movement insiders will need to respond in their own way to such representations, and in their own time, but here I offer one outsider's approach to the ostensive merits and demerits associated with the way Rastafari myths and rituals have entered the public, mediated realm.

Selling Selassie

Whatever cosmological significance is ascribed to His Imperial Majesty, Emperor Haile Selassie I, and we have seen such significance change from generation to generation and from culture to culture, there is no denying that he has become a market entry in many ways in the years since his ascension to Ethiopia's throne. Sometimes Selassie enters the market in an indirect fashion, as with the example of an automobile license plate reference to 'The Lion of Judah,' which not only alludes to Rev 5:5, it stands out as one of the many titles Selassie secured at his coronation, an auspicious signal to Selassie's Solomonic dynasty as well as to his African pride. The same 'Lion of Judah' motif, minus the words, appears via an iPhone case, which, like many of the cultural products online and elsewhere, is saturated with the colors associated with the movement—red, gold, and green. Something similar appears in a 'King of Kings' t-shirt and in a 'Lion of Judah' lavalamp, which, if one examines the lamp's base, seems to be endorsed by Bob Marley's estate.

At other times, Selassie emerges in direct, inventive and, even to the informed scholar, quite puzzling ways. Consider the Nike sneakers that feature a portrait of Selassie himself, as well as the Lion of Judah, artfully festooned in red, gold, and green, an example of Nike's popular shoe customization program. Here an ancient Greek goddess of strength, speed, and victory teams up with the Elect of God, the hope of black liberation, to create a cultural artifact offering a simple message for the new millennium: religious hybridity—just do it!

Selassie as athlete may prove hard for Rastafari to consider. But it is not difficult to imagine Selassie's military might, because examples often appear in photographs, many of which are available online. One such photograph, a picture of Selassie with one foot on top of bombs dropped by Benito Mussolini's Italian forces when they invaded Ethiopia in 1935, is iconic to Rastafari. And yet, I am baffled by Selassie's appearance, dressed in military regalia, on a skateboard and in boxing gloves. I say baffled but reading through *The Trustafarian Handbook*, Brian Griffin's funny yet earnest book, has demystified some things. An astute observer of what he sees as a commodified, countercultural, and mainly white neo-hippie lifestyle inspired by Rastafari, Griffin claims that the skateboard is the Trustafarian's earth-friendly vehicle of choice; and if it is made of organic materials, as some online seem to be, then so much the better, because Rastafari favor whatever promotes ital (read: organic) living. The notion of Selassie-on-a-skateboard may be dismissed as ital chic or ethno-chic for white fashion dreads, as personified by the 'Ras Trent' character featured in an SNL digital short from a few years back, but this product illustrates, if nothing else, how the marketplace has become an influential site for Rastafari religious expression.[2]

Branding Babylon

Anglo, affluent appropriation of Rastafari is not uncommon today. But it was not always so. First-generation Rastafari rejected white dominance, especially in the form of European colonization as well as postcolonial influence, and they hoped for an eventual return to Africa from Babylon, dread talk for the evils of the West.[3] In the last eighty years or so Rasta has become, among other things, a religion of protest against white capitalist values; indeed, it is not unusual to hear Rastas chanting down Babylon, an allusion to weakening Western imperialism either through anticolonial resistance or in seeking an exodus back to Ethiopia. Although the phrase 'Rastafari is a religion of protest' is correct, it tends to tell only one half of the story. As we have seen, Rastafari is also a retrieval of black somebodiness denied by Babylon. How ironic, then, that someone somewhere—market forces?—should co-opt the alleged tools of Babylon, the marketplace and the media, to create something like the 'Babylon Advisory: Revolutionary Content' t-shirt. Now, the English singer-songwriter Billy Bragg once wryly observed that "revolution is only a t-shirt away," which became his lament for how trendy slogans on commercial products have come together to defang social activism's teeth.[4] We do not roll our sleeves up anymore and get on with the task of promoting justice; rather, Bragg implies that we purchase our t-shirts, we wear them loudly and proudly, we craft an identity around our cause, and then we do very little, if anything, at all. What we certainly do, though, is participate in consumer practices. And given what we see in the 'Babylon Advisory' shirt, Rastafari may well ponder: How is Babylon being put on notice, or being 'advised' of the t-shirt wearer's 'revolutionary content,' when the mediated marketplace that supplies the clothing is, in the eyes of many Rastas, the Whore of Babylon?

Rastafari see the ritual use of marijuana ('ganja') as another way to push back against Babylon, something that corporations have been educated to exploit as well as understand. We witness as much when we see the ganja-flecked X-Box 360, which does not reinforce Rastafari, but certainly enables an aspect of Rasta livity to enter the mediated realm, making it possible for young adults to engage an anti-Babylonian religious practice with the aid of one of Babylon's main tools.

Besides smoking ganja, flashing dreadlocks was seen by many first-generation Rastafari as an insult to Babylon, an essential signal of non-conformity. In the commercial world, though, it is part of a profitable business venture, since the design of a spliff-smoking, reggae-listening, dreadlocked lion now appears on everything from shot glasses to bedspreads. When viewed through the lens of Smart's religious theory, this design both blends and brands many dimensions of Rastafari livity—the doctrinal, ritual, mythical, and material dimensions. Lynn Schofield Clark thinks such "religious lifestyle branding" appeals to those of us on a "quest for self-expression" in "today's mediated society." And it seems that entrepreneurs "have discovered that perhaps those who want to figure out how not to eschew but embrace at least part of a religious tradition, the hipper the forms of expression available through religious lifestyle branding, the better."[5]

Marketing Marley

When it comes to Rastafari, there is no one as hip as Bob Marley. Today, his estate stands at the forefront of Rastafari religious lifestyle branding. Imagine pouring Marley's Mellow Mood drink, available at fuel stations throughout North America, into one of the Marley pint glasses, available for order online. With Marley's Mellow Mood, the drink comes advertised as an 'all natural relaxation' drink, an ital mix of green tea and honey, in one version, and, in another, as a decaffeinated dietary supplement designed to reduce stress and relieve tension. Even the word 'ital' appears on the reverse side of the bottle, together with the Marley logo. Given the range of products that the Marley estate has marketed and distributed in recent years, it would seem that the family has intentionally set out to brand Rastafari livity; and some individuals in society, part of a Rasta-identifying subculture perhaps, may consume the products as items that speak to their desire for a life lived in a natural or a simple or an ital way. The 'Mellow Mood' incense sticks only add to the relaxed temperament created by the drink, or so it would seem, and they may even serve as a hip, commercial, and legal way to inhale exotic aromas.

As my selected examples demonstrate, both insiders and outsiders use artistic imagination and business savvy to represent, mediate, and commodify Rastafari in Western capitalist culture. But how should we evaluate this process? Are religion and the marketplace supposed to come together? More specifically, is authentic Rastafari somehow beyond the marketplace, as I suspect many Rastas would declare? And if so, does this mean that the market is a profanation of the Rastafari religion, a Babylonification of Jah? These are all good questions whose answers do not come easily, if they come at all, but, as Stewart Hoover makes clear in several places, religion moves toward the market, and the emergence of what we might call 'Bob Marley, Inc.' is my best evidence that Rastafari is keenly connected to, and increasingly subject to, the media marketplace.[6] This connection yields mixed results, which I will state briefly.

Commodification scholarship notes that the diffusion of goods promises defamiliarization and democratization.[7] On this view, the exoticized Other is domesticated; products carry information, invite clarification, stimulate discussion and thus, in some instances, ignorance diminishes as literacy levels are raised. We all buy more, we all know more. And the more we all know, the better informed we are, especially about Rastafari, one of the world's most misunderstood groups, as Rasta poet Benjamin Zephaniah describes the movement.[8] Still more scholars disagree with this perspective. Vincent Miller holds that "commodification has two interrelated consequences for religion." In the first of these, "elements of religious traditions are fragmented into discrete, free-floating signifiers abstracted from their interconnections with other doctrines, symbols, and practices." So, what does the ganja-flecked X-Box 360 *really* tell us about scriptural and other, related reasons for Rastafari smoking the holy herb? Very little, *really*. "Deprived of their coherence with a broader network of beliefs," such arty abstractions do not serve to deepen awareness; oddly, they only serve "as shallow signifiers of whatever religious sentiment we desire," Miller maintains.[9]

Commodification's second consequence relates to ritual action or religious practices. Miller again: "When abstracted from their conditions of production— that is, from their communities of origin—practices are deprived of their links to the institutional and communal setting in which they shape the daily lives of religious practitioners."[10] Tams, or Rastafari head coverings, provide an instructive example. With their splendid colors of red, gold, and green, they are eye-catchingly cool to many people, especially the Trustafarians I mentioned earlier. Tams look good, the way a person might imagine they do in Montego Bay or Trench Town, and a person might find them attractive enough to buy them. Should they? Besides 'the politics of cultural appropriation' issue which, in our case, questions the right of non-Rastafari to use Rastafari's symbol system for personal effect, there is another concern. When a non-Rastafari sports the symbols of Rastafari with "so shallow an engagement with them," do they not relegate the community that has produced them, and in which the symbols arguably live and breathe, beneath something as superficial as stylish design?[11] I am an outsider to Rastafari, so perhaps it is for insiders to answer such questions and to respond to the numerous artful representations of Rastafari identity in consumer culture. For academics engaged in studying contemporary religion, though, the task is to ponder the place of such religion in our market-driven, media-saturated world.

Notes

1 Copyright clearance concerns makes it impossible to reproduce the images in my book; however, they are online, and my personal website houses all of the images I reference in this chapter, and more. See http://darrenjnmiddleton.com. Accessed March 30, 2014.

2 Brian Griffin, *The Trustafarian Handbook: A Field Guide to the Neo-Hippie Lifestyle— Funded by Mom and Dad* (Avon, MA: Adams Media, 2010), 31. Some scholars are at work on what branding means for and to the Rastafari. See Rivke Jaffe, "Ital Chic: Rastafari, Resistance, and the Politics of Consumption in Jamaica," *Small Axe* 31 (2010): 30–45. Also see Barbara Olsen, "Consuming Rastafari: Ethnographic Research in Context and Meaning," *Advances in Consumer Research* 22 (1995): 481–485.

3 For a more recent account of how Babylon-thinking works among Rastas, see Ennis Barrington Edmonds, *Rastafari: From Outcasts to Culture Bearers* (Oxford and New York: Oxford University Press, 2003), 41–66.

4 This line appears in Bragg's "Waiting for the Great Leap Forwards" song, the lyrics for which are available online. For details, see: http://www.billybragg.com/music/singles. php?singleID=36&songID=47. Accessed March 30, 2014.

5 Lynn Schofield Clark, "Introduction: Identity, Belonging, and Religious Lifestyle Branding (Fashion Bibles, Bhangra Parties, and Muslim Pop)," in Lynn Schofield Clark, editor, *Religion, Media, and the Marketplace* (Brunswick, NJ: Rutgers University Press, 2007), 23.

6 My questions are inspired by observations first made in Stewart M. Hoover, "Afterword," in Clark, editor, *Religion, Media, and the Marketplace*, 308–314.

7 Jean-Christophe Agnew, "The Give-and-Take of Consumer Culture," in Susan Strasser, editor, *Commodifying Everything: Relationships of the Market* (New York and London:
Routledge, 2003), 11. Agnew addresses what commodification appears to inspire in
people, generally speaking.

8 For Zephaniah's commentary, see: http://m.guardiannews.com/commentisfree/2012/
aug/07/snoop-dogg-rastafari. Accessed March 30, 2014.

9 Vincent J. Miller, *Consuming Religion: Christian Faith and Practice in a Consumer Culture*
(New York and London: Continuum, 2003), 3.

10 *Ibid.*, 4.

11 Miller uses the examples of Tibetan prayer flags (4). Pondering what he says, I use
tams as my example of a Rastafari practice—hardly universal but fairly common—that,
through commodification, finds its link to the religious movement that produced it
severed or, at best, weakened. Here, my own observations draw on, or seek to apply,
Miller's own insights.

APPENDIX I

Dr. M's Rasta Riddims Playlist

I am not a reggae historian, though this musical genre has always played an important part in my cultural life, and for many years I hosted my own radio show in Tennessee, where I spun tunes, parsed lyrics, and introduced Rastafari to a Blues-drenched Delta audience. These days I often use reggae in class, either to explain the alliance between protest music and social movements, to stress the Bible's enduring legacy in popular song, or to illustrate Rastafari's material or artistic dimension, and my students regularly ask me to recommend titles to download. What follows is the 250-song list I offer to them. It is a personal inventory—an anthology of word and sound that has proved powerful to me over the years. No doubt different professors will want to remove certain titles and include others. This desire is reasonable, of course, and I urge such folk to do so. My Rasta Riddims Playlist is not comprehensive; rather, it is an omnibus of tunes—crafted by insiders and outsiders—that I think students will find both instructive and fun.

I have selected artists and titles that introduce the listener to one or more dimension(s) of Rastafari religious life. Some artists have made a deep impression on me, which is why I mention two or more of their songs. In the end, though, there is no Bob Marley on my list. This is because I think Marley's music is a given. If it is true that all Western philosophy is a footnote to Plato, then all reggae is a footnote to Marley, which is why I often urge students to listen to him on their own. I advise them to heed his *entire* discography, if possible, and then to take up some, if not all, of the tunes on the following list (arranged alphabetically):

1. Abdoul Jabbar, "Rastaman"
2. The Abyssinians, "Satta Massagana"
3. Alpha Blondy, "Rasta Bourgeois"
4. Ancient King, "Ethiopie"

5. Anita Mahfood, "Woman A Come"
6. Anthony B, "None a Jah Jah Children"
7. Apster, "King Selassie"
8. Army, "Rasta Awake"
9. Artganic, "Rasta Woman"
10. Asante Amen, "Keep Holding On"
11. —. "Only Ras Tafari"
12. —. "Real Rasta"
13. —. "Real Revolutionary"
14. —. "What is This?"
15. Ash Dargen, "Rasta Trance"
16. Aswad, "African Children"
17. —. "Back to Africa"
18. —. "Not Satisfied"
19. Augustus Pablo, "Chant to King Selassie I"
20. Barry Micron, "Rasta Soldier"
21. Benjamin Zephaniah, "Reggae Head"
22. —. "Roots and Culture"
23. Beres Hammond, "One Love, One Life"
24. Biblical, "Psalms & Proverbs"
25. Big Youth, "His Majesty's Teachings" (feat. Joseph Hill)
26. —. "I Pray Thee"
27. Black Dillenger, "Red Gold & Green" (feat. Terror Fabulous)
28. Black Uhuru, "Dread in the Mountain"
29. —. "I Love King Selassie"
30. —. "Peace and Love"
31. —. "Sinsemilla"
32. —. "Utterance"
33. —. "What is Life?"
34. Blakk Rasta, "Ganja Sweet"
35. —. "Rastafari"
36. Boom Shaka, "Rastafari Is The Future"
37. Breeze, "Aid Travels with a Bomb"
38. —. "To Plant"
39. Brother Culture, "Rastafari Army"
40. Bunny Wailer, "Blackheart Man"
41. —. "This Train"
42. Burning Spear, "Black Disciples"
43. —. "Calling Rastafari"
44. —. "Marcus Garvey"
45. Busy Signal, "Modern Day Slavery"
46. Capleton, "Bible Fe Dem"
47. Cat Coore, "Just Rastafari"
48. Chezidek, "Only Rastafari"
49. Chronixx, "Alpha and Omega"

50. —. "Dread"
51. —. "Selassie Souljahz" (feat. Sizzla Kalonji, Protoje, and Kabaka Pyramid)
52. —. "Thanks and Praise"
53. Cocoa Tea, "Holy Mount Zion"
54. Congoes, "Ark of the Covenant"
55. Count Ossie, "Wicked Babylon"
56. Culture, "Why Am I a Rastaman?"
57. Cymande, "Rastafarian Folk Song"
58. Dahweh Congo, "Seek Jah First"
59. Dawit Menelik Tafari, "Rastafari Show I the Way"
60. Deco, "Trenchtown"
61. Dennis Brown, "The Existence of Jah"
62. —. "Promised Land"
63. —. "The Prophet Rides Again"
64. —. "Shashamane Living (Country Living)"
65. Desmond Dekker & the Aces, "Israelites"
66. Don Drummond, "Reincarnation of Marcus Garvey"
67. Dr. Israel, "Israel"
68. Dubmatix, "Repatriation"
69. Dubtronic Kru, "Marcus Garvey"
70. Earl 16, "Marcus"
71. Early B, "Visit of King Selassie"
72. Echo Ranks, "Dreadlocks"
73. Edgar Rebel, "Rasta Concept"
74. Elhadj, "Baay Faal"
75. Empress Ayeola, "Rastafari Works"
76. Errol Dunkley, "Repatriation"
77. Estick & Word Sound Band, "Rasta Woman"
78. Everton Blender, "Is It Because I'm Black?"
79. —. "Leonard Howell"
80. Exco Levi, "Kebra Nagast"
81. Fantan Mojah, "Rasta Got Soul"
82. Fidel, "Negus Negast"
83. Fire Key, "New World Order"
84. Freddie McGregor, "Jah Will Bless You"
85. —. "Peace and Love"
86. —. "Somewhere"
87. Fyah B, "Rastafari Messenger"
88. G Vibes, "Globalization"
89. Garnett Silk, "Kingly Character"
90. —. "Who Is Like Selassie?"
91. —. "Zion in a Vision"
92. The Gladiators, "Roots Natty"
93. Grassman, "Rastafari"
94. The Green, "Power in the Words"

95. Green Lion Crew, "Rasta Road" (feat. Kabaka Pyramid, Chronixx & Dre Island)
96. Gregory Isaacs, "Rasta Business"
97. Haile Maskel, "Ras Blaze"
98. Half Pint, "Greetings"
99. Horace Andy, "Rastafari"
100. —. "Tribute to Bob Marley"
101. I-Roy, "Step On the Dragon"
102. —. "Sufferer's Psalm"
103. Iba Mahr, "Let Jah Lead The Way"
104. Ijahman Levi, "Jah is No Secret"
105. Ini Kamoze, "Ital"
106. Innocent, "Rasta Toka Bongo"
107. Irie Love, "Rastaman"
108. Irie Souls, "Rastafari"
109. Ishence, "Country"
110. —. "Haile Praises"
111. Israel Vibration, "Herb is the Healing"
112. —. "We a de Rasta"
113. The Itals, "Rasta Philosophy"
114. Jacob Miller, "Tenement Yard"
115. Jah & I, "Rasta and Babylon"
116. Jah Cure, "Jah Rule the Universe"
117. Jah Division, "Cuba Cabana"
118. —. "Jah Let Rastaman"
119. Jah Eye, "Rasta Music"
120. Jah Mali, "Blood Thirsty"
121. Jah Mason, "Red Gold & Green"
122. Jah Vinci, "Jah Is My Life"
123. Jah9, "Preacher Man"
124. —. "Reverence"
125. Johnny Clarke, "Rasta International"
126. Johnny Osbourne, "Jah Promise"
127. Judah Eskender Tafari, "Rastafari Tell You"
128. Judy Mowatt, "Black Woman"
129. —. "Warrior Queen"
130. Junior Reid, "Babylon Release the Chain"
131. —. "Emmanuel Calling"
132. —. "Long Road"
133. Kabaka Pyramid, "No Capitalist"
134. Kali, "We Call H.I.M."
135. Katchafire, "I and I"
136. Keida, "Ganja Tea"
137. Keznamdi, "Grade"
138. King Tubby, "Leonard 'Gong' Howell Dub"

139. —. "Natty Dub"
140. Kirkledove, "Livity Riddim"
141. Konshens, "Fake Rasta"
142. —. "Good Life & Livity"
143. Kulcha Far I, "African Rasta"
144. Kush and Bloodfiyah Angels, "Livity"
145. Lee 'Scratch' Perry, "Dreadlocks in Moonlight"
146. —. "Emperor Haile Selassie Light"
147. Linval Thompson, "Don't Cut Off Your Dreadlocks"
148. Little Roy, "Remember Jah"
149. Lorenzo, "Trod in the Valley"
150. Luciano, "Good World"
151. —. "It's Me Again Jah"
152. —. "United States of Africa"
153. Lutan Fyah, "Burn Babylon"
154. —. "Healthy Lifestyle"
155. —. "Rastafari Leads The Way"
156. Macka B, "Conscious Woman"
157. —. "Rasta Postman"
158. Mani Kongo, "Rasta from the Kalahari"
159. Massicker, "New Millennium Rasta"
160. Maxi Priest, "Marcus"
161. Michael Rose, "Babylon A Fight"
162. —. "Trample the Dragon"
163. Michael Rose & Sly and Robbie, "Marcus Garvey" (Dub Mix)
164. Midnite, "Better World Rasta"
165. —. "Bless Go Roun"
166. —. "Supplication to H.I.M."
167. Mighty Diamonds, "Natural Natty"
168. —. "Pass the Kutchie"
169. Mikey Dread, "His Imperial Majesty"
170. Mikey General, "Repatriation"
171. Misty in Roots, "True Rasta"
172. Monty Montgomery, "Rasta Queen"
173. Morgan Heritage, "Hail Rastafari"
174. Mutabaruka, "Any Which Way … Freedom"
175. —. "Spirituality"
176. Mystic Revelation of Rastafari, "Bongo Man"
177. —. "Hundred Years"
178. Mystikal Revolution, "Black Woman"
179. Nakeeba Amaniyea, "Roots Rasta"
180. Natural Ites, "Picture on the Wall"
181. Nechi Nech, "Israeli Rasta"
182. Obeyjah, "Nyabinghi Prayer"
183. Orthodox Issachar, "Prophet Gad"

184. Peter Broggs, "International Farmer"
185. Peter Tosh, "Equal Rights"
186. —. "Legalize It"
187. —. "Wanted Dread or Alive"
188. Prince Alla, "Repatriate Out of Rome"
189. Prince Fari, "Wisdom"
190. Protoje, "Dread"
191. —. "Hail Ras Tafari"
192. —. "I&I"
193. —. "Rasta Love" (feat. Ky-Mani Marley)
194. —. "This Is Not a Marijuana Song"
195. Queen Ifrica, "Calling Africa"
196. —. "Lioness on the Rise"
197. —. "Stand Up for Righteousness"
198. Queen Omega, "Jah Dawta"
199. Radio La Chusma, "Rasta Mexica"
200. Ragga Lox, "Ethiopia" (feat. Mikey General & Jah Lude)
201. Raging Fyah, "Nah Look Back"
202. Ras Dumisani & Afrikhaya Band, "Rastafari"
203. Ras Michael and the Sons of Negus, "Truth and Right"
204. Ras Mikey, "Livity"
205. Ras Shiloh, "Child of a Slave"
206. —. "Rastaman to Africa"
207. Rasta Duke, "Reggae International"
208. The Reggae Bubblers, "St. Croix to Shashemane"
209. Richie Spice, "Jah Provide"
210. —. "Motherland Calling"
211. Rita Marley, "A Jah Jah"
212. —. "One Draw"
213. Rocker T & Version City Rockers, "I-Story"
214. Rocky Dawuni, "African Reggae Fever"
215. —. "Download the Revolution"
216. —. "In Ghana"
217. —. "Jerusalem"
218. Rootikal Riddim, "Rastafari is the Truth"
219. S.N.T. Soundsystem, "Ganja Heal Rasta"
220. Scientist, "Gad Man the Prophet"
221. Sizzla, "Africa"
222. —. "Rastafari Teach I Everything"
223. Skatalites, "Addis Ababa"
224. Soldiers of Jah Army, "Jah Atmosphere"
225. Solo Banton, "Chalice Haffi Blaze"
226. Steel Pulse, "Not King James Version"
227. Sugar Black & Lebanculah, "I Saw Selassie"
228. Sugar Minott, "Herbman Hustling"

229. Sydney Salmon, "Shashemene on My Mind"
230. Tall Rich, "Rastafari Give Us Everything"
231. Tarrus Riley, "Chant Rastafari"
232. —. "King Selassie H.I.M."
233. —. "Love Created I"
234. —. "Rastafari at the Control"
235. Third World, "Reggae Ambassador"
236. Three Plus, "Jah Music"
237. Tomas Doncker, "Jah Rusalem"
238. Toots and the Maytals, "Do the Reggay"
239. Tullo T, "Can't Stop the Ras"
240. Turbulence, "Rastafari Livity"
241. —. "Repatriation"
242. —. "Teachings"
243. U-Roy, "Chalice in the Palace"
244. Vibronics, "Red, Gold and Green"
245. Weeding Dub, "Tribute to the Elders"
246. Yami Bolo, "Haile Selassie"
247. Yasus Afari, "Look to Africa"
248. —. "Meditate"
249. Ziggy Marley (feat. U-Roy), "Fly Rasta"
250. —. "Love Is My Religion"

APPENDIX II

Seven Sacred Sites and Wonders of the Rastafari World[1]

Although pilgrimage is not a prescribed ritual or sacred action for Rastafari, many brethren and sistren often journey to visit certain places of peace and power. Such quests help Rastas ponder or make meaning, and what happens during their stay may eventually play an important part in their specific understanding of livity. The following location list is far from 'official,' yet it recognizes that some believers are like iron filings, inexorably drawn to the magnetic force of particular moments as well as monuments. Even outsiders to the movement feel a tug towards such sites, so it seems fitting to offer an unauthorized guide to seven localities habitually deemed important landmarks in the Rastafari world.

1. *Pinnacle*: Located in the St. Jago Hills high above Jamaica's old capital, Spanish Town, Pinnacle is the first Rastafari commune, which Leonard P. Howell founded in the 1940s. Police raids eventually crushed Pinnacle, and the Rastafari who fled soon resettled in the slums of western Kingston, yet Howell's Dove Cot cemetery epitaph ("No man is indispensable but some are irreplaceable") reminds us that he nurtured an important religious group in its infancy, and that Pinnacle was Rasta's first vision of the 'promised land.'

2. *Western Kingston*: The shanty-town or tenement projects in Jamaica's capital city became home for the numerous Rastas who fled Pinnacle after police burned it down in 1958. The cruel, unsmiling ghettos of Back O'Wall and Trench Town served as Rasta citadels in the early 1960s, ultimately producing eloquent elders like Mortimer Planno and mellifluous musicians like Bob Marley. The tactical seeds of revolutionary reggae were first sown in western Kingston's streets, even if they blossomed elsewhere, from Jutland to Jakarta.

3. *Holy Trinity Cathedral*: This copper-domed, prominent Ethiopian Orthodox cathedral, which is located in Addis Ababa, Ethiopia's capital city, is a fiercely contested site, since Rastas cannot agree on whether or not this place houses His Imperial Majesty Haile Selassie I. The Ethiopian government held a formal reburial of Selassie's remains in November 2000, and Rasta luminaries such as Rita Marley attended the ceremony, but many brethren and sistren refuse to believe the bones belong to Selassie, even if other Rastas journey to the site to pay their respects.

4. *Shashemene*: In 1948, Selassie donated land associated with this town, which is located in central Ethiopia, for the Rastafari. The Jamaican government sent a delegation to Shashemene in 1961. And this group of Rastafari insiders and outsiders spoke to Selassie, who reassured them that he was serious about repatriation for those in the African diaspora. The first settler, Gladstone Robinson, arrived in Shashemene in 1964, and Papa Noel Dyer, the second, arrived in 1965. Selassie reiterated his repatriation invitation during his state visit to Jamaica in 1966, and 2000 Rastas eventually left the Caribbean and settled in Shashemene to reason, to drum, and to chant. The best estimates indicate that 300 Rastas currently reside in Shashemene, which today exemplifies Ethiopia's commitment to sustainable development, but many more visit each year from around the globe.

5. *Bob Marley Museum*: Dedicated to the life and art of Jamaica's most famous reggae musician, and Rastafari's unofficial global ambassador, this museum is located at 56 Hope Road, Kingston 6, Jamaica. In addition to once being Marley's home, and the place where an attempt was made on Marley's life in 1976, it once housed his recording studio and "Tuff Gong" record label. Various mementos line this museum's many walls, a gift shop offers a vast array of Marley merchandise, and those pilgrims who work up an appetite may dine at The Queen of Sheba ital restaurant, which is located nearby.

6. *Bob Marley Mausoleum*: Marley died in Miami, Florida, on May 11, 1981. Later in the same month, in a funeral replete with Rasta pageantry, he was laid to rest in Jamaica's Nine Mile village, where Marley was born in 1945. A reggae-themed gift shop provides pilgrims with Marley keepsakes, and in 2009 *Time* magazine listed the Mausoleum in its list of Top Ten Celebrity Grave Sites. Many visitors journey to the site on February 6, Marley's birthday, which Jamaicans celebrate with a National Holiday.

7. *Bull Bay*: This south-east coastal town in Jamaica's St. Andrew parish is home to one of the largest Rastafari settlements, the Bobo Shanti, on the island. Located at 13 Marcus Garvey Way, Zion Hill, this intimate commune offers a strict liturgical routine in six-hour increments, beginning at 6:00am, and its foremost facilities are genderized. Many of Rastafari's most famous artists self-identify as Bobo Shanti.

Finally, I suspect that the famous Reggae Sunsplash Festival, first held in Jamaica's Montego Bay in 1978 and now an annual event, is the preeminent candidate for the Eighth Wonder of the Rastafari World.

Note

1 I have placed an interactive map for such sites and wonders at my personal website. For details, see: http://darrenjnmiddleton.com. Accessed March 30, 2014.

APPENDIX III

Lois Cordelia: Art, the Bible, Rastafari, and Social Media

An Ipswich-based artist (England) working in cut paper, acrylics, and mixed media, Lois Cordelia has crafted some of the arresting, visual depictions of Rastafari in my book. Additional examples may be found at her personal website: http://loiscordelia.com/. In 2001, she built *Words of Wisdom*, an internet resource that matches reggae song lyrics and scripture: http://homepage.ntlworld.com/davebulow/wow/index.htm. Outsiders often struggle to comprehend the dread talk that reggae singers employ, so my students find this website instructive, and future crowdsourcing will only serve to strengthen its content. I recently invited Cordelia to outline the site's origins as well as to describe the way Rastafari influences her own artistic endeavors; her response appears below.

LC: My love affair with roots reggae began very innocently one evening when I was about seven years old. My proud German mother, having brought me up on the strictest diet of Mozart, Beethoven and the like, had never intended that I should discover anything outside the realm of the Western Classical musical repertoire. But one evening, when my parents had finished the washing-up, they made the fateful mistake of leaving the kitchen radio playing and disappearing upstairs. To me it was a peephole into a forbidden world.

Being broadcast was one of those shows based around a selection of records chosen by the interviewee that he or she would not wish to be without, should they ever chance to be washed up on a desert island. I remember neither the name of the man being interviewed nor the name of the record he chose; I remember only that it grabbed me, almost physically, like a hand laid firmly but warmly on my shoulder as I stood lingering in the corridor, and it wouldn't let go. I had never even heard of reggae at that age. I had no idea what it was that had spellbound me.

Truly, reggae is the music of the heart, for it echoes the gentle, soothing rhythm of the heart's own beat. It was so distinctly different from anything I had ever heard before that I was instantly transfixed. It was earthy, fruity, spicy and sweet, oozing warmth, laughter and playfulness, sun-drenched, sun-ripened, filled with all the exotic scents of the trade winds. To a young and fertile mind, it was like discovering a wonderful new cuisine from a distant land. It was love at first listen.

Several years would pass, however, before I once more chanced to hear that enchanting sound world drifting from the radio. But I wasn't going to let it elude my grasp again. I dropped my homework and paid avid attention. I had to find out what this musical genre was called. Reggae! What a beautiful name. Where did it come from? What was that strange dialect in the lyrics? The more I listened, the more my curiosity grew. As my ears gradually became more attuned to the patois, the music began to speak to my heart on a whole new level. I recognized quotations from the Psalms: *Blessed is the man that walketh not in the counsel of the ungodly … Fret not thyself because of evildoers …* Here was a new dimension, a deep, spiritual dimension that resonated through harmonious and conscious living, peace, positivity, and love. To a passionate young idealist, it was the powerful voice of a revolution that was about to transform my life.

Naturally, my parents were horrified by this bizarre new obsession of mine with 'black music.' Whatever could have happened to their obedient little daughter to cause her to go astray like this? But the more their opposition grew, the more firmly it took root in my heart. *Like a tree planted by the rivers of water, that bringeth forth its fruit in due season; his leaf also shall not wither, and whatsoever he doeth shall prosper.* Reggae became my daily devotional music that lifted my spirits in the morning and played in my heart all day long, a vibrant and energetic song of praise to the Creator, who himself seemed to take on a radical new dimension with a strange and beautiful new name: *Jah Rastafari.*

Moreover, reggae preached the unity of all God's children as brothers and sisters, united in peace and love. *Behold, how good and how pleasant it is for brethren to dwell together in unity!* Naïve, perhaps, but a timelessly powerful and beautiful ideal to fight for, nevertheless. Above all, reggae kindled in me the spirit of rebellion that would inspire me in the coming years to challenge many things that I had been taught to accept as convention. Like any true revolution, it shook my world to its foundations and triggered a period of restless turbulence and discontent, but ultimately paved a new path towards freedom. Redemption songs, as Marley put it. Many of my friends, both black and white, have been baffled at how I came to relate so strongly to this message of emancipation, which after all was supposed to be relevant only to the descendants of black African slaves—surely, no?

But of course, the message of liberation has a timeless and universal appeal to anyone who has ever felt inhibited, thwarted, or repressed, whether physically, emotionally, intellectually, spiritually, or artistically. Hence, reggae inspired me to begin pushing back the narrow confines of my sheltered upbringing in a polite, White, middle-class, Anglo-German family. Not to imply that I rejected my own cultural roots (as my parents seemed to fear), but simply that I was no longer content to be defined and restricted by them. To this day, I defy being put in a box and conveniently labelled as 'Christian,' 'Hindu,' 'Pagan,' or even 'Rastafari.' To hell with 'isms and schisms'! Among the countless spiritual paths I have explored, the Rastafari philosophy is one of the few that strikes a healthy balance—so essential for the modern world—between emphasizing on the one hand the unity of all people and on the other the fierce spirit of individualism.

Perhaps for this reason, Rastafari has influenced me and captured my imagination most deeply in my capacity as an artist. The spirit of rebellion expresses itself time and again in my artwork through the restless energies of a dancing figure, the defiant gaze of a subject's eyes, or the resilience of the human spirit, which, though inhabiting a fragile bodily frame, manifests superhuman strength in the face of opposition. Much of my work has been created while listening to roots reggae; much of my recurring imagery—lions, nomadic prophets, gnarled trees and tree roots, fire, dancing figures, angels—is inspired by the imagery of roots reggae, itself largely drawn from the Old Testament. Ironically, many of the pieces that have been most directly inspired by reggae and Rastafari are among those of my creative efforts that my mother has most praised for their energy!

By this time, I had become fascinated by the significance of the biblical references and allusions in reggae song lyrics, so much so that my curiosity evolved into an ongoing project: *Words of Wisdom*. The website has now been running since 2001, since when I have lost count of the messages of appreciation I have received. I have never consciously considered this labor of love as a 'mission.' I have simply sought to explore and immerse myself in the beauty of Rastafari, and if sharing my discoveries with others has been a source of blessing and inspiration to them also, then my joy is doubled.

Today, anthropologists tell us that Africa was the true cradle of humankind. This seems to evoke a very deep emotional response in many people, even in those who are not of recent African descent. It is easy to dismiss this feeling as the projection of a romanticized ideal of the primordial earthly paradise. But such a widespread resurgence of interest in all things African may suggest some lingering consciousness of a universal African aboriginal identity of humankind.

As the roots of a plant anchor it in the ground and give it stability, the knowledge of one's cultural and spiritual heritage gives a sure foundation on which to build one's sense of identity. It may also engender deep feelings of appreciation, admiration, and respect for those who have gone before and helped to shape our modern world. Thus it may reverse the current trend of dismissing our ancestors as simple-minded folk who believed in magic and miracles and the sacredness of things, so that perhaps ultimately we can learn from them important and refreshing lessons for our secular age.

The prevailing assumption in the West that progress demands us to turn our backs on the past and look instead to the future has caused tradition, myth, and ritual to be forgotten. Such ancient relics appear to have no relation to our present existence. We often speak of them being "stuck in the past." But the Rastafari concept of roots and culture is based on a much more dynamic and flexible understanding of 'tradition' as living, constantly evolving, adaptive and adoptive, the collective experience of communities accumulated by successive generations since time immemorial.

If we look to the past, which is known, rather than to the future, which is unknown, we are not prone to suffer from blindness of vision, and so we gain a true sense of perspective in time, seeing our own place in history. The future need not surprise us unawares, for it is not substantially different from the past: tomorrow contains elements of yesterday and today. Thus the past is the key to the future, just as the awareness of cultural roots is the key to society's progress, and the acknowledgement of one's spiritual roots in God is the key to mystical union with the Most High.

I would never claim to be Rastafari, any more than I would claim to be anything else. But I feel it deep in my heart.

SELECTED BIBLIOGRAPHY

Adams, Norman. *A Historical Report: The Rastafari Movement in England*. London: GWA Works, 2002.

Ahkell, Jah. *Rasta: Emperor Haile Selassie and the Rastafarians*. Chicago: Research Associates School Times, 1999.

de Albuquerque, Klaus. "Rastafarianism and Cultural Identity in the Caribbean." *Revista/Review Interamericana* 10.2 (1980): 230–247.

Alleyne, Mervyn. *Roots of Jamaican Culture*. London: Pluto Press, 1988.

Alston, James Anthony. "The Role of Music in Rastafarian Society in Jamaica, 1930–1995." Thesis (Ph.D.)—University of Pittsburg, 1996.

Alvaré, Bretton. "Fighting for 'Livity': Rastafari Politics in a Neoliberal State." In *Bridging the Gaps: Faith-Based Organizations, Neoliberalism, and Development in Latin America and the Caribbean*, eds. Tara Hefferan, Julie Adkins, and Laurie Occhipinti, 51–68. Lanham, MD: Lexington Books, 2009.

Andwele, Adisa. "The Contribution of Rastafarianism to the Decolonization of the Caribbean." In *Rastafari: A Universal Philosophy in the Third Millennium*, ed. Werner Zips, 7–20. Kingston; Jamaica; Miami: Ian Randle Publishers, 2006.

Appiah, Kwame Anthony and Henry Louis Gates, Jr., eds. *Africana: The Encyclopedia of the African and African American Experience*. New York: Basic Civitas Books, 1999.

Ashcroft, Bill, Gareth Griffiths, and Helen Tiffin. *The Empire Writes Back: Theory and Practice in Post-Colonial Literatures*. London: Routledge, 1989.

Atiba, Alemu I. Jahson. *The Rastafari Ible*. Chicago: Research Associates School Times, 1994.

Augustyn, Heather. *Ska: An Oral History*. Jefferson, NC; London: McFarland and Company, Inc., 2010.

Austin-Broos, Diane J. *Jamaica Genesis: Religion and the Politics of Moral Order*. Chicago: University of Chicago Press, 1997.

—. "Pentecostals and Rastafarians: Cultural, Political and Gender Relations of Two Religious Movements." *Social and Economic Studies* 36.4 (1987): 1–39.

Axford, Barrie. *Theories of Globalization*. Cambridge: Polity Books, 2013.

Aylmer, Kevin J. "Towering Babble and Glimpses of Zion: Recent Depictions of Rastafari in Cinema." In *Chanting Down Babylon: The Rastafari Reader*, eds. Nathaniel Samuel Murrell, William David Spencer, and Adrian Anthony McFarlane, 284–307. Philadelphia: Temple University Press, 1998.

Babatunji, Ayotunde Amtac. *Prophet on Reggae Mountain: Meditations of Ras Shabaka Maasai, Prophet of Jah Rastafari*. Rochester, NY: Garvey-Tubman-Nanny-Nzinga Press, 1994.

Bain, Pauline. "Identity, Protest and Healing: The Multiple Uses of Marijuana in Rastafari." In *Challenges for Anthropology in the 'African Renaissance': A Southern African Contribution*, eds. Debie LeBeau and Robert J. Gordon, 111–122. Namibia: University of Namibia Press, 2001.

Baku, Shango. "Remembering Haile Selassie." *West Africa* 4115 (1996): 2–8.

—. "Seeking His Majesty: Rastas in the Promised Land." *West Africa* 3915 (1992): 1643.

Banton, Michael. *Anthropological Approaches to the Study of Religion*. New York: Frederick A. Praeger, 1966.

Barnes, Natasha. "Dancehall Lyricism." In *Music, Writing, and Cultural Unity in the Caribbean*, ed. Timothy J. Weiss, 287–305. Trenton, NJ: Africa World Press, 2005.

Barnett, Michael. "From Warieka Hill to Zimbabwe: Exploring the Role of Rastafari in Popularizing Reggae Music." In *Rastafari in the New Millennium: A Rastafari Reader*, ed. Michael Barnett, 270–277. Syracuse: Syracuse University Press, 2012.

—. "Rastafari in the New Millennium: Rastafari at the Dawn of the Fifth Epoch." In *Rastafari in the New Millennium: A Rastafari Reader*, ed. Michael Barnett, 1–10. Syracuse: Syracuse University Press, 2012.

—. "Differences and Similiarities Between the Rastafari Movement and the Nation of Islam." *Journal of Black Studies* 36.6 (2006): 873–893.

—. "The Many Faces of Rasta: Doctrinal Diversity within the Rastafari Movement." *Caribbean Quarterly* 51.2 (2005): 67–78.

Barnett, Michael, ed. *Rastafari in the New Millennium: A Rastafari Reader*. Syracuse: Syracuse University Press, 2012.

Barrett, Leonard E. *The Rastafarians*, with a new afterword. Boston: Beacon, 1997; 1988.

Barrow, Steve, and Peter Dalton, *The Rough Guide to Reggae*. London: Penguin, 2004.

Beckford, Robert. *Jesus Dub: Theology, Music, and Social Change*. London and New York: Routledge, 2006.

—. *Jesus is Dread: Black Theology and Black Culture in Britain*. London: Darton, Longman & Todd, Ltd., 1998.

Bedasse, Monique. "Rasta Evolution: The Theology of the Twelve Tribes of Israel." *Journal of Black Studies* 40.5 (2010): 960–973.

Bellegarde-Smith, Patrick. *Fragments of Bone: Neo-African Religions in a New World*. Champaign: University of Illinois Press, 2005.

Benard, Akeia A. "The Material Roots of Rastafarian Marijuana Symbolism." *History and Anthropology* 18 (2007): 89–99.

Bender, Wolfgang, ed. *Rastafarian Art*. Kingston, Jamaica; Miami: Ian Randle Publishers, 2005.

—. "Liberation from Babylon: Rasta Painters in Jamaica." In *Missile and Capsule*, ed. Jurgen Martini, 129–135. Bremen, Germany: Druckerei der Universität Bremen, 1983.

Benjamin, Marcus. *Dub Talking: Selected Poems*. Fort Collins, CO: Rasta Connection L.L.C., 1994.

Bennett, Hazel, and Phillip Sherlock. *The Story of the Jamaican People*. Kingston, Jamaica: Ian Randle Publishers, 1998.

Bennett, Louise. *Jamaica Labrish*. Kingston, Jamaica: Sangster's, 1966.

Bennett, Martin. *West African Trickster Tales*. Oxford: Oxford University Press, 1994.

Bernard, Allan. "A Focus on Sizzla Kalonji: A Leading Influence on a New Generation of Rastafari Youth." In *Rastafari in the New Millennium: A Rastafari Reader*, ed. Michael Barnett, 278–288. Syracuse: Syracuse University Press, 2012.

Besson, Jean, and Karen Fog Olwig. *Caribbean Narratives of Belonging: Fields of Relations, Sites of Identity*. London: Macmillan Caribbean, 2005.

Beyer, Peter. *Religion and Globalization*. Thousand Oaks, CA: Sage Publications, 1996.

Bilby, Kenneth. "The Impact of Reggae in the United States." *Popular Music and Society* 5.5 (1977): 17–23.

Bilby, Kenneth, and Elliot Leib. "Kumina, the Howellite Church and the Emergence of Rastafarian Traditional Music in Jamaica." *Jamaica Journal* 19.3 (1986): 22–28.

Birhan, Farika. *Africa on the Move: A Collection of Afrikan Redemption Poems*. San Jose, CA: Queen Omega Publications, 1983.

—. *Haile Selassie: A Collection of Theocratic Rastafari Poetry*. San Jose, CA: Queen Omega Publications, 1983.

—. *Fari Iyaric: An Introduction into Rastafari Speech*. San Jose, CA: Queen Omega Publications, 1981.

Birhan, I-awta Farika, and Dee Brown, eds. *Sing I a Song of Black Freedom: A Collection of Rastafarian Poetry*. Palo Alto, CA: Penny Press/Zikawuna Books, 1979.

Bishton, Derek. *Black Heart Man: A Journey into Rasta*. London: Chatto & Windus, 1986.

Bisnauth, Dale. *History of Religions in the Caribbean*. Trenton, NJ: Africa World Press, 1996.

Bogues, Anthony. *Black Heretics, Black Prophets: Radical Political Intellectuals*. New York and London: Routledge, 2003.

Bohannan, Paul, and Philip Curtin. *Africa and Africans*. 4th ed. Prospect Heights, IL: Waveland Press, 1995.

Bones, Jah. "Language and Rastafari." In *The Language of the Black Experience*, eds. David Sutcliffe and Ansel Wong, 37–51. London: Blackwell, 1986.

—. "Reggae Deejaying and Jamaican Afro-Lingua." In *The Language of the Black Experience*, eds. David Sutcliffe and Ansel Wong, 52–58. London: Blackwell, 1986.

—. *One Love: Rastafari: History, Doctrine and Livity*. London: Voice of Rasta Publishing House, 1985.

Booker, Cedella. *Bob Marley: An Intimate Portrait by His Mother*. London: Penguin, 1997.

—. *Bob Marley, My Son*. New York: Taylor Trade, 2003.

Booker, M. Keith, and Dubravka Juraga. *The Caribbean Novel in English: An Introduction*. Portsmouth, NH: Heinemann, 2001.

Boot, Adrian, and Vivien Goldman. *Bob Marley: Soul Rebel, Natural Mystic*. New York: St. Martin's, 1982.

Borchert, Sarah. *I-Story: Rastas in Cape Town*. S.I.: S.N., 2006. VHS.

Bowen, W. Errol. "Rastafarianism and the New Society." *Savacou* 5 (1975): 41–50.

Boxhill, Ian, ed. *The Globalization of Rastafari*. Kingston, Jamaica: Arawak Publications, 2008.

Bradley, Lloyd. *This is Reggae Music: The Story of Jamaica's Music*. New York: Grove Press, 2001.

—. *Bass Culture: When Reggae Was King*. London: Penguin, 2000.

Branch, William B., ed. *Crosswinds: An Anthology of Black Dramatists in the Diaspora*. Bloomington and Indianapolis: Indiana University Press, 1993.

Brathwaite, Edward Kamau. *History of the Voice: The Development of National Language in Anglophone Caribbean Poetry*. London: New Beacon Books, 1984.

—. "The African Presence in Caribbean Literature." *Daedalus* 103.2 (1974): 73–109.

Breeze, Jean 'Binta.' *Third World Girl: Selected Poems, with Live Readings*. Northumberland, England: Bloodaxe Books, 2011.

—. "Can a Dub Poet be a Woman?" *Woman: A Cultural Review* 1 (1990): 47–49.

—. *Riddym Ravings and Other Poems*, ed. Mervyn Morris. London: Race Today Publications, 1988.

Breiner, Laurence A. "The English Bible in Jamaican Rastafarianism." *Journal of Religious Thought* 42.2 (1985–1986): 30–43.

Brodber, Erna. "Marcus Garvey and the Politicisation of Some Afro-Jamaicans in the 1920s and 1930s." *Jamaica Journal* 20.3 (1987): 145–160.

Brown, Frank Burch, ed. *The Oxford Handbook of Religion and the Arts*. Oxford and New York: Oxford University Press, 2014.

Brown, Samuel E. "Treatise on the Rastafarian Movement." *Caribbean Studies* 6.1 (1966): 39–40.

Bruder, Edith. *The Black Jews of Africa: History, Religion, Identity*. London and New York: Oxford University Press, 2008.

Brynda, Bianca Nyavingi. *Roots Daughters: The Women of Rastafari*. Toronto: Fari International Productions; Oaks, PA: MVD Visual, 1992. DVD.

Buffonge, Alvin E.G. "Babylon Besieged: The Rastafarian Challenge to the Jamaican Democracy." Thesis (Ph.D.)—Princeton University, 1998.

Burkett, Randall K. *Garveyism as a Religious Movement*. Metuchen, NJ: Scarecrow Press, 1978.

Burnett, Michael. *Jamaican Music*. Oxford: Oxford University Press, 1982.

Busby, Margaret. *Daughters of Africa: An International Anthology of Words and Writings by Women of African Descent from the Ancient Egyptian to the Present*. New York: Pantheon Books, 1992.

Bush, Barbara. "The Dark Side of the City: Racialized Barriers, Culture and Citizenship in Britain, c. 1950–1990s." In *Rastafari: A Universal Philosophy in the Third Millennium*, ed. Werner Zips, 169–201. Kingston, Jamaica; Miami: Ian Randle Publishers, 2006.

Callam, Neville G. "Invitation to Docility: Defusing the Rastafarian Challenge." *Caribbean Journal of Religious Studies* 3.2 (1980): 28–48.

Campbell, Horace. "Rastafari as Pan Africanism in the Caribbean and Africa." *African Journal of Political Economy* 2.1 (1988): 75–88.

—. *Rasta and Resistance: From Marcus Garvey to Walter Rodney*. Trenton, NJ: Africa World Press, 1987.

—. "Rastafari: Culture of Resistance." *Race and Class: A Journal for Black and Third World Liberation* 22.1 (1980): 1–23.

—. "The Rastafarians in the Eastern Caribbean." *Caribbean Quarterly* 26 (1980): 42–61.

Carby, Hazel. *Cultures in Babylon: Black Britain and African Americans*. London: Verso, 1999.

Cariou, Patrick. *Yes Rasta: Photographs by Patrick Cariou*. New York: powerHouse Books, 2000.

Carr, Nicole Racquel. "The Rastafari Presence in Toni Morrison's *Tar Baby, Beloved*, and *Song of Solomon*." Thesis (Ph.D.)—Florida Atlantic University, 2010.

Carson, Roy. *Marcus Garvey: A Giant of Black Politics*. United States: Screen Edge, 2008. DVD.

Case, Charles G. "Rastafari and the Religion of Anthropology: An Epistemological Study." *Religious Education* 78 (1983): 420.

Cashmore, Ellis. "The De-Labelling Process: From 'Lost Tribe' to Ethnic Group." In *Rastafari and Other African-Caribbean Worldviews*, ed. Barry Chevannes, 182–195. New Brunswick, NJ: Rutgers University Press, 1998.

—. "The Decline of the Rastas?" *Religion Today* 1.1 (1984): 3–4.

—. "After the Rastas." *New Community* 9 (1981): 173–181.

—. *Rastaman: The Rastafarian Movement in England*. Boston: G. Allen and Unwin, 1979.

—. "The Rastaman Cometh." *New Society* 41.777 (1977): 382–384.

Cassidy, Frederic G. *Jamaica Talk: Three Hundred Years of the English Language in Jamaica*. London: Macmillan Education, 1961.

Cassidy, Frederic G., and R.B. Le Page, eds. *Dictionary of Jamaican English*. New York: Cambridge University Press, 1980.

Chakravarty, K. Gandhar. "Double Others: The Marginalization of Secular-Spiritual Rastafari Immigrants in Montreal." *Scriptura* 10.2 (2008): 57–74.

Chang, Kevin O'Brien, and Wayne Chen. *Reggae Routes: The Story of Jamaican Music*. Philadelphia: Temple University Press, 1998.

Chawane, Midas. "The Rastafari Movement in South Africa: Before and After Apartheid." *New Contree* 65 (2012): 163–188.

Chevannes, Barry. "Rastafari and the Coming of Age: The Routinization of the New Rastafari Movement in Jamaica." In *Rastafari in the New Millennium: A Rastafari Reader*, ed. Michael Barnett, 13–32. Syracuse: Syracuse University Press, 2012.

—. "Ships That Will Never Sail: The Paradox of Rastafari Pan-Africanism." *Critical Arts* 25.4 (2011): 565–575.

—. *Betwixt and Between: Explorations in an African-Caribbean Mindscape*. Kingston, Jamaica; Miami: Ian Randle Publishers, 2006.

— "Rastafari and the Critical Tradition." In *Rastafari: A Universal Philosophy in the Third Millennium*, ed. Werner Zips, 282–297. Kingston, Jamaica; Miami: Ian Randle Publishers, 2006.

—. "Rastafari and the Exorcism of the Ideology of Racism and Classism in Jamaica." In *Chanting Down Babylon: The Rastafari Reader*, eds. Nathaniel Samuel Murrell, William David Spencer, and Adrian Anthony McFarlane, 55–71. Philadelphia: Temple University Press, 1998.

—. "The Rastafari Abroad." In *America's Alternative Religions*, ed. Timothy Miller, 297–302. Albany, NY: SUNY Press, 1995.

—. *Rastafari: Roots and Ideology*. Syracuse: Syracuse University Press, 1994.

—. "The Rastafari of Jamaica." In *When Prophets Die: The Postcharismatic Fate of New Religious Movements*, ed. Timothy Miller, 135–147. Albany, NY: SUNY Press, 1991.

—. *The Case of Jah Versus Middle Class Society: Rastafari Exorcisim of the Ideology of Racism in Jamaica*. The Hague, Netherlands: Institute of Social Studies, 1989.

—. "Rastafarianism as a Life-Style." In *Black Presence in Multi-Ethnic Canada*, ed. Vincent D'Oyley, 149–165. Vancouver, Canada: Center for the Study of Curriculum and Instruction, Faculty of Education, University of British Columbia, 1979.

—. "The Literature of Rastafari." *Social and Economic Studies* 26 (1977): 239–262.

—. "The Impact of the Ethiopian Revolution on the Rastafari Movement." *Socialism: Theoretical Organ of the Workers Liberation League* 2.3 (1975): 263–289.

Chevannes, Barry, ed. *Rastafari and Other African-Caribbean Worldviews*. New Brunswick, NJ: Rutgers University Press, 1998.

Chevers, Ivy E. "A Study of Rastafarian Culture in Columbus, Ohio: Notes from an African American Woman's Journey." Thesis (Ph.D.)—Ohio State University, 2008.

Chin, Tim. "'Bullers' and 'Battymen': Contesting Homophobia in Black Popular Culture and Contemporary Caribbean Literature." *Callaloo* 20.1 (1997): 127–141.

Chisholm, Clinton. "The Rasta-Selassie-Ethiopian Connections." In *Chanting Down Babylon: The Rastafari Reader*, eds. Nathaniel Samuel Murrell, William David Spencer, and Adrian Anthony McFarlane, 166–177. Philadelphia: Temple University Press, 1998.

Christensen, Jeanne. *Rastafari Reasoning and the RastaWoman: Gender Constructions in the Shaping of Rastafari Livity*. Lanham, MD: Lexington Books, 2014.

—. "The Philosophy of Reasoning: The Rastafari of Jamaica." Thesis (Ph.D.)—University of Colorado, 2003.

Christian, Ijahnya. "Return of the 6th Region: Rastafari Settlement in the Motherland Contributing to the African Renaissance." *CODESRIA Bulletin* 1/2 (2012): 30–42.

Christian, Mark, ed. *Black Identity in the Twentieth Century: Expressions of the US and UK African Diaspora*. London: Hansib, 2002.

Chude-Sokei, Louis. "Roots, Diaspora and Possible Africas." In *Global Reggae*, ed. Carolyn Cooper, 221–240. Kingston, Jamaica: Canoe Press, 2012.

—. "The Sound of Culture: Dread Discourse and Jamaican Sound Systems." In *Language, Rhythm, & Sound: Black Popular Cultures into the Twenty-First Century*, eds. Joseph K. Adjaye and Adrianne R. Andrews, 185–202. Pittsburgh: University of Pittsburgh Press, 1997.

—. "Post-Nationalist Geographies: Rasta, Ragga, and Reinventing Africa." *African Arts* 27 (1994): 80–84.

Clark, Lynn Schofield, ed. *Religion, Media, and the Marketplace*. New Brunswick, NJ: Rutgers University Press, 2007.

Clarke, Peter B. *New Religions in Global Perspective: A Study of Religious Change in the Modern World*. London and New York: Routledge, 2006.

—. *Black Paradise: The Rastafarian Movement*. Wellingborough, UK: The Aquarian Press, 1986.

Clarke, Sebastian. *Jah Music: The Evolution of the Popular Jamaican Song*. London: Heinemann, 1980.

Clough, Brent. "Oceanic Reggae." In *Global Reggae*, ed. Carolyn Cooper, 263–284. Kingston, Jamaica: Canoe Press, 2012.

Collins, Loretta. "*The Harder They Come*: Rougher Version." *Small Axe* 13 (2003): 46–71.

—. "Raggamuffin Cultural Studies: X-Press Novels' Yardies and Cop Killers Put Britain on Trial." *Small Axe* 9 (2001): 70–96.

—. "Daughters of Jah: The Impact of Rastafarian Womanhood in the Caribbean, the United States, Britain, and Canada." In *Religion, Culture and Tradition in the Caribbean*, eds. Hemchand Gossai and Nathaniel Samuel Murrell, 227–255. New York: St. Martin's Press, 2000.

—. "Rude Bwoys, Riddim, Rub-a-Dub, and Rastas: Systems of Political Dissonance in Caribbean Performative Sounds." In *Sound States: Innovative Politics and Acoustical Technologies*, ed. Adelaide Morris, 169–193. Chapel Hill, NC: University of North Carolina Press, 1997.

Collinwood, Dean W., and Osamu Kusatsu. "Japanese Rastafarians: Non-Conformity in Modern Japan." *The Study of International Relations* 26 (Tokyo: Tsuda College, 2000): 23–35.

Collum, Danny. "Jubilee, Rastafarian Style: A Vibrant Human Film on Reggae and Justice." *Sojourners* 9 (1980): 35–36.

Colman, George D. *Oba's Story: Rastafari, Purification and Power*. Trenton, NJ: Africa World Press, 2005.

Cooper, Carolyn. "Reggae Studies at the University of the West Indies." In *Global Reggae*, ed. Carolyn Cooper, 301–314. Kingston, Jamaica: Canoe Press, 2012.

—. "'More Fire': Chanting Down Babylon From Bob Marley to Capleton." In *Music, Writing, and Cultural Unity in the Caribbean*, ed. Timothy J. Weiss, 215–236. Trenton, NJ: Africa World Press, 2005.

—. *Sound Clash: Jamaican Dancehall Culture at Large.* London: Palgrave Macmillan, 2004.

—. *Noises in the Blood: Orality, Gender, and the 'Vulgar' Body of Jamaican Popular Culture.* Durham, NC: Duke University Press, 2000.

—. "'Raggamuffin Sounds': Crossing Over from Reggae to Rap and Back." *Caribbean Quarterly* 44.1/2 (1998): 153–167.

—. "Chanting Down Babylon: Bob Marley's Song as Literary Text." *Jamaica Journal* 19.4 (1986–1987): 2–8.

Cooper, Carolyn, ed. *Global Reggae.* Kingston, Jamaica: Canoe Press, 2012.

Cushman, Thomas. "Rich Rastas and Communist Rockers: A Comparative Study of the Origin, Diffusion and Defusion of Revolutionary Musical Codes." *Journal of Popular Culture* 25.3 (1991): 17–61.

Dalrymple, Henderson. *Bob Marley: Music, Myth and the Rastas.* London: Cari-Arawk, 1976.

Daschke, Dereck, and W. Michael Ashcraft, eds. *New Religious Movements: A Documentary Reader.* New York: New York University Press, 2005.

Davidson, Steed V. "Leave Babylon: The Trope of Babylon in Rastafarian Discourse." *Black Theology: An International Journal* 6.1 (2008): 46–60.

Davis, Kortright. *Emancipation Still Comin': Explorations in Caribbean Emancipatory Theology.* Maryknoll, NY: Orbis Books, 1990.

Davis, Samuel Furé. "Reggae in Cuba and the Hispanic Caribbean." In *Global Reggae*, ed. Carolyn Cooper, 95–125. Kingston, Jamaica: Canoe Press, 2012.

—. "A Voice from Cuba: Conceptual and Practical Difficulties with Studying Rastafari." *IDEAZ* 7 (2008): 28–40.

Davis, Stephen. *Bob Marley.* New York: Doubleday, 1985.

Davis, Stephen, and Peter Simon. *Reggae Bloodlines: In Search of the Music and Culture of Jamaica.* Garden City, NY: Anchor, 1977.

Dawes, Kwame. *Natural Mysticism: Towards a New Reggae Aesthetic in Caribbean Writing.* Leeds, UK: Peepal Tree Press Ltd., 2008.

—. *Bob Marley: Lyrical Genius.* London: Sanctuary, 2003.

—. *Shook Foil: A Collection of Reggae Poems.* Leeds, UK: Peepal Tree Press Ltd., 1997.

Dawes, Kwame, ed. *Wheel and Come Again: An Anthology of Reggae Poetry.* New Brunswick: Goose Lane, 1998.

Daynes, Sarah. "The Musical Construction of the Diaspora: The Case of Reggae and Rastafari." In *Music, Space and Place: Popular Music and Cultural Identity*, eds. Sheila Whiteley, Andy Bennett, and Stan Hawkins, 25–41. Burlington, VT; Aldershot, Hampshire, U.K.: Ashgate Publishing Company, 2004.

DeCosmo, Jan. "'A New Christianity for the Modern World': Rastafari Fundamentalism in Salvador, Bahia, Brazil." In *Rastafari in the New Millennium: A Rastafari Reader*, ed. Michael Barnett, 104–122. Syracuse: Syracuse University Press, 2012.

—. "Globalization and Rastafari Identity in Salvador, Bahia, Brazil." *IDEAZ* 7 (2008): 52–69.

—. "Reggae and Rastafari in Salvador, Bahia: The Caribbean Connection in Brazil." In *Religion, Culture, and Tradition in the Caribbean*, eds. Hemchand Gossai and Nathaniel Samuel Murrell, 37–64. New York: St. Martin's Press, 2000.

Dieng, Cheikh Ahmadou. "Reggae Griots in Francophone Africa." In *Global Reggae*, ed. Carolyn Cooper, 213–220. Kingston, Jamaica: Canoe Press, 2012.

Dijk, Fran Jan van. "Sociological Means: Colonial Reactions to the Radicalization of Rastafari in Jamaica, 1956–1959." *NWIG* 69.1/2 (1995): 67–101.

—. "The Twelve Tribes of Israel: Rasta and the Middle Class." *New West Indian Guide* 62.1 (1988): 1–26.

Dizzy, Ras. "The Rastas Speak." *Caribbean Quarterly* 13.4 (1967): 41–42.

Dollar, John. *The Emperor's Birthday*. New York: Filmakers Library, 1992. VHS.

Donne, Rafella Delle. "'A Place in Which to Feel at Home': An Exploration of the Rastafari as an Embodiment of an Alternative Spatial Paradigm." *Journal for the Study of Religion* 31.1 (2000): 99–121.

Donnell, Alison, and Sarah Lawson Welsh, eds. *The Routledge Reader in Caribbean Literature*. London: Routledge, 1996.

Dorman, Jacob S. *Chosen People: The Rise of Black Israelite Religions*. New York: Oxford University Press, 2013.

Doumerc, Eric and Mutabaruka. "From Page-Poet to Recording Artist: Mutabaruka interviewed by Eric Doumerc." *Journal of Commonwealth Literature* 44.3 (2009): 23–31.

Dovlo, Elom. "Rastafari, African Hebrews and Black Muslims: Return 'Home' Movements in Ghana." *Exchange* 31.1 (2002): 2–22.

Drachler, Jacob, ed. *Black Homeland/Black Diaspora*. Port Washington, NY: Kennikat Press, 1975.

Dunkley, Daive A. "The Suppression of Leonard Howell in Late Colonial Jamaica, 1932–1954." *New West Indian Guide* 87.1–2 (2013): 62–93.

—. *Readings in Caribbean History and Culture: Breaking Ground*. Lanham, MD: Lexington Books, 2011.

Edmonds, Ennis B. *Rastafari: A Very Short Introduction*. Oxford and New York: Oxford University Press, 2013.

—. *Rastafari: From Outcasts to Culture Bearers*. Oxford and New York: Oxford University Press, 2003.

Edmonds, Ennis B., and Michelle A. Gonzalez. *Caribbean Religious History: An Introduction*. New York: New York University Press, 2010.

Edwards, Adolph. *Marcus Garvey, 1887–1940*. London; Port of Spain, Trinidad: New Beacon Books, 1967.

Edwards, Prince Emmanuel Charles VII. *Black Supremacy in Righteousness of Salvation: Jesus Negus Christ*. St. Andrews, Jamaica; West Indies: Ethiopia Africa Black International Congress, n.d.

Edwards, Linda. *A Brief Guide to Beliefs: Ideas, Theologies, Mysteries, and Movements*. Louisville: Westminster John Knox Press, 2001.

Eliade, Mircea. *The Sacred and the Profane: The Nature of Religion*. New York: Harcourt, Brace and Company, 1959.

Erskine, Noel Leo. *Plantation Church: How African American Religion Was Born in Caribbean Slavery*. New York: Oxford University Press, 2014.

—. "Women in Rastafari." In *Ethics That Matters: African, Caribbean, and African American Sources*, eds. Marcia Y. Riggs and James Samuel Logan, 37–49. Minneapolis: Fortress Press, 2012.

—. "The Bible and Reggae: Liberation or Subjugation?" In *The Bible in/and Popular Culture: A Creative Encounter*, eds. Philip Culbertson and Elaine M. Wainwright, 97–109. Atlanta: Society of Biblical Literature, 2010.

—. *From Garvey to Marley: Rastafari Theology*. Gainesville, FL: The University Press of Florida, 2007.

—. *Decolonizing Theology: A Caribbean Perspective*. Maryknoll, NY: Orbis Books, 1981.

Ewarts, James. *Ras tafari*. New York: Insight Media, 2001. DVD.

Eyre, Allan L. "Biblical symbolism and the role of phantasy geography among the Rastafarians of Jamaica." *Journal of Geography* 84.4 (1985): 144–148.

Fala, Tony. "A Riddim Resisting Against the System: Bob Marley in Aotearoa." Thesis (Ph.D.)—University of Auckland, 2008.

Faristzaddi, Mihlawhdh. *Itations of Jamaica and I Rastafari*, three volumes. Miami: Judah Ambesa Ihntanahshinahl, 1991–1997.

Farley, Christopher John. *Before the Legend: The Rise of Bob Marley*. New York: Amistad, 2007.

Ferguson, Bryan J. "Selected Historical Events in the Evolution of Rastafari." In *Arise Ye Mighty People! Gender, Class and Race in Popular Struggles*, eds. Terisa E. Turner and Bryan J. Ferguson, 57–64. Trenton, NJ: Africa World Press, 1994.

Fisher, Robert B. *West African Religious Traditions: Focus on the Akan of Ghana*. Maryknoll, NY: Orbis Books, 1998.

Foehr, Stephen. *Jamaican Warriors: Reggae, Roots, and Culture*. London: Sanctuary Publishing, 2000.

Forsythe, Dennis. *Rastafari: For the Healing of the Nation*. Kingston: Zaika, 1983.

—. "West Indian Culture Through the Prism of Rastafarianism." *Caribbean Quarterly* 26.4 (1980): 62–81.

Foster, Chuck. *Roots, Rock, Reggae: An Oral History of Reggae Music from Ska to Dancehall*. New York: Billboard Books, 1999.

Friday, Michael. "A Comparison of 'Dharma' and 'Dread' as the Determinants of Ethical Standards." *Caribbean Journal of Religious Studies* 5 (1983): 29–37.

Fuller, Robert C. *Spiritual But Not Religious: Understanding Unchurched America*. New York: Oxford University Press, 2001.

Galuska, John D. "Mapping Creative Interiors: Creative Process Narratives and Individualized Workspaces in the Jamaican Dub Poetry Context." Thesis (Ph.D.)—Indiana University, 2007.

Garrick, Neville. *A Rasta's Pilgrimage: Ethiopian Faces and Places*. San Francisco: Pomegranate Communications, 1998.

Garrison, Ken. *Black Youth: Rastafarianism and the Identity Crisis in Britain*. London: Afro-Caribbean Education Resource Project, 1985.

—. *Beyond Babylon: Collection of Poems (1972–82)*. London: Black Star Publications, 1976.

Garvey, Amy Jacques. "Political Activities of Marcus Garvey in Jamaica." *Jamaica Journal* 6.2 (1972): 2–4.

—. *Garvey and Garveyism*. Kingston: United Printers, 1963.

Garvey, Marcus. *The Philosophy and Opinions of Marcus Garvey*. London: Frank Cass & Co. Ltd., 1983.

Gates Jr., Henry Louis. *Black in Latin America*. New York: New York University Press, 2011.

—. *Wonders of the African World*. New York: Alfred A. Knopf, 1999.

Geertz, Clifford. "Religion as a Cultural System." In *Anthropological Approaches to the Study of Religion*, ed. Michael Banton, 1–46. New York: Praeger, 1966.

Geoffroy, Martin. "Theorizing Religion in the Global Age: A Typological Analysis." *International Journal of Politics, Culture and Society* 18.1 (2004): 33–46.

George, Kadja, ed. *Write Black, Write British: From Post Colonial to Black British Literature*. Hertford: Hansib, 2005.

Gibson, Matthew. "Rastafari and Cannabis: Framing a Criminal Law Exemption." *Ecclesiatical Law Journal* 12.3 (2010): 324–344.

Gilroy, Paul. *Postcolonial Melancholia*. Wellek Library Lectures. New York: Columbia University Press, 2006.

—. *The Black Atlantic: Modernity and Double Consciousness*. Cambridge, MA: Harvard University Press, 1993.

Gingell, Susan. "Coming Home through Sound: 'See Hear' Aesthetics in the Poetry of Louise Bennett and Canadian Dub Poets." *Journal of West Indian Literature* 17.2 (2009): 32–48.

Gjerset, Heidi. "First Generation Rastafari in St. Eustatius: A Case Study in the Netherlands Antilles." *Caribbean Quarterly* 40.2 (1994): 64–77.

Glazier, Stephen D. "Being and Becoming a Rastafarian: Notes on the Anthropology of Religious Conversion." In *Rastafari: A Universal Philosophy in the Third Millennium*, ed. Werner Zips, 256–281. Kingston, Jamaica; Miami: Ian Randle Publishers, 2006.

Goldman, Vivien. *The Book of Exodus: The Making and Meaning of Bob Marley and the Wailers' Album of the Century*. New York: Three Rivers Press, 2006.

Gomez, Michael A. *Reversing Sail: A History of the African Diaspora*. New York: Cambridge University Press, 2005.

Gomez, Michael A., ed. *Diasporic Africa: A Reader*. New York: New York University Press, 2006.

Gordon, Joyce, and Roger Hughes. "A Preliminary Rastafari Bibliography." *Caribbean Quarterly* 24.3–4 (1978): 56–58.

Gossai, Hemchand and Nathaniel S. Murrell, eds. *Religion, Culture and Tradition in the Caribbean*. New York: St. Martin's Press, 2000.

Goulbourne, Jean. *Excavation*. Leeds, England: Peepal Tree Press Ltd., 1997.

Graham, Margaret, and Franklin Knight, eds. *Africa and the Caribbean: The Legacies of a Link*. Baltimore, MD: Johns Hopkins University Press, 1979.

Grant, Colin. *The Natural Mystics: Marley, Tosh, and Wailer*. New York and London: St. Martin's Press, 2011.

Greenberg, Alan. *Land of Look Behind*. United States: Subversive Cinema, 2006. DVD.

Griffin, Brian. *The Trustafarian Handbook: A Field Guide to the Neo-Hippie Lifestyle—Funded by Mom and Dad*. Avon, MA: Adams Media, 2010.

Griffin, Glenn A. Elmer. "Come, We Go Burn Down Babylon: A Report on the Cathedral Murders and the Force of Rastafari in the Eastern Caribbean." *Small Axe* 21 (2006): 1–18.

Guadeloupe, Francio. *Chanting Down the New Jerusalem: Calypso, Christianity, and Capitalism in the Caribbean*. Berkeley: University of California Press, 2009.

Gunst, Laurie. *Born Fi' Dead: A Journey Through the Jamaican Posse Underworld*. Edinburgh: Payback Press, 1999.

Habekost, Christian. *Verbal Riddim: The Politics and Aesthetics of African-Caribbean Dub Poetry*. Amsterdam; Atlanta, GA: Rodopi, 1993.

——. *Dub Poetry: 19 Poets from England and Jamaica*. Neustadt, West Germany: M. Schwinn, 1986.

Haim, Monica. *Awake Zion: A Documentary*. New York: Cinema Guild, 2006. DVD.

Hallen, Barry. *A Short History of African Philosophy*. Bloomington: Indiana University Press, 2002.

Hamid, Ansley. *The Ganja Complex: Rastafari and Marijuana*. Lanham, MD: Lexington Books, 2002.

Hannah, Barbara Makeda Blake. *Joseph: A Rasta Reggae Fable*. Oxford: Macmillan Caribbean, 2006.

——. *Rastafari: The New Creation*. 6th ed. Kingston, Jamaica: Jamaica Media Productions, 2006.

——. "Repatriations: Rastafari Pathway to World Peace." In *Rastafari: A Universal Philosophy in the Third Millennium*, ed. Werner Zips, 119–128. Kingston, Jamaica; Miami: Ian Randle Publishers, 2006.

—. "The Meaning of Rastafari for World Critique: Rasta Within a Universal Context." In *Rastafari: A Universal Philosophy in the Third Millennium*, ed. Werner Zips, 1–6. Kingston, Jamaica; Miami: Ian Randle Publishers, 2006.

Hansing, Katrin. *Rasta, Race and Revolution: The Emergence and Development of the Rastafari Movement in Socialist Cuba.* Berlin: Lit Verlag, 2006.

Hardt, Michael, and Antonio Negri. *Empire.* Cambridge: Harvard University Press, 2000.

Haskins, James. *One Love, One Heart: A History of Reggae.* New York: Hyperion, 2002.

Hauiti, Claudette. *Rasta in Aotearoa.* Auckland, New Zealand: Front of the Box Productions, 2004. DVD.

Hausman, Gerald. *The Kebra Nagast: The Lost Bible of Rastafarian Wisdom and Faith from Ethiopia and Jamaica.* New York: St. Martin's Press, 1997.

Hawke, Harry, ed. *Complete Lyrics of Bob Marley.* London: Omnibus, 2000.

Hebdige, Dick. *Cut 'n' Mix: Culture, Identity and Caribbean Music.* London: Routledge, 1987.

Heider, Renée. "The Historical, Social and Political Roots of Reggae: Continuing the Legacy of Resistance in Jamaica." Thesis (M.A.)—California State University, 2000.

Henry, W. "Reggae, Rasta and the Role of the Deejay in the Black British Experience." *Contemporary British History* 26.3 (2012): 355–373.

Hepner, Randal L. "Chanting Down Babylon in the Belly of the Beast: The Rastafari Movement in Metropolitan USA." In *Chanting Down Babylon: The Rastafari Reader*, eds. Nathaniel Samuel Murrell, William David Spencer, and Adrian Anthony McFarlane, 199–216. Philadelphia: Temple University Press, 1998.

—. "The House That Rasta Built: Church-Building and Fundamentalism Among New York Rastafarians." In *Gatherings in Diaspora: Religious Communities and the New Immigration*, eds. R. Stephen Warner and Judith G. Wittner, 197–234. Philadelphia: Temple University Press, 1998.

Hepner, Tricia Redeker, and Randal L. Hepner. "Gender, Community, and Change among the Rastafari of New York." In *New York Glory: Religions in the City*, eds. Tony Carnes and Anna Karpathakis, 333–353. New York: New York University Press, 2001.

Hervieu-Léger, Danièle. *Religion as a Chain of Memory.* New Brunswick, NJ: Rutgers University Press, 2000.

Herzfeld, Anita. "Afro-Caribbean Music as a Cohesion Factor of Identity." In *Rastafari: A Universal Philosophy in the Third Millennium*, ed. Werner Zips, 202–214. Kingston, Jamaica; Miami: Ian Randle Publishers, 2006.

Hess, Robert L. "Toward a History of the Falasha." In *Eastern African History*, eds. Daniel F. McCall, Norman R. Bennett, and Jeffrey Butler, 107–132. New York: Praeger, 1983.

Hill, Oliver. *Coping with Babylon: The Proper Rastology.* Oaks, PA: MVD Visual, 2007. DVD.

Hill, Robert A. *The Rastafari Bible: The Essential Collection of Sacred Writings That Inspired a Black Liberation Movement in the African Diaspora.* San Francisco: Harper, 2005.

—. *Dread History: Leonard P. Howell and Millenarian Visions in the Early Rastafarian Religion.* Chicago: Miguel Lorne Publishers, 2001.

—. "Leonard P. Howell and Millenarian Visions in Early Rastafari." *Jamaica Journal* 16.1 (1983): 24–39.

Hill, Robert, and Barbara Bair. *Marcus Garvey: Life and Lessons.* Berkeley: University of California Press, 1987.

Hodges, Hugh. *Soon Come: Jamaican Spirituality, Jamaican Poetics.* Charlottesville and London: University of Virginia Press, 2008.

Hoenisch, Michael. "Rastafari-Black Decolonization." In *CrossRoutes: The Meaning of 'Race' for the 21st Century*, eds. Paola Boi and Sabine Broeck, 139–148. Münster: Lit; Piscataway, NJ: Distributed in North America by Transaction Publishers, 2003.

—. "Symbolic Politics: Perceptions of the Early Rastafari Movement." *Massachusetts Review* 29 (1989): 432–449.

Holloway, Joseph E., ed. *Africanisms in American Culture*. Bloomington: Indiana University Press, 1991.

Homiak, John P. "Ethiopia Arisen: Discovering Rastafari." *Anthro Notes* 26.2 (2005): 10–18.

—. "Dub History: Soundings on Rastafari Livity and Language." In *Rastafari and Other African-Caribbean Worldviews*, ed. Barry Chevannes, 127–181. New Brunswick, NJ: Rutgers University Press, 1998.

—. "Rastafari Voices Reach Ethiopia: *The Emperor's Birthday* by John Dollar." *American Anthropologist* 96.4 (1994): 958–963.

—. "The 'Ancient of Days' Seated Black: Eldership, Oral Tradition and Ritual in Rastafari Culture." Thesis (Ph.D.)—Brandeis University, 1985.

Hopkins, Dwight N., and Edward P. Antonio, eds. *The Cambridge Companion to Black Theology*. New York: Cambridge University Press, 2012.

Hutton, Clinton, and Nathaniel Samuel Murrell. "Rastas' Psychology of Blackness, Resistance, and Sombodiness." In *Chanting Down Babylon: The Rastafari Reader*, eds. Nathaniel Samuel Murrell, William David Spencer, and Adrian Anthony McFarlane, 36–54. Philadelphia: Temple University Press, 1998.

Isimat-Mirin, Teddy. "Reggae in the French Caribbean." In *Global Reggae*, ed. Carolyn Cooper, 127–148. Kingston, Jamaica: Canoe Press, 2012.

Jackson, Michael. "Rastafarianism." *Theology* 83 (1980): 26–34.

Jacobs, Virginia Lee. *Roots of Rastafari*. San Diego, CA: Avant, 1985.

Jaffe, Rivke. "Ital Chic: Rastafari, Resistance, and the Politics of Consumption in Jamaica." *Small Axe: A Journal of Criticism* 31 (2010): 30–45.

Jaffe, Rivke and Jolien Sanderse. "Surinamese Maroons as Reggae Artistes: Music, Marginality, and Urban Space." *Ethnic and Racial Studies* 33.9 (2010): 1561–1579.

James, William. *The Varieties of Religious Experience: A Study in Human Nature*. New York: Simon and Schuster, 1997.

Johnson, Linton Kwesi. "Writing Reggae: Poetry, Politics and Popular Culture." *Jamaica Journal* 33 (2010): 1–2.

Johnson-Hill, Jack A. "Black Religious Ethics and Higher Education: Rastafarian Identity as a Resource for Inclusiveness." *Journal of Beliefs and Values* 24.1 (2003): 3–13.

—. "Rastafari as a Resource for Social Ethics in South Africa." *Journal for the Study of Religion* 9.1 (1996): 3–39.

—. *I-Sight: The World of Rastafari: An Interpretive Sociological Account of Rastafarian Ethics*. Metuchen, NJ; London: American Theological Library Association and The Scarecrow Press, Inc., 1995.

Jurgensen, Joe. *Bob Marley: The Complete Annotated Bibliography*. Prospect, KY: Haras, 2009.

Kalra, Virinder S. *Sacred and Secular Musics: A Postcolonial Approach*. London and New York: Bloomsbury, 2013.

Kaplan, Louis. "Yahweh Rastafari!: Matisyahu and the Aporias of Hasidic Reggae Superstardom." *CR: The New Centennial Review* 7.1 (2007): 15–44.

Kaslow, Andrew. "The Roots of Reggae." *Sing Out!: The Folk Song Magazine* 23.6 (1975): 12–13.

Katz, David. *Solid Foundation: An Oral History of Reggae*. New York: Bloomsbury, 2003.

Kebede, Alemseghed. "Decentered Movements: The Case of the Structural and Preceptual Versatility of the Rastafari." *Sociological Spectrum* 21.2 (2001): 175–205.

Kebede, Alemseghed, and J. David Knottnerus. "Beyond the Pales of Babylon: The Ideational Components and Social Psychological Foundations of Rastafari." *Sociological Perspectives* 41.3 (1998): 499–517.

Kerfoot, Janice. "Babylon Boys Don't Dance: Music, Meaning, and Young Men in Accra." Thesis (M.A.)—McGill University, 2006. Available as a PDF from this source: http://digitool.Library.McGill.CA:80/R/?func=dbin-jump-full&object_id=99727.

Kessler, Gary E. *Ways of Being Religious*. Mountain View, CA: Mayfield Publishing, 2000.

King, Stephen A. "Protest Music as 'Ego-enhancement': Reggae Music, the Rastafarian Movement, and the Re-Examination of Race and Identity in Jamaica." In *The Resisting Muse: Popular Music and Social Protest*, ed. Ian Peddie, 105–118. Aldershot, England; Burlington, VT: Ashgate, 2006.

—. *Reggae, Rastafari, and the Rhetoric of Social Control*. Jackson, MS: University Press of Mississippi, 2002.

King, Stephen, and Richard J. Jensen. "Bob Marley's 'Redemption Song': The Rhetoric of Reggae and Rastafari." *Journal of Popular Culture* 29.3 (Winter 1995): 17–36.

Kitzinger, Sheila. "Protest and Mysticism: The Rastafarian Cult in Jamaica." *Journal for the Scientific Study of Religion* 8.2 (1969): 240–262.

Klobah, Loretta Collins. "Journeying Towards Mount Zion: Changing Representations of Womanhood in Popular Music, Performance Poetry, and Novels by Rastafarian Women." *IDEAZ* 7 (2008): 158–196.

Knepper, Wendy. "Colonization, Creolization, and Globalization: The Art and Ruses of Bricolage." *Small Axe* 11.1 (2006): 70–86.

Koehlings, Ellen and Pete Lilly. "The Evolution of Reggae in Europe with a Focus on Germany." In *Global Reggae*, ed. Carolyn Cooper, 69–93. Kingston, Jamaica: Canoe Press, 2012.

Kroll, Florian. "Roots and Culture: Rasta Bushdoctors of the Cape, SA." In *Rastafari: A Universal Philosophy in the Third Millennium*, ed. Werner Zips, 215–255. Kingston, Jamaica; Miami: Ian Randle Publishers, 2006.

Kunene, Thandeka, and Pious Tiou Kgomo. *Rastafarians in South Africa*. London: Autograph, 1993.

Lake, Obiagele. *RastafarI Women: Subordination in the Midst of Liberation Theology*. Durham, NC: Carolina Academic Press, 1998.

—. "Religion, Patriarchy, and the Status of Rastafarian Women." In *New Trends and Developments in African Religions*, ed. Peter B. Clarke, 141–158. Westport, CT: Greenwood Press, 1998.

Lakhan, Keith. *Omega Rising: Women in Rastafari*. London: Ceddo Film Video Workshop, 1998.

Lalla, Barbara. *Defining Jamaican Fiction: Maroonage and the Discourse of Survival*. Tuscaloosa: University of Alabama Press, 1996.

Landman-Bogues, Jacqueline. "Rastafarian Food Habits." *Cajanus* 9.4 (1976): 228–233.

Lapperrousaz, Jérôme. *Made in Jamaica*. New York: ArtMattan Productions, 2009. DVD.

Lawson, Winston. *Religion and Race*. New York: Peter Lang, 1996.

Lee, Hélène. *The First Rasta: Leonard Howell and the Rise of Rastafarianism*. Chicago: Lawrence Hill Books, 2003.

Lee, Hélène, and Christophe Farnarier. *The First Rasta*. New York: ArtMattan Productions, 2011. DVD.

Leeman, Bernard. *The Queen of Sheba and Biblical Scholarship*. Trenton, NJ: Africa World Press, 2005.

Levy, Horace, ed. *The African-Caribbean Worldview and the Making of a Caribbean Society*. Kingston: University of West Indies Press, 2009.

Lewis, Linden F. "Living in the Heart of Babylon: Rastafari in the USA." *Bulletin of Eastern Caribbean Affairs* 15.1 (1989): 20–30.

Lewis, Rupert. "Marcus Garvey and the Early Rastafarians: Continuity and Discontinuity." In *Chanting Down Babylon: The Rastafari Reader*, eds. Nathaniel Samuel Murrell, William David Spencer, and Adrian Anthony McFarlane, 145–158. Philadelphia: Temple University Press, 1998.

—. *Marcus Garvey*. Trenton, NJ: Africa World Press, 1988.

Lewis, William F. "The Social Drama of the Rastafari." *Dialectical Anthropology* 19.2–3 (1994): 283–294.

—. *Soul Rebels: The Rastafari*. Prospect Heights, IL: Waveland Press, 1993.

Lieb, Elliott, and Renee Romano. *Rastafari: Conversations Concerning Woman*. New Haven, CT: Eye in I Filmworks, 1985. VHS.

Llosa, Mario Vargas. *The Language of Passion: Selected Commentary*. New York: Farrar, Straus and Giroux, 2003.

Lovelace, Ann. *Values in Action: Exploring Faith Values That Motivate a Rastafarian, a Hindu, and a Christian in Community Work*. London: Christian Aid, 2000.

Lowney, Declan. *Bob Marley: Time Will Tell*. Santa Monica, CA: Immortal, 2006. DVD.

Macdonald, Kevin. *Marley*. Los Angeles: Magnolia Home Entertainment, 2012. DVD.

Mack, Douglas R. *From Babylon to Rastafari: Origin and History of the Rastafarian Movement*. Chicago: Research Associates School Times Publications, 1999.

MacLeod, Erin C. *Visions of Zion: Ethiopians and Rastafari in the Search for the Promised Land*. New York: New York University Press, 2014.

—. "Water Development Projects and Cultural Citizenship: Rastafari Engagement with the Oromo in Shashemene, Ethiopia." In *Rastafari in the New Millennium: A Rastafari Reader*, ed. Michael Barnett, 89–103. Syracuse: Syracuse University Press, 2012.

—. "Leaving Out of Babylon, into Whose Father's Land? The Ethiopian Perception of the Repatriated Rastafari." Thesis (Ph.D.)—McGill University, 2009.

MacNeil, Dean. *The Bible and Bob Marley: Half the Story Has Never Been Told*. Eugene, OR: Wipf and Stock, 2013.

Mais, Roger. *The Hills Were Joyful Together*. Leeds, England: Peepal Tree Press Ltd., 2012.

—. *Brother Man*, special fiftieth anniversary edition, with a foreword by Kwame Dawes. Oxford: Macmillan Caribbean, 2004.

Malloch, Theodore. "Rastafarianism: A Radical Caribbean Movement/Religion." *Center Journal* 4.4 (1985): 67–87.

Manley, Michael. *Jamaica: Struggle in the Periphery*. London: Third World Media, 1982.

Manuel, Peter, Kenneth Bilby, and Michael Largey. *Caribbean Currents: Caribbean Music from Rumba to Reggae*. Philadelphia: Temple University Press, 1995.

Marcus, Harold G. *A History of Ethiopia*. Berkeley, CA: University of California Press, 1994.

Marks, Anthony. *Dancehall*. London: The X Press, 1998.

Marley, Rita, with Hettie Johns. *No Woman, No Cry: My Life with Bob Marley*. New York: Hyperion, 2005.

Marre, Jeremy. *Rebel Music: The Bob Marley Story*. New York: Palm Pictures, 2000. DVD.

Marsh-Lockett, Carol P., and Elizabeth J. West, eds. *Literary Expressions of African Spirituality*. Lanham, MD: Lexington Books, 2013.

Marshall, Wayne. "Bling-Bling for Rastafari: How Jamaicans Deal with Hip-Hop." *Social and Economic Studies* 55.1–2 (2006): 49–74.

Maysles, Philip. "Dubbing the Nation." *Small Axe* 11 (2002): 91–111.

Mazrui, Ali A. "Religious Alternatives in the Black Diaspora: From Malcolm X to Rastafari." *Caribbean Affairs* 3.1 (1990): 157–160.

—. *The Africans: A Triple Heritage*. Boston: Little, Brown, 1986.

Mbiti, John. *African Religions and Philosophy*. London: Heinemann, 1969.

McCutcheon, Russell T., ed. *The Insider/Outsider Problem in the Study of Religion: A Reader.* London: Cassell, 1999.

McKittrick, Katherine, and Clyde Woods, eds. *Black Geographies and the Politics of Place.* Toronto; Cambridge, MA: Between the Lines; South End Press, 2007.

McPherson, E.S.P. *From Rastology to Pan-Ethiopianization.* Bloomington, IN: AuthorHouse, 2008.

—. *An Ethiopian National Front "State of the Nation Address" to South Africa Rastafari & Pan-Africanist Community.* Bronx, NY: Ethiopian National Front Publishers, 2005.

Meeks, Brian. *Paint the Town Red.* Leeds, England: Peepal Tree Press Ltd., 2003.

Mekfet, Tekla. *Christopher Columbus and Rastafari: Ironies of History and Other Reflections on the Symbol of Rastafari.* St. Ann, Jamaica: Jambasa, 1993.

Mengiste, Maaza. *Beneath the Lion's Gaze.* New York and London: W.W. Norton & Company, 2010.

Mhango, Mtendeweka Owen. "The Constitutional Protection of Minority Religious Rights in Malawi: The Case of Rastafari Students." *Journal of African Law* 52.2 (2008): 218–244.

—. "Upholding the Rastafari Religion in Zimbabwe: Farai Dzvova v. Minister of Education, Sports and Culture and Others." *African Human Rights Law Journal* 8.1 (2008): 221–238.

Middleton, Darren J.N. *Theology after Reading: Christian Imagination and the Power of Fiction.* Waco, TX: Baylor University Press, 2008.

—. "As It Is in Zion: Seeking the Rastafari in Ghana, West Africa." *Black Theology: An International Journal* 4.2 (2006): 151–172.

—. "Benjamin Zephaniah." In *The Oxford Encyclopedia of British Literature*, ed. David Scott Kastan, 371–375. Oxford: Oxford University Press, 2006.

—. "Fictional Dread: Two Early Novels about the Rastafarians of Jamaica." *Modern Believing* 41.4 (2000): 23–33.

—. "Riddim Wise and Scripture Smart: Interview and Interpretation with Ras Benjamin Zephaniah." In *Religion, Culture, and Tradition in the Caribbean*, eds. Hemchand Gossai and Nathaniel Samuel Murrell, 257–270. New York: St. Martin's Press, 2000.

—. "Chanting Down Babylon: Three Rastafarian Dub Poets." In *"This Is How We Flow": Rhythm in Black Cultures*, ed. Angela M.S. Nelson, 74–86. Columbia, SC: University of South Carolina Press, 1999.

—. "Poetic Liberation: Rastafarianism, Poetry, and Social Change." *Modern Churchman* 34.2 (1992): 16–21.

—. "Rastafarianism: A Ministry for Social Change?" *Modern Churchman* 31.3 (1989): 45–48.

Middleton, J. Richard. "Identity and Subversion in Babylon: Strategies for 'Resisting Against the System' in the Music of Bob Marley and the Wailers." In *Religion, Culture and Tradition in the Caribbean*, eds. Hemchand Gossai and Nathaniel Samuel Murrell, 181–205. New York: St. Martin's Press, 2000.

Miller, Jacob Killer, Hugh Mandell, Dennis Brown, Errol Dunkley, Augustus Pablo, Sugar Minott, Gregory Isaacs, *et al. Revolutionary Sounds: The Essential Collection of Classic Roots Reggae 1973–1981.* Newton, NJ: Shanachie Entertainment Corp., 1998.

Miller, Marian A.L. "The Rastafarian in Jamaican Political Culture: The Marginalization of a Change Agent." *Western Journal of Black Studies* 17 (1993): 112–177.

Minda, Ababu. "Rastafari in 'The Promised Land': A Change of Identity." *Africa Insight* 34.4 (2004): 31–39.

Mitchell, Mozella G. *Crucial Issues in Caribbean Religions.* New York and Bern: Peter Lang, 2006.

Mongia, Padmini, ed. *Contemporary Postcolonial Theory: A Reader.* London: Arnold, 1996.

Montague, Masani. *Dread Culture: A Rastawoman's Story.* Toronto: Sister Vision Press, 1994.

Morris, Mervyn. *Making West Indian Literature.* Kingston, Jamaica: Ian Randle Publishers, 2005.

—. *'Is English We Speaking' and Other Essays.* Kingston, Jamaica: Ian Randle Publishers, 1999.

—. "Dub Poetry?" *Caribbean Quarterly* 43.4 (1997): 1–10.

Morris, Randall. *Redemption Songs: The Self-Taught Artists of Jamaica.* Winston-Salem, NC: Winston-Salem State University, 1997.

Morrish, Ivor. *Obeah, Christ and Rastaman: Jamaica and its Religion.* Cambridge: James Clarke, 1982.

Morrow, Chris. *Stir It Up: Reggae Album Cover Art.* London: Thames & Hudson, 1999.

Mosely, Leonard. *Haile Selassie: The Conquering Lion.* London: Weidenfeld and Nicholson, 1964.

Moskowitz, David V. *The Words and Music of Bob Marley.* Westport, CT: Praeger, 2007.

Moss, Susanne. *Ras Cuba.* S.I.: Susanne Moss/Sela Photo, 2003. DVD.

Mowatt, Judy. *Rastafari Conversations Concerning Women.* San Diego, CA: Eye in I Filmworks, 1983.

Moyer, Eileen. "Street-Corner Justice in the Name of Jah: Imperatives for Peace among Dar es Salaam Street Youth." *Africa Today* 51.3 (2005): 32–58.

Mulvaney, Rebekah Michele, and Carlos I.H. Nelson. *Rastafari and Reggae: A Dictionary and Sourcebook.* New York: Greenwood Press, 1990.

Murrell, Nathaniel Samuel. *Afro-Caribbean Religions: An Introduction to Their Historical, Cultural, and Sacred Traditions.* Philadelphia, PA: Temple University Press, 2010.

—. "Tuning Hebrew Psalms to Reggae Rhythms: Rastas' Revolutionary Lamentations for Social Change." *CrossCurrents* 50.4 (Winter 2000–2001): 525–540.

—. "*Holy Piby*: Blackman's Bible and Garveyite Ethiopianist Epic with Commentary." In *Religion, Culture and Tradition in the Caribbean,* eds. Hemchand Gossai and Nathaniel Samuel Murrell, 271–306. New York: St. Martin's Press, 2000.

—. "Wresting the Message from the Messenger: The Rastafari as a Case Study in the Caribbean Indigenization of the Bible." In *African Americans and the Bible: Sacred Texts and Social Textures,* ed. Vincent L. Wimbush, 558–575. New York and London: Continuum, 2000.

—. "Who is Who in the Rasta Academy: A Literature Review in Honor of Leonard Barrett." In *Chanting Down Babylon: The Rastafari Reader,* eds. Nathaniel Samuel Murrell, William David Spencer, and Adrian Anthony McFarlane, 429–441. Philadelphia: Temple University Press, 1998.

—. "Woman as Source of Evil and Containment in Rastafarianism: Championing Hebrew Patriarchy and Oppression with Lev 12." *Proceedings of the Eastern Great Lakes and Midwestern Bible Society* (1994): 191–209.

Murrell, Nathaniel Samuel, William David Spencer, and Adrian Anthony McFarlane, eds. *Chanting Down Babylon: The Rastafari Reader.* Philadelphia: Temple University Press, 1998.

Murrell, Nathaniel Samuel, and Lewin Williams. "The Black Biblical Hermeneutics of Rastafari." In *Chanting Down Babylon: The Rastafari Reader,* eds. Nathaniel Samuel Murrell, William David Spencer, and Adrian Anthony McFarlane, 326–348. Philadelphia: Temple University Press, 1998.

Mutabaruka. "Ghana: Africa from Experience." In *Rastafari: A Universal Philosophy in the Third Millennium,* ed. Werner Zips, 106–118. Kingston, Jamaica; Miami: Ian Randle Publishers, 2006.

—. "Rasta from Experience" In *Rastafari: A Universal Philosophy in the Third Millennium*, ed. Werner Zips, 21–41. Kingston, Jamaica; Miami: Ian Randle Publishers, 2006.

—. *The Next Poems (1980–2002)*. Kingston, Jamaica: Paul Issa Publications, 2005.

—. *The Ultimate Collection*. Newton, NJ: Shanachie, 1996.

—. *The First Poems*. Kingston, Jamaica: Paul Issa Publications, 1980.

Myers, Trevor C. *The Essence of Rastafari Nationalism and Black Economic Development*. New York: Vantage, 1989.

Nagashima, Yoshiko S. *Rastafarian Music in Contemporary Jamaica: A Study of Socioreligious Music of the Rastafarian Movement in Jamaica*. Tokyo: Institute for the Study of Languages and Cultures of Asia and Africa, 1984.

Naphtali, Karl Phillpotts, ed. *The Testimony of His Imperial Majesty, Emperor Haile Selassie I, Defender of the Faith*. Washington, D.C.: Zewd, 1999.

Narain, Denise deCaires. *Contemporary Caribbean Women's Poetry: Making Style*. London and New York: Routledge, 2002.

Nelson, Gersham A. "Rastafarians and Ethiopianism." In *Imagining Home: Class, Culture and Nationalism in the African Diaspora*, ed. Sidney J. Lemelle and Robin D.G. Kelley, 66–84. London and New York: Verso, 1994.

Niaah, Jahlani. "The Rastafari Presence in Ethiopia: A Contemporary Perspective." In *Rastafari in the New Millennium: A Rastafari Reader*, ed. Michael Barnett, 66–88. Syracuse: Syracuse University Press, 2012.

—. "Grafting a New History: Rastafari Memory Gems Articulating a 'Hermeneutics of Babylon.'" In *Africa and Trans-Atlantic Memories: Literary and Aesthetic Manifestations of Diaspora and History*, eds. Naana Opoku-Agyemang, Paul E. Lovejoy, and David V. Trotman, 343–369. Trenton, NJ: Africa World Press, 2008.

—. "Sensitive Scholarship: A Review of Rastafari Literature(s)." *Caribbean Quarterly* 51.3–4 (2005): 11–34.

Niaah, Jahlani, and Erin MacLeod, eds. *Let Us Start with Africa: Foundations of Rastafari Scholarship*. Jamaica: The University of West Indies Press, 2013.

Niaah, Jahlani and Sonjah Stanley Niaah. "Jah Cure and Rastafari Celebrity in Contemporary Jamaica." *Wadabagei: Journal of the Caribbean and Its Diaspora* 12.2 (2009): 103–120.

Nicholas, Tracy. *Rastafari: A Way of Life*. Garden City, NY: Anchor, 1978.

Norgren, Jill, and Serena Nanda. *American Cultural Pluralism and Law*. 3rd ed. Westport, CT; London: Praeger, 2006.

Noyce, John L. *The Rastafarians in Britain and Jamaica*. Brighton, England: University of Sussex Press, 1978.

O'Brien, Derek, and Vaughn Carter. "Chant Down Babylon: Freedom of Religion and the Rastafarian Challenge to Majoritarianism." *Journal of Law and Religion* 18:1 (2002): 219–248.

Olaniyan, Tejumola, and James H. Sweet, eds. *The African Diaspora and its Disciplines*. Bloomington: Indiana University Press, 2010.

Oliver, Roland. *The African Experience: Major Themes in African History from Earliest Times to the Present*. New York: HarperCollins, 1992.

Olmos, Margarite Fernández, and Lizabeth Paravisini-Gebert. *Creole Religions of the Caribbean: An Introduction from Vodou and Santería to Obeah and Espiritismo*. 2nd ed. New York: New York University Press, 2011.

Olsen, Barbara. "Consuming Rastafari: Ethnographic Research in Context and Meaning." *Advances in Consumer Research* 22 (1995): 481–485.

Olson, Carl, ed. *Theory and Method in the Study of Religion: A Selection of Critical Readings*. Belmont, CA: Wadsworth, 2003.

Olupona, Jacob K. *African Religions: A Very Short Introduction*. Oxford and New York: Oxford University Press, 2014.

Onishi, Norimitsu. "Uneasy Bond Inside a Promised Land." *New York Times*, 4 August 2001, A4.

Onuora, Adwoa Ntozake. "Exploring RastafarI's Pedagogic, Communicative, and Instructional Potential in the Caribbean: The Life and Works of Mutabaruka as Case Study." In *Rastafari in the New Millennium: A Rastafari Reader*, ed. Michael Barnett, 142–158. Syracuse: Syracuse University Press, 2012.

Oosthuizen, Gerhadus C. "The Rastafarian Movement and Its Appearance in South Africa." *Syzygy: Journal of Alternative Religion and Culture* 2.3–4 (1993): 243–266.

Opoku-Agyemang, Naana Jane, and Paul E. Lovejoy, eds. *Africa and Trans-Atlantic Memories: Literary and Aesthetic Manifestations of Diaspora and History*. Trenton, NJ: Africa World Press, 2008.

Orderson, Kurt. *Chant Down Babylon*. South Africa: Azania Rizing Productions, 2013. DVD.

Otto, Rudolph. *The Idea of the Holy*. 2nd ed. New York: Oxford University Press, 1958.

Owens, Joseph. *Dread: The Rastafarians of Jamaica*. London: Heinemann, 1976.

—. "Literature on the Rastafari, 1955–1974." *Savacou* 11–12 (1975): 86–115.

—. "Ras Tafari: Cult of Outcasts." *New Society* 4.111 (Nov. 12, 1964): 15–17.

Palmer, Delano Vincent. *Messianic 'I' and Rastafari in New Testament Dialogue: Bio-Narratives, The Apocalypse, and Paul's Letter to the Romans*. Lanham, MD: University Press of America, 2010.

Paris, Peter J. *The Spirituality of African Peoples: The Search for a Common Moral Discourse*. Minneapolis: Fortress Press, 1995.

Parker, Victoria. *Benjamin Zephaniah*. Oxford: Heinemann Library, 2007.

Partridge, Christopher H. *Dub in Babylon: Understanding the Evolution and Significance of Dub Reggae in Jamaica and Britain from King Tubby to Post-Punk*. London; Oakville, CT: Equinox, 2010.

Patterson, Orlando. *The Children of Sisyphus*, with an introduction by Kwame Dawes. Leeds, England: Peepal Tree Press Ltd., 2012.

—. "Ras Tafari: The Cult of Outcasts." *New Society* 111.4 (1964): 15–17.

Perasovic, Benjamin. "Rastafarianism in Croatia." *Sociologija i Prostor* 45 (2007): 177–178.

Perkins, Anna Kasafi. "The Wages of (Sin) Is Babylon: Rastafari versus Christian Religious Perspectives of Sin." In *Rastafari in the New Millennium: A Rastafari Reader*, ed. Michael Barnett, 239–252. Syracuse: Syracuse University Press, 2012.

Philander, Lisa Erin. "Hunting Knowledge and Gathering Herbs: Rastafari Bush Doctors in the Western Cape, South Africa." *Journal of Ethnobiology* 32.2 (2012): 134–156.

—. "An Ethnobotany of Western Cape Rasta Bush Medicine." *Journal of Ethnopharmacology* 138.2 (2011): 578–594.

—. "An Emergent Ethnomedicine: Rastafari Bush Doctors in the Western Cape, South Africa." Thesis (Ph.D.)—University of Arizona, 2010.

Philp, Geoffrey. *Benjamin, My Son*. Leeds, England: Peepal Tree Press Ltd., 2003.

Pigou-Dennis, Elizabeth. "Spatial Responses of the African Diaspora in Jamaica: Focus on Rastafarian Architecture." In *Diasporic Africa: A Reader*, ed. Michael A. Gomez, 147–169. New York: New York University Press, 2006.

Pinson, Dovber. "Righteous Reggae—Yearning for Authenticity: Exploring the Musical Phenomenon of Matisyahu." *Parabola Magazine* 31.4 (2006): 92–94.

Plate, S. Brent. *A History of Religion in 5½ Objects: Bringing the Spiritual to Its Senses*. Boston: Beacon, 2014.

Pollard, Velma. "Sound and Power: The Language of the Rastafari." In *Black Linguistics: Language, Society, and Politics in Africa and the Americas*, eds. Sinfree Makoni, Geneva Smitherman, Arnetha F. Ball, and Arthur K. Spears, 60–79. London and New York: Routledge, 2003.

—. *Dread Talk: The Language of Rastafari*. Rev. ed. Montreal: McGill-Queen's University Press, 2000.

Pollard, Velma, and Samuel Furé Davis. "Imported Topics, Foreign Vocabularies: Dread Talk, the Cuban Connection." *Small Axe* 19 (2005): 59–73.

Post, Ken. "The Bible as Ideology: Ethiopianism in Jamaica, 1930–38." In *African Perspectives*, eds. Christopher Allen and R.W. Johnson, 185–207. Cambridge: Cambridge University Press, 1970.

Potash, Chris, ed. *Reggae, Rasta, Revolution: Jamaican Music from Ska to Dub*. New York: Schirmer Books, 1997.

Poupeye, Veerle. *Caribbean Art*. London: Thames and Hudson, 1998.

Prahlad, Anand. *Reggae Wisdom: Proverbs in Jamaican Music*. Jackson: University Press of Mississippi, 2001.

Prahlad, Anand, ed. *The Greenwood Encyclopedia of African American Folklore*. Westport, CT: Greenwood Press, 2006.

Price, Charles. *Becoming Rasta: Origins of Rastafari Identity in Jamaica*. New York: New York University Press, 2009.

Pulis, John W., ed. *Religion, Diaspora and Cultural Identity: A Reader in the Anglophone Caribbean*. New York: Routledge, 1999.

Raboteau, Albert. *Slave Religion*. New York: Oxford University Press, 1978.

Raboteau, Emily. *Searching for Zion: The Quest for Home in the African Diaspora*. New York: Atlantic Monthly Press, 2013.

Ramazani, Jahan. *The Hybrid Muse: Postcolonial Poetry in English*. Chicago: University of Chicago Press, 2001.

Ray, Benjamin C. *African Religions: Symbol, Ritual, and Community*. 2nd ed. Upper Saddle River, NJ: Prentice Hall, 2000.

Ray, Ella Maria. "Standing in the Lion's Shadow: Jamaican Rastafari Women Reconstructing their African Identity." Thesis (Ph.D.)—Johns Hopkins University, 1999.

Reckford, Verena. "Reggae, Rastafarianism and Cultural Identity." *Jamaica Journal* 16 (1982): 70–79.

—. "Rastafarian Music: An Introductory Study." *Jamaica Journal* 11.1–2 (1977): 2–13.

Reddie, Anthony G. *Black Theology*. London: SCM Press, 2012.

Richards, Roosevelt. *Rastafari Voices*. San Diego: Eye in I Filmworks, 1979. VHS.

Robertson-Pearce, Pamela, and Benjamian Zephaniah. *Benjamin Zephaniah—To Do Wid Me: Benjamin Zephaniah Live & Direct*. Tarset, Northumberland: Bloodaxe, 2013.

Rodney, Walter. *Groundings with My Brothers*. London: Bogle L'Ouverture Press, 1969.

Rommen, Timothy. "Protestant Vibrations?: Reggae, Rastafari, and Conscious Evangelicals." *Popular Music* 25.2 (2006): 235–263.

Roskind, Robert, and Julia Roskind. *Rasta Heart: A Journey into One Love*. Blowing Rock, NC: One Love Press, 2001.

Rowe, Maureen. "Gender and Family Relations in RastafarI: A Personal Perspective." In *Chanting Down Babylon: The Rastafari Reader*, eds. Nathaniel Samuel Murrell, William David Spencer, and Adrian Anthony McFarlane, 72–88. Philadelphia: Temple University Press, 1998.

—. "The Women in RastafarI." *Caribbean Quarterly* 26.4 (1980): 13–21.

Rubenstein, Hannah, and Chris Suarez. "The Twelve Tribes of Israel: An Exploratory Field Study." *Religion Today* 9.2 (1994): 1–6.

Runions, Erin. *The Babylon Complex: Theopolitical Fantasies of War, Sex, and Sovereignty*. Oxford and New York: Oxford University Press, 2014.

Saakana, Amon Saba. "The Impact of Jamaican Music in Britain." In *Global Reggae*, ed. Carolyn Cooper, 49–68. Kingston, Jamaica: Canoe Press, 2012.

Salassi, Ray Kalin. *Haile Selassie and the Opening of the Seven Seals*. Chicago: Research Associates School Times, 1997.

Salewicz, Chris. *Bob Marley: The Untold Story*. New York: Faber and Faber, 2010.

Salewicz, Chris, and Adrian Boot. *Reggae Explosion: The Story of Jamaican Music*. New York: Mango Records, 1993.

Salter, Richard C. "Rastafari in a Global Context: Affinities of 'Orthognosy' and 'Oneness' in the Expanding World." *IDEAZ* 7 (2008): 10–27.

——. "Sources and Chronology in Rastafari Origins: A Case of Dreads in Rastafari." *Nova Religio: The Journal of Alternative and Emergent Religions* 9.1 (2005): 5–31.

——. "Religious Group Formation in the West Indies: A Case Study of Religious Change Among Catholics, Pentecostals and Rastafarians in the Commonwealth of Dominica." Thesis (Ph.D.)—University of Chicago Divinity School, 1998.

Savishinsky, Neil J. "Transnational Popular Culture and the Global Spread of the Jamaican Rastafarian Movement." In *Across the Boundaries of Belief: Contemporary Issues in the Anthropology of Religion*, eds. Morton Klass and Maxine K. Weisgrau, 347–366. Boulder, CO: Westview Press, 1999.

——. "African Dimensions of the Jamaican Rastafarian Movement." In *Chanting Down Babylon: The Rastafari Reader*, eds. Nathaniel Samuel Murrell, William David Spencer, and Adrian Anthony McFarlane, 125–144. Philadelphia: Temple University Press, 1998.

——. "Rastafari in the Promised Land: The Spread of a Jamaican Socioreligious Movement Among the Youth of West Africa." *African Studies Review* 37.3 (1994): 19–50.

——. "The Baye Faal of Senegambia: Muslim Rastas in the Promised Land?" *Africa: Journal of the International African Institute* 64.2 (1994): 211–219.

Scheub, Harold. *A Dictionary of African Mythology: The Mythmaker as Storyteller*. Oxford: Oxford University Press, 2000.

Scott, William R. *The Sons of Sheba's Race*. Bloomington; Indianapolis: Indiana University Press, 1993.

Segal, Ronald. *The Black Diaspora*. London: Faber and Faber, 1995.

Semaj, Leachim T. "Race and Identity and Children of the African Diaspora: Contributions of Rastafari." *Caribe* 4 (1980): 14–18.

——. "Rastafari: From Religion to Social Theory." *Caribbean Quarterly* 26.4 (1980): 22–31.

Seyfert, J. Michael. *Rent a Rasta*. S.l.: Yeah But Not Now Productions, 2006. DVD.

Shabazz, Menelik. *The Story of Lover's Rock*. New York: ArtMattan Productions, 2011.

Sharpe, Jenny. "Cartographies of Globalisation, Technologies of Gendered Subjectivities: The Dub Poetry of Jean 'Binta' Breeze." *Gender and History* 15.3 (2003): 450–459.

Sibanda, Fortune. "The Impact of Rastafari Ecological Ethic in Zimbabwe: A Contemporary Discourse." *Journal of Pan African Studies* 5.3 (2012): 59–75.

Simpson, George Eaton. "Political Cultism in Western Kingston." *Social and Economic Studies* 5 (1955): 133–149.

——. "The Ras Tafari Movement in Jamaica: A Study of Race and Class Conflict." *Social Forces* 34.2 (1955): 167–171.

Siwek, Daniel. "Zion Riddims." *Tikkun* 20.2 (March–April 2005): 75–78.

Smart, Ninian. *Worldviews: Cross-Cultural Explorations of Human Beliefs*. 3rd ed. Englewood Cliffs, NJ: Prentice Hall, 1999.

—. *Dimensions of the Sacred: An Anatomy of the World's Beliefs*. Berkeley and Los Angeles, CA: University of California Press, 1996.

Smart, Ninian, Peter Masefield, and Donald Wiebe. *Aspects of Religion: Essays in Honour of Ninian Smart*. New York: Peter Lang, 1994.

Smith, Jonathan Z. *Imagining Religion: From Babylon to Jonestown*. Chicago: University of Chicago Press, 1982.

Smith, M.G., Roy Augier, and Rex Nettleford. *Report on the Rastafari Movement in Kingston, Jamaica*. Mona, Jamaica: University College of the West Indies, Institute of Social and Economic Research, 1960.

Smith, Mikey. *Me Cyaan Believe It*. Island Records, 1982.

Soares, Benjamin F. "'Rasta' Sufis and Muslim Youth Culture in Mali." In *Being Young and Muslim: New Cultural Politics in the Global South and North*, eds. Linda Herrera and Asef Bayat, 241–259. New York: Oxford University Press, 2010.

Soumahoro, Maboula. "Christianity on Trial: The Nation of Islam and the Rastafari, 1930–1950." In *The African Diaspora and the Study of Religion*, ed. Theodore Louis Trost, 35–48. New York: Palgrave Macmillan, 2007.

Soyinka, Wole. *Myth, Literature and the African World*. Cambridge: Cambridge University Press, 1976.

Spady, James G., Samir Meghelli, and Louis Jones, eds. *New Perspectives on the History of Marcus Garvey, the U.N.I.A., and the African Diaspora*. New York: Marcus Garvey Foundation Publishers, 2011.

Spencer, William David. *Dread Jesus*. London: SPCK, 1999.

—. "Chanting Change around the World through Rasta Ridim and Art." In *Chanting Down Babylon: The Rastafari Reader*, eds. Nathaniel Samuel Murrell, William David Spencer, and Adrian Anthony McFarlane, 266–283. Philadelphia: Temple University Press, 1998.

—. "The First Chant: Leonard Howell's *The Promised Key*, with commentary by William David Spencer." In *Chanting Down Babylon: The Rastafari Reader*, eds. Nathaniel Samuel Murrell, William David Spencer, and Adrian Anthony McFarlane, 361–389. Philadelphia: Temple University Press, 1998.

Stafford, Claire. "Reggae and Rastafari: The Popularity of Reggae Music in Ghana, West Africa." Thesis (M.A.)—National University of Ireland, University College Cork, 2007.

Stanley, Cathy S. "Expanding the Small Place: Rastafarians as Knowledge Producers." Thesis (Ed.D.)—Northern Illinois University, 2002.

Steffens, Roger. "Bob Marley: Rasta Warrior." In *Chanting Down Babylon: The Rastafari Reader*, eds. Nathaniel Samuel Murrell, William David Spencer, and Adrian Anthony McFarlane, 253–265. Philadelphia: Temple University Press, 1998.

Steffens, Roger, and Peter Simon. *Roger Steffens and Peter Simons's Reggae Scrapbook*. San Rafael, CA: Insight, 2007.

Stein, Judith. *The World of Marcus Garvey: Race and Class in Modern Society*. Baton Rouge, LA: Louisiana State University Press, 1986.

Sterling, Marvin D. "Gender, Class and Race in Japanese Dancehall Culture." In *Global Reggae*, ed. Carolyn Cooper, 241–261. Kingston, Jamaica: Canoe Press, 2012.

—. *Babylon East: Performing Dancehall, Roots Reggae, and Rastafari in Japan*. Durham, NC: Duke University Press, 2010.

Stewart, Robert J. *Religion and Society in Post-Emancipation Jamaica*. Knoxville: University of Tennessee Press, 1992.

Stokke, Christian. "Unlearning White Superiority: Consciousness-Raising on an Online Rastafari Reasoning Forum." Thesis (M.A.)—University of Oslo, 2005. http://urn.nb.no/URN:NBN:no-11028.

Stolzoff, Norman. *Wake the Town and Tell the People: Dancehall Culture in Jamaica*. Durham, NC: Duke University Press, 2000.

Strasser, Susan, ed. *Commodifying Everything: Relationships of the Market*. New York: Routledge, 2003.

Street, John. *Music and Politics*. Malden, MA: Polity, 2011.

Tafari, Ikael. "Rastafari in Transition: Cultural Confrontation and Political Change in Ethiopia and the Caribbean." *Bulletin of Eastern Caribbean Affairs* 15.1 (1989): 1–13.

Tafari, Jabulani I. "The Rastafari—Successors of Marcus Garvey." *Caribbean Quarterly* 26.4 (1980): 1–12.

Tafari-Ama, Imani M. "Resistance Without and Within: Reasonings on Gender Relations in RastafarI." In *Rastafari in the New Millennium: A Rastafari Reader*, ed. Michael Barnett, 190–221. Syracuse: Syracuse University Press, 2012.

—. "Rastawoman as Rebel: Case Studies in Jamaica." In *Chanting Down Babylon: The Rastafari Reader*, eds. Nathaniel Samuel Murrell, William David Spencer, and Adrian Anthony McFarlane, 89–106. Philadelphia: Temple University Press, 1998.

Tanis, Jonathan, "Babylon by Tro-Tro: The Varieties of Rasta Identity and Practice in Ghana" (2010). ISP Collection. Paper 849. http://digitalcollections.sit.edu/isp_collection/849.

Taylor, Patrick. "Sheba's Song: The Bible, the *Kebra Nagast*, and the Rastafari." In *Nation Dance: Religion, Identity, and Cultural Difference in the Caribbean*, ed. Patrick Taylor, 65–78. Bloomington, IN: Indiana University Press, 2001.

—. "Perspectives on History in Rastafari Thought." *Studies in Religion/Sciences Religieuses* 19.2 (1990): 191–205.

Te Kohu, Edward, and Ian Boxhill. "The Lantern and the Light: Rastafari in Aotearoa (New Zealand)." *IDEAZ* 7 (2008): 70–97.

Thieme, John, ed. *The Arnold Anthology of Post-Colonial Literatures in English*. London: Arnold, 1996.

Thomas, Deborah A. *Bad Friday: Rastafari after Coral Gardens*. New York: Third World Newsreel, 2011. DVD.

Thomas, Michael. "The Rastas Are Coming, the Rastas Are Coming." *Rolling Stone* (Aug. 2, 1976): 32–37.

Thompson, Dave. *Reggae and Caribbean Music*. San Francisco: Backbeat Books, 2002.

Thompson, Winston A. "Reggae Music: An Affective Epistemology." *Union Seminary Quarterly Review* 36.4 (1981): 259–269.

Torres-Salliant, Silvio. *An Intellectual History of the Caribbean*. New York: Palgrave Macmillan, 2006.

—. *Caribbean Poetics: Towards an Aesthetic of West Indian Literature*. Cambridge: Cambridge University Press, 1997.

Tosh, Peter, Edgar Egger, and Nicholas Campbell. *Peter Tosh: Stepping Razor Red X*. Toronto: Music Video Distributors, 2002. DVD.

Toynbee, Jason. *Bob Marley: Herald of a Postcolonial World?* Cambridge, England; Malden, MA: Polity, 2007.

Trost, Theodore Louis, ed. *The African Diaspora and the Study of Religion*. New York: Palgrave Macmillan, 2007.

Turner, Victor. *The Ritual Process: Structure and Anti-Structure*. Ithaca: Cornell University Press, 1969.

Tweed, Thomas A. *Crossings and Dwellings: A Theory of Religion*. Cambridge, MA; London: Harvard University Press, 2006.

Ullendorf, Edward. *Ethiopia and the Bible*. Oxford: Oxford University Press, 1968.

Van De Berg, William R. "Rastafari Perceptions of Self and Symbolism." In *New Trends and Developments in African Religions*, ed. Peter B. Clarke, 159–175. Westport, CT: Greenwood Press, 1998.

Veal, Michael. "Dub: Electronic Music and Sound Experimentation." In *Global Reggae*, ed. Carolyn Cooper, 285–300. Kingston, Jamaica: Canoe Press, 2012.

—. *Dub: Soundscapes and Shattered Songs in Jamaican Reggae*. Middletown, CT: Wesleyan University Press, 2007.

Vidigal, Leonardo. "Reggae Music Documentaries in Brazil." In *Global Reggae*, ed. Carolyn Cooper, 149–168. Kingston, Jamaica: Canoe Press, 2012.

Volkmann, Laurenz. "The Quest for Identity in Benjamin Zephaniah's Poetry." In *Embracing the Other: Addressing Xenophobia in the New Literatures in English*, ed. Dunja M. Mohr, 245–263. Amsterdam: Rodopi, 2008.

Walker, Klive. "The Journey of Reggae in Canada." In *Global Reggae*, ed. Carolyn Cooper, 185–211. Kingston, Jamaica: Canoe Press, 2012.

—. *Dubwise: Reasoning from the Reggae Underground*. Toronto: Insomniac Press, 2005.

Warner, Keith Q. "Calypso, Reggae, and Rastafarianism: Authentic Caribbean Voices." *Popular Music and Society* 12.1 (1988): 53–62.

Warner-Lewis, Maureen. *Central Africa in the Caribbean: Transcending Time, Transforming Cultures*. Kingston: University of the West Indies Press, 2003.

—. "African Continuities in the Rastafari Belief System." *Caribbean Quarterly* 39.3–4 (1993): 108–123.

Waterman, Adam John. "I and Ireland: Reggae and Rastafari in the Work of Sinéad O'Connor." In *Archipelagos of Sound: Transnational Caribbeanites, Women and Music*, ed. Ifeona Fulani, 321–339. Kingston, Jamaica: University of the West Indies Press, 2012.

Waters, Anita M. "Reluctant Candidates?: Rastafarians and Partisan Politics in Jamaica and Elsewhere." In *Rastafari in the New Millennium: A Rastafari Reader*, ed. Michael Barnett, 291–299. Syracuse: Syracuse University Press, 2012.

—. *Race, Class, and Political Symbols: Rastafari and Reggae in Jamaican Politics*. New Brunswick, NJ: Transaction Publishers, 1985.

Watson, Lewelyn. "Patterns of Black Protest in Jamaica: The Case of the Rastafarians." *Journal of Black Studies* 4 (1974): 329–343.

Waugh, Evelyn. *The Coronation of Haile Selassie*. London: Penguin, 2005.

West, Cornel. *Race Matters*. Boston, MA: Beacon Press, 1993.

White, Carmen M. "Rastafarian Repatriates and the Negotiation of Place in Ghana." *Ethnology: An International Journal of Cultural and Social Anthropology* 49.4 (2010): 303–320.

—. "Living in Zion: Rastafarian Repatriates in Ghana, West Africa." *Journal of Black Studies* 37 (2007): 677–709.

White, Timothy. *Catch a Fire: The Life of Bob Marley*. New York: Owl Books, 1998.

Whitney, Malika Lee, Dermot Hussey, and Rita Marley. *Bob Marley: Reggae King of the World*. London: Plexus, 1984.

Wilkins, Verna, and Gillian Hunt. *Benjamin Zephaniah: A Profile*. Northwood: Tamarind, 2008.

Williams, K.M. *The Rastafarians*. London: Ward Lock, 1981.

Williams, N.D. *Prash and Ras*. Leeds, England: Peepal Tree Press Ltd., 1997.

Williams, Prince, with Michael Kuelker. *Book of Memory: A Rastafari Testimony*. St. Louis: CaribSound Ltd., 2004.

Wilmore, Gayraud. *Black Religion and Black Radicalism*. New York: Doubleday, 1972.

Wilson, Gladstone. "Reggae as a Medium of Political Communication." In *Mass Media and the Caribbean*, eds. Stuart H. Surlin and Walter C. Soderland, 429–449. New York: Gordon and Breach, 1990.

Winders, James A. "Reggae, Rastafarians, and Revolution: Rock Music in the Third World." *Journal of Popular Culture* 17.1 (1983): 61–73.

Winslow, Barbara. "The First White Rastafarian: Sylvia Pankhurst, Haile Selassie, and Ethiopia." In *At Home and Abroad in the Empire: British Women Write the 1930s*, eds. Robin Hacket, Freda Hauser, and Gay Wachman, 171–186. Newark: University of Delaware Press, 2009.

Wint, Eleanor, and Carolyn Cooper, eds. *Bob Marley: The Man and His Music*. Kingston, Jamaica: Arawak Publishing, 2003.

Wint, Eleanor, in consultation with members of the Nyabinghi Order. "Who Is Haile Selassie?: His Imperial Majesty in Rasta Voices." In *Chanting Down Babylon: The Rastafari Reader*, eds. Nathaniel Samuel Murrell, William David Spencer, and Adrian Anthony McFarlane, 159–165. Philadelphia: Temple University Press, 1998.

Wisker, Gina. *Post-Colonial and African American Women's Writing: A Critical Introduction*. New York: St. Martin's Press, 2000.

Wittman, Frank. "The Global-Local Nexus: Popular Music Studies and the Case of Rastafari Culture in West Africa." *Critical Arts* 25.2 (2011): 150–174.

Witvliet, Theo. *The Way of the Black Messiah: The Hermeneutical Challenge of Black Theology as a Theology of Liberation*. London: SCM Press, 1987.

—. *A Place in the Sun: An Introduction to Liberation Theology in the Third World*. London: SCM Press, 1985.

Word Sound 'Ave Power: Dub Poets and Dub. Cambridge, MA: Heartbeat Records, 1994.

Wynter, Cadence. "Rodney and Rastafari: Cultural Identity in 1960s Jamaica." In *Rastafari in the New Millennium: A Rastafari Reader*, ed. Michael Barnett, 300–309. Syracuse: Syracuse University Press, 2012.

Yamauchi, Edwin M. *Africa and the Bible*. Grand Rapids, MI: Baker Academic, 2004.

Yawney, Carole D. "Tell Out King Rasta Doctrine Around the Whole World: Rastafari in Global Perspective." In *The Reordering of Culture: Latin America, the Caribbean and Canada in the Hood*, eds. Alvina Ruprecht and Cecilia Taiana, 57–74. Ottawa: Carleton University Press, 1995.

—. "Rasta Mek A Trod: Symbolic Ambiguity in a Globalizing Religion." In *Arise Ye Mighty People!: Gender, Class, and Race in Popular Struggles*, eds. Terisa E. Turner and Bryan J. Ferguson, 75–84. Trenton, NJ: Africa World Press, 1994.

—. "To Grow a Daughter: Cultural Liberation and the Dynamics of Oppression in Jamaica." In *Feminism in Canada*, eds. A. Milles and G. Finn, 119–144. Montreal: Black Rose, 1983.

—. *Lions in Babylon: The Rastafarians of Jamaica as a Visionary Movement*. Ottawa: National Library of Canada, 1980.

—. "Dread Wasteland: Rastafarian Ritual in West Kingston, Jamaica." In *Ritual, Symbolism and Ceremonialism in the Americas: Studies in Symbolic Anthropology*, ed. N. Ross Crumrine, 154–174. Greenley, CO: Museum of Anthropology, University of Northern Colorado, 1978.

—. "Remnant of All Nations: Rastafarian Attitudes to Race and Nationality." In *Ethnicity in the Americas*, ed. Francis Henry, 231–262. The Hague: Mouton, 1976.

Yuajah, Empress. *White Rastafari*. CreateSpace Independent Publishing Platform, 2012.

Zephaniah, Benjamin. *Too Black, Too Strong*. Tarset, Northumberland, England: Bloodaxe, 2001.

—. *City Psalms*. Newcastle upon Tyne, England: Bloodaxe Books, 1992.

—. *The Dread Affair: Collected Poems*. London: Arena Books, 1985.

Zephaniah, Benjamin, and Victor G. Ambrus. *Benjamin Zephaniah: My Story*. London: Collins Educational, 2011.

Zephaniah, Benjamin, and Sarah Symonds. *Wicked World!* London: Puffin Books, 2000.

Zindika, *A Daughter's Grace*. London: Karnak House, 1992.

Ziolkowski, Theodore. *Fictional Transfigurations of Jesus*. Princeton, NJ: Princeton University Press, 1972.

Zips, Werner. "'Repatriation is a Must!': The Rastafari Struggle to *Downstroy* Slavery." In *Rastafari: A Universal Philosophy in the Third Millennium*, ed. Werner Zips, 129–168. Kingston, Jamaica; Miami: Ian Randle Publishers, 2006.

—. "'Global Fire': Repatriation and Reparations from a Rastafari (Re)Migrant's Perspective." In *Mobile People, Mobile Law: Expanding Legal Relations in a Contracting World*, eds. Franz von Benda-Beckmann, Keebet von Benda-Beckmann, and Anne Griffiths, 69–89. Burlington, VT; Aldershot, Hampshire, UK: Ashgate Publishing Company, 2005.

—. "Ragga Cowboys: Country and Western Themes in Rastafarian-Inspired Reggae Music." In *Reinventing Religions: Syncretism and Transformation in Africa and the Americas*, eds. Sidney M. Greenfield and André Droogers, 163–181. Lanham, MD: Rowman & Littlefield, 2001.

Zips, Werner, ed. *Rastafari: A Universal Philosophy in the Third Millennium*. Kingston, Jamaica; Miami: Ian Randle Publishers, 2006.

SELECTED WEBLIOGRAPHY

http://www.africaspeaks.com/
http://black-king.net/english/index.htm
http://www.bobmarley.com/
http://fulfilledrastafari.ning.com/
http://gospelreggaeam.com
http://himchurch.org
http://www.houseofbobo.com/
http://www.imperialethiopia.org/selassie.htm
http://irudder.com
http://www.jah.com/
http://jah-rastafari.com
http://jahworks.org
http://rastafari.dubroom.org
http://www.rastafariglobalcouncil.org/
http://www.rastafari.org/
http://www.rastafarispeaks.com/Selassie/
http://www.rastafarivisions.com
http://www.rastaites.com
http://rastajourney.com
http://rasta-judah.wz.cz/
http://www.rasta-man.co.uk
http://www.rastatimes.com/
http://www.rastavillage.com
http://www.rocktoart.com/rastafari
http://www.tozion.org/
http://worldofjah.com/

INDEX